# Nurturing
# Nonviolent Children

**Recent Titles in
Contributions in Psychology**

# Nurturing Nonviolent Children

## A GUIDE FOR PARENTS, EDUCATORS, AND COUNSELORS

*Elsie Jones-Smith*

Contributions in Psychology
Paul Pedersen, Series Editor

Westport, Connecticut
London

**Library of Congress Cataloging-in-Publication Data**

Jones-Smith, Elsie.
   Nurturing nonviolent children : a guide for parents, educators, and counselors /
   Elsie Jones-Smith.
       p. cm. – (Contributions in psychology ; no. 50)
   Includes bibliographical references and index.
   ISBN: 978–0–275–98403–8 (alk. paper)
1. Violence in children–Prevention. 2. Nonviolence–Study and teaching. 3. Children and violence. I.
Title.
HQ784.V55J665 2008
649'.64—dc22          2008009006

British Library Cataloguing in Publication Data is available.

Library of Congress Catalog Card Number: 2008009006
ISBN: 978–0–275–98403–8
ISSN: 0736–2714

First published in 2008

Praeger Publishers, 88 Post Road West, Westport, CT 06881
An imprint of Greenwood Publishing Group, Inc.
www.praeger.com

Printed in the United States of America

The paper used in this book complies with the
Permanent Paper Standard issued by the National
Information Standards Organization (Z39.48–1984).

10 9 8 7 6 5 4 3 2 1

# Contents

# Illustrations

# Series Foreword

All behaviors are learned and displayed in a cultural context. Therefore, accurate assessment, meaningful understanding, and appropriate intervention requires that we focus our attention on the context of any situation we hope to influence. As each country and culture learns of the power of multicultural awareness as a bottom-up, consumer-driven revolution of modern society, it becomes important for them to learn from the others about what works and what does not work.

This book seeks to guide us through a learning experience toward increased multicultural awareness of violence and of nurture. Culture provides the foundation of identity and therefore the basis of all communication. Each behavior is displayed in a cultural context of learned values, expectations, and perceptions of reality. Multicultural awareness, therefore, is the process of learning about the assumptions that control behavior and the perception of reality. Each person's decisions are based on those culturally learned perceptions.

Dr. Smith does an excellent job of presenting real examples of violence among children and youth and examples of nurturing nonviolence through understanding the violence in its cultural context. Newspaper stories are full of examples where apparently meaningless and senseless violence has occurred involving children and youth. The causes of violence are complex and not simple, but intentional parenting provides an important foundation for managing the causes of violence more effectively. For a variety of reasons there seems to be more violence among youth especially than a decade or two ago. Smith does a good job of explaining both the reasons for increased violence and the reasons for decreased resources to manage that violence more harmoniously. Each chapter targets a specific psychological construct, so after reading the book one can have a meaningful grasp of what is needed for nurturing nonviolent behavior in children and youth.

Dr. Smith's book is very classroom-friendly. Each chapter has a separate theoretical focus, provides case examples to illustrate the constructs being discussed, lists extra reading for going into more depth than would be possible in a single book, offers structured exercises and activities where experiences for multicultural learning occur, and raises questions for classroom discussion on the topic. This fits with the other books in the Contributions to Psychology book series with Greenwood/Praeger.

Psychology is to this millennium what theology was to the previous millennium as an "engine of change." The fields of psychology are going through rapid and radical alterations to match the changing society in which psychology is applied. While there is some disagreement about the paradigm shift, there is almost universal agreement that profound changes are taking place in the field of psychology. The books in this series have been selected to help chart the progress of psychology as a discipline going through these changes. To the extent the changes are being mediated by controversy, this series will be controversial. In any case, the emphasis is on applications of psychology to particular social problems. Some of the social problems addressed in the series have included identity issues, moral development, ethical thinking, self-representation, culturally competent therapy, and hostage trauma. Dr. Smith's book, *Nurturing Nonviolent Children,* fits precisely within the context of this series.

*Paul Pedersen*
Professor Emeritus Syracuse University and Visiting Professor,
University of Hawaii Department of Psychology

# *Preface*

This book was written because of my deep concern about the spiraling youth violence in our nation. Too many young people are dying from homicide committed by other youth. Increasing numbers of youth are afraid to go to school because of threats of violence. Each year more American youth are killed by violent acts than soldiers are killed in both Iraq and Afghanistan. Likewise, increasing numbers of youth are deciding that life is so unbearable for them that they no longer want to live; so they end it all by committing suicide. Homicide is violence directed outward toward the world, while suicide is violence directed inwards toward the self. Young people are crying out for adult help. Yet, for far too many of them, the adults in their lives are simply distant bystanders who shield themselves from their pain and violence.

There are no easy answers or quick fixes for reducing youth violence. In fact, researchers are beginning to trace violence to the earliest days of a child's life, particularly the attachment experiences with a primary caregiver. This book is based on the author's 25 years of working with youth from various economic, social, and cultural backgrounds. It is designed to help parents learn how to nurture their children so that they are nonviolent. It is founded on the premise that parents need to be attuned to the emotional needs of their children. They need to spend time truly listening to their children, and they need to help them find the emotional words to describe their feelings. We all have a role to play in helping youth to become nonviolent. The nurturing of children is both a journey and a process that requires the support of families and the entire village in which they live.

# *Acknowledgements*

This book is dedicated to Geneva and Richard, my mother and father, for their loving nurturing and guidance. I am deeply grateful to them for their modeling integrity, perseverance, hope, gratefulness, and forgiveness so that I might exemplify these characteristics in my life and pass them along to my son, Travis, and grandchildren, Elisha, Zion, Rejoice, and Travis Jr. I also extend a special thanks to my brothers, Richard and Eli, for all of their support for my very meaningful and rewarding journey in life.

I also want to acknowledge the helpful editorial assistance of Deborah Carvalko and the many youth who have taught me what it feels like to be a child trying to make his/her place in the world.

# Introduction

The seeds for writing this book were sown many years ago when my son and I sat glued to the television watching the aftermath of a violent stabbing on a school bus in the city in which we lived. I felt a deep sense of sadness, first for the teenage boy who was murdered and second for the family of the boy who had committed this horrible act. There were no winners in this scene; everyone lost. What could ever lead a human being to think that taking another's life was an acceptable answer to a problem? What had gone so terribly wrong?

The teen who had done the stabbing looked dazed and disoriented as the police escorted him handcuffed and shackled from their van to the holding center. His face was stained with his tears, and he kept mumbling to himself: "They just wouldn't leave me alone . . . they just wouldn't stop calling me names and hitting me. I tried to get them to stop, but they wouldn't . . . . I didn't mean to hurt nobody . . . ."

Days later, the newspaper pieced together what had happened. The teen charged with the murder had been bullied unmercifully. Although he had initially sought help from teachers and other adults, unwittingly they minimized what he was actually feeling. "You can handle this, can't you? Come on. You're not going to let words get to you, are you?" The adults in that child's village had failed him miserably, and the consequences for their failure were catastrophic.

Clearly, young people who commit violent acts must ultimately accept responsibility for their own actions. We cannot blame the rest of the world for our actions and behavior. Violence is a choice—a decision that some people make to deal with their hurt. Nurturing nonviolent children is all about teaching parents how to raise their children so that they make the right decisions about how to handle their anger and the flip side of their anger—their pain.

Nurturing nonviolent children requires a shift in our thinking and actions. We must change from talking only about youth's problems to emphasizing their

strengths and possibilities. We must move from managing violent crises to building a shared national vision to prevent youth violence. I believe that increasing
parents', schools', and the public's understanding of attachment, children's
needs, risk factors, protective factors, strength, and resiliency offer the potential-
ity of providing a framework for such a national vision.

Parenting is a spiritual journey that requires us to look inward as we raise our
children. We relive parts of our own childhood as we discipline and comfort our
children. Parenting should be an intentional journey—that is, a very deliberate
sort of undertaking that we spend time thinking about both before and after we
embark upon the journey. To parent effectively, we have to commit our time
and our energy and value the parenting journey.

This book was written to help parents, teachers, counselors, and educators
learn how to nurture nonviolent children. Nurturing nonviolent children is the
best violence prevention tool. Chapter 1 provides an overview of the issue of violence. The reader is introduced to Eric, who at a little more than two years old
had already begun to hit others, including his mother, when he did not get what
he wanted. Eric comes from a middle to upper middle class background; yet he
hears his parents arguing frequently as he grows up. It is suggested that perhaps
part of Eric's violent temper can be traced to domestic violence, which is no
respecter of ethnicity, social class, occupation, or any other factor. The majority
of Chapter 1 provides statistics on violence. A section is written on parenting as
a spiritual journey, and I ask the reader to come along on this journey with me.

Chapter 2 focuses exclusively on attachment, primarily because I believe, as
do a growing number of psychologists, that the seeds for violence are planted in
the child's earliest of attachment relationships with his mother or primary caregivers. Chapter 2 has a wealth of exercises at the end of the chapter. For instance,
the reader is provided with a chart labeled "My Child's Chart: Attachment to
Whom." The reader is also given an opportunity to examine his/her attachment
relationships on a scale from secure to insecure attachments.

Chapter 3 deals with children's needs and developmental stages. It uses
Maslow's Need Hierarchy and Erickson's psychosocial stages of development
as primary theoretical frameworks. Parents need to know what to look for in their
children's development, so as not to expect too much too early from them. This
chapter begins with a brief scenario with a child named Matt who soils his
clothes just as his mother is getting ready to turn on the security alarm so that
they can leave the house for work and day care.

Chapter 4 addresses the topic of anger. It traces the origin of anger and how
it can be expressed in appropriate ways. The importance of children learning
emotional self-regulation is emphasized. Parents are asked to think back to their
earliest experiences with anger.

Chapter 5 examines school violence. It explores the impact of gangs and
drugs on school violence. Parents will find useful sections on how to tell if
your child is a member of a gang or is on drugs. Young people's dating relationships and violence are discussed. The basic principles for conflict resolution

are discussed. Exercises to help families use conflict resolution are also provided.

Chapter 6 delves into the impact of television and the media on violence in children. It points out that by the time the average American child reaches 18 years old, he will have witnessed on television 200,000 acts of violence, including 40,000 murders. The reader is given simple tests to determine if he/she is addicted to a media form.

Chapter 7 is designed to help parents raise responsible children. It discusses such things as recognizing the difference between logical consequences and punishment, assigning chores, making a family mission statement, attending family meetings, and enforcing appropriate boundaries within the family.

Chapter 8 focuses on the resilient youth. It examines nine characteristics of resilient children. This chapter recommends that parents become involved in emotional parenting. It provides an exercise labeled "Resiliency Builders."

The theme of Chapter 9 is that it takes a village to raise a nonviolent child. The village is a network of families, teachers, clergy, business people, and community leaders committed to protect the health, safety, and welfare of our children. The village consists of four types of families: (1) First, the birth or adoptive family, which consists of the mother, father, and siblings; (2) second, the extended family, which consists of blood relatives, friends, and mentors; (3) third, the school (including teachers and school personnel), neighborhood, community, and state in which one grows up; and (4) the nation and the global world or the human family. We have different responsibilities in each of these families, but they converge on one point and that is, the nurturing of nonviolent children who learn to get their needs met in acceptable ways.

# 1

# Many Roots and Causes for Children's Violence

*When we nurture our children, we lay the foundation for our future.*

Raising a child is one of the most rewarding, but challenging, jobs a person can have. Most parents want to be the best parents they can be. They read the headlines about young people killing their parents and classmates, and they shudder to think that a tragedy like that could ever happen with their own children. No one wants to raise a child who becomes violent later on in life. Yet, some parents have few clues about what it takes to nurture a nonviolent child.

Parents' lack of knowledge and understanding about what it takes to raise a nonviolent child is reflected in their concerns about the behavior of their own children. One parent complained:

> I've spent my entire life trying to control Eric, and nothing seems to work. I'm afraid that one night a few years from now, I'll hear a knock on my door, and it will be the police looking for Eric because he has bashed someone's head in. I've tried everything, and I don't know what to do or where to turn any more.

Eric's parents do not live in a high crime, inner-city neighborhood. On the contrary, they live in a middle to upper middle class, suburban neighborhood with graceful tall elm trees that line a street of four-bedroom brick homes and neatly manicured lawns with three car garages. Eric's parents have good-paying jobs, and neighbors consider them to be respectable citizens. Yet, violence has visited their home many times. Eric has been awakened in the middle of the night by his parents' loud arguing. He has sat scared, huddled at the top of the stairs, listening to accusations by both of his parents about who is right and who is wrong. Sometimes he has felt like hitting his father to protect his mother. On other occasions, he has felt like hitting his mother just to shut her up, in the hope that all the yelling would stop and the family would get back to being a family again.

Eric's parents are not unusual. The vast majority of parents have never been given any training on how to raise a nonviolent, responsible, and caring child. Parenting, one of the most challenging jobs in the world, is often left up to what we observed our parents doing rather than what is developmentally appropriate for our own child. As a result, parents tend to pass on to their children how they were treated and what they learned from being in a family.

Eric's parents are deeply concerned about their son's behavior, and they should be. At the age of two, he started hitting his mother when he could not get his way. In the beginning, Eric's father thought that his hitting behavior was cute, and he laughed at it, especially as Mom was hit. Later, when Eric was attending a reunion with them, his parents were embarrassed when family members called attention to his violent behaviors. "You shouldn't let your kid hit you," a family member cautioned. Eric's mother ignored the early warning signs of potential later violence and dismissed his behavior on grounds that, "He is just going through his terrible twos." Yet, Eric did not stop his outbursts. As he grew older, he lashed out by hitting his brother in the head when he did not let him play with his toys. He fought the kids in his class when they made fun of him because he got into trouble.

Violence is an equal opportunity caller. It visits people of all ages, from both gender groups, and from all ethnic, socioeconomic, and political groups. American children encounter a continuum of exposure to violence, ranging from being a witness, victim, and/or perpetrator. Violence touches the lives of some children more directly and critically than others. In New Haven, Connecticut, almost 39 percent of the sixth, eighth, and tenth grade students had seen someone shot at in the preceding year.[1] In Miami, Florida, more than 90 percent of the high school students witnessed community violence, and 44 percent had been a victim of a violent crime.[2] In Richmond, Virginia, 88 percent of the children in one neighborhood heard gunfire near home, and 25 percent saw someone killed. It has been estimated that 9 million youth have witnessed serious violence during their short lifetimes.[3]

Youth witnessing violence is only part of the problem; young people are also the perpetrators of violence. Each year, nearly 4 million American adolescents are the victims of a serious physical assault.[4] One in 12 high school students is threatened or injured with a weapon each year.[5] Data from a survey of eighth and ninth grade students revealed that 25 percent had been victims of nonsexual dating violence and 8 percent had been victims of sexual dating violence.[6] Nationally, 9 percent of students reported they had been hit, slapped, or physically hurt by their boyfriend or girlfriend in the 12 months prior to being surveyed.

Where does such youth violence come from? Do most violent youth perpetrators begin like Eric, by hitting family members? Do children exposed to domestic violence later engage in killing sprees, date violence, or bullying? The answers to these questions vary, depending upon with whom one speaks. Even when parents take care not to argue and fight in front of their children, violence may intrude its presence almost imperceptibly into their homes—via television and video games.

In many respects, the media mirrors our culture of violence. Violence in the media, in our neighborhoods, and in our schools can make our children feel frightened, anxious, unsafe, and insecure. Yet, there is still hope. If parents, caring school teachers, and counselors take an opportunity to talk with children about violence, fears may not take root, and violence may be reduced. As the first-ever Surgeon General's Report on Youth Violence[7] has maintained, youth violence is not an intractable problem. It can be reduced by establishing programs that address preventing broken homes, teaching parents to provide love and support to their children, improving parents' use of discipline, and restricting children's exposure to violent media.

The focus of this book is about nurturing nonviolent children. Nurturing is defined as caring actions that provide sustenance for living, that help one to grow or develop, or that educate, cultivate, or train. A basic theme is that we nurture children to become nonviolent by helping them to realize their developmental assets, by teaching them how to resolve conflicts constructively, by helping them to develop healthy relationships with their family members, peers, and teachers, and by modeling skills in empathy, problem solving, communication, and anger management. I maintain that teaching a child to be nonviolent is a learning process that begins very early in life, far younger than many parents typically imagine. Such learning takes place in our homes, at school, and within communities, as well as in countless everyday situations that we often fail to acknowledge or even remember. It begins with the daily behavior children observe in their families, especially between their parents. This book helps the reader to understand the continuum of violence as it occurs in our lives and in the daily lives of children. The next section begins by providing a working definition of violence.

## Definition of Violence

What is violence? Violence is defined as an act carried out by an individual with the intention of causing another person to experience physical or psychological pain or injury.[8] Violent behavior in children encompasses a wide range of behaviors, including temper tantrums, physical aggression, fighting, threats or attempts to hurt others, homicidal thoughts, use of weapons, cruelty toward animals, fire setting, and intentional destruction of property and vandalism.

Physical injury is not a necessary requirement for a behavior to be classified as violent. A child who kicks, hits, or bites a parent because the parent has demanded that he go to his room wants the parent to feel real pain. Therefore, the parent's lack of physical injury does not exempt the child's behavior from being labeled violent. The American Psychological Association[9] has maintained that children who show early aggressive behavior warrant immediate attention. Violent behavior in preschool children may be a precursor of what is to come, if nothing is done to correct it. Typically, children living with family violence use hitting as their initial method to solve problems.

Violence is a learned behavior, even though there is some research to suggest that biological factors may predispose a person to become violent.[10] Children learn violence from the people around them. Each year, 3 to 10 million children witness domestic violence. Early childhood exposure to family violence and sexual and physical abuse are factors strongly associated with adolescent and adult violence.[11] Girls who observe their mothers being hit by their fathers or boyfriends may learn that victimization is inevitable and consequently become withdrawn, passive, and dependent. Later on in life, they may choose boyfriends who also victimize them on dates, and some see such abuse as inevitable.

# *Many Fingers of Blame*

What causes violence among children and adolescents? What makes a young child strike another because he has taken his favorite toy? What prompts a child to hit his mother because she will not let him stay out late with his friends, or a teenager to carry a shotgun to school for the purpose of blowing away other students and teachers? Rage? Anger? Are some children born to be violent? Who is to blame when a child or adolescent becomes violent? Do we blame the parents? After all, they are the ones who raised the violent child. If they had just handled certain situations differently, would there would have been different results, such as a more controllable and nonviolent child? Maybe or maybe not.

A case in point is the situation of Columbine High School in Littleton, Colorado, on April 20, 1999. Columbine represents the worst incident of public high school violence in U.S. history.[12] Two White, middle class youth, 18-year-old Eric Harris and 17-year-old Dylan Klebold, let loose an assault inside Columbine High School that left a number of their classmates and a beloved teacher dead. They shot and killed 13 people and injured another 20 before they took their own lives. By most American standards, Eric and Dylan were living the good life. They lived in a middle class, White suburban community, where some residents had fled to in order to escape the violence in city schools. There were no reports of domestic violence between either boy's parents.

Many Americans challenged the Columbine parents' claim of ignorance regarding their sons' intentions. Instead, they pointed the finger directly at the parents and asked loudly and accusingly why they never picked up on the clues of their children's anger, despair, and violence. Why did the parents not go into their own children's bedrooms to see what was going on? Perhaps they would have become aware of their plans.

In response to the numerous criticisms that they had been ineffective and poor parents, Eric and Dylan's parents answered they had simply been ignorant of the signs and effects of bullying against their own children and of their children's alienation from school and their peers. They were unaware of just how much pain their children were in because of the teasing they were experiencing at school. They put their faith in teachers, who, for whatever well-intentioned reasons, also looked the other way as the two boys' classmates ostracized and ridiculed them. Should the teachers at Columbine be blamed for not stopping the attacks on the already troubled adolescents? What about the principal at Columbine? And what about the students whom the two boys felt humiliated them? Do they share any blame for what happened? Solely blaming the parents of the Columbine perpetrators does not bring back one murdered youth, nor does it bring back the teacher who died protecting students.

The answer to the question of whom we should blame is complicated. If blame is what we want, there is enough to go around so that no one really feels left out. Families do not raise their children in isolation from the rest of society. The American Psychological Association[13] has maintained that everyone who comes into contact with children—including parents, educators, child care providers, the community in which they live and grow up, their peers, television, video games, and the music media—may potentially contribute to their attitude toward violence and their inclination toward violent behavior. Hence, there is no single factor that reveals the entire story for any one given child. Violent behavior results from multiple factors converging over a period of time. In response to the question, who is to blame for youth violence, researchers have identified factors that contribute to a child's violence risk profile, including biological factors, ineffective parenting, disrupted emotional and cognitive development, sex role socialization, economic inequality (poverty), and media influences.

This book takes a close look at factors associated with violence, including domestic violence, and child abuse and neglect. The first part of Chapter 1 examines some statistics on youth violence. Second, it probes some causes of youth violence. Third, I maintain that if we are to reduce violence, we need to reconceptualize parenting as a spiritual journey that we take not only with our own children but also with our parents—or what I call "the parents in our heads." To prevent violence in children and adolescence, I assert that parenting should be intentional rather than sporadic. Intentional parental tips for preventing violence are presented at the end of the chapter.

# Statistics on Violence in the United States

Violence is a public health concern because intentional interpersonal violence disproportionately involves young people as both perpetrators and victims.[14] Every day 10 American children are murdered; 16 children die from guns; 316 are arrested for crimes of violence; and 8,042 are reported abused or neglected. Researchers have estimated that more than three American children die each day as a result of child abuse or neglect. Of this number, 78 percent are under five years of age at the time of their death. A U.S. Department of Justice report, *Safe from the Start,*[15] indicated that of the nation's 22.3 million children between the ages of 12 and 17, nearly 1.8 million have been victims of a serious sexual assault; 3.9 million have been victims of a serious physical assault.

One national survey reported that for every teen arrested, at least ten were involved in violence that could have seriously injured or killed another person.[16] Approximately one in three high school students reported they had been involved in a physical fight during the past year, and about one in eight of those students required medical attention for injuries.[17] In 2002, more than 877,700 young people ages 10 to 24 were injured from violent acts, with 1 in 13 requiring hospitalization.[18]

## Homicide Rate

Violence in America is epitomized by its high homicide rate. The United States has the highest homicide rate of any Western industrialized nation in the world.[19] More than 25,000 Americans are murdered each year, making homicide the tenth leading cause of death in our nation.[20] In 2005, the most recent year for which figures are available, 30,694 people were killed by firearms in the United States.[21]

Within the past two decades, homicide has become associated with youth. In 1997, six young people under the age of 18 were murdered each day; 56 percent of the victims were killed with a firearm. Nearly one in eight people murdered each year in the Untied States are younger than 18 years of age. About 9 percent of murders in the United States were committed by youth under 18 in 2000. An estimated 1,561 youth under the age of 18 were arrested for homicide in 2000.[22] The Centers for Disease Control has reported that 73 percent of all deaths for young people 15–24 years of age result from only four causes: motor vehicle crashes, other unintentional injuries, homicide, and suicide.[23]

In 2004, 5,292 young people ages 10 to 24 were murdered—an average of 15 each day.[24] Among homicide victims ages 10 to 24 years old, 81% were killed with a firearm. Among this age group, 85% (4,518) of the homicide victims were male and 15% (774) were female. This country's homicide rate among males 15–24 years of age is 10 times higher than in Canada, 15 times higher than in

Australia, and 28 times higher than in France or Germany.[25] Only in such South American countries as Columbia and Brazil, and in actual war zones, is there a higher homicide rate among young males. If the United States were to reduce gun homicide to levels similar to those of other westernized nations, youth homicide rates would decline significantly.

Homicide is the number one cause of death of young African American males ages 15–24; the second leading cause of death for Hispanic youth; and the third leading cause of death for American Indians, Alaskan Natives, and Asian Pacific Islanders.[26] A young African American male is 11 times more likely to die by homicide than a non–African American male. The probability of a young African American female dying by homicide is four times that of a White female.

In *The Good Son,* Michael Gurian[27] described how violence is primarily associated with American male children. He made the case that American sons are an endangered species. Gurian described his experience of working with boys and men in classrooms, in prisons, and in his therapy practice over the past two decades. According to him, this country has the most violent nonwar population of children in the world. More people in the United States commit violent acts each day than anywhere else in the westernized world, and 90 percent of those who commit such crimes are males. After Russia, more American citizens are in prison than in any other country in the world, and 90 percent of those in prisons are males.

Gurian[28] asserts that violence threatens the welfare of American boys. He posits that this nation does a poor job of providing nurturing environments for boys because boys form the majority of children who are homeless, are murdered, live in foster care, are neglected, and are institutionalized. Such deficit-based nurturing environments for male children provide fertile ground for their elevated mental disorder levels, which in the American male population per capita is one of the highest in the world. It is unclear to what extent the higher rates of violence among American males are related to their higher levels of mental disorders.

## Growing Girl Violence in America

Violence among young girls is growing at a rate that has caught some communities by surprise. In the past, violence among girls was understudied, partly because girls were usually the victims of violence and partly because fewer girls have traditionally been involved in violence.[29] Within the past decade, however, girls have become perpetrators of violence. According to Peters and Peters,[30] during the 1990s, there was a substantial increase in the numbers of young adolescent females who were involved in gangs, a disproportionate number of whom were members of a minority. In 1997, the most serious offenses referred for juvenile delinquency cases involving females were property offenses (50 percent), person offenses (25 percent), public order offenses (20 percent), and drug offenses (7 percent). Heimer and De Coster[31] have observed that although there is a substantial gender gap in violent crimes committed by boys and by girls, girls do engage in a significant amount of violent delinquency.

According to James Garbarino,[32] American girls are being arrested in record numbers. National arrest statistics for simple and aggravated assaults by girls have been on the rise for two decades. The FBI's Uniform Crime Reports indicate that the female percentage of total juvenile assault arrests increased from 21 percent to 32 percent between 1990 and 2003.[33] Some researchers trace the surge in the number of arrests for girls to increased pressures emanating from breakdowns of family, church, community, and school.[34] Other researchers argue that girls are more likely to act out because of changing gender-role expectations. Violence by girls is also depicted in the media. Even in a recent Harry Potter movie, a girl character—Hermione Granger—hits a boy, only to say afterwards: "Boy, that felt good."

In addition, there are differences in the types of violent acts girls and boys commit.[35] Boys are two to three times more likely to carry and to use guns, whereas girls tend to use knives in violent acts. Girls commit murder as a result of a conflict with a person—especially within the family. Typically, their violence problems are related to sexual abuse, partner violence, and early motherhood. In contrast, boys' violence tends to be related to territorial issues, larceny, and theft.[36]

## Suicide: Violence Directed Inward

Suicide forms a special kind of homicidal violence. It is homicide directed inward toward the self. More people die from suicide than from homicide in the United States. Whereas the American public responds quickly and negatively to youth violence turned outward (homicide) at others, it is much slower to respond to youth who turn violence inward toward the self (suicide). In 2000, suicide was the third leading cause of death for young people 10 to 19 years of age, with 1,921 young people taking their lives by suicide.[37] More American teenagers die from suicide than from cancer, heart disease, AIDS, birth defects, stroke, pneumonia and influenza, and chronic lung disease combined. Survey data from 2001 show that 19 percent of high school students had seriously considered attempting suicide, nearly 15 percent had made plans to attempt suicide, and about 9 percent had made a suicide attempt during the year preceding the survey.[38]

Suicide is the second leading cause of firearm-related deaths among children and adolescents, constituting 33 percent of those deaths, and alcohol is involved in 70 percent of adolescent suicides.[39] White male adolescents and youth residing in rural areas are more likely than other youth to take their lives by gun suicide. Male teens are almost five times more likely than are females to die by suicide, even though females are more inclined to attempt suicide. Although White male youth have the highest suicide rate (60 percent), the rate for African American males 10 to 19 has doubled over the past 20 years.[40]

Likewise, suicide rates may also vary according to teens' sexual orientation. Studies have found that gay, lesbian, and bisexual teens are much more likely to consider and attempt suicide than are heterosexual teens.[41,42,43] Gay teens may experience higher rates of discrimination due to the social stigmatization of homosexuality in American culture, and they may suffer mental health consequences due to such stigmatization. Another reason for gays' elevated suicide rate is that they report a higher rate of problems with substance abuse and depression than do heterosexuals.[44,45]

Child abuse, a family history of suicide, and psychiatric disorders also contribute to youths' taking of their own lives. In one study, youthful attempters were three to six times more likely to have suffered sexual or physical abuse at home.[46] Other factors that contribute to teen suicide include poor impulse control, the physical and sexual changes and pressures of adolescence, family discord or violence, school-related or social events that bring shame, humiliation, or rejection, and such trigger factors as alcohol, drugs, or access to firearms.[47] Additional risk factors for teen suicide include pressure to succeed, family problems, low self-esteem, and the loss of someone close to the youth who has committed suicide.

Parents and counselors must be concerned about cluster or copycat suicides for adolescents, events that occur when youth take their lives in a manner that follows or imitates another suicide.[48] After one youth takes his life, another youth who is experiencing despair may begin to view suicide as a legitimate response to feelings of depression and hopelessness. For this reason, parents should be particularly vigilant after television or a newspaper has publicized an adolescent's suicide or after a teen suicide has taken place in their school or community.[49]

## School Violence

Less than 1 percent of all homicides among school-aged children (15–19 years of age) occur on or around school grounds or on the way to and from school. Parents should be aware that school violent deaths tend to occur at certain times of the day. More than 50 percent of all school-associated violent deaths occur at the beginning or end of the school day, or during lunch.[50] Youth who have the greatest chance of being killed in school-associated violence are those from a racial or ethnic minority, senior high schools, and urban school districts.

What are some reasons for school violence? According to Petersen, Pietrzak, and Speaker,[51] the major reasons for the increase in school violence are the following: lack of family rules or family structure, lack of personal supervision, violence acted out by parents, parental drug abuse, student drug or alcohol use, violent movies, poor self-concept or emotional disturbance, violence in television, and gang activities.

Shubert, Bressette, Deeken, and Bender[52] studied the shootings in schools that took place in Pearl, Mississippi; West Paducah, Kentucky; Jonesboro,

Arkansas; Edinboro, Pennsylvania; and Springfield, Oregon. These researchers found that: (1) peers believed that the shooters had serious emotional problems as well as a disregard for human life; (2) the shooters were virtually estranged from family and friends; (3) all shooters had talked about violence and the killing of others prior to the shootings, and these discussions were ignored; (4) all shooters had average or above average intelligence; and (5) on the days of the shootings, the perpetrators appeared to be acting from a plan because they acted in organized and deliberate ways.

Moreover, the profile of the shooters was not typical of the children who are usually associated with violent acts in school; the shooters were not bullies or young people who had been previously identified as aggressive. Instead, they were what the researchers described as the "invisible kids," because they were easy to ignore and because they were unknown by many of the school personnel prior to the shooting incidents. The invisible kids were frequently identified as "nerds" or "geeks" and as students who were bullied and picked on by more powerful students. Their violent outburst carried the message that they had had enough and that they would no longer tolerate bullying.

## Violence Costs

It has been estimated that 3 percent of the medical spending in the United States can be attributed to interpersonal violence.[53] Firearm injuries alone cost this nation between $1.4 and $4 billion dollars annually in direct medical costs, plus another $19 billion in indirect costs, such as lost earnings. Cook and Ludwig[54] estimate that the total annual cost of gun violence in the United States is $100 billion, of which $15 billion involves the costs of gun violence against children and youth.

# Some Causes of Youth Violence

Given the staggering cost of violence, it is important for policy makers and others to understand the causes of youth violence. Myles and Simpson[55] have asserted that violence among children has increased for the following reasons: (1) American society has more violence than before, and children who are exposed to violence on a consistent basis become desensitized to the meaning of violence. (2) There is an increased number of seriously disturbed children who are being mainstreamed into regular classrooms. (3) There are more negative influences in a child's life than previously (gang activity, child abuse and neglect, family violence, and violent neighborhoods that offer few positive role models for children).

What do youth think causes violence among their peers? Anderson[56] conducted interviews with youth in the nation's most violent neighborhoods. Children cited the following top causes of violence: (1) media; (2) substance abuse; (3) gangs; (4) unemployment; (5) weapons; (6) poverty; (7) peer pressure; (8) broken homes; (9) poor family environment or bad neighborhoods; and (10) intolerance or ignorance. The ensuing sections examine various factors that researchers have found to be associated with youth violence. I explore, for example, biological factors, family factors, and neighborhood socialization factors. Separate chapters of this book are devoted to television and media violence, school violence, and gangs.

## Violent Brains: Biological Factors Contributing to Violence

Millions of American young people are exposed to family strife, television violence, and guns, without becoming violent themselves or without killing their classmates and teachers. What combination of factors causes one child to lash out with violence, while another who has faced similar circumstances deals with his environment in a nonviolent manner? In *Ghosts from the Nursery: Tracing the Roots of Violence,* Robin Karr-Morse and Meredith Wiley[57] posit that biological factors, such as premature birth, the effects of drugs in utero, birth trauma, tiny brain hemorrhages, attention deficit hyperactive disorder (ADHD), or a difficult temperament can make a baby vulnerable to later violence. Biological deficits, such as low birth weight, and head trauma during delivery have also been associated with later childhood violence. One study revealed that 43 percent of juvenile murderers experienced serious head trauma, which may have led to the etiology of their murderous behavior.[58]

## The Infant's Brain and Nurturing

Parents need to know some basics about their children's brain development if they are to nurture them to be nonviolent. Children are born with 100 billion brain cells, which are connected through electrochemical structures called synapses.[59] These electrochemical brain structures help infants to become who they are and who they will be in the future.[60]

Although genes predispose an individual toward certain traits, environmental factors, such as care, nutrition, surroundings, and stimulation, also influence the dynamics of brain development.[61,62] The manner in which caregivers plan children's contact with their environment affects their formation of brain neural pathways. Parents who promote positive interactions with their babies will greatly enhance their children's developing patterns of brain neuronal connections.[63,64] Play exchanges and positive interactions between parent and infant are critical to the infant's brain formation and biochemistry.[65]

The current prevailing view is that there is a critical window for children's brain and emotional development.[66] PET scans have shown increased activity in the brain's frontal cortex between six months and two years. Between 10 and 18 months, a baby's emotional intelligence is wired.[67] Such emotional arousal becomes closely linked with long-term memory. The brain is an organism that craves experience and association. Therefore, whatever experiences a parent nurtures will become permanent. To nurture healthy frontal cortex development and positive brain associations, it is important that parents develop positive emotional bonds with their children from birth onward so that their children's neurological brain connections will remain intact. If children are cared for and loved by people sensitive to their unique personalities, the pleasure of such relationships will help "trigger" their "social brain."

The orbitofrontal and the prefrontal cortex play major roles in managing children's social brains and their emotional lives. This area of the brain picks up on social cues, helps them to empathize with others, and allows them to restrain aggressive impulses.[68] People are not born with the capacity to empathize or to pick up on social cues. This part of the brain develops almost entirely postnatally. Yet, there is nothing automatic about a baby's development of an orbitofrontal cortex so it can begin to relate well to others. On the contrary, the kind of brain that each baby develops is one that evolves out of his or her experiences with other people. Love nourishes a massive burst of connections in the orbitofrontal cortex between 6 and 12 months. If babies are neglected between 6 and 12 months, their prefrontal cortex development may be reduced.

Equally important, early parental care of babies establishes the way that they deal with stress later on in their lives.[69] Babies have a stress response, which is a complex chain of biochemical reactions. In essence, each child's stress response is most likely "set" like a thermostat very early in life by their parents and caregivers. Babies depend on their parents to soothe their distress and to restore equilibrium to them when they are in distress. With nurturing parents, the baby's stress response remains an emergency response. Babies need to be held and cuddled. They need someone to be there consistently for them, to notice how they feel, to smile at them lovingly, and to set things straight when distress occurs. When parents or caregivers convey hostility or resentment toward supplying a baby's needs, or when they ignore or leave a baby in a state of distress for longer then he can bear, they may be causing their baby's stress response system to become overly sensitive.

Scientists have found clear links between harsh treatment in the first two years of life and children's later development of antisocial behavior.[70] Harsh environments that ignore babies' cries or punish them for distress produce children who are prone to aggression and are relatively insensitive to others' feelings. Inadequately nurtured children are those who have been described as being "mean" to others, who hit and blame other children, who fail to cooperate with their teachers, and who are intolerant of frustration. Their "social brains" have been inadequately developed, and this may lead to later aggression and violence. Hence, some consequences parents may foster due to inadequate nurturing of their children include:

• Hindering their children's development of critical neuropathway brain connections,

- Failing to help develop their children's social brain,
- Setting a stress response syndrome that makes their children tolerate little frustration, and
- Transmitting aggression (smacking) and antisocial behavior to their children.

## Nurturing and Inherited Vulnerability

Appropriate family nurturing can reduce the negative impact of inherited biological factors that predispose youth to violence. For example, Stephen Suomi[71] of the National Institute of Child Health and Human Development has completed extensive research with rhesus monkeys demonstrating how nurturing and genes interact. Suomi found that for some rhesus monkeys a variation in one of their genes appeared to predispose them toward aggression and poor impulse control. The aggressive monkeys drank a great deal of alcohol at "monkey happy hour," and they were more likely to engage in binge drinking than other less aggressive monkeys. The aggressive monkeys were not well liked or accepted by the other monkeys.

Suomi's studies have revealed that strong mothering can eliminate the negative impact of risky genes and even turn certain of those genes into an advantage. When the genetically "at-risk" monkeys were raised in supportive environments, their harmful aggressive behavior began to disappear, as did their excessive binge drinking. In supportive environments, the at-risk monkeys not only survived, but they flourished. They were able to make their way near the top of the rhesus monkey social hierarchy. Suomi[72] concluded that an improved social environment can change an inherited vulnerability toward aggression into a positive, behavioral asset.

Debra Niehoff has provided some evidence that a person's brain keeps track of life experiences. In *The Biology of Violence,* Niehoff[73] asserted that the biggest lesson scientists have learned is that violence is the result of a lifelong interaction between the brain and the environment. Each person's brain keeps track of his experiences through a language of chemistry and the hormones of the nervous system, and especially the circuitry for emotion and our responses to stress. When an individual interacts with a new person, he brings to that relationship a neurochemical profile that is based on answers to such important questions as the following: Is the world a safe place? Are people I meet trustworthy? An individual's reactions to these questions set off emotional reactions, and these reactions form his chemistry of feelings, which are translated into responses to everyday life experiences.

Niehoff has maintained that what a child understands about how safe the world is and what he learns about correct social behavior is critical in violence prevention. She recommends three steps parents can take to protect their children from the development of violent behavior. First, parents acknowledge each child's individuality and temperament and learn how to work with these two conditions. Second, parents identify high risk situations for themselves and their children and take steps to intervene before trouble takes place. Third, parents learn how to intervene as early as possible when children are not developing socially for their age group.

## The Prefrontal Cortex and Adults' Brains

Much of the exciting research being conducted on babies' brains and the nurturing of nonviolent behavior among children is based on early studies conducted on adults' brains. These studies have found that specific regions of the brain may play a vital role in human violent tendencies. One such study involved Phineas Gage. In 1848, a 25-year-old American railroad worker named Phineas sustained a nasty head injury when a construction explosion blasted an iron rod up into his face and through his head. Amazingly, he recovered from this injury and lived another 12 years, but as a psychologically changed man.[74] Damage to the frontal part of his brain completely altered his personality from "intelligent and respectful" to "fitful, impulsive, and rude."

The prefrontal cortex forms the brain's foremost outer region, and it is located right behind the eyes. It is vital in emotion, arousal, and attention, and it houses the mental machinery that helps people to restrain themselves from acting on all of their impulses.[75] Scientists have postulated that the prefrontal cortex functions to suppress impulse behavior, particularly violence. The prefrontal cortex is also said to be central to a child's ability to learn to feel remorse, conscience, and social sensitivity. While violent video games, music, peer pressure, and bad parenting have all taken the blame for school violence, scientists are now beginning to assert that abnormalities in a young person's brain region may, in some cases, trigger violent behavior.

When the brain is not functioning properly, rage can spin out of control. Prefrontal cortex damage can result from birth defects, problems in birth delivery, head injury, stroke, and alcohol or drug abuse. Teens may be at risk for manifesting violent behavior simply because the prefrontal cortex does not fully mature until age 20 or 21. People with a prefrontal injury often show an array of disturbing behaviors, such as difficulty holding a job, planning ahead, and making poor decisions. It is important for parents to consider prefrontal cortex damage when assessing their children's behavior.

## The Brain's Amygdala and Violence

The amygdala is a key brain structure for mediating violence.[76] It is part of the limbic system that is known best for its roles in fear, vigilance, and aggression. The amygdala is also involved in memory and specific basic motivations. Destroying the amygdala has a calming effect on otherwise mean-spirited people. In contrast, electrically stimulating the amygdala can trigger aggressive behavior. Scientists have noted that animals that had their amygdala removed were remarkably tame and showed little fear.[77] When youth show signs of violence that have not been there before, parents might consider having a brain scan completed to rule out any damage or a tumor on their child's amygdala.

A brain scan of Charles Whitman may have saved the lives of 15 people and spared injury to more than 30 others. Whitman was a 1966 sniper who lay on the University Tower at the University of Texas at Austin and killed people at random as they walked by unsuspectingly. During the spring of 1966, Charles's mother left his father and moved to Austin to be near her oldest son. On March 29, 1966, Whitman sought medical and psychiatric advice at the university health center, but he did not return as the counseling center had requested. On July 22, 1966, he and one of his brothers visited the University of Texas tower observation deck. During the early morning hours of August 1, 1966, Whitman killed his mother in her apartment and his wife at their residence. Next, he bought a shotgun and ammunition, and at about 11:30 AM he went out to the university tower. At the tower, he clubbed the receptionist who later died, killed two people, and wounded two others.

For 96 minutes, Charles Whitman held police at bay, as he opened fire on people crossing the campus and walking on nearby streets, killing ten more people and wounding an additional 31, one of whom died a week later. At 1:24 AM, a police officer and a deputized private citizen reached the observation deck and killed Whitman. They discovered that Whitman had left behind a note that begged people to examine his brain for possible dysfunction. His autopsy showed that he had a tumor pressing into his amygdala. Medical authorities disagreed over the effect of the tumor on Whitman's actions.[78]

## Differences between Boys' and Girls' Amygdala

There are important noteworthy differences in the amygdala for males and females. The male amygdala is larger than the female amygdala. Because the amygdala is the primary aggression center of the brain, the larger male amygdala creates more active aggression in males compared to females. This biological fact may predispose boys to become more engaged in aggressive or violent behavior than girls. In comparison to girls, boys are more likely to hit, to curse, or to compete with another person to get what they want.

Gender differences in the size of the amygdala alone cannot account for difference in aggression and violence between boys and girls. Culture plays an important role in the expression of violence. Globally boys have larger amygdalas and exhibit more aggression than girls, but in some countries males are less violent than American males. In Japanese culture, there is a heavy emphasis placed on making sure children are raised to be nonviolent. Such an emphasis may be based partially on the fact that the Japanese tend to live in close quarters. Eastern cultures in general have lower violence rates among males, partly because a great deal of emphasis is placed on raising a child nonviolently.

As a parent, you need to be aware of brain differences between boys and girls and the impact that such differences may have on their aggressive and violent behavior. This comment is not meant to excuse violent behavior perpetrated by boys, but merely to point out that what some parents may view as willful violations of their rules about aggression can be traced, in part, to differences in the size of boys' amygdala.

## Boys' and Girls' Hormones and Violence

It is not just damage to the amygdala that predisposes one to violence. Body hormones have also been linked with aggression and violence.[79] Progesterone is the human bonding hormone that allows us to form bonding and close connections with others. It is part of the reason that some people believe that women and men are basically different in their views of the world. Females in general are driven by the progesterone bonding hormone. Therefore, they are more likely to seek "bonding outcomes" in their intimate and love relationships. In contrast, the dominant hormone for males is testosterone. Testosterone is a hormone that drives an individual toward increased sexual copulation and aggression.

It has been proposed that males are more aggressive than females because of their higher testosterone level.[80] One consequence of males' higher testosterone level is that males are more inclined to seek a physically or intellectually competitive experience, and they place less emphasis on bonding relationships. Research has found that the higher the testosterone level, the higher the likelihood that an individual will climb the corporate ladder quickly and the more likely he will turn violent and hurt others. In addition, studies have found that one can manipulate aggression in animals by changing their testosterone levels and that high testosterone males are more likely to be socially aggressive than are their low testosterone counterparts; however, there is no evidence that they are more violent.[81]

Parents need to be aware of the influence of boys' high testosterone level on their aggressive behavior. Males have up to 20 times more testosterone than females, but they have limited amounts of estrogen and progesterone—facts that make it difficult for them to feel empathy as an initial response to an external stimulus. Whereas boys may spend more time trying to control early aggressive responses, females are inclined to focus on providing empathic responses to others.

Differences between males and females in their levels of progesterone, estrogen, and testosterone can have a significant impact on children's moral and disciplinary development. Under stress, a young girl's progesterone and estrogen guide her toward more direct bonding responses with friends, family, and other potential emotional allies. When young girls are under stress, they are more likely to seek help or to cry, simply because of increases in their levels of progesterone and estrogen. In contrast, boys under stress experience an increase in their testosterone level; therefore, they are guided less toward immediate bonding responses and more toward aggressive, or at worst, violent responses. Whereas girls are inclined to pull closer to others, boys tend to pull away. Moreover, boys are ten times more likely than a female to use their bodies destructively, especially the power of their bodies' muscle mass. A boy's response to being emotional stressed or to being abused psychologically or physically is to strike out by punching a wall or yelling at another person. Such a response may be frightening for parents and for the community.

What are some parenting implications of these biological and hormonal differences between boys and girls? Parents may have to train males constantly and directly about empathic rather than aggressive responses to events. Boys require more help from parents in controlling their aggressive tendencies than do girls. Helping boys to understand what is taking place in their bodies is a beginning first step. Consider the fact that most classrooms are taught by female teachers who may not be aware of differences in the size of boys' amygdalas and that their testosterone levels may be silent behavioral influencers in the classroom. Johnny cannot be like Suzy because they are wired differently from birth.

## The Male Brain and Aggression

Boys and girls also manifest differences in their brain system. Men and boys take longer to process feelings through the brain system than do females. The male's brain, which includes the corpus callosum, the limbic system, and the prefrontal lobes, is set up better for externalized responses as opposed to internalized responses. The externalizing impulse of the male brain predisposes boys to search for more rough-and-tumble play, including physical action, such as climbing on objects and running. In classrooms, boys are more physically impulsive. During recess or playtime, they play by creating externalized play with trucks or blocks. Watch boys and girls playing, and you will hear boys making all kinds of sounds with trucks that seemingly only small boys can make. In contrast, girls are more inclined to pick dolls and other objects with which they can create an internalized dialogue or conversation. Their play is quieter because they are having conversations with various toys.

The male brain has also been conceptualized as the hunting brain because it is more spatially oriented than the female's brain. The hunting brain pursues objects of prey. This theory has been partially supported by studies that show that boys score better on spatial problems that involve depth perception, three-dimensionality, and direction than do girls. Some believe that boys' spatial brain system causes them to externalize more of their feelings.

## Boys' and Girls' Serotonin Level and Violence

Neurotransmitters in the brain have also been linked with aggression and violence.[82] The neurotransmitter serotonin has a key role in mediating aggressive and violent behavior.[83] Serotonin modulates the brain's response to external stimuli. Usually, when an event catches the brain's attention, neurons begin to fire. Serotonin is an inhibitory neurotransmitter that helps reduce this response.

Hence, serotonin operates like brakes in a car. It puts a brake on human behavior. Individuals with a history of impulsive, violent behavior, such as arsonists and criminals, and those who die by violent methods of suicide evidence low levels of serotonin in their cerebral spinal fluid.

Coccaro, Kavoussi, Hauger, Cooper, and Ferris[84] reported that serotonin, along with other neurotransmitters, assumes a critical role in the development of such behaviors. Coccaro et al.[85] found that treatment with fluoxetine, a drug that keeps serotonin levels high, improves aggressive adult behavior. Data on serotonin and children are limited; however, a two-year study conducted by Kruesi and colleagues[86] found that among children diagnosed with disruptive behavior disorders, their low serotonin level predicted aggression.

In addition, there are gender differences with serotonin production. The female brain produces more serotonin than the male. Because of their lower levels of serotonin, boys have less natural impulse control than girls. Medical doctors have reported that male fetuses are more physically impulsive than female fetuses, kicking Mom more in the uterus. Boys' lower impulse control continues throughout their childhood, adolescence, and adulthood. Impulsive children get into more behavioral difficulty than do those who are less impulsive. Because of their tendency toward impulsivity, boys may need to have clear limits and discipline, plus a large dose of forgiveness, forgiveness, and more forgiveness.

Moreover, researchers concur that there most likely exists a genetic component to aggression because violent behavior tends to run in families.[87,88] Violent fathers tend to produce violent sons. While it is possible to inherit a predisposition to violence, psychologists have emphasized that modeling aggressive behavior in the home provides the basis for most violent children.[89,90] Thus, the next section explores the role of the family and the impact that the family has on producing violent youth.

## The Family Environment as a Cause of Youth Violence

Family violence is intergenerational. In dysfunctional families, either the victim or the perpetrator may participate in child maltreatment and neglect or violence. Most abusive parents have experienced some form of abuse in their childhood. Children raised in dysfunctional families tend to be unable to acquire socially appropriate problem-solving skills, and they are likely to become aggressive toward people in authority and toward their peers.[91,92] Other intergenerational factors associated with violence in families include poverty, mental illness, and drug and alcohol abuse. In the United States, one out of five families lives in poverty, and the shortage of such social resources as money for shelter, food, clothing, and health care may contribute to family violence.[93]

This book distinguishes between the family violence and domestic violence. Ordinary families, with little hint of overt domestic violence, may contribute to youth violence by the manner in which parents communicate with each other and discipline their children. The family is the alpha and the omega for learning about violence for young children. It can create a supportive environment that helps young people to turn inherited biological characteristics toward violence into developmental assets, or it can become part of the violence problem.[94]

Although the United States is one of the greatest countries in the world, the condition of children in this country is precarious. According to the Children's Defense Fund,[95] 1 in 2 American children live in a single parent family at some point in childhood; 1 in 3 is born to unmarried parents; 1 in 4 lives with only one parent; 1 in 8 children is born to a teenage mother, and 1 in 25 lives with neither parent. These family conditions put American youth at risk for violence, both as victims and as predators.[96]

There is a growing body of research that indicates parents should be concerned about their children's violence, if only from the perspective of their own safety.[97] Children and adolescents are committing an increasing number of assaults within the family. Instead of being afraid for children, some Americans are increasingly becoming afraid of their own children. Statistics have shown that 20 percent of the murder victims in the United States are killed by family members.[98]

## Violence Against Mothers

Much of family violence tends to be against mothers, because they are frequently targets for domestic violence.[99] As children mature in violent homes, sympathy toward the battered mother is often replaced by overt hostility and actual battering by her children. Children's violence against mothers is often hidden in the closet, until it becomes unbearable for the victim.[100] Bandura's[101] social learning theory has been used to explain children's greater violence toward mothers than toward fathers. According to social learning theory, boys are more physically aggressive toward their mothers because their fathers served as violent role models against their mothers. For instance, Cornell and Gelles's[102] early research found that sons were more likely to hit their mothers if the mothers had been victims of partner violence. Using reasoning from social learning theory, women who stay in physically abusive relationships for the sake of their children are only increasing the likelihood that their children will become violent toward them.

## Parental Discipline and Violence

Although observing violent behavior between their parents is a key factor in children's later development of violent behavior, what forms an equally important impression on children is when their own parents hit them out of anger or out of efforts to discipline them for some wrongdoing. Over 90 percent of children ages three to five in the United States, are hit by their mothers and fathers.[103] Such parental hitting of children provides powerful modeling for violence. One study found that each increase in the amount of parent-to-child violence, beginning even with one or two instances of corporal punishment in the previous 12 months is associated with a substantial increase in the percentage of children who hit their mothers. When mothers used one or two instances of corporal punishment in the previous 12 months, 30 percent were hit by their children that year, and only 13 percent were so hit when mothers did not use such punishment in the previous 12 months. Children's hitting rate against their mothers increased to 47 percent when they hit the children with an object, punched, or kicked them.[104]

Children's hitting of their mothers declines as they move from toddler stage to adolescence.[105] As children mature, they exercise greater control over their behavior, with the possible exception of adolescent boys who increase their violence as they acquire the physical skills to carry out more severe assaults on parents.[106]

## The Family and the Intergenerational Transmission of Violence

Violence sometimes begins and ends in the family. Struder[107] has asserted that the family is the most violent institution in our society. Moreover, Myers[108] has reported that 17–20 percent of all homicides in the United States take place within a family situation. The term "family violence" includes a broad set of familial relationships. It encompasses a wide range of behaviors that harm someone within the family, such as child abuse and neglect, domestic violence, elder abuse, and abuse of people with handicaps. Such harm may be physical abuse or psychological abuse in the form of hurting words, intimidation, economic manipulation, and sexual threats. The cycle of violence theory[109] maintains there is an intergenerational transmission of violence. Violent behavior is first learned in the family and then passed on from one generation to the next. A childhood survivor of violence passes on the violence to his new family, thereby creating a never-ending cycle of violence.

In contrast to family violence, domestic violence is relationship specific. Domestic violence has been defined as a pattern of assaultive and coercive behaviors, including physical, psychological, sexual, and economic coercion that adults or adolescents use against their intimate partners.[110] The conscious or unconscious goal of such behavior is to establish power and control over a spouse or a significant other with whom one has been in a romantic relationship.[111] Domestic violence perpetrators use psychological abuse, for example, by providing put-downs, creating public humiliation, shaming, ridiculing, insulting valued beliefs, telling lies such as saying that the victim caused the hurtful act, isolating someone from friends and family, and threatening the victim or the victim's loved ones, particularly children.

Physical domestic violence entails hitting, punching, slapping, shoving, kicking, or choking a person, locking someone in or outside the house, harming family pets, and stalking the victim. Sexual domestic violence includes accusing someone of affairs or boasting about affairs, and calling someone names like "whore," "bitch," or "frigid"; or it may result in coercing a person into unwanted sexual acts or rape. Domestic violence may also be economic, such as making all financial decisions without allowing input from one's partner, prohibiting a partner from working, or taking a person's money.

Each year an estimated 3 to 10 million children witness domestic violence in their families and homes.[112] Studies have found that child abuse takes place in 30–60 percent of the domestic violence cases that involve families with children. Between 4 percent and 30 percent of women who enter emergency hospital care departments suffer from a domestic violence injury.[113] Nearly 47 percent of the men who beat their wives do so at least three times per year. Each year, 6 percent of all pregnant (240,000) women in the United States are battered by the men in their lives.[114] Battered pregnant women suffer a number of complications during pregnancy, including anemia, infection, maternal depression, suicide attempts, and illicit drug use. African American women suffer a 35 percent higher rate of intimate partner violence than do White women. Moreover, women who are illegal immigrants or whose immigration status depends on her partner may be battered and isolated by cultural dynamics that prevent them from seeking assistance from the legal system.

Female homicides in which race was identified (1,194 victims) included 1,204 White females, 659 African American females, 30 Asian or Pacific Islanders, and 21 American Indian or Alaskan natives.[115] Overall, African American women (3.64 per 100,000) were murdered at a rate more than three times higher than white women (1.06 per 100,000).

## Effects of Domestic Violence on Children

Children who observe domestic violence in their homes are secondary victims of violence, even if they are not hit or otherwise abused. Some may even develop a post-traumatic stress disorder or a conduct disorder. Exposure to domestic violence encompasses watching or hearing the violent acts and direct involvement, which may take the form of having the children fighting the perpetrator or intervening in some manner. It may also include witnessing the aftereffects of the violence, such as seeing bruises on one's mother or observing maternal depression.[116,117] In addition, children may be forced to leave their homes and to live in community shelters.

Another consequence of domestic violence is that battered mothers are oftentimes less emotionally available to their children because they are preoccupied with their own safety or because they are experiencing depression from violence.[118] Studies of domestic violence have produced conflicting results about how battered women treat their children. While some studies have shown no differences in mothers' patterns of affectionate or aggressive conduct toward their children, others have reported that battered women may use more punitive child-rearing strategies toward their children.[119]

The specific effects of domestic violence on children vary, depending on the children's ages, the nature and severity of the violence, and the risk factors in the children's lives.[120] For instance, infants exposed to an environment in which there may be frequent fighting, yelling, and arguing may cry excessively, manifest irritability, suffer sleep disturbances, show regression in toilet training, exhibit language retardation, and have digestive problems.[121,122] Infants or toddlers exposed to violence often develop a lack of trust in relationships. Children may become afraid to go near the scene of the violent act they witnessed, or they may wake up at night with nightmares, screaming and yelling for their parents.

School-age children who have watched domestic violence may have difficulty paying attention and concentrating in school because they are distracted by intrusive thoughts. They may worry about being safe, feel jumpy, and be scared of ordinary circumstances. Further, school-age children who frequently observe domestic violence are likely to be aggressive toward others. They learn their aggression by seeing it (observation learning), by receiving rewards (greater stature in a community), or by punishments for it (whippings). Aggressive children may be given a diagnosis of conduct disorder or antisocial behavior.[123] Such children have difficulty understanding how to achieve positive behavior through prosocial means. Violence may be the primary source of power they use and admire.

The effects of domestic violence on adolescents can lead to the death of the perpetrator and imprisonment for the children. Children sometimes take steps to end violence against their mothers. Almost 62 percent of young men between the ages of 11 and 20 who were serving time for homicide killed their mother's batterer. Fantuzzo and Mohr[124] concluded that children in domestic violence households are not just witnessing the violence; they are sometimes a part of it. Adult perpetrators sometimes use children to bring on violence in the house, or they may be asked to call 911, or they act to end the cycle of violence.

## Child Abuse, Neglect, and Violence

Both child abuse and child neglect have long been considered to be powerful causes for youth violence. Child abuse has been defined as any behavior directed toward a child by a parent, caregiver, other family member, or other adult that endangers or impairs a child's physical or emotional health and development. It occurs in all segments of society and in all cultural, ethnic, and religious groups.[125,126] In the United States, more than 2.5 million reports of child abuse are made each year, with hundreds of deaths connected to such abuse.[127] A majority of runaway teens, adolescent prostitutes, and teenage delinquents have stated they were victims of child abuse.

Child abuse may be divided into four categories: physical abuse, sexual abuse, emotional abuse, and neglect. Physical abuse involves external injuries to the child, and it is more easily detected than other forms of abuse. Child neglect is the repeated failure to provide a child with the necessary care and protection, including adequate shelter, food, clothing, and medical care. Lack of appropriate supervision for a young child for extended periods of time also constitutes child neglect.[128,129]

Emotional abuse involves both verbal assaults and the withholding of positive emotional support. Parents who use emotional abuse daily harm their children with words that demean, shame, threaten, blame, or intimidate; they criticize their children relentlessly. Emotional abuse destroys children's self-confidence and self-esteem. Emotionally abused children exhibit patterned behavior that is extreme (e.g., lying, stealing, fighting), or they are overly aggressive and act out inappropriately.[130]

Sexual abuse can be physical (fondling, intercourse, and rape) or nonphysical (indecent exposure and obscene phone calls). Sexual abuse of children leaves lasting emotional scars. For instance, they may develop addictions, particularly sexual addictions.[131] People who sexually abuse children typically suffer from an emotional or psychological disorder, usually as a result of their own prior sexual victimization.[132] The majority of child molesters are men who abuse both boys and girls.[133] Women form only a small percentage of those who sexually abuse children. The majority of all sexual molestation is perpetrated by someone whom the child knows or trusts, such as a father, family member, relative, babysitter, neighbor, or other authority figure.

The vast majority of sexually abused children do not become violent, although sexual abuse has been linked to criminal behavior in adulthood. Experiencing childhood abuse and neglect, however, increases a young person's likelihood of an arrest by 53 percent and the chances that he will commit a violent crime by 38 percent.[134] Perhaps most telling is the fact that children who are abused or neglected are likely to abuse their own children later on in life. Why do parents abuse or neglect their children? Contrary to popular beliefs, parents who abuse their children may love them very much, but they may not love them appropriately. Otherwise, good-intentioned parents sometimes engage in child abuse when they themselves are immature and lack an understanding of child development.

Parents abuse their children for a variety of reasons, including their abuse as children and their lack of a successful role model for parenting and family life.[135] Child abuse also occurs when parents' lack of understanding of child development leads to unrealistic expectations for their children's behavior. When children fail to meet parental expectations, parents may become frustrated and become abusive toward the child.

Abusing parents are often isolated from their families and the community in which they live.[136] Such isolation may lead to their excessive dependence on their children to satisfy their unmet emotional needs. Parents who are overwhelmed and unable to cope because of financial pressures, poor housing conditions, and unemployment are more likely to abuse their children than are those who do not have these difficulties. Alcohol and substance abuse increase parents' chances for loss of control, for eruption of violent behavior, and for abuse of their children.[137] Sixty percent of domestic violence incidents involve drinking.[138]

Effective parenting can serve as a protective factor against a child's becoming violent. Similar to violence, nonviolence is a learned behavior. Parents can avoid rearing a violent child or adolescent if they are not violent toward each other and if they model peaceful ways of resolving conflict between themselves. The most important protective factor that a child can have against the negative effects of exposure to violence is a strong relationship with a competent, caring positive adult, who, hopefully, is a parent.[139] Professionals who have consistent contact with children and adolescents, including teachers, social workers, law enforcement officers, and court personnel should receive ongoing training on domestic violence and its impact on children.

## Poverty, the Culture of Violence and Violence Socialization

Conditions associated with poverty, such as high levels of transience and unemployment, crowded housing, firearm and drug infested neighborhoods, high school dropout and pregnancy rates, have been highly correlated with violence.[140] In poor neighborhoods, young people may be socialized into violent behavior in early childhood and throughout adolescence.[141] The violence socialization theory maintains that children have early experiences in antisocial or aggressive behavior that are reinforced by peers or family members.[142] Children receive support or rewards for their aggressive behavior, and they subsequently seek out others who evidence similar behaviors in order to be accepted and reinforced by the social group. They may be socialized into violence at a later age by peers.

Neighborhoods that have a high rate of violence also have what researchers label "low social capital." Coleman[143] used the term "social capital" to refer to the quality and the depth of relationships between people in a family or in a community. According to Coleman, the social capital of a community resides in the actual social relationships that exist among parents in the parents' relations with the institutions of the community. Social capital also refers to the family's or the community's ability to work on behalf of the child's well-being and its ability to work toward a common good.

In some African American inner city neighborhoods, there is low social capital for the community and its members. Over the past 30 years, some African American inner city neighborhoods have become isolated and cut off from the rest of the American society. These neighborhoods experience what sociologist Julius Wilson[144] has labeled as the "concentrated effects of poverty." African American youth find themselves trapped in economically devastated neighborhoods, with few employed adults, few stable families, and a large number of households headed by single mothers.[145] Such youth internalize aggression and violence in order to survive.[146] They may become involved in predatory violence, that is, violence that usually involves a stranger trying to take something of value by using physical threats or direct violence. Predatory violence also comes from nonfamily interpersonal conflicts, such as with acquaintances involved in a drug conflict.[147,148] Drive-by shootings are part of the new predatory violence in some communities.

When violence repeatedly takes place in a community, parents may become overprotective of their children. The children may not be allowed to explore their environment because it is not safe. Sometimes their homes or apartments become their own prisons, as they find themselves locked behind windows with bars placed over them for their own safety. Even with bars over the windows and doors, some inner-city families still do not feel safe.[149,150] The parents suffer because the neighborhood violence interferes with their ability to raise their children in the manner they believe is best.[151] The children suffer because their parents' failure to satisfy their own basic safety needs in their community diminishes their ability to form close attachment relationships required for later healthy, emotional maturity.[152] Young people living in "urban war zones" experience post-traumatic stress disorder symptoms similar to that of counterparts of their age living in actual war zones.[153,154,155]

When adolescents are exposed to chronic community violence, they exhibit high levels of aggression and acting out, behavioral problems, school problems, truancy, and revenge seeking.[156] Moreover, adolescents who suffer from chronic exposure to violence have a different sense of their own mortality. They tend to express a sense of hopelessness and inability to make plans for their future. Many state they do not expect to live beyond 25 or 30 years of age.[157] Such beliefs may lead to high risk-taking behavior among youth because they cannot imagine the long-term consequences of their actions, and because they do not feel that they have control over their environment. Further, adolescents attach themselves to gangs as sources of protection from the violence. Adolescents who have experienced chronic community violence may find it difficult to extricate themselves from a web of violence. They may become violent themselves, as reflected in the high prison rates for many minority males.[158]

## Drugs and Substance Abuse as a Cause of Youth Violence

Substance use and abuse are key features of a violent lifestyle.[159,160] Parker and Auerhahn[161] found that youths' use of alcohol is a major factor in their violence. Young people's use of drugs tends to increase their violence toward others and themselves. Although youths' use of alcohol declined between 1978 and 1993 and has fluctuated within a limited range since then, 31 percent of high school seniors, 24 percent of tenth graders, and 14 percent of eighth graders reported heavy drinking in the two weeks preceding a 1998 survey.[162] One reason drug use increases youth violence is that it is associated with an increase in youths' carrying of firearms. In the United States, 40 percent of youth who drank alcohol at school also carried a weapon at school compared with 4.4 percent of those who did not drink. Half of the youth homicide victims have elevated blood alcohol levels on autopsy.[163] A similar situation exists for youth who commit homicide and are apprehended in time to test for substance abuse. Drugs also increase youth violence because they alter their perceptions, all the while increasing their impulsivity. Nearly 50 percent of youth who are arrested test positive for illicit drugs. Moreover, youths' efforts to get money to support a drug habit increase their participation in burglaries and robberies.

## Gangs as a Cause of Violence

Gangs are responsible for a disproportionate share of all youthful criminal offenses. Currently, gang problems have spread to jurisdictions previously thought exempt from such activities, including rural and suburban areas. As a result, the numbers of White gang members outside of big cities have increased. Similarly, there has been an increase in the number of female gang members.[164] Gangs have a direct influence on violence because there is also a link between gang activity and guns. Quinn and Downs[165] found that movement from nongang membership to gang membership resulted in increases in the use of guns. Nearly 68 percent of the sample said that their gang regularly bought and sold guns, and 61 percent described "driving around shooting at people you don't like" as a regular gang activity.

## Television and Media Violence as a Cause of Youth Violence

The vast majority of evidence from more than 3,000 research studies over two decades shows that the violence portrayed on television influences the attitudes and behavior of children who watch it. The American Psychological Association has provided evidence that the level of violence on commercial television has remained fairly constant for the past two decades. During prime time, there are five to six violent acts per hour; and on Saturday morning, there are 20 to 25 violent acts per hour on children's programs. In homes that have MTV, cable television, and VCRs, there may be a much higher rate of media violence. According to the American Academy of Pediatrics:

- The average child watches three hours of TV a day—two hours of quality programming is the maximum recommended by the Academy.
- Active play time is needed to develop mental, physical, and social skills.
- Children who watch violence on TV are more likely to exhibit aggressive behavior.
- Young children do not know the difference between programs and commercials.

A more in-depth discussion of mediation violence is presented in Chapter 6. It is important to reiterate that both children and parents see media violence as a major cause of youth violence.

## Warning Signs for Violence

Parents need to be aware of warning signs in order to recognize tendencies toward violence in their children. No single warning sign can predict violence; however, in 1998, the U.S. Department of Education published a report entitled *Early Warning, Timely Response: A Guide to Safe Schools*[166] that detailed warning signs of youth violence. A child's previous history of violence is the strongest developmental predictor of his violence. For instance, a child's aggression toward his peers shows considerable consistency and predictability over a period of time. What should a parent look for in young infants for early warning signs of a possible violent temperament? In general, children who demonstrate a fearless, impulsive temperament very early in life may have a predisposition for aggressive and violent behavior. Likewise, children who are hard to soothe when they are infants, who manifest a pattern of repeated, out-of-control temper tantrums, and who refuse to follow simple early rules are also at risk for aggressive and delinquent behavior. This does not mean that every child who has a temper tantrum is going to become violent later in life. One has to examine the frequency of such temper tantrums.

Boys, rather than girls, are at a greater risk of committing violent acts. At this point, it is unclear to what extent gender differences in violence are attributable to biological factors and to what degree they can be explained by differences in sex role socialization. Parents might take notice of settings in which children operate. The most significant settings for a child's development for aggression are in the home and in the school. Children's aggression in the home is usually, but not always, related to their aggression at school. A child's aggression in school is most often directed at peers. Typical school fights between youth are about retaliation, rules of the games, or possession of toys, equipment, or territory. Physical aggression by boys in schools predicts later antisocial acts, delinquency, and violent offending in the community.[167]

# Parenting Is a Spiritual Journey

Parenting is a spiritual journey that involves travels inward toward the self and back out again to the world. We look inward for answers to nagging questions about who we really are, what we actually want out of life, and what we are willing to give to ourselves, our children, and our families. Sometimes the journey inward can be frightening because we are not quite sure what we will find. After all, our own childhood and adolescence are over. Why go back over ground well traveled? We made it out okay.

Whether we like it or not, parenting our own children sends us back repeatedly to our own childhoods. As Benjamin Spock once said:

> All the time a person is a child he is both a child and learning to be a parent. After he becomes a parent, he becomes predominantly a parent reliving childhood.

It is inevitable that we revisit our childhood as we parent our own children. In fact, such a revisit is almost obligatory and occurs in the strangest of moments, such as right after we have disciplined our child. We hear ourselves asking silently: "Did I actually say that? Where did that come from? Oh, my God, I think I just heard my mother talking, but it was me." And then we see ourselves as little kids again. If the revisitation is not all that pleasant, we might say with a sigh of quiet relief: "I thought I had put all that behind me. What brought it up again?"

This book is then about the spiritual journey that we embark upon when we have children. Most of us are not aware that we are about to go on a spiritual journey when we become parents. In fact, we often see the hospital delivery room as the end of a nine-month journey, but in reality, it is only the beginning. Many of you, hopefully, will get a chance to see the effects of your parenting when your children become adults.

## The Inward Spiritual Journey

The inward journey brought on by parenthood consists of all the stored memories, the pictures of you as a little child, the smells of your home, the young pictures of your parents, your brothers and sisters (if any), your teachers, and your friends. All that you thought you left behind comes back to you in bits and pieces as you parent your own children. The inward journey is important because it helps you to understand why you want to parent the way you are guiding your children.

One of the underlying premises of this book is that all life consists of energy. Our thoughts are energy. Our life experiences consist of negative and positive energy. The struggle in life for most people is learning how to transform negative life energy into positive life energy. The transformation process is not easy. Sometimes we are forced to go back to the very beginning when our life force energy was first created and either nurtured by our parents or left to struggle for itself on the vine.

The parental spiritual journey involves finding your unconscious parent, your inner child, and your adult or independent conscious parent. Your unconscious parent consists of the internalized personalities of your mother and father. Their attitudes and views become the voice for your unconscious parent. Quite frequently, people say when they are young that they will never treat their children in the same manner that their parents treated them; yet, it is difficult to quiet completely the voices of our parents. We hear their voices in our heads. We even sometimes carry on conversations with them in our heads. Your inner child is you as a young child and the opinions you formed regarding your parents and the world. Today, this child still exists, even though you may have grown much older. Oftentimes, the unconscious parents and the inner child still debate what is right and wrong and how children should be raised.

Becoming an adult often means trying to find your independent adult parent. Your adult parent is the parent you are trying, or in some instances struggling, to be. The adult parent operates at the conscious level of awareness. You have some understanding of your parenting strengths and weaknesses. You are aware of how you are parenting and why.

## Conscious and Unconscious Parenting

We all engage in both conscious and unconscious parenting. Conscious parenting takes place when you are aware of your guidance or behavior on your children. There is a certain intentionality involved with conscious parenting. Unconscious parenting takes place when you parent without awareness of your behavior or words on your children. You can compare unconscious parenting to driving while having the car on cruise control. You are there, and you can take the cruise control off any time you want, but it is so much better not having to worry about the changing of your speed, especially when there is a straightaway. A great deal of parenting involves unconscious parenting, where you are not even aware of the underlying needs that cause you to parent one way or another.

Unconscious parenting takes place when you require your child to do something without actually understanding why you are making the requirement. It is like the TV commercial where a father folds his peanut butter sandwich over, and the daughter asks: "But why do you do that?" And the father answers: "I don't know. I guess because that's the way my dad made his sandwiches." And then the little girl responds: "That's silly." She turns her back and folds her sandwich in the exact same way. The father looks at her, laughs, and realizes that he has just passed down a family tradition for making peanut butter sandwiches.

Unconscious parenting takes place when parents lack a vision of what they want to accomplish by parenting and when their energies are scattered on so many things that they and their children lose focus. There is something of the feeling: "Where are we supposed to be tonight?" Or, "What's wrong, we're all together tonight? Did we miss someone's practice?" Cruise control parenting happens when parents just let things happen, and when they have gotten into a reacting mode.

When you parent unconsciously, you tend to parent the way your parents did. The unconscious pilot is in actuality your own parents directing how you should interact with your children. For instance, a father tells his teenage son to do something, and the teen responds with a "Why?" The father responds: "Just because I said so, that's why." A few minutes later the father actually does ask himself his son's question of why, and he finds that try as he might, he cannot answer the question. When parents do not know why they take a certain action toward their children, there is a good chance that the unconscious parent is in control.

In conscious parenting, parents are more inclined to be meeting their own unrecognized needs rather than their children's needs. For instance, parents who have a deep-seated need for control may later discover that such a need extends to controlling their children. They may find it difficult to let their children form their own opinions. Similar situations may be said to occur for parents who have unresolved, unconscious power needs. In this instance, parenting becomes a means to dominate one's children—all under the guise of the principle of building obedience to one's elders.

Parents need to take inventory to understand to what extent their parenting meets their own needs rather than those of their children. When you parent in the unconscious mode, you are inclined to meet your own needs rather than those of your children. One goal of this book is to help make parents aware of when their unconscious parent or their independent adult parent is in control of their interactions with their own children.

## Understanding Your Own Parenting Spiritual Values

An Indian proverb states that everyone can be compared to a house with four rooms—physical, mental, emotional, and spiritual. Most people spend the majority of their time in only one or two rooms. Few live fully in all four rooms. This book is intended partly to help you find ways to enter your spiritual parenting room.

The journey for spiritual parents begins long before you become a parent. One way to get clues to your early spiritual parenting journey is to ask yourself: What is my earliest memory? Who is there with you in your earliest memory? Is it your mother? Father? What is going on in this memory? How are you being treated? What are you feeling in this scene? How does this earliest memory relate to current issues that are going on in your life? If you were given a chance, would you change anything in your earliest memory? If so, what would that be? What does this remembered life scene tell you about your earliest spiritual views on parenting? How are you viewing parenting, and what are your views on how children should be treated?

The above questions are designed to help you recover the experiences that led to your current views on parenting. The belief is that our earliest memories symbolize the current themes in our lives. What we remember becomes figured in our lives. We remember how we were treated by our parents. If you are fortunate, your earliest memory is positive. All too often, however, our earliest memories are fraught with conflict, struggles, and negative relationships.

Moreover, the job of parenting requires that you look inward to determine what your values are, what your hopes and dreams are for your child, and how you would like to guide your child through part of his journey. What do you believe that parenting is? What is the purpose of parenting? What do you hope to pass on to your child and how? Carl Jung, the famous psychologist, once said:

> If there is anything we wish to change in the child, we should first examine it and see whether it is something that could better be changed in ourselves.

Are you going to parent unconsciously on cruise control with mainly the direction of how your parents raised you? Are you going to parent with your inner child being in control? Or, are you going to parent as an independent adult who has spent some time learning about the developmental needs of children and how to respond to such needs? Another way of presenting these questions is: To what extent will your parenting of your child be conscious or unconscious?

What would make you feel successful as a parent? And how do you intend to reach your goals? Would you be happy if your children get good jobs or even become wealthy? The Dharma spiritual philosophy of parenting is that you should detach yourself from the seeming successes and failures of your children. By doing so, you become able to be at one with them at all times. The principle is that parents should not live their lives through their children. Let them be free to find their own true fulfillment in life. A similar sentiment is expressed in Tao philosophy.

The Tao states:

*The wisest person*
*Trusts the process, without seeking to control.*
*Takes everything as it comes,*
*Lives not to achieve or possess,*
*But simply to be*
*All he or she can be*
*In harmony with the Tao.*

# *Intentional Parenting*

One goal of this book is to help you parent intentionally or with a purpose in mind. Have you ever thought about what it means to be an intentional parent? An intentional parent understands what you want for your child because you have spent some time thinking about it. An intentional parent is an on purpose parent. When you parent intentionally, you make a commitment to parenting and all the time that it requires to do it right. Your children gain when you parent them intentionally. The following are recommended steps for critical parenting.

Step one for an intentional parent is to imagine what you want your relationship with your child to be like.

Step two is to consider what you would like for your child's relationships to be with others once he has reached adulthood. Try to get a picture in your mind of your child reaching adulthood. How is he acting, talking, accomplishing in the outside world? What values does your child have? How internal is your adult child's sense of reference? Is he able to establish boundaries with others? How would you rate his level of self-esteem? Is your child violent, or does he have control over his emotions?

Step three is to imagine what legacy you want to leave to your child. What legacy would you like for your child to leave to his children? How instrumental have you been as a parent in helping your child build upon a positive legacy that he could leave with his own children?

As parents, we are inclined to parent our children "in between" so many different things. Rarely do we plan in advance how we want to parent our children. Our goal as parents should be to give our children intentional gifts—that is, gifts that we believe will be useful to them on their life journey. Intentional parents made decisions about what kind of health practices they will have with their children—for instance, whether or not to allow refined sugar in their diet. Intentional parents should also parent consciously about what they would like to impart regarding their children's emotional, social, and educational development.

You are practicing parenting with a purpose when you

- Have a clear vision of what you want to accomplish with parenting your child
- Establish communication patterns you adhere to with your child
- Understand what kind of power relationships you want to establish with your child
- Identify personal qualities you would like your children to have as adults
- Identify a wide range of strategies for strengthening your family
- Prepare a plan to organize your family to meet life's challenges
- Decide whether your family will have its own motto to show what it stands for
- Create a vision for your family and an action plan for the future

Intentional parenting does not mean that you can take your child and fashion him such that he turns out to be whatever you desire. Nor does it mean that you should rescue your children from every adversity. One of the Dharma lessons on wisdom and compassion is appropriate for giving clues about raising children. The story is that a traveler was walking down the road and saw a butterfly trying to emerge from its cocoon. The butterfly was struggling to set itself free. Filled with compassion for the butterfly, the traveler reached down and broke open the cocoon to free the butterfly from its struggles. To the traveler's amazement, the freed butterfly fell to the ground unable to fly and died. The traveler did not have the wisdom to know that the butterfly's struggle against the cocoon strengthens its wings enabling it to fly. Without the struggle, the butterfly's wings did not work. In raising children, parents are continually faced with the question of whether or not they should free them from the problems of life. The next few chapters are designed to help you understand your child's developmental stages and the issues that these stages present for parenting.

# Chapter Summary

Violence in America is a public health concern. This chapter has reviewed the many roots and causes of young people's violence, including biological factors, family influences, and neighborhood socialization practices. There is no single cause of youth violence. Instead, there are many fingers of blame. Warning signs for youth violence were presented. The chapter discussed parenting as a spiritual journey and compared cruise control parenting with intentional parenting.

# Intentional Parenting Tips

This section contains a series of quizzes and tips to help parents determine to what extent violence is a factor in their homes. These quizzes are not scientific, but merely point to issues parents might want to consider.

## Is Violence a Problem for My Child?

Answer the questions below to find out your child's violence or violence potential. Your response will determine if you believe your child is at risk and needs your intervention.

_____ 1. Does your child frequently become angry?

_____ 2. Does your child become out of control if he does not get his way?

_____ 3. Does your child use abusive language toward you or other family members?

_____ 4. Has your child's temper gotten him into trouble at school?

_____ 5. Is your child frequently out late without your permission?

_____ 6. Is your child defiant when you tell him to do something?

_____ 7. Has your child been involved in fights in your neighborhood?

_____ 8. Does your child tend to make friends with kids who are having problems at school or who may be using drugs?

_____ 9. Has your child destroyed property in your home in an angry rage?

_____10. Has your child been violent toward anyone at home?

_____11. Has your child observed either one of his parents acting violently?

_____12. Is your child's acting out behavior affecting your marriage or the family in a negative way?

_____13. Does your child like to listen to music that has violent lyrics?

_____14. Does your child like to watch sadistic and violent movies?

_____15. Are you satisfied with your child's ability to manage his anger?

_____16. Are you afraid of your child's hitting or hurting you?

If you answered yes to more than three questions, your child might be having a problem with anger and violence. You may have suspected that your child has a problem with emotions or behavior. Some parents minimize their teen's behavior or deny that there is a problem. They make excuses for their child and blame others, such as the school, teachers, family, or friends. They may be "fixing" problems the child creates. They may be giving in to their child's demands and compromising their own values just to keep the peace at home. Sometimes, parents may not take steps to get help with their angry or out-of-control child because they have guilty feelings for separation, divorce, or drinking. If you are a parent of an angry child, you may feel isolated and think that your family is the only one with a child who is out of control. That is simply not true.

## How Nurturing I Am As a Parent Quiz

The following is a quiz for parents to discover how nurturing they are as parents. Use the following numbers to indicate the degree to which you agree with each of the statements below: 4 = strongly agree; 3 = agree; 2 = disagree; and 1 = strongly disagree.

_____ 1. I know the developmental stages my child goes through as he matures.
_____ 2. I am aware of my child's needs.
_____ 3. I am able to understand how other people feel.
_____ 4. I am able to understand the reasons other people behave the way that they do.
_____ 5. I know how to manage my children without hitting them.
_____ 6. I am aware of my own needs and how they affect my parenting.
_____ 7. I feel good about my children.
_____ 8. I have decided not to spank my children.
_____ 9. I am confident that I know how to bring out the best in my children.
_____10. I feel good about being a parent.
_____11. My children and I have a good relationship.
_____12. I take time to really listen to what my children are saying.
_____13. I spend time playing with my children.
_____14. I help my children to express their feelings toward me and others.
_____15. I encourage my child and help him to focus on his strengths.
_____16. I have formed a strong, positive bond with my child.
_____17. I set aside private time each day with my child.
_____18. My child has formed a strong positive bond with me.
_____19. My child trusts me.
_____20. My child likes me.

Add up your total points. The higher the score, the higher your nurturing potential is as a parent.

## Domestic Violence Quiz

True or False—Answer true or false to the questions below.

_____ 1. Verbal abuse is not a form of domestic violence.

_____ 2. If a mother is abused by her children's father, the children are also likely to be abused.

_____ 3. Most people will end a relationship if the boyfriend or girlfriend hits them.

_____ 4. People who are abused often blame themselves for the abuse.

_____ 5. A pregnant woman is at even greater risk of physical abuse than those who are not pregnant.

_____ 6. Most men who abuse their partners grew up in violent homes.

_____ 7. Most rapes are committed by strangers who attack women at night on the streets.

_____ 8. Teenagers often report abuse to their parents or to school authorities.

_____ 9. The victims of sexual violence do not usually know their attackers.

_____10. The motive for rape is not the result of uncontrollable sexual urges. Rather, it is the need to gain control over the victim.

_____11. If my child or a child I know was being sexually abused, he would tell me right away.

_____12. Possessiveness is a common warning sign of an abusive relationship.

_____13. My partner questions my whereabouts, who I talk with, and/or why I want to be with my friends or family.

_____14. I feel pushed or forced into having sex.

_____15. My partner tells me he is sorry after he hits me.

## Parental Attitudes toward Children

Are you a violent or a nonviolent parent? The questions below help you to discern how you handle anger in relationship to your child and other family members.

_____ 1. My child often gets on my nerves.

_____ 2. I wish I did not have a child.

_____ 3. I feel very angry toward my child.

_____ 4. I feel ashamed of my child.

_____ 5. Parenting is an honor and privilege.

_____ 6. I believe that hitting a child is the best way to correct undesirable behavior.

_____ 7. I do not believe that parents should hit children, even when they misbehave.

_____ 8. I believe that children should be seen and not heard.

_____ 9. Parents should not spend time playing with their children. It spoils them.

_____10. Parents should forge a close bond with their children.

## How Angry Is Your Child!

_____ 1. My child does not know how to explain how he is feeling when he is upset.

_____ 2. My child has frequent angry temper tantrums, even over minor issues.

_____ 3. My child has difficulty calming down after he becomes angry or frustrated.

_____ 4. My child talks about violence or writes about or draws violent or aggressive acts.

_____ 5. My child cares only about his or her feelings.

_____ 6. My child has difficulty adapting to changes in routines or changes in life.
_____ 7. My child often acts without thinking, and sometimes behaves reckless recklessly.
_____ 8. My child has trouble bouncing back from a frustrating situation.
_____ 9. My child frequently fights or hits others.
_____10. My child blames others and does not accept responsibility for his actions.

This quiz is designed to help you examine how your child handles anger and frustration. There is no total score that will tell you if your child has a problem. If you checked two of these items, it may be a warning sign that your child needs help dealing with anger. Consider recording and tracking some of your child's angry behavior to see if he is having a more difficult time coping at a particular time of the day or when certain things are happening.

## Getting in Touch with Who You Are

It is important to know and understand yourself as you begin the parenting journey. You might try examining your own childhood, what you found valuable about your parents' raising you and what you might want to change with your own child.

### I AM

1. I am _____.
2. I need _____.
3. I love _____.
4. What I liked most about my parents' raising me was
   _____.
5. What I liked least about my parents' raising me was
   _____.
6. I fear
   _____.
7. I would like to achieve
   _____.
8. I would like my legacy to the world to be
   _____.
9. I believe in
   _____.
10. I appreciate
    _____.

# Reading List for Chapter 1

## Story Books That Deal with Domestic Violence and Child Abuse

*A Safe Place*
Maxine Trottier
Childwork/Childsplay—(800) 962-1141

*A mother escapes to a domestic violence shelter with her young daughter, where she builds up her strength and gains the courage to begin a new life. As they leave, the little girl gives hope to a frightened boy just entering the shelter. This picture book has illustrations in colored pencil. It is appropriate for children 5–9 years.*

*Clover's Secret*
Christine Winn and David Walsh, PhD
Minneapolis, MN: Fairview Press
(800) 544-8207/ FAX (612) 672-4980
http://fairviewpress.org/

*In an imaginary land where people can fly, two girls form a friendship that helps one of them deal with the problems she faces at home. This book is a picture book with colored pencil illustrations. It is appropriate for children 4–10 years.*

*Daddy, Daddy, Be There*
Candy Dawson Boyd and Floyd Cooper
New York City: Philomel Books Division of Putnam & Grosset

*This book represents children's moving pleas for a father's love and support. This easy-to-read story touches on all that children want from their father—emotionally—as they go through the life span together. This book only touches on domestic violence, but its use as a tool for assessment and for exploration of wish fulfillment cannot be denied. The book is a picture book with multicultural illustrations in pastels, 3–10 years.*

*The Dragon and the Mouse*
Steven Timm
Available exclusively from:
Touchstone Enterprise
2108 South University Drive
Fargo, ND 58103
(701) 237-4742

*A mouse lives with a dragon who is abusive to him emotionally, physically, mentally, and socially. In the end, the mouse leaves the living arrangement, but continues to be friends with the dragon. This picture book has vivid illustrations. It is appropriate for children 4–11 years.*

*I Wish the Hitting Would Stop*
The Rape and Abuse Crisis Center of Fargo-Moorhead
Fargo, ND: Red Flag Green Flag Resources
(800) 627-3675 / FAX (888) 237-5332
http://www.redflaggreenflag.com/

*Actually a workbook that can be used as a story book, it is written from the perspectives of young persons living in violent homes. Their feelings and thoughts about parental violence are explored. Safety-planning and coping skills are addressed as well. A 68-page facilitator's guide is also available, which includes discussion questions, related activities, and a resource section listing books, films, and games for children and adults, as well as "Cycle of Violence" and "Myths and Realities of Domestic Violence." This soft cover book has simple black and white drawings suitable for coloring, 6–14 years.*

*Something Is Wrong At My House*
Diane Davis
Seattle, WA: Parenting Press
(800) 992-6657 / FAX (206) 362-0702
http://www.parentingpress.com/

*A boy tells about the violence in his home and how it affects him. For younger children, just a text below the illustrations can be read. Advice for children on coping is included. This book is small and has pencil sketch illustrations. It is appropriate for children 3–10 years.*

Also in their Books to Help Protect Children series (Spanish versions of these are also available):

- *Loving Touches* (a book about positive, nurturing touches)
- *The Trouble with Secrets* (helps young children decide whether to keep or share a secret)
- *Something Happened and I'm Scared to Tell* (for sexual abuse victims)
- *It's My Body* (sexual abuse prevention)

*When Mommy Got Hurt—A Story for Young Children about Domestic Violence*
Ilene Lee and Kathy Sylvester
Charlotte, NC: KIDSRIGHTS
(800) 892-5437 / FAX (704) 541-0113

*A young (androgynous) child tells this story about the parents' fight, how the mother and child leave to live somewhere safe, and the conversations the mother has with this child afterward. The story focuses on four points: Violence is wrong, it is not the child's fault, it happens in many families, and it is OK to talk about it. This is a large, soft cover book with simple black and white drawings suitable for coloring, 3–9 years.*

# 2

# *Attachment*

*Other than life, the gift of parental attachment and bonding is perhaps the greatest gift that a parent can give a child.*

Kathy sat in the doctor's office on the worn leather couch. She was desperately trying to piece together all the bits and pieces of raising Paden that might have a bearing on his angry and often violent outbursts that were directed primarily toward her. She was tearful and struggled with her own accusing thoughts that she had somehow failed in raising Paden. Part of her wanted to defend herself with "I did the best I could raising Paden. It wasn't easy, you know." Instead, she recounted the circumstances of Paden's birth. "He had to have an operation, and I was discharged while he had to stay in the hospital for an extra week," she said. "And the doctor said that it was best that I not come to the hospital during the week so as not to upset him when I left. So, I did that. I did what I was told to do, and now I'm learning from you that what I did was wrong. . . . I can't believe this. . . . I mean how could a doctor tell me to do something that would harm my son? I can't believe this . . . this thing you're calling an attachment disorder was created by my leaving him in the hospital right after he was born?"

Kathy started to cry. The therapist tried to console her with some kind of psychological junk about "I know you are feeling upset right now, but. . . ." "How the hell can you know how I am feeling?" she replied. "Why should I even listen to you? . . . Maybe . . . maybe you're like that other doctor. You don't know what you're talking about either." But there was something about the therapist's diagnosis of Paden that rang true. He was superficial in most of his relationships, always lying and trying to be someone other than himself. Sometimes he would have these deep conversations with people he barely knew. Kathy wondered how she could have been so stupid to have done what the doctor told her to do.

Deep down inside she felt betrayed and wanted to scream at the top of her lungs, but she knew that would not do any good.

Many parents are just like Kathy. They know little about infant attachment and the impact that it can have on a child's development. In fact, a good number of parents fail to form an early attachment relationship with their children more so out of ignorance than out of any ill will toward their children. Attachment issues can be caused by such factors as a child having to stay in the hospital away from a mother, a primary caregiver being called away to take care of an ailing relative for weeks or months, poor day care, domestic violence, or drug use.

This chapter is about children's attachment and the role that this bond or the lack of it has on producing angry and violent children. Some of the most violent children in this country are those who are suffering from attachment issues. They have not ever formed a real bond or attachment to anyone in their lives, including their parents. Therefore, they have difficulty showing empathy toward others.

Recently, a 21-year-old male was on television describing how he killed two of his friends. He had been in and out of foster homes for most of his life. He confessed and told the arresting detective how he killed his two friends. "Jamie begged for her life and cried. She actually thought that I was going to let her go. I shot her in the back of the head." The detective asked: "Don't you feel anything about killing your friends?" "Me," he replied. "I ain't got no feelings for nobody. I don't trust nobody. Going to jail? That don't mean nothing to me." Attachment disordered children can be very violent and unforgiving of any offense. They feel angry and betrayed by the world. Charles Manson, a mass murderer, is a prime example of an attachment disordered child.

The significance of early infant attachment cannot be overstated. Attachment is at the center of healthy child development. It lays the foundation for the child's ability to relate intimately with others, including his own future spouse and children. The results of infant attachment are long term and can be handed down to future generations.

# *Definition of Attachment and Bonding*

Attachment can be defined as the psychological connection between two people that allows them to have relational significance to each other. It is an affectionate bond between two people that endures through time and that serves to join them emotionally together, regardless if they are near or far from each other.[1,2,3,4] Attachment is a biologically based strategy that provides both emotional and physical protection for children.[5,6] Bonding provides our emotional glue to another human being.[7]

Mothers typically have some kind of bond to the child after having carried him for nine months. Yet, even before birth, the umbilical cord provides the foundation for the bond between a mother and her child. Research shows that babies in the womb have emotional and intuitive capabilities to sense their parents' love. Prenates can see, hear, feel, remember, taste, and even think before birth.[8] It is extremely important for the infant and the mother to be alone together right after the birth to establish a strong bond. If there are too many people in the room right after birth, the natural process of attachment can be disrupted, and this disruption can have long-lasting effects on the relationship between the child and the mother or primary caregiver.[9]

What are bonding acts between a mother and a child? Bonding experiences include holding, rocking, feeding, singing, gazing, kissing, and other nurturing behaviors that occur as a part of caring for infants and young children. Factors critical to bonding include the time the caregiver and child spend together (in childhood, the quantity of time does matter), face-to-face interactions, eye contact, physical proximity, touch, and other sensory experiences such as smell, sound, and taste.[10,11]

# John Bowlby: The Father of Attachment Theory

John Bowlby is considered to be the father of attachment theory.[12,13] Bowlby, an English psychiatrist who trained initially as a Freudian psychoanalyst, wrote in 1969 the first of three influential books on attachment and loss. He believed that attachment begins at infancy and continues throughout life, and that there are several innate behavioral control systems that are needed for survival and procreation.

Bowlby noticed, along with other clinicians, that there was a somewhat predictable sequence of behaviors in young children's response to loss: (1) the child responded with anger and rage; (2) the child became depressed and evidenced despair; (3) the child became detached from people and the surrounding environment. In his first major work on attachment, Bowlby argued that an infant's social, psychological, and biological capacities cannot be understood apart from its relationship with its mother.

There were three basic components of Bowlby's attachment theory: (1) instincts; (2) physical factors; (3) emotional and social factors. Bowlby proposed that instincts have a major influence on an infant's attachment to his or her mother or primary caregiver. Infants' first instincts are the instincts to survive, to be social, and to be adaptable to the environment. Bowlby described instinctive behaviors that do not achieve the desired results as deviations in evolutionary adaptedness. Such deviations can produce maladaptive patterns. When maladaptive patterns take hold, the child begins a negative cycle. He or she slips farther and farther away from the instinctive goal of connection with other people. The physical factors that influence attachment include the brain, the central nervous system, and other aspects of human physiology, including hormones.

Physical touch is extremely important in the infant's ability to form an attachment with the primary caregiver.[14]

According to Bowlby, the mother-infant attachment relationship is "accompanied by the strongest of feelings and emotions, happy or the reverse," and that such interaction takes place within a context of "facial expression, posture, tone of voice, physiological changes, tempo of movement, and incipient action," and that further the attachment interactions provide the basis for the emergence of a biological control system that functions in the organism's "state of arousal."[15] The infant forms a secure attachment bond of emotional communication with the mother. This early socioemotional learning then becomes internalized in the form of an enduring capacity to regulate, to generate, and to maintain states of emotional security.[16] Social reciprocity is one goal of attachment.

Bowlby maintained that the capacity of an infant to cope with stress is connected to early nurturing maternal behaviors that are recorded in the brain and neuropsychological structure. He termed the manner in which a child begins to understand his or her surroundings as "inner working models." The inner working model that a child develops influences his perceptions about himself and others from early childhood well into adulthood.[17]

Bowlby's attachment theory can be summarized into eight crucial steps. First, the infant elicits social responses from a wide array of stimuli. These stimuli gradually narrow, and after several months they become confined to one or more individuals. Second, the infant develops a bias to respond more to certain kinds of stimuli than to other kinds. Third, the infant develops an attachment as he or she experiences more and more positive interactions with the primary caregiver. Fourth, as the infant has repeated exposure to the primary caregiver's face, he engages in a process of discrimination related to the attachment figure.[18]

Fifth, the timing of the attachment is critical and should be developed during the sensitive period within the first year of life. Sixth, the sensitive phase begins after six weeks. Seventh, at the end of the sensitive period, the infant responds to nonattachment figures with a fear response, making it difficult for him to attach after one year. Eighth, once infants become strongly attached, they prefer this person to all others, despite separation. Infants and children develop a preference to discern certain patterns and movements. They show preference for the familiar. They adopt approach behavior when they receive positive behavior, while negative feedback results in reduced approach response and then becomes withdrawal behavior.[19]

# Attachment and the Role of the Right Hemisphere of the Brain

There is a connection between the right hemisphere of the brain and attachment. During infant development, the right hemisphere of the brain connects into both the limbic system[20] and the autonomic nervous system (ANS). The right hemisphere is central to the control of vital functions that support survival and that help the infant to cope with stresses and challenges.[21] It is specialized for inhibitory control and feelings of violence that can develop later on in life. The right hemisphere is also dominant for unconscious processes. It weighs on a moment-to-moment basis the threat of external stimuli.

In growth facilitating environments, children's positive contact with the mother causes a burst of matured connections within the limbic system. Conversely, in growth inhibiting environments, early inadequate caregiving experiences have long-standing effects on the neurochemicals released by children's brains. When children have severely compromised attachment relationships with their primary caregivers, their brain development may become inefficient in regulating their affective states related to anger and self-control.[22]

Recent neuropsychological studies have revealed that the emotional experience(s) of the infant are disproportionately stored or processed in the right hemisphere during the formative stages of brain ontogeny.[23] The infant relies primarily on its procedural memory stems during the first two to three years of life,[24] and the right brain contains the cerebral representation of one's own past and the substrate of affectively laden autobiographical memory.[25] These recent studies suggest that the infant's early attachment relationship is processed and stored in implicit procedural memory systems in the right cortex, the hemisphere dominant for implicit learning.

Developmental neuroscientific studies on the effects of attuned and misattuned parental environments have revealed subtle, but important differences in brain organization among securely and insecurely attached individuals.[26] According to Mary Main,[27] a leading figure in the continuing development of attachment theory, we are now, or will soon be, in a position to begin mapping the relations between individual differences in early attachment experiences and changes in the neurochemistry of their brain organization.

## Why Is Attachment So Important?

Children's attachment to a primary caregiver is absolutely critical for the foundation of a healthy personality. The parent/child bond is instrumental for later bonding with society and the social institutions within a society. Attachment also helps one to be able to handle fear and worry, and to cope with stress and frustration. Poor attachment militates against a child's commitment to long-term goals.

When a parent responds to a child's cry for food or for a dry diaper with "shut up" or, worse yet, by slapping the child, he is quieted by the caregiver's slap. Hence, at the height of the child's emotional state, he has learned that his needs are fulfilled by abuse. Abuse has replaced loving care, and if the abuse is severe, the child may use such abuse as a source of gratification. For instance, some children may respond to a caregiver's slap by banging their heads on the floor, by pulling out their hair, or by some other method of destructive, self-abusive behavior. These children have learned that they can only trust themselves and that they can cause others to respond to them with anger. Such children soon become the masters of control, manipulation, and anger. They feel secure in their anger and in their own self-abusive behavior.

Since Bowlby's early work,[28] researchers and clinicians have come to believe that attachment and bonding are at the heart of explaining some of the most fundamental psychological and social problems. Key among these beliefs is that attachment and bonding issues produce violent children. Cline[29] has written:

> Our society is producing a generation of severely disturbed children who lack conscience...these children grow up unattached—incapable of caring about themselves and others, unable to distinguish right from wrong, unable to form loving relationships, unable to accept responsibility.

Children who experience attachment problems frequently target the mother as the one who has to be broken and controlled. Violence toward mothers takes place because they are the ones who are usually responsible for disciplining their children. Moreover, attachment problems can be transmitted from one generation to the next. Children who lack secure attachments may grow up to be parents who experience difficulty in establishing an attachment relationship with their own children.

Attachment is important because it is critical for the foundation of a healthy personality and because it is necessary for an individual to develop a conscience. A child's lack of conscience may be caused by his lack of trust in others. Positive attachment also helps individuals to cope with stress, to handle perceived threats to the self, to form adult intimate relationships, and to later parent their own children. Children's positive attachment to a primary caregiver has the following functions:

1. Infants and children learn basic trust and reciprocity, which serves as a guide for all future emotional relationships.
2. Securely attached infants explore the environment with feelings of safety and security (secure base), which leads to their positive mental and cognitive development.
3. They develop the ability to self-regulate, which results in their effective management of impulses and anger.
4. They form a personal identity, which includes a sense of competency, dependence, and autonomy.
5. They establish a prosocial moral framework, which includes empathy and compassion for others.

6. They develop a core belief system that contains appropriate cognitive appraisals of themselves, their caregivers, and the others who come into contact with them.

7. They develop a defense against stress and trauma and are resilient.

Attachment is important because it is critical for the foundation of a healthy personality and because it is necessary for an individual to develop a conscience, to be able to cope with stress and frustration, to handle perceived threats to the self, to form adult intimate relationships, and to later parent his own children.

# *The Attachment Cycle*

The attachment system involves a number of behaviors intended to maintain proximity between the child and the caregiver. When the attachment system is activated, the child will engage in behaviors to establish proximity to the caregiver. Once proximity is established, the child's behaviors are deactivated. Attachment also serves a social function and holds a child's felt security as the final goal. The child's attachment behavioral system is activated by both internal and external conditions. For instance, the child's internal conditions of hunger, illness, and fatigue may activate his attachment behavioral system. Similarly, the attachment system can also be activated by external conditions within the environment, such as loud noises (baby's startled response), loneliness, and physical threats to the child.

The child engages in some form of cognitive appraisal with respect to his attachment behavioral system. The child's cognitive appraisal of a situation influences his proximity seeking or internal activation of the attachment system. If the child views an external or environmental stimulus as a threat (such as a stranger), his attachment behavioral system may also be activated. Children's repeated experiences with proximity seeking for caregivers become internalized at some point, and they adopt an internalized working model of attachment that may guide their behavior for the rest of their lives.

A child's working model of attachment is an internalized sense that his parent or caregiver will be available when he needs the caregiver's proximity. The internalized sense is not just that the parent will become available but rather that his presence will provide the child with a sense of felt security that meets his needs. Children develop a mental representation of the caregiver as a secure base from which they can venture at a safe distance. Once children form a clear mental representation of self and caregiver in relationship, they no longer need the concrete physical reassurance they previously held. Instead, they carry a mental image inside themselves as they explore, go to school, meet new people, and form intimate relationships in adult life.

Thus, children's internalization of a close emotional bond actually facilitates their growing sense of independence. This mental representation becomes the foundation of our capacity to form, sustain, and commit to close relationships in the future. Later on, after the mental working model has been established, the child is able to tolerate separation due to its internalized reminder of the relationship. Thus secure attachment promotes not only children's exploration and independence, but also their independence and the formation of an autonomous self capable of forming meaningful relationships.

Children develop an attachment exploratory system that is related to their felt sense of security with a primary caregiver. This exploratory system provides the basis for their interaction with the environment and their world. Secure attachments promote children's positive exploration of their world. Children and parents do not always agree on an acceptable level of distance between them. Moreover, children develop a sociable system related to their attachment experiences. The sociable system represents children's survival-based tendency to become affiliated with others. Children who are securely attached to a caregiver are inclined to develop a positive social system; however, this social system may be compromised if they do not have sufficient opportunities to spend time with their peers.

The attachment cycle may be described in this manner. When a baby cries, the mother or primary caregiver picks the child up and holds it. The primary caregiver may then stroke or talk to the baby who is being fed, diapered, or soothed. After a few days, the child learns that if he cries, the caretaker will respond. The child grows familiar with the person who meets the need. When the baby is soothed, he has an increased sense of security and trust. If the child's needs are met consistently, a secure attachment occurs between the infant and the caregiver. This cycle represents a healthy cycle of attachment. Illustration 1 is a schematic view of the attachment cycle.

Illustration 1

Moreover, the amount of time that the mother spends with the child is highly significant. In an early study, Trowell[30] found that children whose mothers were given an extra five hours of contact a day for the first three days of life have significantly higher IQ scores. By age five, these children scored higher on language and comprehension tests than did children whose mothers had not given them the extra time. Mothers who spent more time with their children showed more soothing behavior toward their infants, made more eye contact with the child, and had more physical contact with them.

## The Window of Opportunity for Bonding: The First Three Years of Life

There is a window of opportunity for bonding experiences to take place. Bonding experiences lead to healthy attachments when they are provided in the first three years of a child's life. During the first three years of human life, the human brain develops to about 90 percent of adult size and develops the majority of systems and structures that will be responsible for all future emotional, behavioral, social, and physiological functioning for the rest of one's life.[31] Child trauma experts maintain that there are critical periods during which bonding experiences must be present for the brain systems responsible for attachment to develop on a normal basis. One such critical period is during the first year of life, and it is defined by the capacity of the child and the caregiver to form a positive interactive relationship.

What happens if a parent misses the first year window of opportunity? The impact of impaired bonding varies among children. Children without sufficient touch, stimulation, and nurturing from a primary caregiver can actually lose the capacity to form any meaningful relationship for the rest of their lives.[32] Most children do not encounter such a devastating impaired attachment experience; but such experiences can create problems that range from mild interpersonal discomfort in social settings, to deep social and emotional problems, to violence. It may take many years of therapy to help repair the damage that resulted from only a few months of neglect in infancy. After the age of three, children may still learn to attach, but such learning is more difficult to bring about. Children who are learning to attach may be influenced by three factors: (1) their genetic disposition; (2) the conditions under which they are nurtured or taught; and (3) the qualities of their caretakers or parents.

Healthy attachments are based on the nature of the relationship between the child and the primary caregiver. The attachment bond between a child and a caregiver is a type of affectional bond. The criteria for such affectional bonds are that they are usually focused on one person, are persistent, and are emotionally significant for the child, and that the child experiences a desire for proximity to the caregiver. If such proximity is not granted, the child experiences distress related to the involuntary separation. The infant initiates such attachment behaviors as crying, gazing, touching, and seeking.[33]

## Summary of Factors That Influence the Attachment of the Growing Child

Children who are learning to attach will be influenced by three primary factors:

1. *First, the child's genetic disposition:* While some children have an easygoing disposition that draws people to them, others have a more temperamental disposition. Some children who suffer from autism or Asperger's syndrome have disorders that make it difficult for them to form attachments.

2. *Second, the conditions under which the child is taught* have a great deal to do with his ability to attach to a caregiver. Children whose needs have been met on a consistent basis find it easier to trust their world and their caregivers. Children's ability to trust their caregivers provides the basis of their forming attachment relationships. Parents who have had their own issues with attachment, perhaps as a result of adoption, drug use, domestic violence, or mental illness, may be unavailable as attachment objects.

3. *Third, the sensitivity of the child's parents* also has an influence on his attachment.

What causes problematic attachment of a child to a primary caregiver? Do only poorly educated, low-income parents produce children with attachment difficulties? The answer is no; most parents know very little about attachment disorders. Some may even believe that children who have been orphaned or abused and neglected are the primary victims of poor bonding and attachment in the early years. Yet, a child does not have to be an orphan to develop an attachment disorder. Two working parents may put children at risk for developing an attachment disorder. Often parents have more money than time to spend with their children. As a result, children may be raised in a financially secure, but emotionally empty home, with little discipline and structure. Such homes are neglectful homes even though the child's biological needs are provided for in a consistent manner.

Yet, many parents have not been educated about the critical importance of the child's experiences during the first three years of life. It has been estimated that such ignorance of attachment and bonding issues has led to one in three people having an avoidant, ambivalent, or resistant attachment with their caregiver. Despite their insecure attachment, these people will eventually form and maintain relationships, but with difficulty and crises.[34]

# Fathers and Attachment

Children receive a richness of care when they are nurtured by both a mother and a father. Fathers and mothers bring unique strengths to their relationships with children, different parenting styles, and quite different links to the outside world. Whereas mothers form an attachment to their children during the course of their pregnancy, fathers establish a bond with their infants after they are born. To establish a bond with their infants, it is important that fathers be available during the immediate postdelivery situation. Klaus, Kennell, and Klaus[35] found that fathers who have early delivery room contact with their children have a stronger attachment with them in the months following their birth.

Despite the fact that women are traditionally the primary caregivers for children, research has found that fathers also form attachment relationships with their children and that they can be just as responsive to their babies' needs as are their mothers.[36] When fathers spend time with their babies, they come to understand exactly what each of their baby's signals mean. Such familiarity helps fathers to respond sensitively to infants' various needs. Fathers evidence strong attachment toward their children by holding them. For instance, a study on parent-infant attachment found that fathers who were affectionate, spent time with their children, and overall had a positive attitude were more likely to have securely attached infants than did fathers who spent less time with their infants.[37]

Another study found that fathers who had spent more time with their children without the presence of the mother tended to have children who showed greater responsibility and exploration than did children who spent little time with their fathers.[38] In a study of 75 toddlers, Esterbrooks and Goldberg[39] found that children who were securely attached to their fathers were better problem solvers than children who were not securely attached to their fathers. A study assessing the level of adaptation of one year olds reported that when left with a stranger, children whose fathers were highly involved were less likely to cry, worry, or disrupt play than other one year olds whose fathers were less involved.[40]

Father/infant interactions are typically focused on affiliation and play, while mothers' interactions are viewed as more nurturing and affectionate toward the child.[41] One researcher found that fathers' play interactions are more exciting and pleasurable to children than play interactions with the mother. As babies grow older, many come to prefer playing with their fathers who provide unpredictable, stimulating, and exciting play. Such father stimulation and attachment behavior is important because it fosters healthy development of the baby's brain and can have long-term effects on children's social, emotional, and intellectual development.[42,43,44]

When infants become toddlers, their parents must adhere to addressing two basic needs: (1) supporting their toddler's exploration, and (2) setting appropriate limits with their children. As noted, fathers spend a larger proportion of their time playing with their children than do mothers. They also tend to be more boisterous and active in their play. Studies have found that children enjoy this kind of boisterous play.[45,46] Thus even if fathers spend less personal caregiving time with their children than their mothers, fathers become important, meaningful, and special to their children through play.[47]

Through rough-and-tumble play, fathers teach their children how to interact with the world by creating obstacles for them and by demanding respect for the limits and boundaries that they set in play. Simultaneously, fathers challenge their children and encourage them to explore their own strength, their ability to do new things, and their impact on their world. For instance, toddlers who must learn how to retrieve a ball that is just out of reach in their father's hand or how to wrestle their father to the ground are practicing important problem-solving skills. Studies have found that when fathers are good at playing with their children, they score higher on tests of thinking and problem-solving skills.[48,49]

Fathers' playing with their children also helps in developing their children's emotional knowledge and in their being able to identify their own feelings as well as those of others. Toddlers must accomplish a number of developmental tasks.[50,51] They must learn emotional regulations; they must learn how to express their emotions responsibly; and they must learn how to control their behavior. When children understand their emotions and learn how to control them, they become more popular with other children. For instance, consider a toddler who engages in a temper tantrum and hits his younger sibling. Contrast this with a four year old who is disappointed because he cannot go outside to play because it is raining. Instead of creating a temper tantrum at the rain, he decides to play inside with his younger brother.

Fathers teach their children emotional regulation through direct instruction and daily interactions with them. Research has found that when fathers are affectionate and helpful, their children are more likely to get along well with their brothers and sisters.[52] When children have fathers who are emotionally involved and who acknowledge their children's feelings, they score higher on tests of "emotional intelligence." Fathers' attachment behavior and involvement in their children's lives can last well into adulthood. Hence, fathers have a major influence on helping their children to build strong social relationships during the toddler and early childhood stage, as well as later in life.[53]

It is important to note that statistics about children who do not live with their fathers can be extremely negative. On virtually every major outcome that has been investigated, including educational achievement, self-esteem, responsible social behavior, and adjustment as adults, children do better when they live with both of their parents. As one scholar who reviewed 28 studies of father absence has stated: "The major disadvantage related to father absence is lessened parental attention."[54]

## *Ainsworth's Patterns of Attachments*

Mary Ainsworth[55,56] outlined different patterns of attachment using the research "Strange Situation," which was a laboratory experiment that recorded the interaction between mothers and their children prior to, during, and after a brief separation. The Strange Situation is a widely used laboratory procedure for assessing the quality of attachment between one and two years of age. It takes the baby through eight short episodes in which brief separations from and reunions with the parent take place. Mary Ainsworth and her colleagues reasoned that securely attached infants and toddlers would use the parent as a secure base from which to explore an unfamiliar playroom, and that when a parent leaves, an unfamiliar adult would be less comforting than the parent. Observing infants responses to these episodes, researchers (for the past several decades) have identified a secure attachment pattern and several patterns of insecurity. Ainsworth identified the following three categories:

- Secure attachment—the child protested when the mother left the room, and looked for her while she was gone. She greeted the mother with delight when the mother returned, and she explored more when the mother was present.

- Anxious attachment—the child protested when the mother left and showed little relief when reunited with the mother. The child was highly anxious before, during, and after separation. The child was not inclined to explore her environment, even when the mother was present.

- Avoidant attachment—the child was relatively indifferent to the mother, rarely cried when she left, and showed little positive response upon her return to the room. The child's curiosity was unaffected by the mother's presence.

# Secure Attachments

Infants' secure attachment to a primary caregiver provides a secure base from which they can explore the world, be resilient to stress, and form meaningful relationships with themselves and others.[57,58] To develop a secure attachment, infants must have a primary adult who responds to their needs in sensitive ways. Because infants vary in what it takes to calm and soothe them, each attachment takes place in a unique manner.[59]

Most infants (about 65 percent) are securely attached. Relationships between caregivers and infants that are characterized by secure attachment have the following attributes: (1) the adult aligns his own internal state with that of the infant or child and communicates this alignment in nonverbal ways that the child understands; (2) the communication between the child and the caregiver forms a bond

Illustration 2   Characteristics of a Secure Attachment

| As Children | As Adults |
|---|---|
| Able to separate from parent | Have trusting, long-term relationships |
| Seek comfort from parents when frightened | Tend to have good self-esteem |
| Show positive emotions upon return of parents | Are comfortable sharing feelings with friends and partner |

of trust between the two (for instance, the child cries, and the mother attempts to soothe the child's crying, or the infant smiles and kicks, and the mother responds with play of her own); and (3) the aligned interactions between the mother and child encourage the child to feel safe enough to interact positively with others.

Emily represents an example of a one year old who is securely attached to her mother. When her mother drops her off, initially she is hesitant to leave her mother. However, when she sees something she wants to play with, she leaves her mother to explore. Emily checks back a couple of times to make sure her mother is watching, and then continues to explore by playing with toys. When her mother leaves the day care center, Emily says, "bye bye," but she does not fuss, and she continues to play happily while her mother is absent. When her mother comes to pick her up, Emily greets her warmly.[60]

## The Benefits of Secure Attachment—Infancy through Adulthood

In securely attached infants, there is an expectation that the homeostatic disruptions they have experienced will be set right.[61] As Rutter[62] has maintained, infants and, later, children develop an internal model based on their early child-parent attachments that contains their set of expectations about their own relationship capacities and about other people's resources to meet their social and biological needs. These internal models contain cognitive and affective components that help children guide appraisals of their experience. A securely attached child believes: "I am a good person." "I am worthwhile and lovable." "My life is safe and comfortable."

Both society and children benefit when they are securely attached to a primary caregiver. Children with secure attachment relationships have been found to take better advantage of their opportunities in life, are better liked by their peers, have superior leadership and social skills, and are more confident than insecurely attached children.[63,64] Kesner[65] studied preschool-age children and found that securely attached children had better conflict management skills than their insecurely attached peers. He theorized that this situation occurred because children who lack the social skills to manage conflict often resort to aggressive behavior. Risk factors of single parent status, low socioeconomic status, and gender were not significant predictors, as was not security of relationship to the teacher. The children's attachment to their parents was the sole predictor of their conflict management skills.

In an earlier study within the Minnesota Preschool Project, Sroufe[66] found that preschool children who had been rated securely attached as infants had several advantages over anxiously attached children. The securely attached children were more ego resilient, had higher self-esteem, and had relationships with their teachers that were characterized by autonomy and less dependence. In addition, securely attached children who had their emotional needs met by an adult were more positive, less aggressive, less angry with others, and more compliant within a classroom setting.

The benefits of a secure attachment continue from preschool throughout adolescence. Young people with secure attachment backgrounds do better than insecurely attached children in their emotional health, leadership skills, morality, prosocial behavior, self-reliance, and self-control at each stage of development —early childhood, middle childhood, teenage years.[67,68] School-age children who are securely attached are more cooperative with their parents, more inclined to explore their environment, and more likely to get along with their peers.[69,70] Children's early secure attachments have an impact on their later parenting behavior as adults because parenting behaviors are transmitted intergenerationally.[71]

Securely attached children mature into parents who are both responsible and sensitive to their own children's psychological and emotional needs. Researchers have found that parental attachment histories and their level of understanding of their attachment histories correlated highly with their parenting styles and marital interactions.[72] Moreover, fathers' attachment history predicted their children's externalizing behaviors, while mothers' attachment history predicted their children's internalizing behaviors.

# Insecure Attachments

What causes insecure attachments to a primary caregiver? Do only poorly educated, low-income parents produce children with attachment difficulties? The answer is no. Most parents know very little about attachment disorders. Some may even believe that children who have been orphaned or abused and neglected are the primary victims of poor bonding and attachment in the early years. Sometimes children can be raised in a financially secure but emotionally empty home, with little discipline and structure. Such homes are neglectful, even though the child's biological needs are provided for in a consistent manner.

Insecure attachments take place when repeated experiences of failed communication between a parent and child happen or when the bond between child and primary caregiver does not occur with sufficient regularity. A large body of research studies shows that the mother's sensitivity in responding appropriately to her baby's needs is a principal determinant of the baby's attachment pattern. Studies of mothers with personality disorders, depression, bipolar disorders, or schizophrenia support the view that the disturbances in caregivers' personalities predict anxious, insecure attachments in infants.

In addition, the mother's representational model of attachment relationships is a good predictor of her baby's attachment pattern. Representational models are unconscious mental representations of the self and others, based on early experiences in first relationships. People's representational attachment models set the stage for interactions with new social partners and have long-term consequences for shaping personality, organizing behavior, and developing close relationships. Bowlby maintained that it is not uncommon for a person to hold conflicting internal models of an important relationship—"I love my mother, and I also hate her." One model may develop largely from a child's direct experience with his mother (for instance, negative experience such as slapping or hitting), while another model may result from the mother's cognitive input—for instance, statements from the mother that do not support the child's experience. An example of this conflicting model develops when a mother repeatedly states that she loves the child, but she hates being with the child and spends as much time as possible avoiding him.

As children develop, they can experience changes in their attachment behavior and in their representational models of attachment relationships. Attachment modifications can take place as a result of changes in children's experiences with an attachment figure or within their environment. For instance, changes in a

Illustration 3   Challenges to Infant Attachment

| Multiple disruptions in caregiving for your child | Postpartum depression causing an emotionally unavailable mother | Hospitalization of the child causing separation from the parent and/or unrelieved pain—for instance, child placement in a hospital intensive care unit or repeated hospitalizations during infancy |
|---|---|---|
| Parents who have experienced their own relational trauma, leading to neglect, abuse (physical, sexual, or verbal), or inappropriate parental responses not leading to a secure or predictable relationship | Caregivers whose own needs are not being met, leading to overload and lack of awareness of the infant's needs | Drug or alcohol use by mother during pregnancy |
| Caring for the infant on a timed schedule or other self-centered parenting | Sudden abandonment or separation from mother (death of mother, illness of mother or child, or adoption) | Physical, sexual, or emotional abuse |
| Neglect of physical or emotional needs | Several family moves | Inconsistent or inadequate care or day care |
| Unprepared mothers, poor parent skills, inconsistent responses to your child | Mothers with depression | Undiagnosed or painful illnesses (ear infections, colic, surgery) |

child's attachment can stem from the birth of a sibling, a death, divorce, or his entry into a day care nursery or school. Insecure attachments are passed down from one generation to another, unless therapeutic repair or some intervention to correct the situation takes place.

It has been estimated that because many parents have not been educated about the importance of attachment and bonding during the first three years of their children's life that many well-meaning and concerned parents will raise children who have one of the following types of insecure attachments: ambivalent, avoidant, or disorganized. Children and parents face challenges in forming healthy, secure attachments. If a child experiences any of the following factors in the first three years of life, he is at risk for developing an attachment disorder.[73]

Although basic attachment is typically completed by age three, children's attachment to a parent is affected by the day-to-day parental interactions. If children perceive that the parent or primary caregiver rejects them by refusing to acknowledge their worth and the legitimacy of their needs, then continued attachment may be impaired. Such rejection may have taken many different forms, including some of the examples provided here:

### Rejection Behavior of Parents or Caregivers that Hinders Attachment

- Abandoning the child
- Expressing the wish that the child had never been born or that the pregnancy had been aborted
- Excluding the child from family activities
- Refusing the child's overtures of affection—attempts to hug or to kiss the mother, father, etc.
- Punishing the child for expressions of emotion

### Isolation Behavior of Parents or Caregivers that Thwarts Attachment

- Preventing the child from engaging in socializing behaviors, such as forming friendships, causing the child to feel alone in the world
- Leaving children and infants in a room unattended for long periods of time
- Denying the child access to loved ones
- Prohibiting or failing to encourage the child from participating in clubs, after school programs, intramural sports, dating, music, etc.
- Ignoring the child's achievements or his presence
- Failing to show up when child or teachers request help in resolving problems

### Terrorizing the Child Hinders Attachment

Terrorizing the child includes threatening him or her with vague but sinister punishment; or it may involve increasing fear and a climate of unpredictable threat for the child. Additionally, parents might harm children by setting unreasonable expectations for the child and then punishing him for not meeting the expectations, and by destroying their treasured objects, such as pets. Other examples of terrorizing behavior include:

- Forcing the child to choose between two competing parents
- Threatening to reveal to others intensely embarrassing information (for example, you wet in your clothes)
- Publicly humiliating the child
- Using derogatory terms toward the child
- Alternating episodes of rage with periods of affection for the child

## *Ambivalent Attachment*

Ambivalently attached children experience the caregiver's communication as inconsistent. Because they cannot depend upon the parent for emotional alignment, they develop anxiety and feelings of insecurity. About 10 to 15 percent (of most samples) are categorized as ambivalent infants. Infants or children who are ambivalently attached are anxious, and they manifest their anxiety and mixed feelings about the attachment figure. At reunion after brief separations in an unfamiliar environment, ambivalently attached children evidence openly angry behavior with their attachment behavior.

Ambivalent infants are often less persistent, less enthusiastic, and less compliant as toddlers than those classified as secure. Ambivalent infants express more anger and frustration. Preschoolers in this category have been found to become victims of exploitation in interaction with peers. They tend to elicit mixed responses from their peers that perpetuate their own ambivalent feelings and expectations about relationships.

A mother's (or primary caregiver's) inconsistent, unpredictable responding (such as ignoring the child's signal at times, being intrusive at other times, or responding sensitively on one occasion) produces ambivalent attachments. Mothers of children with ambivalent attachment are often caught up in their own attachment issues. During the attachment interview, they may angrily report events from the past as if these events were current. They tend to ramble from one topic to another without being able to focus clearly on the issue at hand. These mothers' preoccupation with their own attachment issues hampers their ability to respond consistently and appropriately to their children's needs. They are said to have preoccupied states of mind with regard to their children's attachment.

A child who has an ambivalent attachment shows sadness on the mother's departure. On the mother's return, she shows some ambivalence, signs of anger, reluctance to warm to her and return to play. Jennifer is a one year old who screams loudly when her mother tries to leave her at the day care center. In contrast to Emily, she clings to her mother, crying, and screams louder as her mother walks out the door. The other adults at the day care center find it difficult to comfort Jennifer, and she makes little attempt to explore the environment and interact with other children. When her mother returns to pick her up, Jennifer at first runs to her mother for the comfort she has been wanting all day long. Yet, she also soon feels anger about her mother's leaving her, and she pushes her mother away. Jennifer has internalized an anxious-ambivalent attachment to her mother.

## Avoidant Attachment

About 20 percent of infants in most American samples are categorized as avoidant. Babies with avoidant attachments are anxious about the primary caregiver's responsiveness and have developed a defensive strategy for managing their anxiety. Upon the attachment figure's return after moderately stressful events, the avoidant babies manifest a mild version of the "detachment" behavior that characterizes many infants after separations of two or three weeks. They greet the mother, ignore her overtures to them, and act as if she is of little importance to them. A number of studies, both in the United States and in Europe, have reported that the mother's rejection of the baby, especially rebuffing the baby's attempts for contact, prompts the development of avoidant defenses.

Children who have an avoidant attachment style evidence behavior that is characterized by their detachment, restricted emotional awareness, masked feelings, and difficulty in expressing negative emotions. Such children adopt a defensive posture to their relationships with others. Avoidant children do not request practical assistance or emotional support because they lack the trust that people around them will respond positively. Children in this category play most often with objects, have restricted fantasy play, and are unable to admit normal imperfections.

There are a number of ways parents might be rejecting to their children, without being completely aware of the impact of their actions. For instance, a boy falls off his bike and runs to his mother crying. Instead of hugging and comforting her child, the mother says to the child: "You're a big boy. Big boys don't cry. Go get your bike." Another mother might say: "Didn't I tell you that you might fall riding that bike?" In both instances, the child has gotten the message that he will not be comforted and reassured when hurt. If the mother's response is typical of her responses to her child when he gets hurt, the child will then develop the expectation that his mother will not be available when he is hurt or distressed.

Avoidant children tend to first look to the mother (or primary caregiver) when in difficulty and then turn away abruptly, as if remembering that they should not look to the parent for reassurance. Or, they may appear to be indifferent to their mother's presence. Avoidant attachment children's strategy is adaptive to the extent that they ask no more of their parent than the parent is willing to give.

Mothers of children with an avoidant attachment style are frequently dismissing or devaluing of their own attachment experiences. When they are asked to talk about attachment figures in their lives, they are inclined to describe them in idealized ways. For instance, they may characterize their father as "wonderful and loving," but when asked to give examples of such loving behavior, they are not able to provide specific examples. These mothers are uncomfortable talking about problems they faced in attachment or in connecting the influence of their earlier attachment on their current functioning. They have dismissal states of mind with regard to attachment.

Tara is an example of an avoidantly attached, one-year-old child. She moves away from her mother as soon as she enters the day care center. Although Tara explores the environment, she rarely interacts with the other children. Unlike Emily, who also did much exploring, Tara does not check to see if her mother is watching her. She appears to ignore her mother completely. Tara does not acknowledge when her mother leaves or when she returns to pick her up. There is no visible reunion between Tara and her mother because she is avoidantly attached.[74]

## Disorganized Attachment

Recently researchers have added a disorganized attachment category, which is said to take place when the child's need for emotional closeness goes unrecognized or ignored. It is estimated that approximately 10 to 15 percent of infants are disorganized in their attachment style. Children who experience child abuse, serious maternal psychopathology, and unresolved caregiver mourning tend to have disorganized infant attachments. Children in this category appear to have no consistent strategy for managing separation from and reunion with the attachment figure.

When primary caregivers act in frightening ways to children, children tend to show a breakdown in attachment strategy when they are distressed and in their parents' presence. Such children have an irreconcilable dilemma. They are frightened of the person to whom they look for reassurance. Parents can be frightening to children when they threaten to or actually do harm them. In addition, children can also be frightened of parents who say they are going to leave them or who play too harshly with them. Moreover, children who have a disorganized attachment style appear to be clinically depressed. These infants are often seen in studies of high-risk samples of severely maltreated, very disturbed, or depressed babies. One well-executed study found that infants with disorganized attachments were at risk for showing hostile or aggressive behavior problems at age five.

In studies of institutionalized babies who had no regularly present caregiver, researchers found that a high percentage of babies died despite good physical care. Those children who survived such care later became socially indifferent or developed "affect hunger," which is an insatiable need for attention and affection from indiscriminant sources. These young people were not able to form meaningful attachments to caretakers or peers. As adolescents, they were aggressive and impulsive, and they engaged in antisocial behavior. The following categories of children are at a high risk for insecure, disorganized attachment:

children of teen mothers, those with neurological disorders (cerebral palsy, autism, Down syndrome), and those who have been abused, neglected, or exposed to domestic violence.[75]

# Consequences of Insecure Attachment

This book suggests that it is disorganized attachment that has the most significant risk for later psychopathology. Although it would be good if all children could develop secure attachments, children with avoidant and ambivalent attachment patterns typically developed adaptive strategies for dealing with the world. Both avoidant and ambivalent attachment patterned children tend to be at an increased risk for anxiety disorders. Ambivalently attached children tend to grow into dependent children.

Boys who were categorized as avoidant were found to be the most aggressive and the most likely to be conduct disordered when they grew up. Avoidant girls were inclined to turn the aggressiveness inward and to become depressed.[76] Sroufe's study found that conduct problems in adolescence were predicted by both avoidant and disorganized attachment relationships in early childhood. Lyons-Ruth[77] has reported that disorganized attachment behaviors are the forerunners of coercive childhood behavior, and that insecure and disorganized attachment relationships contribute to conduct disorders and oppositional defiant disorder in young people.

Research suggests, then, that disorganized attachment is associated with a range of later problems, including especially dissociative symptoms (seeming to be in a fog or out of it, or detached), but also internalizing symptoms (e.g., depression and anxiety as well as externalizing symptoms—acting out, violence). Hence, it is disorganized attachment that parents and child care workers should work especially hard to remediate.

# Attachment and Middle Childhood

During the early and middle school years, children seek alternate attachment figures from their parents. Usually, such people are similar to them in status or friends that they find in their neighborhood or school. Young people explore their physical and social world with their best friends. Middle school children also turn to these friends for comfort when they are faced with moderate to low threat.[78] These children are still exploring their environment; so, they run home to Mommy for protection and comfort whenever they feel threatened. Young children seek autonomy while maintaining their ability to go to their caregiver for support. In contrast, adolescents are primarily concerned with separation and individuation from their parents, while still seeking their parents' acceptance.

# *Adolescent Attachment Development*

By adolescence, young people have formed their internal attachment model that will become their guide for building friendships and intimate relationships for their adolescence and adult life. It is important to compare attachment during adolescence with how it develops during some of the younger stages. In infancy, the relationship between the infant and the attached caregiver is characterized by the vast power differentials. Infants explore their world from their attachment caregivers when they feel safe, and they return to them when they feel threatened or uncomfortable. In the preschool years, children begin to challenge the power and authority of their parents.

Adolescence is, then, a period of reorganization of young people's attachment alliances. Parent-children relationships undergo great transitions. Adolescents spend decreased time with parents. There is a psychological shift from dependency to mutual reciprocity with their friends.[79,80,81,82] Parents who support their children during this stressful transition period tend to have children who have a positive adolescent attachment adjustment.

Adolescent attachment changes are related to their own emerging sexuality, the growth in the importance of their peers in their lives, and their need to develop autonomy from their parents. The major attachment change is that adolescents form romantic relationships that shift their allegiance from parents to their romantic partner. During adolescence, attachment involves a high level of intimacy with another individual—an exploration of oneself with another. Adolescents explore their shared interests with their attachment partner.

Intimacy in adolescence is influenced by the kind of working model of attachment that an adolescent has internalized. Problems can sometimes be created if the adolescent's transition to a peer attachment figure takes place too soon or with an unsuitable partner. The selection of an attachment partner is one of the central outcomes of adolescent development.[83,84] In later adult relationships, each person becomes both the attached person and the attachment figure for the partner.

The frequencies of some of the major attachment patterns (secure, insecure, avoidant, ambivalent, or disorganized) in samples of adolescents and adults are very similar to those for infants. In older groups, as in infancy, each category of attachment is about as common among males as among females. Secure adolescents and adults describe their most important love experiences as happy, friendly, and trusting. On average, their relationships last longer than those for anxiously attached people.

Anxiously attached adolescents and adults are described as "distant," with few close friends or long-term love relationships. Their relationships are often marked by fear and jealousy. Anxious-ambivalent adolescents and adults report love relationships that involve obsession, extreme sexual attraction, desire for union, and extreme jealousy. Individuals in this category report self-doubts, they feel misunderstood and underappreciated, and they have high scores on loneliness.

Studies have found that patterns of attachment may even help to predict or explain the adult's approach to work and success or failure in the job setting. For instance, secure adult attachments are inclined to approach their work somewhat compulsively to avoid their difficulties and deficiencies in interpersonal relationships. Anxious-ambivalent adults tend to be preoccupied with unmet attachment needs; therefore, they often permit interpersonal involvements to interfere with their work.

Patterns of attachment are often transmitted from generation to generation. Parents with secure or balanced representational attachment models are better able to give sensitive care to their babies, and therefore, they rear securely attached children.

# Cross Cultural Issues in Attachment

Most children are securely attached to the mother in virtually every culture. Yet, cultures have different infant care practices that underlie their definitions of secure attachment. Scholars have pointed out that there is evidence of cultural variations on attachment and that attachment theory is ladened with Western values and meaning. These researchers emphasize that comparisons of the United States and Japan challenge three basic attachment theory assumptions, namely that caregiver sensitivity leads to secure attachment, that secure attachment leads to later social competence, and that children who are securely attached use the primary caregiver as a secure base for exploring the external world.

Attachment theorists use measures of sensitivity, competence, and secure base that are biased toward Western ways of thinking because such measures emphasize the child's autonomy, individuation, and exploration. In Japan, sensitivity, competence, and secure base are valued differently; therefore, this finding calls into question the universality of some of the tenets of attachment theory.

# Attachment Parenting: A Spiritual Journey

Attachment parenting is raising your child the way you wish you had been treated during your childhood. It is truly a spiritual journey. As a parent, you have to decide the kind of relationship you will have with your child. Are you going to be the kind of parent who likes to keep your child close to you? What kind of bond do you want to form with your child? What promotes that bond, and what hinders it? How do the childhood bonds that you formed with your parents influence the quality of the attachment you are able to form with your own child?

It is not easy to be a parent. We all make mistakes. We must learn to forgive ourselves for our mistakes and move on. Most of us were not given any instruction booklets on how to be a good parent. Whatever knowledge we have typically has come from our own parents, our relatives, the few psychology courses we took in college, and whatever self-help books we sought once we learned we were going to become parents. So we struggle with our own issues leftover from childhood, hoping that somehow they will not interfere with our parenting our own children.

We want the best for our children, and we want them to have a better life than what we had. Most of all, we just want to be good parents. Attachment parenting focuses on the bond between parent and child, regardless if that child is a five year old, an adolescent, or an adult struggling to raise his own children. There are some activities parents can engage in with their children to promote bonding. For instance, parents might play games together to increase fun time and to encourage eye contact. It is common for children who have not formed good attachments to avoid eye contact with their caregivers and others. Try playing a game of peekaboo with your child.

Reading is another activity in which parents can participate with their children that promotes bonding between them. Sharing a book with your child provides an opportunity for you to cuddle with him. Singing songs is another activity that builds a bond with your child. Try singing songs like "Old McDonald" and "London Bridge." Talk and listen carefully, not absently, to your child. Talk during bath time and when you and your child are watching television. Do not forget touch, which is so important for bonding with children. Babies benefit from resting skin to skin on the mother or on Dad's chest. Apply lotion to your baby during the day and especially at nighttime. You might consider carrying your baby in a Snugli or fabric carrier on your front to increase touch and eye contact with your child.

Spend sufficient time with your child in nurturing activities. Consider limiting your time away from your baby. In fact, you might do well to not leave your child for overnight trips for the first year. Try to meet your child's needs on demand rather than on a fixed schedule. Feed on demand and quickly respond to your baby's signs of fussing. Put aside 30 minutes each day for play with your child. Keep a calm but interesting home, one that contains ample stimulation for your child. Explain to your child your relationship with him. Say such things as: "Mommy loves you very much." "Mommy will always come back when she has to go out for groceries."

Remember attachment is an interactive process. Our brains are structured to connect to one another. The attachment process changes the brains of both parent and child. Fostering a secure attachment begins with attending to your child's needs. Pay attention to your child's cues, such as his crying or holding arms out to you. Then respond quickly to those cues and needs. Children learn to trust when someone responds quickly and consistently to their needs. Very young children simply do not understand "waiting" for someone. Express warm, positive, and caring responses as you interact with your child.

# What Can Be Done When Attachment Has Been Disrupted?

When attachment has been disrupted, the most important first step is to begin the process of building a secure attachment with the child. It is important to remember that the basic needs of your child are still unmet if he is insecurely attached. Such needs include: (1) the need to be understood and responded to; (2) the need to be held; and (3) the need to be enjoyed and admired. It is important to hold your child as often as possible and to maintain eye contact when holding him. Children with attachment issues may resist being held. Yet, holding can be achieved in such ways as sitting with children, tucking them into bed, and staying with them when they appear to be afraid of the dark.

The primary caregivers need to spend time with their children. A great portion of the time should be focused on communicating with your child, even if your child cannot quite understand what you are saying. Children respond positively to smiles, snuggles, and cooing. The goal is to try to repair the attachment breach as soon as possible before it becomes a full-blown attachment disorder. Consider therapy for you and your child.

# Types of Attachment Disorders

Children who have an attachment disorder tend to exhibit antisocial behavior throughout their childhood (including preschool age). They may be intimidating, violent, or aggressive toward others. They evidence a low ability to learn from social experience (including punishment or restrictions). They display a lack of guilt and remorse, blaming others only when confronted. Such children will be charming and trustful toward new, unfamiliar people, and may contact people at random. They are unable to distinguish emotionally between familiar and unfamiliar persons, and will oftentimes reject the love of people who have known them for a long time over the anticipated affection of their so-called "new friends." These children have short, unreliable, and superficial contact patterns.

Moreover, children with attachment issues will have difficulties developing social competencies in building meaningful relationships with others. These children encounter negative reactions from others on a daily basis. Therefore, their intellectual learning capacities may not develop fully. As a consequence of school failure or lack of school achievement, many develop secondary problems such as criminal activity and drug abuse. Adolescent and adult attachment styles influence substance abuse.

## Reactive Attachment Disorder

There are two primary attachment disorders: (1) Reactive attachment disorder (RAD) and (2) separation anxiety disorder. The most frequently diagnosed and serious attachment disorder is RAD. As described in the Diagnostic Criteria from the American Psychiatric Association's DSM-IV-TR, a reactive attachment disorder (313.89) is a disorder characterized by a markedly disturbed and developmentally inappropriate social relatedness in most contexts, which begins before age five years and is evidenced by the child's persistent failure to respond appropriately in social situations. The DSM-IV attributes a reactive attachment disorder to a child's having multiple caregivers. Some of the signs of a reactive disorder are provided in Illustration 4.

Children who have a reactive attachment disorder have symptoms that may be placed in five categories: (1) *Behavior*—oppositional and defiant, destructive, lying and stealing, aggressive and abusive, hyperactive, self-destructive, cruel to animals, irresponsible, and fire-setting; (2) *Emotions*—intense anger and temper, sad, depressed and hopeless, moody, fearful and anxious, irritable, inappropriate emotional reactions; (3) *Thoughts*—negative beliefs about self, relationships, and life in general (negative working model), lack of cause-and-effect thinking, attention and learning problems; (4) *Relationships*—lack of trust, controlling ("bossy"), manipulative, no giving or receiving of genuine affection and love, indiscriminately affectionate with strangers, unstable peer relationships, blaming of others for own mistakes or problems, and victimizing of others or victimized; (5) *Physical*—poor hygiene, accident prone, high pain tolerance, genetic predispositions (hyperactivity); and (6) *Moral/spiritual*—lack of faith, compassion, remorse, meaning, and other prosocial values.

A number of factors may cause reactive adjustment disorder if they occur within the first two years of life, including maternal drug and/or alcohol during

Illustration 4    Reactive Adjustment Disorder Signs

| Is manipulative, superficially engaging, or charming | Lacks direct eye contact | Becomes indiscriminately affectionate with strangers | Lacks ability to give and receive affection |
|---|---|---|---|
| Is destructive to self and others, animals, material things | Lacks self-esteem | Is unable to develop and maintain friendships | Is alienated from and oppositional with parents, caregivers, and other authority figures |
| Becomes aggressive and violent | Has difficulty with genuine trust, intimacy, and affection | Lacks empathy, compassion, and remorse | Has behavioral and academic problems at school |
| Engages in crazy, chronic lying | Has poor peer relationships | Has anger management issues | Lacks impulse control and cause-and-effect thinking |

pregnancy, premature birth, abuse (physical, emotional, sexual), neglect; sudden separation from the primary caretaker (illness or death of mother, chronic illness or hospitalization of the child); frequent moves or placements, chronic maternal depression, and teenage mothers with poor parenting skills.

## Separation Anxiety Disorder

Separation anxiety disorder is characterized as excessive anxiety about being away from home or separated from people to whom one is attached. The onset is before 18 years, and it is usually triggered by life stress, such as the death of a relative, friend, or pet, geographic move, or a change in schools. Separation anxiety disorder lasts at least a month, and it causes significant distress or impairment in the child's functioning. A child suffering from anxiety disorder may:

- Experience great distress (crying, clinging, panic) when separated from home or people to whom he is attached
- Need to know the whereabouts of attached people
- Be preoccupied with fears that something terrible will happen to him
- Be uncomfortable traveling alone
- Refuse to attend school or camp or to visit a friend's house
- Have difficulty at bedtime
- Be reluctant to sleep alone
- Experience nightmares that reveal the anxiety
- Experience physical problems (nausea, stomachaches, and dizziness)

Children suffering from a separation anxiety disorder may be placed on medication to allow them to return to school. Both psychodynamic play therapy and behavioral therapy have been found to help reduce anxiety disorders. From a psychodynamic approach looking at oriented play therapy, the therapist works with the child to help him express the anxiety through play. In behavior therapy, the child learns to overcome fear through gradual exposure to separation from the parents.

# Effects of a Child's Attachment Disorder on the Family

Children who suffer from an attachment disorder may present challenges to the family. Parents may mistakenly believe that their love and understanding will solve all the child's problems. Love is not enough for children suffering from an attachment disorder. Children who are insecurely attached may not be able to respond to their parents' overtures of love. As a consequence, the parents may become frustrated at their inability to receive reciprocal love and bonding from their children. Many children suffering from a reactive adjustment disorder are angry at the world. They have difficulty with loving and with obeying the simplest of family and school rules. They fight others to protect themselves.

Oftentimes children who have an attachment disorder do not trust enough to do things a parent's way. They are not sure that things will work out for them. They may try to make the parent angry by pushing their buttons and using grossing out behaviors—creating a mess such as defecating over themselves and parts of the house. Attachment disordered children engage in such behaviors because they do not want you to love them. They want to keep you emotionally distanced to feel safe; however, deep down inside such children feel bad about themselves. They may even hate themselves.

To make matters worse, schools, churches, friends, and relatives may become critical of the parents' form of discipline and inability to control the child's behavior. In fact, some parents of attachment disordered children have been put through the wringer of criticism from therapists, the schools, and social service programs. Typically, they are blamed for their children's acting out problems. As a result, they may become deeply frustrated in their attempts to get help for their children and themselves. They become angry with their child, feel guilty for their own anger and parenting inadequacy, and sometimes consider giving their children up for someone else to raise.

In response to such criticism, the family becomes controlled by the child's antics and acting out behavior. As a consequence, the parents may withdraw from normal social functions because they can never be sure about the child's behavior. The attachment disordered child may target and threaten siblings with violence, and he may attack family pets. Attendance at family events may be characterized by outbursts of the child's reactive anger. The child may vent hatred toward the mother. Traditional parenting does not work because there is no normal point of reference for dealing with the child.

To help their attachment disordered children, parents must begin to view their children as deeply wounded who were denied the very basics in life—a mother's love and protection. Parents have to stop focusing on their own hurt feelings and dashed dreams of having a "perfect child" and redirect their energies to helping their children find their way back from the very beginning. Even at their children's advanced age, they must start the attachment cycle again and help them to heal their broken hearts. Healing the child might be possible with the appropriate therapy, family support, and parental love. Yet, there is no guarantee that all will work out well. There is just a chance that all will eventually be all right, and for many parents, holding on to such hope is critical because hope is all they have.

# Working with the Anger of Attachment Disordered Children

Children suffering from attachment issues are prone to become intensely angry children. To be effective, therapists and parents must address children's anger. As pointed out in an earlier section, attachment disordered children's experience of early trauma leads to their hypersensitivity to arousal in the face of threat. Their responses to such arousal typically take the form of either aggressive reactivity or dissociation. To work effectively with such young people, parents, teachers, and counselors must undermine the legitimacy of aggression as a response to the perceived provocation and threat. Parents and school authorities should avoid power assertion whenever possible to reduce the experience of threat and thus maintain the youth in a nonaggressive state. Attachment disordered kids require a calming environment to reduce their hyperarousal response.

Parents can promote trust in adult authority by creating a highly controlled environment in which their youth rationally conclude that they are safe at home and can now relinquish their defensive posture. A family's involvement in the church and parents' teaching of spiritual values give youth a sense that life is not meaningless.

Frequently, attachment disordered violence represents a youth's attempt to achieve the justice that he believes he was wrongly denied. To help a child come to terms with violence that is related to his attachment disorder, parents need to engage their child in a conversation about his perceptions of injustice and his subsequent violence. The desired end result is that parents help their child to achieve higher stages of moral reasoning—for instance, the use of violence may not produce the justice that he desires; other nonviolent actions may be far more effective in getting justice. Finally, because empathy is the enemy of aggression, parents promote their child's development of empathy through role modeling (helping him to understand the feelings of others) and by communicating respectfully with their own child. When dealing with an attachment disordered child's anger, remember to:

1. Protect the child from hurting himself or others when he is in a rage or has a tantrum.

2. Help the child to understand that his coping strategy has broken down and that he needs help in restoring his coping ability.

3. Redirect the child's energy so that he focuses on positive ways to achieve the justice that he seeks.

4. Help the child understand the other party's point of view toward justice.

5. Choose carefully which negative behaviors to change. Decide which present safety concerns or which are likely to be the most dysfunctional in the long

run. Work at changing no more than three negative behaviors at one time. Otherwise, the child becomes overwhelmed by negativity.

6. Obtain support from organizations or counseling groups.

## Evidenced-Based Therapeutic Approaches to Attachment Disorder

Evidence-based approaches do exist for the effective treatment of reactive adjustment disorder. Research studies have found that dyadic developmental psychotherapy is highly effective in the treatment of RAD.[85] Dyadic developmental psychology is an effective and evidence-based treatment developed by Daniel Hughes.[86,87] This therapeutic approach focuses on both the caregivers' and the therapists' own attachment strategies. It emphasizes the importance of the caregivers' and therapists' state of mind for the success of dyadic therapy. The therapist and caregiver must be attuned to the child's subjective experience and reflect this back to the child. Through their attunement strategies, the therapist and caregiver establish a connection with the child. Because attachment has to do with family relationships, it is important that the family be included as part of the therapeutic approach. James[88] has identified five steps in the treatment of attachment disorders: (1) teaching; (2) self-identity work; (3) affect modulation; (4) relationship building; and mastering behavior.

## Therapy for Adolescents and Attachment Issues

Therapy for adolescents must take into account the fact that adolescence is a time period of reorganization for youth because it entails developmental change and disruption of the behavioral organizations constructed in earlier developmental periods. A guiding principle underlying attachment-based therapy is that the therapist functions as a transitional attachment figure or object in the adolescent's zone of proximal development. In Vygotsky's theory, this includes a range of tasks that a young person cannot yet handle alone, but can do with the help of more skilled partners, such as parents or a therapist. The therapist partially fulfills the functions of parents as attachment figures. As such, the therapist is available to provide protection and comfort, specifically located within the adolescent's zone of proximate emotional development.

Those things that the adolescent manages competently are left to his determination, whereas those things that are beyond the adolescent's zone of proximal development, such as his areas of emerging competencies, form the arena within which therapy will take place. For instance, adolescents might need help in their proximal zone of development related to abstract thinking about their own and others' behaviors or responses toward them. Hence, parents would spend time helping their adolescents to understand their behavior in forming relationships with others.

Disturbed adolescents have different zones of proximal development. Their competencies may be delayed, or impaired in such a manner that they make the transition to adolescence and to adulthood difficult. One might say that their zone of proximal development can be characterized as falling somewhere between the distorted relationships they experienced with their parents and the more balanced or healthy relationships they might potentially develop with partners in the future. Therapy should help adolescents to reorganize their attachment relationships so that they form satisfying, positive interpersonal relationships with others.

# Finding Help for Your Child

One of the first steps to take with a child experiencing attachment disorder symptoms is to find help for your child. If you are living with an attachment disordered child, know that you are not alone. Networking is essential; there are other parents out there who feel alone and failing as parents because they may not understand the symptoms of attachment disorders in children and because they may be struggling with their own attachment issues. The Internet contains a number of sites of organizations that provide intensive therapy for children experiencing attachment disorders. Try not to feel guilty or dumb because you found out about attachment disorders so late in your child's or teenager's life. Although it is difficult, attachment issues can even be dealt with in adult children if children and parents want to take steps to repair their relationship.

Specialized parenting skills are usually necessary to be successful in working with children who are diagnosed with a reactive adjustment disorder. Parents' or caregivers' own attachment histories play an important role in their treatment of their children. Parents must become aware of how their own prior family-of-origin issues currently influence their parenting difficulties and practices. The therapeutic challenge is to reignite parents' motivation to try again with their children and to give them some measure of hope. Because traditional parenting techniques may not work with attachment disordered children, parents have to learn new concepts and techniques that have proven to be effective with children similar to theirs.

Effective parenting for attachment must provide a balance of structure and nurturance. Attachment parental training involves the four R's. Parents are taught that children must learn how to be responsible, respectful, resourceful, and reciprocal.[89] Children are held accountable for their choices and their actions, including their responsibilities for chores as family members. Good treatment programs focus on providing a support group for parents, giving them hope that their child can be helped and teaching them specific parenting skills. Therapy goals for children include helping them to:

- Develop the capacity to form secure attachments and reciprocal relationships: the ability to give and receive love and affection

- Develop the internal psychological resources to make healthy choices, solve problems, and manage adversity effectively
- Construct a positive and realistic sense of self and self in relation to the world
- Learn to identify, manage, and express emotions in a constructive manner
- Learn prosocial values and morality, as well as the self-discipline and self-control needed to function successfully in society
- Develop the capacity for joy and positive, purposeful meaning in life

Parents cannot magically fix a child, even with therapy. They can, however, create a positive, healthy environment that promotes the secure attachment of their children. Effective therapeutic approaches emphasize teaching parents how to analyze their own attachments and how to nurture and to love their own children. Such approaches give parents assistance in establishing clear family rules and expectations, and specific consequences for actions that violate family rules. These parental skills help children feel safe and secure and give them an opportunity to learn from their mistakes. In addition, effective therapeutic approaches teach parents how to set the emotional tone in their families, model effective communication, solve problems, set boundaries, cope with stress, manage emotions and conflict, and care about others.

# *Chapter Summary*

Attachment theory is above all else a theory about the nature of all human beings. It touches on several critical elements of an individual's emotional life—the tendency to form attachment bonds; the role of the caregiver; the anxiety and anger that separation and loss evoke; and the process of grieving for the loss of an attachment. Second, this theory categorizes the nature of a child's first attachment as secure, insecure, avoidant, or disorganized and attempts to describe the impact of these patterns on subsequent behavior and relationships.

The most significant quality of human beings is their capacity to form and maintain relationships. Such relationships are essential for individuals to survive, to learn, to work, to love, and to procreate. The most pleasurable and painful of these relationships involve the family, the place where individuals create their first attachments and bonds. Each family establishes its own emotional glue that is shared with other members. In turn, each individual family member passes on this emotional glue or its lack thereof to his offspring, and so the human challenge to love one another continues.

This chapter has examined children's attachment to primary caregivers within the family. In no way can this chapter be considered an exhaustive treatise on attachment and the issues of violence. Its intent was to trace violence in human beings to its earliest beginnings—to attachment to a primary caregiver

or the lack of it. We nurture our children intentionally when we create uncondi-
tional loving bonds that give them strong roots and wings for them to fly.

# Reading List for Chapter 2

These are books that you might like to read to your child while bonding with
him.

*All Fall Down* by Helen Oxenbury. Little Simon, 1999.

*Baby Rock, Baby Roll* by Stella Blackstone. Holiday House, 1997.

*Big Fat Hen* by Keith Baker. Harcourt Brace, 1994.

*Brown Bear, Brown Bear, What Do You See?* by Bill Martin Jr. and Eric Carle.
    Henry Holt, 1992.

*Brown Sugar Babies* by Charles Smith. Jump at the Sun, 2000.

*I Love Colors* by Margaret Mille. Simon & Schuster, 1999.

*Twinkle, Twinkle, Little Star* by Jeanette Winter. Red Wagon, 2000.

*Welcome, Baby! Baby Rhymes for Baby Times* by Stephanie Calmenson.
    HarperCollins, 2002.

# Intentional Parenting Tips

Attachment parenting is not something that you do on a catch-as-catch-can
basis. The best results for children occur when we intentionally use attachment
parenting. Healthy attachment provides young children with an internal experience that helps them develop trust, self-control, and problem-solving skills.
When an infant's needs are met in a consistent manner, he will develop trust in
others. This section contains quizzes you can use to assess and improve your
attachment relationship with your child. An adult romantic attachment scale is
included for you to assess your own attachment style.

## Parental Attachment Rating Scale

You might consider completing this exercise on a weekly or perhaps even a
daily basis using the following parental attachment rating scale. Rate yourself on
a scale of 1 to 4 (with 1 = never, to 4 = often) regarding how frequently you are
responsive to your interactions with your child by checking the box that applies:
(1 = never; 2 = seldom; 3 = sometimes; and 4 = often).

_____1. *Availability:* I make myself physically available to my children often and focus
    on them when we are together.

_____2. *Knowledge:* I try to learn more about and gain experience with children through reading, classes, or other opportunities.

_____3. *Attentiveness:* I am aware of my child's cues for help. I understand what my child's cues mean, and I respond in a way that comforts my child.

_____4. *Consistency:* I respond quickly and consistently to my child's cues and needs.

_____5. *Warmth:* I respond to my child in a warm, caring, and positive manner rather than roughly or harshly.

_____6. *Sensitivity:* I pay attention to my child's signals and respond in appropriate ways.

_____7. *Cooperation:* I know my child's interests and try to help him develop such interests rather than try to force him to follow my own preferences.

_____8. *Avoid overstimulation:* I take care not to frustrate my child.

## Attachment Quiz—True or False

The following statements assess your knowledge of attachment with children. Answer each question by marking either true or false next to the item number.

_____1. Young children bond easily with a wide variety of caregivers in the first two years of life.

_____2. The type of relationship a parent forms with a young child has little effect on how the child's brain forms.

_____3. Infants in the first six months who cry for food or comfort should not be picked up every time because they will be spoiled.

_____4. Young children really enjoy interaction, but parents need to be careful not to "overstimulate" them.

_____5. Young children who have not formed healthy attachments often can overcome this challenge though intensive and caring attention.

The answer to the first three statements is FALSE; the answer to the last two statements is TRUE.

## My Child's Attachments

This exercise is designed to focus on what you think about the quality of your child's attachment with you and with others. It is important for you to note with whom your child has formed attachments and how they might be improved.

Illustration 5    My Child's Chart: Attachment to Whom

Fill in the names of those with whom you feel your child has a primary (main) attachment relationship. Then fill in the names of those who you believe are important secondary (supportive) attachment relationships for your child. This chart then represents your child's hierarchy chart of attachment relationships.

Primary Attachments: Names        Relationship to Child
1. _____    _____
2. _____    _____
3. _____    _____
Secondary Attachment: Names     Relationship to Child
1. _____    _____
2. _____    _____
3. _____    _____

Illustration 6    Type of Attachment Relationship: Secure to Insecure

Consider an attachment continuum from secure to insecure. Given what you understand about attachment, place yourself and your child somewhere on this continuum. Put "me" for parent, "child" for your child, the name of another person.

Primary Attachment
Relationship 1.

| Secure | Insecure: Avoidant | Insecure: Ambivalent | Insecure: Disorganized |
|---|---|---|---|

Primary Attachment
Relationship 2.

| Secure | Insecure: Avoidant | Insecure: Ambivalent | Insecure: Disorganized |
|---|---|---|---|

Primary Attachment
Relationship 3.

| Secure | Insecure: Avoidant | Insecure: Ambivalent | Insecure: Disorganized |
|---|---|---|---|

Secondary
Attachment
Relationship 1.

| Secure | Insecure: Avoidant | Insecure: Ambivalent | Insecure: Disorganized |
|---|---|---|---|

Secondary
Attachment
Relationship 2.

| Secure | Insecure: Avoidant | Insecure: Ambivalent | Insecure: Disorganized |
|---|---|---|---|

Secondary
Attachment
Relationship 3.

| Secure | Insecure: Avoidant | Insecure: Ambivalent | Insecure: Disorganized |
|---|---|---|---|

Illustration 7    Ways to Improve My Child's Attachment Relationships

List three ways that you might improve your attachment relationship with your child.

1. _____

2. _____

3. _____

List three ways that you might work to promote better attachment relationships between your child and his other primary attachment figures.

1. _____

2. _____

3. _____

List three ways that you might promote better attachment relationships between your child and his secondary attachment figures.

1. _____

2. _____

3. _____

# 3

# Understanding Needs, Developmental Stages, Developmental Tasks, and Violence

*Forcing a rose to bloom before it is ready harms its petals.*

Nicole ran downstairs again, grabbed her coat, checked to make sure the alarm was on and gently pushed Matthew toward the door. "Come on, we've got to go. Hurry! Mommy put the alarm on." But Matthew just stood there looking at her. "Come on," Nicole, urged. "For once we're getting out early enough so I won't be late for work."

"Potty, Matt go potty."

Nicole looked at him in disbelief. "I asked you earlier if you had to go, and you said no." Nicole could hear her voice getting louder. "I just put your coat and everything on, and now you tell me you have to go potty. Why do you do this to me, Matt?" she began yelling. "Why?" As she moved toward him, Nicole realized that Matt had already gone to the bathroom in his clothes. His day care had a rule that no child could be brought in with soiled clothing. She would have to change him and sponge him off.

Nicole turned off the alarm and threw her purse down on the sofa. Tears filled her eyes as she realized that she was going to be late again for work. "I'm sick of it. I can't take this anymore. I'm going to lose my job because of you Matt. It's not fair! Why do you always do this to me?"

Matt began to cry as Nicole snatched on his arm to take him back upstairs. "You should cry," Nicole yelled. "Go on and cry. You're nothing but a big cry baby anyway. I'm sick of you. You went to potty in your clothes on purpose. You wanted to make me late for work."

Attending to children's needs makes demands on a scarce commodity—your time. Sometimes meeting your children's needs may be difficult and trying because their needs conflict with meeting your own. In the case just described, Matt's desire for elimination conflicted with Nicole's responsibility to go to work. The case could have easily have been about a sick child and a parent having to go to work. Should the mother stay home with the child, take him to the day care sick, or try to get someone else to come in and stay with the child while she goes off to her job? What should parents do?

In the case of Nicole and Matt, Nicole attributed several things to her child. For one thing, she accused him of willfulness and purposefulness in his behavior. It is highly unlikely that her two-year-old son actually planned to "potty" in his pants to make Nicole late for work. Nicole also engaged in name calling when she called Matt a "big cry baby." Matt was simply trying to get his needs met, and he did so at an inconvenient time for Nicole. Nicole became angry because Matt's needs were conflicting with her need—namely to get to her job on time.

Nicole became upset and angry partly because she was more aware of her own needs than she was aware of her own child's needs. Children do not plan going to the potty or to become sick with colic. In a quieter moment, Nicole would easily have admitted the lack of purposefulness in Matt's potty behavior. As parents, we find it challenging, and sometimes draining, to meet the needs of our children. Sometimes all we need is a quiet moment to reflect on the situation or a supportive hand to help us through the problem.

This chapter is designed to help you become more aware of your children's needs and how you can anticipate and plan for them so that they do not become figured negatively in their lives. The models developed by Abraham Maslow[1,2] and Eric Erikson[3] are used to assist you in understanding children's needs. Everyday issues that parents face with raising their children are discussed, including such areas as children's fears, bedtime issues, including nightmares, anxiety disorders, and children's school refusal issues. An entire section is presented on the importance of childhood friendships and tips for helping children to form friendships.

# *Maslow's Hierarchy of Needs*

Maslow's hierarchy of needs posits that our actions are motivated by a series of increasingly complex needs. These needs occur whether one is a child or adult. The theory asserts that the order in which these needs present themselves is universal and that as soon as one need is satisfied, a person will move on to the next. Maslow postulated that people have only five categories of needs that they spend their entire life trying to satisfy. He envisioned a pyramid that began at the bottom with the basic need for sustenance and culminated toward transcendence.

All human beings have a hierarchy of needs based on two basic groupings: deficiency needs and growth needs. The first four levels of the pyramid contained deficiency needs, which only manifest themselves when people are lacking in a particular need. Within the deficiency needs grouping, our lower needs must be met or satisfied before moving to the next higher level of needs. The following contains a brief description of the deficiency needs that make up the first four rungs of the pyramid and the growth needs:

- *Physiological needs: Level 1 of the hierarchy.* This level contains our need for the things that keep our bodies alive—food, water, air, rest, elimination, etc. These needs come first. We meet these needs or we die.
- *Safety/security needs: Level 2 of the hierarchy.* All human beings experience a need to stay alive and a need to be safe. There are two kinds of safety needs: the need to be physically safe and the need to be psychologically safe or secure.
- *Belongingness and love needs: Level 3 of the hierarchy.* This level deals with our need to affiliate with others, to be accepted. Once we are alive and feel safe, we then try to satisfy our social needs, our needs to be with and to be accepted by other people. We discover our need for love.
- *Esteem needs: Level 4 of the hierarchy.* This level involves our need to achieve, to be competent, to gain approval, and to receive recognition. After our first three need levels are fairly well met, we try to satisfy a fourth need. This is a need for recognition, respect, and reputation. This need has two parts: self-esteem (thinking well of ourselves) and gaining the esteem of others.
- *Self-actualization (growth needs): Level 5 of the hierarchy.* This level contains the growth needs for self-actualization or personal fulfillment—the reasons that people give for climbing mountains, spending hours writing, or playing the stock market—in essence for the challenge, to see if they can do it. Maslow categorized self-actualization as "being needs." Within this grouping, people are not motivated by a deficiency of anything, but by the need to grow, to be something better, greater than what they were before. Individuals are ready to act upon their growth needs only if their deficiency needs have been met.

Self-actualized people have been described as: (1) being problem-centered; (2) incorporating an ongoing fresh appreciation of life; (3) having a concern about their own personal growth; and (4) having the ability to have peak experiences. Later on in life, Maslow[4] differentiated the growth need of self-actualization into two lower-level growth needs that occur prior to a person's reaching a general level of self-actualization.[5] These additional growth needs are the following: (5) cognitive, a person's need to know, to understand, and to explore; (6) aesthetic, an individual's need for symmetry and order; (7) beauty, an individual's need to find self-fulfillment and to realize one's potential; and (8) transcendence, a person's need to help others find self-fulfillment and to realize their potential. Maslow theorized that as individuals become more self-actualized and transcendent, they develop wisdom.

There is no way to quantify the level of any one need, nor is there an exact definable point at which a need has been satisfied. People do not have to be 100 percent satisfied in one level to begin focusing on another level. Maslow suggested that people could have 85 percent of their physiological needs, 75 percent of their safety needs, and 90 percent of their belonging needs, but he did not provide any method to calculate, for example, what 75 percent would represent.

Each human being is trying to meet needs on a given level during any one time in his life. A person seeking to meet needs for food and water will not be looking to meet needs of belonging, love, or self-esteem. Each of us moves up and down our need pyramid every day. We move down the pyramid each time we become hungry or tired. We move toward our belongingness needs each time we try to impress somebody else or when we try to join a particular group.

## The Basic Needs of Children

Maslow's need hierarchy provides a means for understanding children and their behavior, whether the child is a toddler or a teenager. A strong foundation must first be built in order for children to proceed from one level to the next. At the lowest rung of the needs pyramid, children's physiological needs must be cared for and supplied. They must be fed, clothed, and sheltered.

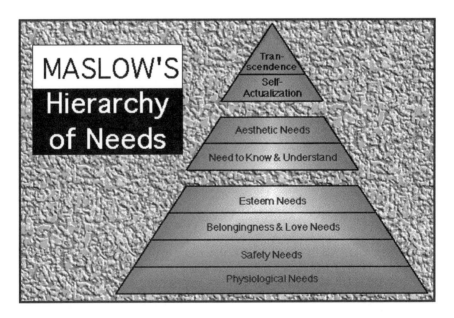

Illustration 8    Maslow's Hierarchy of Needs

Children require a sense of safety in order for them to feel secure and to grow. A child's sense of safety comes from trusting that his physiological needs (hunger, thirst, pain, air, rest, and noise) and protection from danger needs will be met reliably. Children who live in dysfunctional families and abusive situations, foster care, or any other unstable conditions do not usually develop feelings of security and safety. For some children, a sense of security might be going through the day without worrying: "Will Daddy or Mommy hit me again?" "Will Mommy work late again?" "Will I be beat up again in school?"

After the physiological and safety needs are met, children's needs become more internal and more emotional. Children want to feel that they are accepted and that they belong to a family and to a community. They experience a desire to be loved within their family and in other groups. The combined efforts of parents, school, and community are important in helping children to develop a sense of safety. Moreover, children have to feel that they belong to a social group in order to feel comfortable with their surroundings. Extracurricular activities, such as being on a swim or a basketball team or taking part in community programs, can provide opportunities for children to develop new skills and to gain feelings of acceptance among their peers. Children who have a diagnosed disability, such as attention deficit hyperactivity disorder, are sometimes rejected by other children because they lack appropriate behavioral controls. Likewise, those with physical disabilities are sometimes rejected because they look or walk differently than their peers. Children's belongingness needs will be satisfied only if they feel accepted and truly welcome. If their belongingness needs are not met, they experience a deep sense of loneliness and isolation.

Maslow's theory provides that people can be handicapped at one level if they endure a long period of great need during their youth. For infants, being left alone by themselves for extensive periods of time may produce within them a sense of deep alienation and isolation. Survivors of a low nurturance childhood who were shamed as young children often endlessly search for the specialness and praise they never received at home or at school. Children who grow up in poverty might spend a good part of their adult life fixated or stuck on whether they have enough money to supply their needs. Children traumatized by divorce can sometimes spend their adult lives unable to form intimate relationships. They become paralyzed by the fear that the partner will leave or abandon them just as their parent did.

Finally, children require a sense of their own self-esteem as well as that of others in their environment if they are to experience positive development. They achieve a sense of self-esteem by hearing encouraging words, by being praised by their parents and teachers, by feeling they are loved by their families, and by finding purpose and competency in their lives. Children thrive when they feel they believe they have good qualities and can accomplish their goals.

It is important for parents to examine their relationship with their children to determine to what extent their basic physiological, safety, belongingness, esteem, and self-actualization needs are being met within the family and at school.

Children whose lower order needs are not being met are prime candidates for having behavioral problems in the school classroom. Some children become violent if their needs for belongingness and self-esteem are continually frustrated by parents, teachers, school officials, and other students. For instance, there appears to be some evidence that the two students who killed others during the Columbine massacre may have done so because they felt that their belongingness and self-esteem needs were being repeatedly frustrated and violated by others. The Columbine killers turned their anger and violence, first outward with the murder toward others and finally inward toward themselves—suicide.

Although Maslow's need theory has relevance for all children, regardless of their socioeconomic status or ethnic or cultural background, it has particular relevance for children who live in economically challenged, inner-city neighborhoods. Statistics indicate that these children tend to reside in single parent homes with a sole provider who is working one or more jobs just to put food on the table and keep a roof over the family's head. Single parents who work one

Illustration 9    Children's Version of Maslow's Hierarchy of Needs

or more jobs might not be available to help their children with homework because they may be working when the child comes home or because they may lack the academic skills to help their children with schoolwork. This situation does not necessarily mean that these parents do not care about their children's education. Instead, it suggests that educators might have to take into account a number of family and socioeconomic factors when working with children in schools.[6]

Maslow's theory maintains that if deficiency needs (such as physiological, esteem, love, and safety needs) are not met, growth needs such as the need to know and understand life cannot be fulfilled. Inner-city children who grow up in violence-ridden neighborhoods may not have parents available to reassure them that they are safe when they come home from school. Hence, such children have a harder time (than suburban children) learning in school. They may not be able to concentrate or to pay attention because their deficiency needs have not been met.

What can a school and guidance counselor do to help children in resource-challenged home environments? Studies on the home-school connection for increasing reading or literacy of children have found that schools can be enlisted to respond to literacy needs that are not being addressed at home.[7] Students enrolled in the home-school connection program learned the reading material better than those enrolled in the regular school program. The key was increasing the home-school connection and responding to children's needs. Many of the negative behavioral problems and academic failure associated with inner-city schooling can be eliminated or kept to a minimum if children have a positive attachment to a close adult.[8] Such attachments do not necessarily have to be a parent, but a positive adult role model is essential.

Children are biologically hardwired for two important traits sometimes lacking in their families and schools: (1) enduring attachments to other people; and (2) the search for moral and spiritual meaning.[9] They search instinctively for deeper meaning in their lives and in learning. They seek positive role models to see how that meaning is portrayed in society.

Childhood has been identified as the most significant time for developing an altruistic orientation.[10] True education for children engages and develops their altruistic identity, and, by achieving this, motivates them to a higher level of skill development. A well-maintained and caring work or school environment helps young people to empathize with others by encouraging them to first know themselves.[11]

## Why Is Meeting Children's and Adolescents' Needs So Important?

If children's and adolescents' needs are met in positive ways, they develop good methods of relating to others as well as sound character. Youth who experience belonging in a positive manner are inclined to be trusting and friendly toward others. Youth who have been given a chance to experience mastery of a skill or a task have good self-esteem and subsequently become problem solvers who are motivated and achievement-oriented.

Conversely, if children's and adolescents' needs are not met or are met in negative ways, their original needs remain unsatisfied. These unmet needs then become the defining factor in their lives. For instance, youth whose belonging needs are not met positively oftentimes join gangs. Youth who have their love needs unsatisfied sometimes end up as prostitutes or promiscuous people. Youth who lack opportunities to connect meaningfully with others become isolated and sometimes suicidal or even antisocial.

## Needs Theory Applied to Other Areas

Maslow's hierarchy of needs can be used to describe the kinds of information that children and adults seek at different need levels.[12] For instance, children at the lowest level seek coping information to meet their basic needs. Such children seek information in finding out how they can be safe and secure. Therefore, individuals at the safety level rung require helping information. People seeking enlightening information to meet their belongingness needs turn to books or other materials on relationship development. People functioning at the esteem level seek empowering information. Those in the growth levels of cognitive, aesthetic, and self-actualization seek edifying information.

Although Maslow's theory of human motivation is one of the most popular in psychology, there has only been conflicting research evidence to support his theory.[13] Deci and Ryan[14] suggested three, unordered needs: (1) the need for autonomy; (2) the need for competence; and (3) the need for relatedness. Thompson, Grace, and Cohen[15] proposed that the most important needs for children are connection, recognition, and power. Differences among theorists regarding the number and types of needs people have are a result of their different philosophies rather than differences among people.[16] A person's explanatory or attributional style will alter his list of basic needs.[17]

John Burton[18] has applied needs theory to current social and political conflicts. He examined protracted social conflicts to ascertain how universal human needs often are neglected and why some groups attempt to satisfy their needs with violence. Burton has argued that education and culture lead parties to dehumanize the other group.

Marshall Rosenberg's[19] approach stresses that human needs are universal and meeting them is critical to human survival and well-being. Rosenberg places the needs in subgroups and acknowledges that needs might exist beyond those he has identified. His view is that our education and culture sometimes alienate us from connecting with our real needs. Rosenberg has proposed a nonviolent communication model for connecting with our needs and those of others. He has used this approach in mediation in several countries.

Human perception plays a critical role in understanding needs and conflict.[20] Our culture, education, and society influence how we perceive our needs and the manner or style in which we satisfy them. Violence, for instance, is often perpetrated against others because we create enemy images that convince groups and individuals that their needs can only be met by certain strategies and that other people or groups are obstacles to getting their needs met. Some groups' lack of trust and enemy images of the "other" person or group lead them to believe that the only acceptable solution is to destroy the other or to create a separate state. In a multiethnic society, it is important for counselors to build trust among conflicting groups and to deconstruct enemy images.

One contribution of needs theory to conflict issues is that it focuses on the source of the conflict, examining how best the parties can have their needs met. Identifying strategies to meet underlying needs helps nations to reduce the occurrence of wars and peacekeeping operations throughout the world. Another contribution is that it emphasizes the common threads that motivate people to feel the same way that they do.

# Maslow's Hierarchy of Needs and Violence

Human needs theorists such as Maslow,[21] Burton,[22] and Rosenberg[23] argue that Maslow's Hierarchy of Needs is a useful tool for examining how violence develops in children and adolescents. They maintain that conflicts, especially those that are violent, are caused by unmet human needs. Although conflicts between people and groups take place over subsistence issues such as food, most conflicts have to do with other unmet human needs, such as protection (safety), identity, recognition, participation, and understanding.

Violence takes place when people and groups do not see any other way of meeting their needs and when people lack understanding, respect, and consideration of their needs. When we experience deficits in any of Maslow's four deficiency levels, we become at risk for perpetrating violence on others. When we are afraid, we enter a space that feels dangerous and threatening to our welfare or survival.

We expel our fears for self when our basic physiological needs have been met, as well as when we experience safety, have self-esteem, accept ourselves as we are, feel that we matter, and feel that we have a place and space to belong. Fear for self produces violence toward others. Fear of others is essentially anxiety for self. Sometimes children and adolescents do not effectively recognize wounds that arise from trauma or unfulfilled needs in the five levels. Within some families, cycles of fear may cut across generations and become encoded in the very fabric of the family. Children's construction of the other begins very early in life.

Instead of perpetrating violence on others, children can be taught how to negotiate when their needs are threatened in any of the levels described. They can learn to recognize their alarm or fight or flight response and to identify the physiological signals that accompany an alarm state. They can be taught to take care of themselves without feeling threatened, and they can be instructed how to recognize their fears and not to run away from them. They can discover how to sit with a fear, to see what it feels like, and to determine if it is real or imagined. When they enter a space that is threatening to them, they can be taught to ask: At what level, if any, does the threat actually exist?

The seeds of violence begin with constructions of those whom we call "other"—that is, other people, outsiders, or enemies. Children's construction of outsiders and enemies begins very early in life. As they grow in age, "the others" they have constructed in their minds become frightening. Parents, teachers, and counselors can help students question their constructions of the other and how such constructions keep them in a fear and an alarm state.

# Children's Needs and Fears: Impact on Their Development

Many parents have questions about how to deal with children during bedtime and with their fears. Should they ignore their baby's cries at night? What do you do with children who seem to want to be held continually? What happens when parental needs conflict with those of their children?

## Bedtime

Do not ignore your children's cries during the night. Infants and young children are emotional beings rather than rational ones. They do not understand why their cries for help are being ignored by you. Even with the best of intentions, ignoring children's cries leads them to feel abandoned, and they have a good chance of becoming insecure, unhappy children. You will not spoil your children by responding to their cries. Infants cry for a reason that we may not know. If a baby cries at night, it may be because he is hungry, thirsty, sick, uncomfortable, agitated, lonely, or frightened by a nightmare. Whatever the problem, the fact that babies cry indicates that they are unable to solve their problem alone and that they need the assistance of their parents.

It is unreasonable for parents to expect that their children will self-soothe themselves. When parents respond positively to their children's cries and comfort them by trying to help them overcome whatever it is that is bothering them, they are more capable of dealing with their fears. Do not let children cry it out when they are in bed at night. When babies are forced to cry themselves to sleep, they learn that they cannot trust their parents to respond to their needs. Children who feel that they cannot trust their parents to respond to their needs have low self-esteem, feel insecure, and feel emotionally abandoned. The best way to help your children become secure, independent, and emotionally healthy people is to respond to their needs rapidly and to provide nurturing care.

If you truly believe that your child is crying because he is spoiled rather than because of a real problem, ask yourself why your child might be spoiled. You might want to eliminate stressful things from your child's daily activities. Do not expect your young infant to sleep through the night because he is biologically required to feed several times during the night. Infants should not be expected to use adult sleeping patterns.

As your toddlers and older children lie in bed at night, it is important that you plan for tomorrow. Encourage your children that tomorrow will be a good day, and they will learn to be optimistic. Your words to your child should be positive, supportive, and loving. You want to convey to your child that you love him and that he is important to you. No matter how old children are, they hear "love messages." Frequent reminders of your love will encourage them to become secure, balanced, self-assured, and confident.

Physical affection is especially important to your child at night. Touch, hold, hug, and kiss your child before saying good night. Children need physical affection and bodily contact with their parents for their own mental health. Research studies have demonstrated that children with insufficient touch and loving holding develop emotional difficulties in their subsequent relationships with others. The physical touch of a loving parent or a caregiver releases endorphins—painkilling chemicals in a child's brain—which encourage him to relax.

## Toddlers and Older Children's Fears and Anxieties

Fear is a necessary alarm system for our survival. If we accept Maslow's theory that our natural inclination is toward growth and development, we also have to acknowledge that we would not survive very long as a species if it were not for our ability to appraise a situation and avoid danger. Fear, then, is a protective mechanism, and it is a part of our normal development. Fear can be conceptualized as an emotional response that takes place in the interim between confronting a new situation and actually mastering it.

Children's fears are increased by their active imagination as they try to understand a new situation. Temporary fears are a natural part of life. Young children may fear the bogeyman or a monster that they have seen on cartoons. They cry to Mommy and Daddy to protect them from the monsters they have viewed on television. Similarly, adults may lock themselves in their homes with bars over their doors and their windows to keep burglars out. Sometimes, however, the very protective devices adults have purchased and installed to protect their fears end causing their own death—i.e., when the fire company cannot get to them.

Hence, for both children and adults anxiety is an intense emotional state that takes place when you cannot predict the outcome of a situation or guarantee that you will not receive an undesirable result. Children sometimes have fears because their safety needs are not being met. Fear arises in children during the second half of the first year. This rise in fear keeps newly mobile babies close to their mothers. Babies use their mother or primary caregiver as a base of support and as a point from which they can safely explore the world. Older infants oftentimes hesitate before playing with a new toy. Infants who have just learned to crawl show a fear of heights. Children's most frequent expression of fear is to unfamiliar adults, a response called stranger anxiety.

Children change the focus of their anxiety as they mature and encounter new experiences that they have not yet mastered. For instance, babies are afraid of a loss of support and loud noises. Toddlers are afraid of separation and things bigger than themselves, especially at night—monsters, burglars, and bad people. As toddlers' cognitive development increases, they become capable of discriminating between threatening and nonthreatening people and situations. Hence, stranger anxiety declines as do other fears of the first two years. Fear decreases as toddlers learn more strategies for coping with it.

Although children's fears of the dark, thunder and lightning, and supernatural beings persist into middle childhood, their anxieties are also directed toward new concerns. Once children begin to understand the dangers of the world and the possibility of personal harm (being robbed, stabbed, or shot), their sense of safety becomes challenged. Other common childhood fears include academic failure, parents' health, physical injury, and peer rejection. Adolescents fear not being accepted by their peers and begin to look to the world community toward issues related to war and their own future success as an adult.

Severe childhood fears and anxiety may arise from living in negative situations, such as inner-city ghettos and war torn areas of the world. In violent neighborhoods and in families that have domestic violence, many children suffer from post-traumatic stress disorders from the violence. Their safety needs are severely compromised.

It is important that you ask your child about his fears. Anxious children often have unrealistic ideas about how others perceive them or how friendships are supposed to be. Parents need to find out about the beliefs behind their children's fears and to help them challenge such fears in their daily lives.

## Anxiety Disorders: When Children's Fears Become Excessive

Anxiety disorders have been traced to a number of different sources, including genetics, children's temperament, and family enhancement of a certain anxious thinking style. Researchers have established some support for the genetic transmission of anxiety. For instance, children of anxious parents are seven times more likely to develop an anxiety disorder than are children of nonanxious parents. Scientists have indicated that genetics account for about 30 to 40 percent of all transmission of anxiety disorders. Panic disorders provide the greatest evidence for a genetic transmission of anxiety. It is believed that a set of genes affects how different cells in the body's alarm system respond to sensitivities. Even though genetics make a significant contribution to children's development of an anxiety disorder, the vast majority of children with anxious parents do not develop such disorders. Instead, genetics influence primarily children's overall vulnerability to anxiety.

There is concern that some children are wired in their brains for worry. The amygdala functions to alert us to danger, but it is not always accurate. We can think that we are in danger when in reality we are not. The amygdala quickly assesses the emotional significance of cues and activates nearly every system in the body to survive a perceived threat. Our bodies become poised for flight or fight. During the time of fear alert, serotonin, a neurotransmitter or brain messenger chemical, also plays a role. When danger and all-clear messages are not transmitted accurately or efficiently, the child may experience prolonged distress. Selective serotonin reuptake inhibitors, or SSRIs, are the medications most prescribed for anxiety disorders. Children's anxiety becomes a disorder when they automatically exaggerate risks and underestimate their ability to cope with a given situation. Excessive anxiety can become debilitating to children and can result in chronic fatigue and somatic body complaints as well as decreased academic achievement and school attendance.

A child's temperament is also a factor in anxiety disorders. Many children are sensitive to change and risk from birth. Therefore, they are less inclined to explore their environment. Children's temperament predisposition influences how they resolve to meet their needs and experiences. Some develop an extremely cautious style called behavioral inhibition. Children who have a strong behavioral inhibition react to even the most minor changes in their environment with signs of distress (new baby bottle), while other infants respond with excitement or delight to the same changes.

Moreover, children who have experienced a traumatic event in their lives are twice as likely to develop an anxiety disorder or depression. Children who encounter stressful or traumatic situations experience periods of great sensitivity that may lead to clinging behavior or regression to earlier developmental stages. Such regression behaviors are normal and adaptive to the extent that they enable them to get the nurturing they need to recover emotionally and physically. Children who have experienced such stressors as having an illness, dealing with the death of a loved one, being the victim of violence, losing a best friend, or facing parental separation or parental divorce may have prolonged periods of anxiety. Such stressful life events may become too much for the child and turn what started as an occasional anxiety into a full blown anxiety disorder.

## *Parenting Behaviors that Promote or Hinder Anxiety Disorders*

Family and child interactions can also enhance an already slightly anxious child's perceptions of a situation. For instance, some parents hover over their children at the slightest indication of a minor accident. The child then becomes anxious about participating in those activities that cause their parents to worry. Studies have reported that children with anxiety disorders describe their parents as more controlling, less cohesive and supportive, and more conflictual than families of children without such a diagnosis. The following parenting behaviors are associated with anxiety in children:

- *Parental overcontrol:* The parent is intrusive, exerting control in conversation, limits autonomy, and limits independence in conversation.

- *Parental overprotection:* The parent provides excessive parental caution and protective behavior without reasonable cause for using strict cautions.

- *Modeling of anxious interpretation:* The parent agrees with the child's distortion of the risk in a given situation, and thereby reinforces the child's belief that normal, everyday things in the world are too frightening to approach.

- *Tolerance or encouragement of avoidance behavior:* The parent repeatedly suggests to the child or agrees with the child that he should not try something difficult.

- *Rejection or criticism:* The parent repeatedly uses disapproving judgment and critical or dismissive responses to the child's efforts to do something on his own.

- *Conflict:* Some studies reported that fighting, arguing, or disharmony in the child's family was associated with higher levels of anxiety

Researchers have also found that there exist certain positive parenting behaviors that buffer a child's stress and anxiety. Some positive parenting behaviors that can prevent children's development of anxiety disorders are the following:

- *Reward children's coping behavior:* Parents should focus on a child's efforts, not necessarily the ends or results. Parents encourage children to take on challenges, and they recognize partial success.

- *Extinguish excessive anxious behavior:* Parents can extinguish their child's anxious behavior by not responding to it excessively, either with concern or anger.

- *Manage their own anxiety:* Parents reduce or limit their displays of emotional distress. Parents are careful not to introduce their own worries into the child's.

- *Develop family communication and problem-solving skills:* Parents who talk with their children and who encourage them to engage in problem solving have children who are less anxious.

## Children's Security Needs and Nightmares

Children's nightmares can be caused by a number of factors, including their sense that they are not safe—security needs. The raw terror that children experience as a result of a frightening nightmare may accentuate their insecurity and bring on anxiety for hours or days afterward. Sometimes children become afraid to go to bed, while others develop sleep disturbances and sleep phobias.

Nightmares may have a silver lining because they can sometimes point to issues that are most upsetting to children, when they are unable to express what is actually bothering them. Every nightmare contains within it important information about the emotional issues in children's lives. Children who dream repeatedly about someone chasing them may be overwhelmed about what is taking place in their lives. When children are plagued by repeated nightmares, parents might examine how much stress and change their little ones are currently experiencing. Too much change in children's lives may leave them unable to cope and produce nightmares that indicate they are overwhelmed by stress.

For most children and people in general, nightmares are a normal part of coping with changes in our lives. For instance, children have nightmares in response to such events as entering school, moving to a new neighborhood, or dealing with a divorce or remarriage—primarily because these events require them to adjust to change in their lives. Nightmares diminish as children grow older, partly because they learn how to master their fears and gain more control over their world. During a period of stress or family crisis, parents should anticipate that their children might have more nightmares. If children suddenly have a marked increase in nightmares, they are telling you that they are feeling overwhelmed and insecure.

Oftentimes, people's nightmare symbols emerge early in childhood and continue throughout their entire life span. For instance, one day when Sarah was about three years old, she was frightened by a baby bird that had fallen out of its nest and landed on her head. She ran to her mother yelling and screaming, terrified that the bird would eat her or harm her in some way. After the bird incident, Sarah began to have repeated dreams of being chased by birds who tried to peck her. Subsequently, Sarah would have her bird dream whenever she was upset— for example, when her mother was going on a business trip and when her baby brother was born. Her bird dreams had become symbolic of events that threatened her sense of security. Recurrent dream patterns can also be influenced by television programs, family fears, cultural stereotypes, and current events.

What can we learn from recurrent dreams? For one thing, they serve as warnings of lingering unresolved, psychological conflicts. Each person develops his own repertoire of dream symbols. Research on people who kept dream journals for as long as 50 years has found that certain dream scenes and dream figures are repeated from early childhood throughout a person's life. Sometimes children of divorce dream that their parents are reunited, and abuse survivors have dreams in which they are the victims of violence.

When children experience a change in the content of their recurring dreams, they are usually signaling an improvement in their psychological functioning. For instance, in working with young children, a therapist might ask your child to revisualize the dream and see himself turning around and chasing the scary monster. Your kid then chases the monster and calls the police who come to get the monster out of the closet where he ran to hide. Parents can help their children with nightmares if they reassure them and if they recognize that some basic security need has been threatened. The next time your child has a scary dream, do not try to put him back to bed and dismiss the dream. Instead, tell your child that if he is experiencing the dream, he must get up and come to your bedroom and the two of you will deal with the scary monster. Such direction gives your child a sense of empowerment. He does not have to be afraid to go to bed at night out of fear of the nightmare.

When your child comes to your bedroom, remain calm and determined that the two of you are going to handle that monster so that he will never come back again. Have your child recount the dream as it appeared, and then have your child reframe the dream with him as a triumphant survivor instead of a victim. Your child refuses to run. Instead, he says something like: "You cannot scare me anymore. You better get out of here before I chase you out of here and call the police." Adults can also use this technique to deal with nightmares. The parent returns the child to his own bed once he has been empowered to deal with the scary dream.

## Three Stages of Resolution in Children's Recurring Dreams

Parents can help a child by identifying for themselves and possibly for the child (depending on his age) three stages of resolution in recurring dreams. These are the following:

- *Threat:* In the dream, a main character is threatened and unable to present a defense to stop the threat. For instance, one adolescent complained of being paralyzed in her dream while lying next to a big snake.
- *Struggle:* The dreamer's attempts to confront figures in the nightmare are partially successful in fending off the person or symbol. An example would be a ghost comes into a child's room, and he throws something at the ghost, making it run out of the room.
- *Resolution:* The nightmare demon or figure is defeated, and the dreamer is able to get on with his life. Children can be helped by telling them to pretend that they have a magic wand and it will defeat the monster or the shadowy figure. Parents should examine and emphasize a degree of mastery over the demon or monster in the dream. As children mature emotionally and cognitively, they increase their ability to solve problems and to handle situations independently. As children gain control in their dreams, they may also acquire control over their conscious, waking lives.

# Children's Needs and Choosing a School

Your child's attending preschool and kindergarten are two major transitions that may interfere with his security needs. There are four basic fit factors to consider in choosing a school for your child, and these are the following: (1) What your child learns—these are aspects of your child that influence what subjects and at what level your child should be taught at school—your child's basic learning capability, his interests; (2) How your child learns, which includes your child's learning style, motivational level, mental health challenges, learning disabilities and disorders; (3) Social issues, your child's need for social contact; and (4) Practical matters, the school's extracurricular activities. Some signs that indicate a school is a good fit for your child are listed in Illustrations 10 and 11.

## School Refusal Behavior and Your Child

If your child persistently complains that he does not want to attend school, try to find out what is going on at school to give your child such feelings. Sometimes children and adolescents develop school refusal. About 28 percent of school-aged children in this country refuse school at some point during their education. School refusal is equally common among boys and girls. While children between the ages of 5 and 17 may refuse to attend school, most young people who refuse are 10–13 years old. Peaks in school refusal behavior are typically seen during times of transitions, such as 5–6 and 14–15 years as children enter new schools.

Parental training and psychological treatment may be necessary if your child persistently evidences school refusal behavior. For instance, if your child's reason for school refusal is that he is attempting to escape from some negative effect of school such as separation anxiety, generalized anxiety, or fears, you might consider training in somatic management skills—breathing retraining (progressive muscle relaxation), self-efficacy training, or gradual reintroduction

Illustration 10    Signs that School Is a Good Fit for Your Child

| |
|---|
| Your child is eager to go to school, preschool, or day care. |
| You see tremendous progress in your child's overall development—academic, physical, and social throughout the entire school year. |
| Your child feels that his abilities and interests are appreciated at the school. |
| Your child is achieving and performing at the level for which he is capable, and he is being challenged appropriately in the school. |
| Your child has friends and acquaintances who like and accept him at school. |

Illustration 11   Signs that School Is a Poor Fit for Your Child

| |
|---|
| Even well into the school year, your child is adamantly opposed to going to school, and the stressful events in his life do not explain his opposition. |
| Your child has made little progress during the year, either academically, socially, or emotionally. |
| Your child is not performing academically as well as you think he can or as well as his test results suggest. |
| Your child often says that teachers of other kids do not understand him or do not like him. |
| Your child does not seem to have any close friends or friendly acquaintances. |

to school. Other techniques include establishing routines, using rewards and pun-ishments for school attendance and school refusal. If your child wants to escape from aversive social and evaluative situations (such as test anxiety, public speak-ing fears, shyness, and social skills deficits), try role-playing and cognitive restructuring of his negative self-talk. It is important to get help with a child's school refusal if it is a persistent pattern. Stay connected to your child's school work.

# Children's Friends and Belonging Needs

It is heartbreaking for a parent to hear his child say that "nobody likes me" or "I don't have any friends." Parents want their children to be well-liked and to be able to get along with others. Children's friendships are responsive to their belongingness needs. When these needs are satisfied, they like going to school to meet and be with their friends. Conversely, when children feel that other chil-dren do not like them or make fun of them, they sometimes hate going to school. Children's friendships are not inconsequential matters. Everyone wants to belong. Most children want a friend. Think back to your childhood. Did you have a best friend? Who was he? What did that friendship mean to you?

Some children have a natural knack for making friends. They join groups easily, and they attract others to their circle of play. They like to talk, and they get good opportunities to build their verbal skills as children surround them. In contrast, other children have difficulty making friends. For instance, children with attention deficit hyperactive disorder often miss the social cues needed to have friends, and therefore, kids are likely to exclude them from their play. Shy children experience discomfort approaching others; anxious children put a great deal of attention into managing their fears and worries rather than making friends. Whatever the particular case might be, it hurts when one does not have a friend.

How do children form friends? As children mature cognitively and socially, they become increasingly self-aware. They also get better at communicating and understanding the thoughts and feelings of others. Likewise, their skill of interacting with other children improves. Peers give young children learning experiences that only they can provide. For one thing, peers act on an equal footing with each other. Unlike their conversations with adults, children must work at keeping a conversation going with other children. They must learn to cooperate and set goals with each other if they want to play together peacefully. Children form friendships with each other—that is, special relationships that are characterized by attachment and common interests.

Mildred Parten,[24] who was one of the early pioneers to study peer sociability among children ages two to five, noticed a dramatic increase with age in joint, interactive play. She maintained that social development and friendships are governed by a three-step process. First, it begins with nonsocial activity—where the child is an onlooker and engages in solitary play. Then the child shifts to parallel play, in which a child plays near other children with similar materials but does not try to influence their behavior. At the third and highest level of play are two forms of social interaction. One is associative play, in which the children participate in social activities but exchange toys and comment on one another's behavior. The other is cooperative play, where children orient themselves toward a common goal, such as playing doctor.

Preschoolers seem to use parallel play as a means to get respite from the complex demands of social interaction and as a bridge to new activities. Although nonsocial activity among children declines with age, it is still the most frequent form among three to four year olds and accounts for a third of kindergartners' free play time. Solitary and parallel play remain relatively stable from three to six years of age, and these account for as much of the child's play as cooperative interaction.

Sometimes parents wonder if a preschooler who spends a great deal of time playing alone is developing normally. Only certain kinds of nonsocial activities should concern parents, and these are aimless wandering, hovering near peers, and functional play involving repetitive motor activity. Children who watch peers playing without trying to join in may be temperamentally inhibited, that is, high in social fearfulness. Moreover, children who participate in solitary, repetitive behavior (such as banging blocks, making a doll jump up and down) are inclined to be immature, impulsive children who find it hard to regulate anger and aggression. Consequently, their peers tend to ostracize them.

Yet most preschoolers with low rates of peer play interaction are not socially anxious. They just like to play by themselves, and their solitary play activities are usually positive and constructive. For instance, some children who prefer solitary play like to play with art materials, puzzles, and building toys. These children are typically well adjusted. Children may be rebuffed by their peers if they play with toys that are usually associated with the opposite gender.

Children's first friendships are formed as a result of their play activities. Preschoolers view a friend as someone "who likes you" and with whom you spend a lot of time playing. Four to seven year olds regard a friend as someone with whom you play and share toys. During this time, friendship does not have a long-term, enduring quality based on mutual trust. One importance of early childhood friends is that they offer social support. Studies have found, for example, that children who begin kindergarten with friends in their class or readily make new friends adjust to school more favorably.[25]

## Why Are Childhood Friendships Important?

Friendships help children to integrate themselves into a school's learning environment that promotes both academic and social competence. First friendships serve as important contexts for children's social and emotional development. Parents influence their children's early peer relationships directly by arranging informal play activities. Preschoolers whose parents frequently use their homes for informal children activities tend to have children with large peer networks, and their children are more socially skilled. Children learn how to initiate their own peer contacts when their parents host play activities for their friends. Such parents are present to teach children how to enter play groups and how to resolve conflicts nonviolently.

Childhood friendships are important because they satisfy children's belongingness needs, their need for social support, and their validation by others. Children give parents clues to their ability to form friendships by the manner in which they engage in play activities. Those who have insecure attachments to parents and other family members may be less knowledgeable about how to interact sensitively with their peers; consequently, they do not expect kindness from others. Children's ability to keep positive friendships is closely related to positive outcomes in adulthood—especially in terms of having good relationships at home and at work. In addition, the quality of children's friendships can affect their success in forming positive relationships with the rest of their peers.

Children who are rejected by their peer group are at risk for a variety of negative outcomes that have implications for their psychological well-being as adults. They are at increased risk for depression, anxiety, and low self-esteem. Childhood friendships are powerful predictors of social adjustment in adulthood. Close friendships are marked by affection, a sense of reliable alliance and intimacy—the sharing of secrets and personal information. When children and adolescents have a friend to confide in, they develop feelings of trust, acceptance, and a sense of being understood. Therefore, friendship mediates the link between acceptance and loneliness.

Young children have on-again, off-again friendships and group acceptance. By the age of 10, children's patterns of acceptance, friendship, and psychological adjustment are pretty much set in place. During these transitional years, intimacy is more important in peer relations for girls than for boys. It has been estimated that 70 percent of teens report having stable friendships.

Parents should be concerned if their child is unable to make any friend at all. Warning signs that children do not have close friends include the inability to name specific close friends (or naming kids not really their friends), lack of incoming calls or invitations from peers, hanging out with friends who are significantly older or younger, and lack of regular peer contacts outside of school. Although direct parental involvement with their children's friends decline as children age, parents still need to monitor their friendships. It is important that parents know who their children's friends are, where they are, how to contact them, and what they may be doing.

## Tips for Helping Children to Form Friendships

Good friendships do not just happen. Studies indicate an association between parental involvement in arranging children's peer contacts and the social and academic adjustment of preschoolers and kindergartners. Parents who arrange play dates, enroll their children in structured activities, and monitor peer interactions have children who are socially competent. Sometimes children need help in making friends. Parents can help their children by teaching them social competence or ways to engage others. People who form friendships score high on likability measures. Therefore, parents need to understand how to help their children increase their "likability quotient." Suggestions for helping children develop friendships include:

- Have your child look for opportunities to help others. Research shows that helpfulness correlates more strongly than any other attribute to being liked. Teach your child to become aware of other people's needs and to offer assistance spontaneously, before others ask for it.
- Teach your child how to say "hello" first and to smile. People who smile are viewed as nice and approachable. When children smile and are optimistic about whatever they are doing, others are drawn to then.
- Have your child put a curb on displaying various moods, complaining, and blaming others. Children distance themselves from peers who are consistently negative and pessimistic about life.
- Show your child how to introduce himself and to make contact with peers.
- Encourage your child to ask to join in the fun when approaching a group that is already engaged in play or in an activity. It is better to approach one person in the group than to ask the entire group for permission to join it. Make sure that your child says "thank you" to the person and the group for letting him join the activity. If your child is turned down, teach him to say, "Okay, maybe next time."
- Help your child not to take rebuffs from other children personally. The child who was rude may have been having a bad day.

- Teach your child basic body language skills. Children's body language helps them to be considered likeable to others. Assist your child in understanding the importance of eye contact, standing up straight, and honoring other children's personal space.
- Make sure that your child dresses in the clothing styles of his peers. One mother went to school and discovered that she was sending her son to school in clothes that were seriously out-of-date, while the majority of the kids wore hoodies and baggy pants to school.
- Support your child's involvement in extracurricular activities. By joining clubs or teams, your child can meet others who share the same interests. Children find it easier to connect when they have something in common to talk about.
- Observe your child to find out if he has any behaviors that may be causing a problem. Is your child too bossy or aggressive? If so, help him to recognize the problem and develop different behaviors.

Children's friendships are training ground for adult relationships. Social aptitude can make or break careers and relationships in the adult world. Poor social skills put a person more at risk in the work world than poor spelling. It takes only one best friend to stave off a child's loneliness and depression. Even if a child is not accepted by the larger group, one close friendship can serve as a buffer to loneliness and depression.

# Children's Security Needs and Divorce

Children's security needs are threatened by family disruption, especially divorce. When parents divorce, the child may feel that his world is threatened and will never be the same again. There are ways that parents can respond that lessen the impact of divorce and make the child feel more secure during the changes. First, parents need to talk with their children about the divorce, depending, of course, on the child's age and level of maturity. Children's response to a divorce are based partly on how their parents informed them of their decision to part. Whenever possible, the entire family should meet together so that both parents can answer children's questions. This strategy is designed to help parents avoid blaming each other for the divorce, and it also is responsive to children's needs for safety and security.

When you first talk with your child about the divorce, limit your discussion to the most essential and immediate issues. Children want to know that their basic needs will be met, that someone will be there to fix them breakfast in the morning, that a parent will still help them with their homework, and that a parent will tuck them into bed at night. Children also need to be reassured that their relationship with both parents will continue. Divorce requires them to make many changes; therefore, children need to hear what will remain the same as well as what will change.

During these family discussions, it is important that children understand that the divorce is final and that their parents will not be getting back together again. Oftentimes children secretly harbor fantasies that their parents will reunite. Children need to hear from parents that the divorce is not their fault. Some children believe that the divorce happened because of something that they did or did not do. For instance, they may believe that the divorce is taking place because they misbehaved or did not do well in school.

To aid children during a divorce, parents should ask their children what their concerns and fears are about their lives. If the children are caught off guard about the divorce, the parents might give them some time to think about their concerns and bring them to the next family meeting. It is especially important that parents convey to their children that they understand the impact of the divorce on their lives. The concerns and feelings of some children and adolescents are captured below:

### What I Need from My Mother and Father

- "I need both of you to stay involved in my life, even if you don't live close by each other. Please keep in contact with me by writing letters, calling me on the phone, and spending time with me. When I don't see you or have contact with you, I feel as if I don't really matter to you and that you don't love me."

- "Please stop fighting with each other because it upsets me a lot. I would like for the two of you to agree on matters related to me and my needs. When you fight about me, I feel torn apart."

- "Please don't ask me to take messages back and forth from the two of you. That's distressing to me because I am not sure if I am always saying the right thing. Sometimes I might mess up the message."

- "Please don't ask me to spy on the other parent. I am not a detective, and I don't want to get involved in who's going out with whom and other matters."

- "Please don't talk bad about or run the other parent into the ground with bad statements about what the other person did wrong in the marriage. I want to respect and feel good about the both of you."

Because parental divorce shatters children's sense of safety and security concerns, it is important that parents keep their children's normal schedules and routine as much as possible. Make sure your child has access to all of his familiar belongings at both houses. Reassure them of your continued presence with love and hugs. Let them know repeatedly that their needs will be met. Read books to younger children about divorce, and do not bring a new romantic partner to your home or to children's special events. Keep your problems about the divorce to yourself. Instead of using your child as a confidant, find a friend or a counselor to discuss your issues; but do not force your child to deal with your problems. Make sure the child has access to both parents. Children should know how to contact the noncustodial parent should they want to talk with him.

# Children's Security and Belonging Needs and Moving

Moving is a major stressful life event. Children experience a deep sense of loss when they move and leave familiar surroundings and friends. Two of the young people who shot others at schools complained that they were angry because their parents had divorced and they were forced to move and leave their friends. Eight-year-old Stephan and his six-year-old younger sister were moving from the only home that they had ever known. Both Stephan and Rachel had made many close friends at their school and in their upscale, middle class neighborhood. Before the family moved, Stephan began having nightmares. He kept on dreaming that he was running, running, and running from someone who was chasing him. He was terrified of the person, but he did not know who the person was.

His mother tried to comfort him and asked if he were concerned about his moving to a new city and making new friends. Stephan started to cry. He pleaded with his mother that he did not want to leave his old home and friends. He loved his teacher and his school. Stephan's mother reassured him that he would make new friends in his new city.

Frequently, when people have dreams about running from an unknown person, they are experiencing anxiety about the unknown. Stephan's dream symbolized that he was overwhelmed by the move and frightened by the loss of his familiar home, old friends, and school. In addition, Stephan's dream was an indication that he was insecure about the move and that he was already experiencing deep-seated loss of all those things and people whom he loved. What he needed was reassurance from his parents.

It is important that parents encourage their children to express their emotions about the move and that they help allay their fears. Encourage children to create a scrapbook of their former home, school, and friends. If possible, involve the children in some of the decision-making about the move. To help children cope with their anxiety about moving, parents might hold a farewell party for the children and plan a theme with party favors that reflect something the children have shared. Have the children visit the school they will attend before moving and have them meet their teachers. When arranging the new home, organize the children's room first so that they will feel settled as soon as possible.

Children require time to adjust to new homes, schools, and communities. In an effort to cope with the moving change, they may regress to earlier developmental stages. Parents should understand that such regression may represent effective coping strategies for some children and that it takes them at least six months to adjust to a move. If a child begins to show signs of depression or extreme mood changes, major changes in sleeping or eating, it is best to contact

Illustration 12   Children's Need Assessment Chart

| Needs | What Is Blocking Needs from Being Met | Resources Needed to Meet Needs | Steps to Take to Meet Needs |
|---|---|---|---|
| Physiological | | | |
| 1. | | | |
| 2. | | | |
| 3. | | | |
| Safety and Protection | | | |
| 1. | | | |
| 2. | | | |
| 3. | | | |
| Belongingness and Love Needs | | | |
| 1. | | | |
| 2. | | | |
| 3. | | | |
| Self-Esteem Needs | | | |
| 1. | | | |
| 2. | | | |
| Self-Actualization and Reaching Potential Needs | | | |
| 1. | | | |
| 2. | | | |
| Most Pressing Need | | | |

a mental health professional or a guidance counselor in the school. Help your child make friends at his new home.

# Assessing a Child's Hierarchy of Needs

Each person within a family has a fluctuating group of psychological, physical, spiritual, and mental needs. Helping family members to identify and to fulfill their primary needs promotes harmony within a family. List your child's unmet needs. For each unmet need, indicate what is blocking its fulfillment, what resources are needed to satisfy it, and what steps you believe need to be taken to remedy the situation.

# Family Needs Assessment

Families should also consider examining the needs of the family as a whole. They develop strategies for dealing with outside threats to members' survival.

Illustration 13    Family Needs Assessment

| Needs | What Is Blocking Needs from Being Met | Resources Needed to Meet Needs | Steps to Take to Meet Needs |
|---|---|---|---|
| Physiological | | | |
| 1. | | | |
| 2. | | | |
| 3. | | | |
| Safety and Protection | | | |
| 1. | | | |
| 2. | | | |
| 3. | | | |
| Belongingness and Love Needs | | | |
| 1. | | | |
| 2. | | | |
| 3. | | | |
| Self-Esteem Needs | | | |
| 1. | | | |
| 2. | | | |
| Self-Actualization and Reaching Potential Needs | | | |
| 1. | | | |
| 2. | | | |
| Most Pressing Need | | | |

They might determine that the overall safety needs of its members necessitate that an alarm system is purchased for the home or that a fire evacuation plan be instituted. To increase belongingness, a family plans and participates in family vacations or family reunions. In the chart, list your family's unmet needs and indicate what is blocking each one's fulfillment. Moreover, determine what resources are needed to satisfy these unmet needs, and what steps should be taken to remedy the situation.

## Meeting Lower Order Needs Insufficient for Happiness

Research has found, however, that meeting Maslow's physiological and safety needs are not a necessary prerequisite for self-actualization (finding self-fulfillment and realizing one's own potential). A study on a group of homeless men found fewer differences than anticipated on the self-actualization scores of homeless men involved in a daily battle for shelter, food and safety over an extended period and college students.[26] More than 39 percent of the homeless men described themselves as happy. The words of Mother Teresa are instructive for understanding the fact that meeting a person's basic needs does not necessarily translate to their feeling happy in life. She stated:

> In every country there are poor. On certain continents poverty is more spiritual than material. . . . Perhaps in rich countries people aren't hungry for bread as they are in India or Africa. . . . I think it is much easier to give a plate of rice or a piece of bread to a hungry person than to eliminate loneliness, and the feeling of being unwanted—a feeling that many rich people have who spend their days alone. I think that is great poverty.[27]

# Contributions of Erikson's Psychosocial Theory

Erikson's theory of psychosocial development[28,29,30] is one of the best known theories in psychology. Similar to Freud, Erikson proposed that a persons' personality develops in a series of stages. Freud focused on psychosexual stages of development. He believed that people develop through stages based upon a particular erogenous zone—for instance, the mouth during infancy becomes the erogenous zone of pleasure. In contrast to Freud, Erikson's[31,32] theory emphasizes the importance of one's social experiences across the entire lifespan. Each stage in Erikson's theory is concerned with the individual's becoming competent with a critical developmental issue.

Erikson[33] believed that people experience a conflict that functions as a turning point in development. The individual's conflict is centered on either developing a psychological quality or failing to achieve that quality or state. During the psychosocial stages of development, an individual's potential for growth is high, and so is his potential for failure. If the person handles the issue well, he will develop a sense of mastery. Conversely, if the individual manages the stage poorly, he will emerge with a sense of inadequacy. Erikson's stages related to children and adolescents are presented for brief discussion.

## Children Are Different at Different Ages and Stages

### Psychosocial Stage 1—Crisis: Trust or Mistrust (Birth to 1 Year)
The first stage of development is labeled trust vs. mistrust. It occurs between birth and one year of age. It is the most fundamental stage of life because an infant is completely dependent on a caregiver, who is usually a parent. The primary question the infant must answer is this: Is my world safe, predictable, and supportive? An infant develops trust based on the dependability, consistency, and quality of care provided by caregivers. Children develop a sense of trust if their caregivers are responsive to their needs on a consistent basis. Children who develop basic trust feel safe and secure in the world; they have a sense of

hope and confidence and the belief that things will work out well in the end. They also develop the enduring belief that they can attain their deep and essential wishes. The ego quality that the child develops is hope.

In contrast, when caregivers are emotionally unavailable, inconsistent, or rejecting, children develop a sense of basic mistrust of the world. When children fail to develop trust, they see the world as fearful or unpredictable and inconsistent. Later on in life, they may suffer from depression, withdrawal, and paranoia.

The concept of trust vs. mistrust pervades an individual's entire life. If an individual does not develop an adequate sense of trust, he may be unable to form healthy and long-lasting relationships with others or even themselves. Adults who never developed a sense of trust and hope find it extremely difficult to believe that they can succeed during difficult times or crises in their lives. An individual's belief in hope is critical to his survival in an ever-changing world.

### Psychosocial Stage 2—Crisis: Autonomy vs. Shame and Doubt (2–3 Years)

The second stage of Erikson's theory of psychosocial development takes place as the child attempts to establish a sense of autonomy. This stage focuses on children developing a greater sense of personal control. The main question asked is this: Can I do it by myself, or will I always need assistance? This question becomes important with the child during toilet training. Erikson believed that learning to control one's bodily functions results in children developing a sense of control and independence from their parents. If children are praised and guided firmly, they will develop a sense of will that will help them to accomplish and build self-esteem as children and adults. The ego quality that children develop during the second psychosocial stage is will and the determination to exercise free will and self-control.

If parents are too permissive, harsh, or demanding, children can feel defeated and experience extreme shame and doubt. Consequently, they grow up to engage in neurotic attempts to regain feelings of control, power, and competency. Sometimes children develop obsessive/compulsive disorders. When children are given no limits or guidance, they can fail to gain any shame or doubt and become impulsive. If they are denied autonomy, they turn their urges to manipulate and discriminate. Shame develops within their self-concept. Children who complete this stage successfully feel secure and confident, while those who do not are left with a sense of inadequacy and self-doubt.

### Psychosocial Stage 3: Crisis: Initiative vs. Guilt (4–5 Years)

Erikson described early childhood as a period of "vigorous unfolding." Once children develop a sense of autonomy, they become less contrary than they were as toddlers. Their energies are now free to deal with the psychological conflict of the preschool years: initiative vs. guilt. As the word initiative implies, children develop a sense of purposefulness. In addition, they begin to develop their conscience.

Erikson believed that a primary purpose of children's play is that it provides a means by which they learn about themselves and their social world. Play gives preschoolers an opportunity to try out new skills and to practice work-related activities performed by their parents. Children around the world act out highly visible occupations during play (e.g., doctor and nurse in the United States; rabbit hunter and potter among Hopi Indians), thereby developing a sense of initiative.

In contrast to Freud, Erikson believed that one negative outcome of early childhood is that some children develop an overly strict superego that causes them to feel too much guilt because they have been overly punished by parents. If parents are supportive of children's efforts to show initiative, they develop a sense of purpose. The central question children ask is this: Am I good or bad? Children set goals and act in ways to reach them. If children are punished for attempts to demonstrate initiative, they develop a sense of guilt, which in the excess can result in feelings of inhibition. Children who are successful at this stage feel capable and able to lead others. Those who fail to acquire these skills develop a sense of guilt, self-doubt, and lack of initiative. If children develop too much purpose and no guilt, they may turn out to be ruthless in their interactions with others and achieve their goals without caring about whom they hurt or step on in the process.

## Psychosocial Stage 4: Crisis: Industry vs. Inferiority (6–12 Years)

Erikson maintained that if children's previous experiences have been primarily positive, they enter middle childhood prepared to redirect their energies from the make-believe of early childhood into realistic accomplishment. He asserted that the combination of parental expectations and children's drive toward mastery lay the foundation for the psychological conflict of middle childhood: industry vs. inferiority, which is resolved positively when children develop a sense of competence at useful skills and tasks.

A central question children ask is this: Am I successful at what I do, or am I worthless? The ego quality the child seeks to develop is competence. Some developmental tasks children seek to master are building friendships, learning in school, playing on teams, and performing self-evaluation. Children who are encouraged by their parents and teachers develop a feeling of competence and belief in their skills. Those who receive little or no encouragement from their parents, teachers, or peers will doubt their ability to be successful. Hence, the danger at this stage is that children will develop a sense of inferiority, which is reflected in their pessimism about their ability to do well. As children participate in activities together, they become more aware of each other's unique talents and come to view themselves as responsible and capable. Children develop a sense of inadequacy when parents have not prepared children well for school or when teachers and peers destroy children's feelings of competence with negative comments.

## Psychosocial Stage 5: Crisis: Identity vs. Role Confusion (Adolescence: 12–18 Years)

Erikson believed that identity is the major personality achievement of adolescence and that crystallizing who you are as a person is a critical step toward becoming a productive adult. In order for individuals to construct an identity, they must define who they are, what they value, and what directions they want to pursue in life. Adolescents seek to develop several different types of identities: a personal identity, a sexual or gender identity, and a career identity. They become very concerned about developing an identity with their peers and with separating from their parents. Young people mature physically and socially during adolescence, and such maturation has a profound impact on how they view themselves and others.

Erikson called the conflict of adolescence identity vs. role confusion. According to him, in complex societies, adolescents go through an identity crisis, which can be conceptualized as a temporary period of distress as they experiment with alternative identities. For instance, adolescents go through a number of changes as they search for a personal identity that fits them. They color their hair or dress differently from their parents. Instead of getting upset with young people about their purple hair, parents should view such hair coloring as an attempt to establish their own individual identity. From Erikson's perspective, a healthy identity is experienced as a sense of physical, psychological, and social well-being—a feeling of being at home in one's own body and a sense of knowing where one is going. If adolescents successfully pass this stage, they develop fidelity, which is the ability to sustain loyalties despite differences in the value systems of the people with whom they associate. They learn to be friends with different people.

If they fail to resolve the psychosocial crisis, they develop identity confusion. Their sense of self is unstable and threatened. For some youth, the identity search is traumatic, but for the majority the typical experience is one of exploration followed by commitment. Young people who lack a firm sense of self or a personal identity will find it difficult to experience intimacy or the self-sharing in Erikson's early adult stage.

Erikson's theoretical model has provided a way of conceptualizing developmental work with young people. When we meet children's needs appropriately, they are able to grow and develop optimally. Erikson believed that a child's development must not be rushed or emotional harm would be done to them. Therefore, it is important that you learn the stages of your child's development and what to expect with each stage.

## Understanding Your Child's Needs during Transitions

Young people face two major sources of transitions: (1) transitions from one developmental stage to a higher one; and (2) transitions from one school to another. On average, children move from one developmental stage to another without much fanfare. Yet, sometimes parents forget that transitions cause children to adjust to change and change produces stress in human beings.

More than 88 percent of public school students experience moving from an elementary to a middle school in this country. This period of transition elicits a wide spectrum of emotions, behaviors, and concerns for young people and their families. Transition to middle school is characterized by several key changes in educational practices. In most elementary schools, children are taught in self-contained classrooms with a familiar set of peers and one or two teachers. Once students graduate to middle schools, where they move from class to class with different teachers and students, they must interact with more peers and more teachers, as well as deal with increased expectations for their academic performance.

Subsequently, children begin to experience problems in transitions during middle childhood. Middle school children encounter a number of pressures, including puberty and peer pressure. As their bodies change, middle schoolers attempt to assert themselves socially. Because middle school brings with it the onset of puberty, middle schoolers experience self-doubt, anxiety, and confusion that they did not face in their younger grades. These changes help make middle school stressful for many young people.

In looking back over their lives, young people tend to indicate that they met their greatest challenges during middle school rather than during high school. Middle school is often associated with a decline in academic achievement, performance motivation, and self-perceptions. It is also a time when young people are most likely to experiment with at-risk behaviors. During this phase, parents should become knowledgeable about the needs and concerns of young adolescents in transition, and they should maintain strong family connections with them.

It is noteworthy that a number of the violent shootings that occurred in American schools over the past decade were conducted by middle schoolers. Several killed over the loss of a girlfriend or disciplinary tactics the school used in response to some behavior they exhibited. Hence, it is important to consider the issues that middle schoolers face if we are to prevent their acts of violence.

Adolescence is the second major developmental stage that young people experience adjustment problems in great numbers. This situation occurs because adolescents must focus on developing several identities, including a personal identity, a sexual identity (gay or straight), and a work or college-related identity. Choices have to be made for these various types of identities, and having to make choices causes stress for many adolescents.

## Spiritual Journey of Parenting and Understanding Children's Needs

You relive your early childhood as you parent your own children during their school years. Sometimes the memories can be quite happy; on other occasions, they can be painful. Some parents expect that children will fulfill the fantasies and hopes they had for themselves when they were kids. So they push their children to become the cheerleader, basketball player, or swimmer that they either once were or once had hoped to be. How do parents go about fulfilling their needs and those of their children? Whose needs should be filled first—those of children or of parents? Parents struggle with their need to control rather than to guide their children.

# Chapter Summary

It is important that parents, caregivers, teachers, and counselors understand children's needs and their psychosocial stages of development. Children's needs vary with their age, stage of development, attachment to their family and care-givers, and their reaction to what is taking place around them. Sometimes parents forget that it is not easy going through the changes and transitions young people experience. For most young people, a key developmental issue is finding one close friend they can take with them on their life journey.

# Parent Reading List

*Helping Children Cope with Separation and Loss* by Claudia L. Jewett. B. T. Batsford, 1997.
*Helping Your Child Handle Stress* by Katherine Kersey. Acropolis Books, 1995.
*Making Divorce Easier on Your Child: 50 Effective Ways to Help Children Adjust* by Nicholas Long and Rex L. Forehand. Contemporary Books, 2002.
*What to Do When You're Scared and Worried* by Dr. James J. Crisp. Free Spirit Publishing, 2004.

## Suggested Reading for Children

*The Best Friends Book* by Todd Parr. Little Brown Young Readers, 2006.
*Big Ernie's New Home: A Story for Young Children Who Are Moving* by Teresa Martin and Whitney Martin. Magination Press, 2006.
*Squishy Turtle and Friends* by Roger Priddy. Priddy Books, 2003.
*We're Moving (First-Time Stories)* by Heather Maisner and Kristina Stephenson. Kingfisher, 2004.
*Where Is My Friend?* by Simms Taback. Blue Apple Books, 2006.

## Using Books to Talk with Children about Divorce

*It's Not Your Fault, KoKo Bear* by Vicky Lansky (1998). Book Peddlers, 1998.
*Two Homes* by Claire Masurel and Kady Macdonald. Candlewick, 2003.

*The Most Important Thing* by Rhonda Roth and Shane Grajczyk. Crossing Guard Books, 2006.

*What Can I Do?: A Book for Children of Divorce* by Danielle Lowry and Bonnie J. Matthews. Magination Press, 2001.

# Intentional Parenting Tips on Children's Needs

This section is designed to help parents pursue their goal of intentional parenting using Maslow's need hierarchy. A number of quizzes are presented that will help parents consider what kind of nurturing environment they are providing for their children. The section begins with a comparison of nurturing and non-nurturing experiences.

## Parental Questionnaire on My Child's Need Hierarchy

Below is a brief questionnaire that measures your perceptions of how well your child's home and school situations are currently satisfying or failing to satisfy your child's needs.

Directions: Place a true or false next to each of the following statements as they apply to your child's current life situation.

_____ 1. My child's needs for food, shelter, and rest are being met satisfactorily within our family.

_____ 2. My child feels a sense of safety in our home.

_____ 3. My child feels safe at his school.

_____ 4. Sometimes, I am not able to meet my child's basic needs for food and shelter.

_____ 5. My child feels loved, needed, and accepted by others in our family.

_____ 6. My child feels connected and bonded at his school.

_____ 7. My child has been able to make friends at his school.

_____ 8. My child's need for respect, recognition, and positive regard are being met within our family.

_____ 9. My child sometimes acts out because he does not feel accepted by others.

_____10. My child feels good about himself.

_____11. My child's teachers encourage him to do well in school.

_____12. My child is achieving in his grade at school.

_____13. My child has a sense of attachment to me and other family members.

_____14. I love my child.

_____15. I do not hit my child to discipline him.

_____16. My child feels he has a place in our family.

## Framework for Assessing Children's Needs: Degree to Which Need Has Been Met

The following assessment protocol is designed to help parents, teachers, and counselors to assess children's needs. Indicate the extent to which you feel your child's needs are being met in each category. Use 1 = unmet needs; 2 = fair meeting of needs; 3 = good meeting of needs; and 4 = optimal meeting of child's needs.

_____ 1. Physiological needs—food, clothing, shelter, sleep, and health.

_____ 2. Safety needs—protection, security, sense of safety.

_____ 3. Safety needs—the need for structure, predictability, and stability.

_____ 4. Social needs—belongingness, love

_____ 5. Social needs—child gives and receives affection in a group.

_____ 6. Identity needs—self-esteem.

_____ 7. Identity needs—child can identify himself in relation to the outside world.

_____ 8. Identity needs—child's identity is recognized, valued.

_____ 9. Cultural identity needs—child's culture, religion, customs are valued and recognized.

_____10. Spiritual needs—child has a sense of purpose in life.

_____11. Spiritual needs—child has a sense of hope about himself and the future.

The higher the total score, the more the child's needs are being met. If the total score is low, evaluate the extent to which the child is at risk for not having his needs met. You might also consider if the child's needs in specific categories are or are not being met. What can you do as a parent, teacher, or counselor to help the child fulfill his unsatisfied needs?

## Parental Thoughts and Actions

1. "I'd like to be able to be more _____ with my child."

2. "I resolve to be more _____ with my child."

3. "My relationship with my child is _____."

4. "Most of my child's behavior is directed toward satisfying _____ needs."

5. "I wish my relationship with my child could be more _____."

6. "If I could change one thing about my relationship with my child, it would be to _____."

7. "I am working on eliminating _____ behavior with my child.

Illustration 14    A Comparison of Nurturing and Non-Nurturing Environments

| Nurturing Environment | Non-Nurturing Environment |
|---|---|
| Developing close attachment or connections to parents and other significant adults | Developing poor attachment or connections with parents or other adults |
| Experiencing warm consistent discipline—explaining why poor behavior needs to change and enforcing good behavior without violence | Experiencing cold or harsh, inconsistent discipline—frequent beatings and spankings |
| Growing up in a home where disagreements are discussed without parents' use of threats or violence | Witnessing violence in the home, watching a parent getting hit or beat up —omestic violence |
| Having parents place controls on watching media violence | Witnessing violence repeatedly on television—early and prolonged exposure to media and television violence |
| Being taught how to calm down bullies and handle street conflicts | Being taught to fight if another starts a fight. |
| Having been taught at home and in school nonviolent techniques for handling conflicts, such as asking questions, explaining your side of the problem, offering a compromise | Having few skills for handling conflicts nonviolently |
| Living in a neighborhood, school, or organization where bullying is not tolerated | Living in a neighborhood, school, or organization where bullying is tolerated |
| Playing with few violent toys | Playing with many violent toys |
| Living in a home with no firearms present | Living in a home with firearms present |
| Having low genetic incidence for violence (family heredity factors) | Having high genetic incidence for violence (family heredity factors) |
| Living in reasonable family socioeconomic conditions, low poverty rate, dual parenting. home, employment of parents. | Living in combination of stressful family socioeconomic factors (poverty, single parenting, marital breakup, unemployment, loss of support from extended family) |

## *See the World from Your Child's Eyes*

Try to imagine the world from your child's perspective, purposefully letting go of your own. Practice this exercise every day in the evening or after a crisis to remind you of who this child is and what he faces in the world.

## *Your Expectations of Your Child*

Think about your expectations for your child and ask yourself if they are truly in your child's best interests. List at least two ways that you communicate those expectations and consider how they affect your children.

## *Keeping Your Child's Trust*

Whenever you have betrayed your child's trust, apologize to him. Apologies help heal hurt feelings.

## *Makeups*

One technique parents can use to discipline their children is to allow them to do makeups. A person who has harmed another may sometimes say: "What can I do to make things up to you?" They want a second chance, an opportunity to get themselves back into the person's good graces.

Both children and parents can ask for makeups. For instance, a parent may have forgotten to pick up a child from basketball practice. The parent picks the child up and asks what he can do to make up for his mistake? Similarly, children want to make up for their errors. For example, if child forgets to do a chore, he asks the parent for a makeup, and the parent decides that he has another week of chores.

## *Five Things that Children Respond to Well*

- Sharing your feelings with them.
- Showing that you trust them.
- Spending quality time with them.
- Remembering special events in their lives.
- Telling them that you like them.

## *A Parent's Spiritual Journey: My Own Needs*

1. Analyze three things you need in your life.
2. Analyze which categories your three needs fall under in Maslow's hierarchy of needs.
3. Explore what is blocking you in meeting or satisfying these needs.
4. List three resources you might use in meeting these needs.
5. List three steps you might take to meet or satisfy these needs.

# 4

# Helping a Child Learn How to Deal with Anger

*Teach your child how to control his anger and emotions, and you have taught him part of what is needed to chart his own destiny.*

Jonathan had been excited all week about going to the concert with Stan, his new best friend. For the past year, he had been somewhat lonely attending St. Michaels because he did not have anyone to hang out with the way the other kids did. Jonathan's teacher had asked him to show Stan around, and he felt pretty good about doing that.

Friday finally rolled around, and Jonathan brought Stan over to his house so that they might decide what they were going to do about the concert. At age 15, Jonathan was feeling pretty grown up, especially since his father had moved out of the house. His parents were getting a divorce, and he was assuming a more grown-up role in the house.

"I'll get my mother to drive us there and pick us up," Jonathan told Stan.

"Do you think she'll take us?" Stan asked. "It will take us a good half hour to get there."

"Sure, she said she would earlier this week," Jonathan said shaking his head with assurance. "My mom's cool. Now that my dad is not here, I get to do pretty much what I want."

Jonathan's mother, Susan Winters, came downstairs and entered the den with a puzzled and irritated look on her face. "Did I just hear you say that I was going to take you to the concert? I'm exhausted. I've worked all day, and I'm dead tired. Maybe next time you can go."

"But you promised, Mom. You promised."

"I didn't promise. I said maybe, maybe if I weren't too tired. . . . You should have reminded me yesterday and maybe. . . ."

"But you promised, Mom, you promised. I brought Stan over, and now you treat me like I'm some little boy, telling me I can't go to the concert because you're tired. What the hell. . . ."

"Don't use that tone of voice and language with me, young man . . . maybe Stan should leave and you should go to your room to cool off. You're definitely not going anywhere now."

"I think I'd better go," Stan interrupted looking nervous as if he had just stepped in the middle of a family argument. "Call me tomorrow, Jonathan." With those words, Stan grabbed his jacket off the couch and headed out the door.

"Wait, come back. We can still go . . . I"

But Stan did not come back. Instead, he mumbled something about Jonathan needed time to talk things over with his mom.

Jonathan turned toward his mother yelling at the top of his voice: "Do you see what you did to me, Mom? You treated me like a little boy in front of my friend. I hate you, hate you, hate you." And as Jonathan turned to leave, his eyes caught sight of his mother's favorite vase. "You embarrassed me in front of my friend. . . . Ok, and with those words, he threw the vase on the floor breaking it into small pieces."

Susan Winters looked in amazement and started screaming: "My mother gave me that vase . . . that's the only thing I have left that she gave me . . . how could you. . . ."

"Oh, your feelings are hurt now . . . well let me see if this hurts too, and with that he swept his arm across the entire fireplace mantle and broke everything that his mother had placed there so proudly. He then took the poker and put two large gapping holes in the wall of the den. "How does that make you feel? Does this hurt? You embarrassed me, Mom. You embarrassed me in front of my friend, and now everyone will probably know in school that Jonathan's a little boy and his mother would not let him go to the concert because she was tired. I hate you, Mom. I hate you." And with those words, Jonathan grabbed his jacket and ran out of the house.

Susan looked at her mother's vase all broken up in little pieces, the pictures of the family that had been on the mantle that were strewn across the floor, also broken. What had happened? One minute everything was okay, and just because she said she was tired, there was now all this damage. She could not believe that Jonathan had done this, destroyed their den . . . the big gaping holes in the wall. She started to cry. Her whole world was coming apart . . . the divorce . . . Jonathan out of control. How was she going to handle this? Should she call Jonathan's father? And what would he say: "I told you couldn't handle that boy all by yourself. Maybe I should come back home." For a brief moment, Susan thought about calling the police.

The next day Susan made an emergency appointment with a psychologist to help her sort things out. She learned that maybe things had been brewing for a long time and that Jonathan needed to be in anger management counseling. But there was something else. The psychologist had done a couple of impromptu role playing sessions with her to help her get some clarity on what was happening with her son. Although she had not meant to do it, she had humiliated Jonathan in front of his new friend, and such humiliation to a teenager could be experienced like someone put a ton of bricks on his chest. Saving face is very important to a teen trying to show that he is all grown up and can do things on his own.

Maybe it would have been better if she had asked to speak with Jonathan privately. Maybe she could have called her husband to see if he were busy. The more that she thought about it, there were a number of things she could have done other than to have dismissed Jonathan's concert as if he were still a five year old.

Susan also learned something else. Behind anger is hurt, and in Jonathan's case deep psychological hurt. He had finally found a person who wanted to be his friend, and he had planned something that they could do together that was cool. Jonathan did not plan to get angry with his mother and destroy the den. It happened so quickly. One moment everything was all right, and the next minute the situation was out of control. Susan also learned that she was struggling with her own anger, only she had expressed it differently by destroying Jonathan's plans.

Children's anger presents challenges to parents and teachers.[1,2] All children become angry at some point because their perceived wants or needs are not being met. It happens at every age. We have all probably seen a toddler having a meltdown tantrum in a grocery store. We have read newspaper stories about young people murdered over girlfriends. This chapter begins with an examination of the nature of anger, and then it explores how a child is influenced by both heredity and environment to deal with anger. Children's temperaments are believed to influence their response to the world, including their reaction when things do not go their way.

# The Nature of Anger

Anger is a normal, usually healthy human emotion; it can be useful, necessary, and even healing. It is an emotion characterized by feelings of hostility or displeasure. It can range from mild irritation to intense fury and rage. On the positive side, anger can focus our minds and strengthen our resolve. It is what gives us the courage and the power to confront the fear that things will never change. Sometimes we need our anger to motivate us to the next level.

In addition, anger is a signal that some part of us feels threatened or hurt. It is a natural, adaptive response that alerts us that part of the self is in danger. It also helps us to become aware of our underlying feelings and emotions about a situation. We ask ourselves: "Why am I angry with my partner?" Typically, the answer comes back because our partner has hurt our feelings, betrayed our trust, etc. Expressing our anger appropriately helps us to redefine who we are and to reinforce our boundaries and our values. Anger is good for identifying problems, but not for solving them.

# The Three Components of Anger

Anger is believed to have three components: (1) the emotional state of anger; (2) the expression of anger; and (3) the understanding and management of anger.[3] Within these three components, there are subcomponents. There is also a certain amount of overlap between these three components.

### The Emotional State of Anger: First Component

The first component of anger is the emotion itself. Anger is an arousal state, or a feeling experienced when a goal is blocked or needs are frustrated. The emotional part of anger has also been termed the psychological component. Anger also has a physiological dimension, which refers to how your body responds to anger. For instance, you may develop muscle tension or experience an increase in heart rate and blood pressure as your body releases adrenaline—the fight-or-flight hormone.

Anger may be caused by problems that have either an internal (inside of us) or an external source. When we fail to achieve our expectations of ourselves, we can create an internal sense of anger—anger at the self. When this occurs, we say such things to ourselves as: "I really should have been able to get that promotion or to pass that test." Or, I am angry at me because I should have been able to see through his deceptions. How could I be such a fool?" On other occasions, we become angry at external events such as a traffic jam or a canceled flight. Memories of traumatic events or past injustices can also trigger angry feelings.

### The Expression of Anger: Second Component

The second component of anger consists of its expression. Individuals use a number of both conscious and unconscious processes to deal with their angry feelings. The three primary approaches are (1) expressing; (2) suppressing, and (3) calming. Expression entails conveying your anger. It takes place along a continuum, from having a rational discussion to erupting into out-of-control violence. For instance, children express anger through facial expressions, crying, sulking, or talking, but do little to try to solve a problem or confront the provocateur. [4] Others actively resist by physically or verbally defending their positions, self-esteem, or possessions in nonaggressive ways. Still some children express anger with aggressive revenge by physically or verbally retaliating against the provocateur. They tell the offender that he or she cannot play or is not liked. Children also express anger through avoidance or attempts to escape from or evade the provocateur or they come to parents and teachers for answers.

Expressing angry feelings in an assertive rather than an aggressive manner is the healthiest way to express anger. To express anger assertively, you have to make clear what your needs are, and how you want to get them met without hurting others. Jonathan's expression of anger was inappropriate and completely out of control. In fact, his anger had turned to rage before even he recognized it. Jonathan needs to learn more acceptable ways of expressing anger so that he is in control of his anger rather than it being in control of him.

Moreover, anger can be suppressed and then converted or redirected. This situation takes place when you hold in your anger, stop thinking about it, and focus on something positive. The goal is to inhibit or to suppress your anger and then to convert it into more constructive behavior. You may think that you should not be angry or that you will lose control if you let yourself feel anger. The danger in suppressing your angry is that if it is not allowed outward expression, your anger can turn inward—on yourself. Trying to suppress your anger can lead to such health problems as headaches, stress, depression, or high blood pressure.

Unexpressed anger can lead to other problems. It can result in pathological expressions of anger, such as passive-aggressive behavior (getting back at people indirectly, without telling them why, rather than confronting them head-on), or a personality that seems to be cynical and hostile most of the time. Cynical and hostile people who put others down and criticize everything have not learned to express their anger constructively.

### An Understanding of Anger: Third Component

The third component of the anger experience is understanding—that is, interpreting and evaluating the emotion of anger. The ability to regulate the expression of anger is linked to an understanding of the emotion.[5] Because children's ability to reflect on their anger is somewhat limited, they need guidance from teachers and parents in understanding and managing their angry feelings. This book chooses to view anger as a signal that one needs to take action and as an indication that a goal is being blocked and that frustration is building. How children and their parents learn to respond to their angry signals will determine ultimately whether they manage anger or anger controls them.

When you explode with anger, there are usually a lot of feelings behind your response. Your personal history feeds your reactions to anger. Your angry reaction to losing a parking space may be supported by years of built-up feelings of being unheard, ignored, sad, frustrated, or disrespected. We learn to let our anger be out of control. An anger management class is a way to teach people how to express their anger in a controlled, healthy way.

It is important to learn the sequences of anger. Buying time allows us to gain control of and moderate our thoughts. Angry feelings are not actually caused by situations and events, but rather by the thoughts we have about those situations and events. Once the thoughts about an event are identified, those thoughts can be replaced with different thoughts as one method for controlling anger.

Understanding the emotion behind anger is extremely important. Jonathan's anger had turned to rage toward his mother because he felt that she had humiliated him in front of his new friend. In his mind, she had forced him to return to his former dreaded state of being a dwork. "You're a dwork, Jonathan," the kids used to mock as he was changing classes in the hall. "No one wants to be with you, you Dwork, you geek—you mamma's boy."

The deep emotion behind Jonathan's utter destruction that day in the den was caused by the real words he heard in his head—"you dwork, geek, mama's boy." If only Jonathan had taken a moment to examine the emotion behind his anger, perhaps he would have responded differently to his mother. He might have said something like: "I know you're tired, Mom. And I want you to know that I am deeply appreciative that you're always there for me. I wouldn't ask you to take us to the concert, if it weren't really important to me. All the rest of the kids will be going, and I don't want to not go and act like the 'geek' that they call me. You do me this one favor, and I promise you that I will do my chores next week without complaining one bit." Jonathan's mother might have responded differently if he had approached her in this manner.

Yet, Jonathan's mother was also angry with herself for being in the situation in which she found herself, angry at her husband, the stress of the divorce, and the fact that she was exhausted and there was no one there to help her. Susan failed to even acknowledge that part of her anger was caused by overhearing Jonathan tell Stan that he could do pretty much what he wanted now that his dad was no longer living in the house. She was also upset because her husband, Adam, was always the one who drove Jonathan to different places.

Susan was only half honest when she said she was completely surprised by Jonathan's response to her refusal to take the teens to the concert. She had an idea of how much going to the concert meant to Jonathan because he had mentioned it several times during the week. It was convenient for her to deny any responsibility for what had taken place because, after all, she was not the one to lose control of her anger. That was Jonathan's fault. She was just an innocent victim of her son's anger. Besides kids are supposed to be respectful of their parents, and Jonathan had shouted at her and even cursed.

Yet, Susan sensed deep down inside that she had egged the situation on with Jonathan. She had played the game of trumping Jonathan with her parent control card. "I'll show you who's boss around here, you son of a . . . I'll take something away from you that will really hurt."

The difference between Jonathan and Susan was in the manner in which each one expressed anger. Susan had expressed her anger in such a way that she could even lie to herself. She was not angry and trying to get back at Jonathan. She was just tired and exercising her rights as a parent to discipline her child. Jonathan had used his rage of destruction to assert his own power. "You don't let me go to the concert. I destroy some of what you love. Now who's in control." Anger out of control can destroy a family, and the same situation exists when it is denied and never expressed. We need to have a plan to deal with anger so that we can limit its intensity and prevent any destruction that it may cause.

In anger management classes, participants are taught what constitutes anger, how to recognize it, and how to keep it under control. They may be asked to complete an anger sequencing chart, which consists of event, thoughts, feelings, and substitute thought. Some people blame their outbursts on others. Someone can push your angry buttons and you may feel that he made you angry. In actuality, how you express anger is your responsibility. You are responsible for your own feelings and reactions to what other people do. Sometimes changing your environment is helpful.

Teachers can use child guidance strategies to help children express angry feelings in socially constructive ways. Children develop ideas about how to express emotions[6,7] primarily through social interaction in their families and later by watching television or movies, playing video games, and reading books.[8] Some children have learned a negative, aggressive approach to expressing anger[9] and, when confronted with everyday conflicts, resort to using aggression in the classroom. A major challenge for early childhood teachers is to encourage children to acknowledge and to express anger in positive and effective ways.

# Parents' Knowledge of Children's Social and Emotional Development

In 1998, an organization named Zero to Three commissioned a national research study for parents of children younger than three years old to determine: (1) what they knew and believed about early childhood development; (2) where they sought information and support; and (3) how receptive they were to new information on child development. A major finding was that most parents' knowledge of child development is limited and that this deficit was a barrier to better parenting. They did not understand fully how specific parenting practices shape their children's social, emotional, and intellectual development.[10]

Parents knew least about children's emotional development, and they did not understand fully how to determine if their children's development was on track. Only 38 percent felt totally sure they could tell if their children's emotional development was healthy and on target for their age. Only 37 percent knew the milestones of children's social development, and only 44 percent could tell if their children's intellectual development was on track.[11]

The report noted that parents' desires to obtain information on how they can best support their children's development are strongest before their first child is born (from birth to eight months) rather than later. This finding suggests that it is important to get information on child development to new and expectant parents as early as possible. The report concluded that parents are hungry for specific information about how they can become better parents.

# Children's Temperament: A Beginning Window to Their Anger Response

Children's temperament is key to understanding their response to anger as illustrated in the following case. Patricia stood staring out her kitchen window as if she were in a trance. She kept shaking her head, and her deep sighs indicated that something was wrong. Nothing she did seemed to work with her son Justine, who was nine going on 30. She thought that she had planned a perfect day for them to spend some time together. Did not all kids love going to an amusement park? But when she surprised Justine with the news, there was a slight frown on his face that he tried to hide. Justine did not like surprises or what some might call spontaneous events. He did not want to go to the park. With Justine, everything had to be planned out weeks in advance, or he would have a fit. Justine had reacted this way ever since he had come home from the hospital. Mother and son were so different, and those differences got them into power struggles.

"We never seem to click," Patricia murmured to herself. "I can't seem to figure out what's wrong." Patricia felt that Justine was continually trying to be difficult for her. She interpreted all his refusals to do things that she knew she had enjoyed growing up as part of his contrariness. She even wondered if Justine had a negative personality or, worse yet, that he was somehow possessed. Deep down within, Patricia suspected that Justine secretly hated her. "No," she said shaking her head. "I know he loves me. It's just that sometimes . . . I dunno. I dunno what's wrong."

Although the situation between Justine and his mother sounds irreconcilable and doomed to future conflict, this does not have to be the case. Justine was not deliberately trying to be stubborn or negative toward his mother. He just did not like doing the things that she liked to do. They were wired differently from birth. What Patricia was experiencing with Justine was a clash of different temperament styles. Parents tend to want to raise kids using activities that they found to be fun, but the truth is that kids come into the world with their own style of temperament, which means that they might be hardwired from birth to enjoy doing some activities more so than others.

Moreover, kids are inclined to gravitate toward and forge alliances with the parent who is closer to them in temperamental style. They prefer one parent because both share similar temperament styles. For instance, both enjoy the same kinds of activities, such as being active in sports. Another child might also prefer a particular parent because the two approach the world in similar ways. It is important, then, that parents have some knowledge about their own temperament styles, those of their partner, and those of their children.

## Children's Temperaments

Temperament describes how we perceive the world. It is our first and natural response to situations in our lives. It includes how sensitive we are to things in our environment, how we react to new things, and how easily we shift from one thing to another; our activity, intensity, and persistence levels are also considered. Temperament is not learned from our parents, nor can we easily force ourselves to be one way rather than another way. A baby does not decide to be active or inactive; he just is one way or another. Infants manifest a temperament shortly after they are born. Some are fussy, sensitive to noises, easily startled, and others are calmer and easier to manage.

Parents who have several children see differences in their children's persistence, distractibility, and energy levels. They understand that while one child may be typically outgoing and enthusiastic, another may be shy and low-key. When we describe children as easygoing, difficult, or prone to angry outbursts, we are referring to their temperament, which may be described as early appearing, stable individual differences in reactivity and self-regulation. Certain temperaments may be more susceptible to angry outbursts and meltdowns.

## Why Is Temperament Important!

Differences in parents' temperament and that of their children's may be a major reason behind the power struggles between them. For instance, children may be slow or quick to adapt because of their temperament. Children who are slow to adapt as an orientation to the world hate surprises and a great deal of change in their lives. They have difficulty shifting from one thing to another. Conversely, children who are quick to adapt may not even notice the transitions they are encountering. Instead, they are viewed as welcome changes that bring excitement to their lives. By understanding temperament, you will be able to:

- Understand the emotions you and your child are experiencing, such as the emotional distress that your slow-to-adapt child feels when she has to leave her friend's house, or the exhaustion of the active child who's been forced to sit inside for long periods of time.
- Predict potential triggers that set you and your child off related to differences in temperament.
- Choose the most effective strategies to help you eliminate or minimize anger triggers.
- Maximize the pleasure and reduce the frustrations of working with your child.

## What Research Tells Us about Temperament

In 1956, Alexander Thomas and Stella Chess[12] began the New York Longitudinal Study, which investigated the development of temperament that followed 141 children from early infancy well into adulthood. The results showed that temperament can either increase a child's chances of experiencing psychological problems or, conversely, protect a child from the negative effects of a highly stressful home. Shortly thereafter, Thomas and Chess[13] found that parenting practices can modify children's temperaments a great deal. These investigators' findings stimulated a growing body of research on temperament that studied its stability, biological roots, and interaction with child-rearing experiences.

Thomas and Chess created the first influential model of temperament. They identified three different types of temperaments that children exhibit. About 35 percent of the children manifested unique blends of temperamental characteristics. The temperament types are the following:

1. The easy child (40 percent of the sample) quickly establishes regular routines in infancy, is usually cheerful, and adapts easily to new experiences.
2. The difficult child (10 percent of the sample) is irregular in daily routines, is slow to accept new experiences, and tends to react negatively and intensely.
3. The slow-to-warm-up child (15 percent of the sample) is inactive, shows mild, low-key reactions to environmental stimuli, is negative in mood, and adjusts slowly to new experiences.

The difficult temperament pattern has engendered the most interest because it puts children at high risk for adjustment problems—both anxious withdrawal and aggressive behavior in early and middle childhood.[14,15] In comparison to difficult children, slow-to-warm-up children present fewer problems in the early years. Instead, they tend to evidence excessive fearfulness and slow, constricted behavior in the late preschool and school years, when they are expected to respond actively and quickly in classrooms and peer groups.[16]

## Ten Components of Temperament

Thomas and Chess[17] also identified ten dimensions of temperament based on their research with children and families. These dimensions provide a framework for describing individual differences in temperament. On a scale of one to five, most children will score very high or very low on at least one dimension, but on no more than seven of the temperament traits. The more extreme the ratings, the more challenging the child will be to raise. It is valuable for children to learn about their own temperament so that they can tell people their needs. A child might say: "Mommy, you are rushing me. I need more time." The ten dimensions of temperament are described below:

- *Sensory threshold* refers to how sensitive a child is to each of the senses, touch, taste, smell, hearing, and vision. For instance, children with a low sensory threshold might not be able to wear bright colors, such as red, because they believe that they look funny. In contrast, children with a high sensory threshold will be able to wear virtually any color.

- *Activity component of temperament* refers to the amount of physical energy that tends to drive a child's behavior. Highly active children find it difficult to sit still, feel restless on days they have to stay inside and act impulsively, oftentimes getting into trouble. In contrast, children with low activity levels move at a slower pace and prefer inactive pastimes, such as coloring, playing quietly with toys, or watching TV.

- *Intensity component of temperament* refers to how much energy and strength a child uses to express emotions. While some children are loud or dramatic, others react quietly and respond with reserve to interactions.

- *Rhythmicity/regularity dimension of temperament* deals with the predictability of a child's sleep, hunger, and elimination patterns. Children who have irregular patterns tend to get tired or hungry at different times each day. Conversely, a highly regular child is predictable and can get into schedules quickly.

- *Adaptability component of temperament* examines how much time a child needs to adjust to people or circumstances. Children who adapt fast to people or circumstances tend to be followers and are compliant and cooperative. At the other end of the spectrum, children who adapt slowly may act stubborn, strong willed, or headstrong. Slow to adapt children may feel that they are being rushed by parents and teachers.

- *Mood dimension of temperament* explores the way a child generally views the world. Negative mood children see the world with a glass that is half-empty or pessimistic lenses. Positive mood children see the glass as half full and note the positive side of things.

- *Approach/withdrawal dimension of temperament* refers to how a child responds to a new experience, such as meeting a person, tasting a food, or being in an unusual situation. Children whose temperament is approach jump right into the thick of things. Withdrawing children hold back cautiously until they feel safe.

- *Persistence dimension of temperament* indicates how a child responds when something becomes difficult. High persistence children tend to keep trying, even when they are confronted with a task that goes beyond their skill level. Low persistence children become frustrated, ask for help quickly, or simply give up.

- *Distractibility* indicates how easily a child's attention is distracted by things happening around him. Highly distractible children have short attention spans and can get sidetracked easily. Children with low distractibility focus intently on what they are doing and might not notice immediately changes in their surroundings, such as a person coming quietly into a room in which they are working on a project.

- *Emotional sensitivity dimension of temperament* refers to how easily a child displays emotions, such as hurt, embarrassment, worry, sorrow, empathy, or fear.

## Temperament Stability

Children's temperament is low to moderately stable over time.[18] Temperament itself develops with age. As infants learn to regulate their attention and emotions, those who seemed irritable can become calm and content, depending upon the parenting techniques used with them. Long-term predictions about children's early temperament are most accurately made after age two. Children's temperaments rarely change from one extreme to another after age two. Shy toddlers do not magically become highly sociable, and irritable toddlers seldom become easygoing.

## Temperament and the Goodness-of-Fit Model

Thomas and Chess proposed a goodness-of-fit model to describe how temperament and environment can produce favorable outcomes. Goodness-of-fit entails creating child-rearing environments that recognize each child's temperament. Children with a difficult temperament (those who withdraw from new experiences and react negatively and intensely) oftentimes experience parenting that fits poorly with their dispositions, putting them at high risk for later adjustment problems. Typically, by the second year, parents of difficult children often use angry, punitive discipline, which undermines the child's development of effortful control. The child reacts with defiance and disobedience, and the parents become increasingly angry and stressed.[19] Consequently, the parents continue their coercive parenting tactics and discipline inconsistently, vacillating between rewarding the child's noncompliance and giving in to it.[20] Such parental child-rearing and discipline tactics only maintain and even increase the child's irritable, conflict-ridden style. Conversely, parents who are positive and sensitive to the needs and struggles of their children help them to better regulate their emotions. As a result, the child's disruptive behavior declines.

The goodness-of-fit model teaches us that infants have unique temperamental dispositions that adults must accept. Parents cannot be blamed for their children's temperament, but they can help a child learn how to build upon his strengths. Parents who learn how to work with children who have difficult temperaments may be able to prevent problems with their children at school. It is the goodness-of-fit between parent and child that matters the most.

## How Temperament Affects Family Life

The goodness-of-fit between parents' and children's temperaments can lead to positive or negative interactions and sometimes even to conflict situations within the entire family. Children within the same family often have different temperaments. Understanding temperaments may provide insight into conflict between and among siblings. An active, impulsive child may bother an older sibling who likes to read quietly in his room. A child who is distractible and low in persistence can frustrate parents' efforts to get him to complete his homework or to finish a household chore.

Learning about your child's temperament may help you to reframe how you interpret your child's behavior and influences the way you think about the reasons for his behavior. If you see your child's intense behavior as disruptive and purposeful, you may become irritated, even angry, and you may even respond punitively. Conversely, if you see your child's behavior as temperament related rather than as due to willful misbehavior, you can reduce your negative reactions to it. It is important to recognize individual differences in your children's temperament and to help them understand their temperament's impact on other family members.

## Early Cues to Infants' Emotional States and Anger Responses

Besides temperament, there are other early cues to infants' emotional states and how they might eventually respond to anger. Infants' earliest emotional life consists of two global arousal states: attraction to pleasant stimulation and withdrawal from unpleasant stimulation. Gradually their emotions become clear, well-organized signals.[21] When parents mirror their baby's emotional behavior, this helps the baby to construct discrete emotional expressions that more closely resembles those of adults.[22]

From four months on, infants' angry expressions increase in frequency and intensity. By six to eight months, infants' expressions of basic emotions are well organized and vary with environmental events. Infants start to become angry more often and in a wider range of situations, including when an object is taken away. From 8–12 months, infants' understanding of the meaning of others' emotional expressions improves, and social referencing appears. Infants laugh at subtle elements of surprise. From 18–24 months, toddlers develop self-conscious emotions of shame, embarrassment, guilt, and pride. They construct a vocabulary for talking about feelings, and subsequently, their emotional self-regulation improves. Toddlers begin to develop the first signs of empathy when they learn that others' emotional reactions may differ from their own.

Infants' angry reactions increase with age because they experience improvements in their motor and cognitive abilities. As infants age, they become capable of intentional behavior. Older infants improve at identifying who caused them pain or who removed a toy. Their new motor development enables them to defend themselves (hit) or overcome an obstacle.[23] An infant's anger may motivate the caregiver to relieve his distress. When parents act to alleviate infant's distress, the child's behavior is reinforced.

## Children's Self-Development for the First Two Years

Infants' development of the self is central to their developing an anger repertoire. Infants sense they are physically distinct from their surroundings almost at birth. Newborns, for instance, have a capacity for intermodal perception. They began to feel their own touch, they watch their limbs move, and they feel and hear themselves cry. These intermodal matches help them to differentiate their own body from the world and the people who surround them. Gradually over the next few months, infants begin to distinguish their own bodies from those of others, thereby increasing their own self-awareness.

During their second year, toddlers become consciously aware of the self's physical features. When they see their image in a mirror, they may act silly or coy, playfully experimenting with the way the self looks.[24] At about age two, self-recognition, the identification of the self as a physically unique being, is well under way. Children point to themselves in pictures and refer to themselves by name or with a personal pronoun ("I" or "me"). Self-awareness develops as infants and toddlers begin to recognize that their own actions cause objects and people to react in predictable ways.[25] When infants interact with their environment, they notice effects that help them sort out self, other people, and objects. They are developing a clear sense of the self and how the self responds to situations.

## The Importance of Self-Referencing in Children's Development of Emotions

Infants engage in self-referencing in which they actively seek emotional information from a trusted person in an uncertain situation. Studies have found that a caregiver's emotional expression (angry, happy, or fearful) influences whether a one year old will be wary of strangers or play with an unfamiliar toy.[26,27] For instance, in one study an adult showed 14 and 18 month olds broccoli and crackers and acted happy with one food but disgusted with the other. When the infants and toddlers were asked to share the food, the 18 month olds gave the adult whichever food he appeared to like, regardless of their own preferences.[28] Children use signals from family members to guide their actions and to discover others' internal states and preferences.

Children also learn a second set of higher-order feelings that include guilt, shame, embarrassment, and pride. These emotions are labeled "self-conscious emotions" because they involve injury to or enhancement of our sense of self. We feel guilty when we have harmed another and want to correct the situation. We feel pride when we have accomplished something, and we are inclined to tell others what we have achieved.

Self-conscious emotions emerge in the second half of the second year, as 18–24 month olds become aware of themselves as separate, unique individuals. Toddlers manifest shame and embarrassment by lowering their eyes, hanging their heads, and hiding their faces with their hands. Pride also emerges around this time, and envy appears by age three.[29] Parents play an important role in children's development of self-conscious emotions. They provide adult instruction to toddlers regarding when to feel proud, ashamed, or guilty. Parents begin this instruction when they make such statements as: "Look how well you ate your food. Good boy." Self-conscious emotions assume central roles in children's achievement-related behavior and moral behaviors.

There is also a cultural context for children's development of self-conscious emotions. In the United States, children are taught to feel pride because of their personal achievement, such as their being able to throw a ball the farthest, winning a game, or getting the highest grades in a course. Yet, in group-oriented or collectivist-oriented cultures, such as China and Japan, calling attention to only personal success results in embarrassment. Violating cultural standards by failing to show concern for others, such as a parent, teacher, or employer, results in intense shame for members of some Asian cultures.

### Children's Cognitive Development and Their Emotions

As children develop cognitively (ability to think and reason), they become increasingly aware of their own and others' emotions. Before the age of two or three, children express emotions primarily nonverbally, that is, through facial expressions, vocal sounds, and gestures. Once children develop the ability to use their words to express how they are feeling, they become better able to regulate or explain both their own emotions and those of others.

Children's emotional language develops around 20 months and increases rapidly during their third year. By age three, children refer to different feeling states in themselves and in others. They also acquire the words for naming the emotions they are feeling. Gradually, children's improved ability to think helps them to understand anger. Preschool children may not be able to put their frustrations into words, so they express their anger by hitting a person or animal, or by damaging an object. Some children become angry when someone takes something away from them or when they are asked to do a task they do not want to do. As children learn to speak and to communicate with words, they may express anger verbally and physically. Older children may hit, tease, yell at, and bully others. In addition, children's memory improves substantially during early childhood, enabling them to better remember different aspects of previously experienced anger-arousing interactions.

Children who have developed negative ideas of how to express anger may try to use the earlier unhelpful strategy. Teachers may have to remind some children two or three times about the less aggressive ways of expressing anger. Talking about emotions helps young children understand their feelings. Children's overall language ability predicts their understanding of emotion. Therefore, parents need to take into consideration their children's overall cognitive and language ability when trying to teach them techniques to manage anger. Parents can do a great deal to help children use words to describe their emotions. Ashley's mother saw her crying and asked her why she was so sad. Her mother had defined Ashley's emotional state as sad. When parents repeatedly expose children to these emotional labels, such experiences can lead to improvements in how children experience and express emotions.

# Children's Development of Self-Regulatory Behavior

Emotional self-regulation refers to the strategies we use to adjust our emotional state to a comfortable level of intensity in order to achieve our goals.[30]

When you tell yourself that an anxiety-provoking event will soon be over, suppress your anger at your child's behavior, or decide not to confront a co-worker, you are engaging in emotional self-regulation. Self-regulation can be conceptualized as controlling one's impulses, tolerating frustration, and postponing immediate gratification. Emotional self-regulation involves voluntary, effortful management of emotions. Children's capacity for effortful control improves gradually with the development of the cerebral cortex and the help of caregivers, who guide them in managing intense emotion and teach them strategies for controlling emotions.

Individual differences in control of emotion are clear as early as infancy. During the first few months of life, infants have only a limited capacity to regulate their emotional states. They are easily overwhelmed by things within their environment, and they depend on the soothing interventions of caregivers—for instance, lifting the distressed baby to the shoulder, rocking him, and talking softly to him. The infant's rapid development of the frontal lobes of the cerebral cortex increases his tolerance for stimulation.[31] Between two and four months, caregivers build on this capacity when they initiate face-to-face play with their infants. As you interact with your infant, your baby's tolerance for stimulation increases. By four months, infants develop the capacity to shift their attention, and this helps them to control emotion. Research has found that babies who more readily turn away from unpleasant events are less prone to distress.[32] By the end of the first year, infants' ability to crawl and walk helps them to regulate their feelings by approaching or retreating from various situations.

Parents and caregivers provide infants with lessons about socially approved ways to express their feelings. As early as the first few months of life, parents encourage infants to suppress negative emotions by imitating their expressions of interest, happiness, and surprise more often than their expressions of anger and sadness. Typically, boys are taught to limit their expression of emotions, especially crying. Consequently, a sex difference in emotional expression is created at a young age, with girls being more emotionally expressive than boys.

Somewhere between 12 and 18 months, children gain a clear awareness of parents' wishes and expectations; they can choose to obey or to disobey simple requests and commands. One way toddlers assert their autonomy is by resisting adult directives. Toddlers' compliance efforts may lead to their self-correcting verbalizations by saying "No can't" before reaching for a treat or picking up a treasured item. As toddlers increase their sense of self-control, parents expand the rules they expect them to obey, from safety and respect for property and people to family routines and manners. Toddlers who experience parental warmth and encouragement experience an increase in their self-control.

As the end of the second year approaches, toddlers have developed a vocabulary for talking about their feelings—"happy," "surprised," "scary," "yucky," and "mad." Toddlers are able to redirect their attention from distress in the presence of supportive adults. For instance, while listening to a story about happiness, Jenny yelled, "happy." Jenny's mom said, "yes," put the book down, and gave her a big hug. To act in a self-controlled manner, children must have some ability to think of themselves as separate, autonomous beings who can direct their own actions. In addition, they must have the representational and memory capacities to recall a caregiver's directive (for example, "Elisha, don't touch that light socket") and apply it to their own behavior.

Children are first able to understand that people can experience two consecutive emotions (e.g., feeling scared and then feeling happy) at age six. Shortly thereafter, they learn that two emotions can co-occur. As children develop the capacity to take the perspective of others, they become increasingly aware of other people's feelings, such as grief and sadness. Their growing sense of self-awareness also contributes to their effortful control or the extent to which they can inhibit impulses, manage negative emotions, and behave in socially acceptable ways. As they gain a firmer sense of themselves, they are better able to exert effortful control.

## Helping Children Develop Compliance and Self-Control

Most children misbehave at some point; that is simply part of finding out what appropriate behavior is and where the limits are. Hence, children may throw tantrums, test the rules, start fights, refuse to cooperate with family routines, use bad language, etc. It is the parents' responsibility to teach appropriate behavior, desired social rules, and boundaries. The goal of discipline is to help a child to develop self-control and a sense of limits, to experience the consequences of his behavior, and to learn from his mistakes. Discipline does not have to mean punishment or conflict between parent and child. All children need the security of knowing what the rules and the boundaries of behavior are. Without such rules, they flounder and become lost.

Parents set up the foundation for discipline during their children's early years when they establish family interaction patterns. As toddlers begin to move around, they test their independence, and they need to be helped to understand what is safe, what they can do, and what they cannot do. Initially, toddlers are focused on satisfying their own needs rather than interests of others. Toddlers begin to learn that there are rules. To help toddlers develop compliant behaviors, give advanced notice when they must stop an enjoyable activity. Toddlers find it difficult to stop a pleasant activity that is already under way. Offer them many prompts and reminders. Keep in mind that toddlers' ability to remember and to comply with rules is limited. They need continuous adult oversight and repeating of family rules.

Moreover, children's development of attention is related to self-control. Those who can shift their attention from a captivating stimulus and focus on a less attractive alternative are better at controlling their responses. Respond to children's self-control behavior with verbal and physical approval. Praise and hugs reinforce the desired behavior, increasing the likelihood of such behavior occurring again.

## Strategies for Dealing with Children's Aggression toward Parents

At about a year or 18 months of age, some parents notice a change in their children's behavior. They turn from a lovable cuddly infant to an aggressive toddler.[33] Toddlers go through a stage of biting, kicking, and hitting. Although this aggressive stage is not pleasant, it is quite normal for many young children. Toddlers often say "no" and want to do things for themselves and become independent. They have difficulty controlling themselves, partly because they do not have the words or vocabulary to describe their emotions and desires.

If your child hits you, stop the aggression immediately. Do not let him hit you repeatedly. Grip his wrist firmly, and say with firmness: "No hitting. You do not hit me. You can be angry, but you may not hit." Do not let go of the child's wrist until you can feel the tension subside. You may have to explain: "I won't let you go until you put your hand down and stop hitting." When the child stops struggling to hit you and relaxes, praise and encourage him. You might say: "That's better. I knew you could do it." Release the child gently. Give the child a hug and say to him: "Hands are not for hitting; hands are for hugging." Then quickly move on to the next activity. "All right. Let's have a snack or let's read a story."

## Understanding Temper Tantrums

Temper tantrums are often associated with the "terrible twos"; yet, rarely do they begin on a child's second birthday and end on his third. Some children never have a temper tantrum, while others are still having them at age 50. Parents may see a tantrum as a form of disobedience or a child out of control and, therefore, fail to handle the tantrum appropriately.

Temper tantrums are a normal way for toddlers to express feelings of frustration, anger, and tiredness. The first step is to understand what kind of tantrum is in force. Is the tantrum manipulative or temperamental? Does it express verbal frustration? Manipulative tantrums take place when the child does not get his way. It will stop if it is ignored. If at home, the parent can walk away from the tantrum. Some parents remove the child to another room and indicate that the child can rejoin the family when the tantrum is over. "When you are finished with your tantrum, I will come and get you to join the rest of the family."

The grocery store is one of the more difficult locations with which to deal with a child's manipulative tantrum. You might try stepping out of line to deal with your child's behavior. Another technique is to offer your child an alternative and tell him that you will not get back in line until the behavior stops. Before you go on your next shopping trip, let your child know that you will not be taking him. After your child has missed one or two shopping trips, you might say: "I am going to the grocery store today, and I am taking you with me. You won't be buying anything. You can push the cart." Help your toddler to understand that his tantrum will not work.

Temperamental tantrums take place when your toddler's inherited or learned disposition is out of control. You might try holding your child and giving him hugs, or you might use a distraction, such as a song, a book, or a favorite activity. As noted earlier, it is important to help a child to use words to describe what he is feeling. "Use your words to tell Mommy what is upsetting to you." You might also teach your child deep breathing techniques. "Can you show Mommy how you can take a deep breath to feel better?" Focus on your toddler's positive behavior. This helps teach toddlers the correct behavior and also gives them the attention and affection they desire.

Establish routines for your child to reduce the incidence of tantrums. Children need to feel secure, and they also like to know what is coming next. Routines are reassuring to children because they structure their lives and such structure gives them a sense of safety. Children need clearly established mealtimes, snack times, bath times, and bedtime. If you have established a routine of reading your children a story after they have had a bath and snack, they will recognize that it is story time after they have had their baths. Once you have established routines to minimize tantrums, evaluate how you react to your children's tantrum and plan your most effective means of controlling your reactions to such outbursts.

## Parenting Style, Discipline, and Teaching Children Self-Regulating Behaviors

Parenting style refers to the broad overall pattern of parental actions, rather than any single parental action. Diana Baumrind[34] was one of the first researchers to describe parenting styles in detail. She and other researchers examined children who had the qualities most of us would like in our children: independence, maturity, self-reliance, self-control, curiosity, friendliness, and achievement orientation. The researchers then interviewed the parents of these children to determine which elements of parenting promoted these qualities. They identified two components: (1) parental responsiveness, or warmth and supportiveness, and (2) demandingness and behavioral control. The parenting styles also differed in such parental control practices as inducing guilt feelings from their children, withdrawing love from them to control behavior, or shaming them in front of family members and friends. Psychological control is developed through such practices as guilt induction and withdrawal of love.

Authoritarian parenting style is an extremely strict style where parents are highly controlling. Such parents emphasize obedience to authority and discourage discussion. They expect their orders to be obeyed and do not encourage give and take with their children. These parents evidence low levels of sensitivity. The authoritarian child-rearing style is low in acceptance and involvement, high in coercive control, and low in autonomy granting.

Authoritarian parents appear to be cold and rejecting. To exercise control, they yell, command, criticize, and threaten. They state: "Do it because I said so." They make decisions for their children and expect them to accept their orders without question. If the child resists, authoritarian parents use force and punishment. Such parents often use psychological control methods that intrude upon the child's ability to develop his individuality; they rarely listen to the child's point of view; and they do not engage in autonomy granting.

Children of authoritarian parents tend to be anxious, unhappy, low in self-esteem and self-reliance, and they react with hostility when frustrated. Boys manifest high rates of anger and defiance. Girls also engage in acting-out behavior, but they are more likely to be dependent and to become overwhelmed by challenging tasks.[35] Children subjected to psychological control manifest adjustment problems, and they are inclined to be withdrawn, defiant, and aggressive.[36]

In contrast, the authoritative parenting style is the most successful approach to child rearing. Such parents are warm, attentive, and sensitive to their child's needs, and they give reasons for their actions and expectations. Authoritative parents provide gradual autonomy to their children; they allow children to make decisions and to express thoughts, feelings, and desires. Authoritative parenting is linked to a number of positive developments for children, including an upbeat mood, self-control, task persistence, cooperativeness, high self-esteem, social and moral maturity, and favorable school performance.[37]

What makes authoritative child rearing effective is that it creates an emotional context for positive parental influence in young people's lives. Warm, involved parents who are secure in the standards they maintain for their children serve as role models of caring people. Moreover, children are more likely to comply with and internalize parental control that appears fair and reasonable, rather than arbitrary. Authoritative parents make demands and participate in autonomy granting that matches their children's ability to take responsibility for their own behavior. Such actions promote a sense of competency within children.

In the permissive parenting style, parents are overindulgent or inattentive. They exercise little control over their children's behavior, and they permit children to make many of their own decisions at an age when they are not yet capable of doing so. Children raised by permissive parents are inclined to be impulsive, disobedient, and rebellious, and they show less persistence on tasks. The research shows that boys raised by permissive parents tend to be dependent and nonachieving.[38]

The uninvolved parenting style uses low acceptance, little control, and general indifference to autonomy granting. Frequently, these parents are emotionally detached, depressed, and overwhelmed by life stress. Neglect is the extreme form of uninvolved parenting. Children and adolescents who are raised by uninvolved parents manifest many problems, including poor emotional self-regulation, poor school achievement, and antisocial behavior.[39]

# Dealing with the Angry Child

It is also important to distinguish between anger and aggression. Anger is a temporary emotional state caused by frustration. Aggression is typically an attempt to hurt a person or to destroy property. It will be easier to deal with children's anger if we get rid of the notion that anger is bad. The goal of parents, teachers, and counselors is not to repress or destroy angry feelings in children or in ourselves but rather to accept the feelings and to help channel and direct them to constructive ends. Parents, teachers, and counselors must permit children to feel all their feelings. Adult skills can then be focused on showing children acceptable ways of expressing their feelings. Children's strong feelings should not be denied. Angry outbursts are not always signs of serious problems.

Our actions toward angry children should be guided by the need to protect and to teach, not by a desire to punish. Parents and teachers show a child that they accept the child's feelings, while suggesting other ways to express the feelings. An adult might say, for example, "Let me tell you what some children might do in a situation like this." It is insufficient to tell children what behaviors they find unacceptable. Parents must teach their children acceptable ways of coping and appropriate ways of handling their anger.

## What Does Work with Helping Children Deal with Anger?

The following techniques help children to deal constructively with their anger: praising for appropriate behavior, reasoning, giving consequences, withholding privileges, enforcing time out, and teaching a child to express anger in constructive ways.[40] What you say to an angry child will either increase or decrease the possibility of his anger becoming out of control the next time. Children who act negatively on their anger need to hear correction statements phrased in positive language. You can help children by interrupting their negative thinking patterns and, in a nonthreatening manner, helping them to process what happened and what could be different next time. Children are ripest for change immediately after they have expressed their anger in a high arousal situation.

### Respond to your child's sense of fair play after a conflict or angry situation.

Try to understand what your child feels is out of her control or unfair. You might say: "If you could change one thing about this situation, what would it be?" "I want to understand why you are upset. Can you use your words?" First, show your child the consequences of her actions on the other person. Second, give your child a choice. Third, ask her to make a value judgment on what she did. Fourth, provide her with information on how she might act in more positive ways. Fifth, leave your child with her self-esteem still intact and give her hope that she will understand how to deal effectively with anger in future conflict situations.

Some children who have difficulty with anger management externalize their anger. When parents confront them about hitting their brother or sister, they may shrug it off with an "I don't care" attitude. The child rationalizes his angry behavior with some form of "He made me do it. If he hadn't . . . I would not of . . . So it's his fault." With this kind of defense, the child externalizes blame to someone else. This pattern of dealing with anger is typically learned from parents, and the cycle of anger is often repeated down through generations of families. The research indicates that people engage in cognitive distortions when they are angry. That is, they minimize, justify, or rationalize their angry outbursts and destructive behavior. This situation occurs because their pain may be great and their defenses so ingrained that they cannot see their own part in the conflict. They can only see the fault of others.[41]

You can help your children with externalization of blame and rationalization of their behavior if you get them to feel their vulnerability and show them that you are on their side. "Stan really hurt your feelings by calling your stupid, didn't he? It's not nice to hurt another person's feelings." Then you might help your child understand that it is okay to be sad or mad. Anger is an appropriate feeling to have when others hurt you. Angry feelings are part of being a human being. However, it is not okay to respond with our fists when others say mean things to you. Establish the following anger management rules with your child.

- Explain that people are not to be hurt.
- Encourage the child to use words to work out anger. You might tell your child: "I understand that you are angry, but I can't permit you to show your anger by kicking the wall or throwing things at me. Instead, you can use your words to tell me what you are angry about." Talking helps a child to exercise control and reduces acting-out behavior.
- Explain that no one can make a good choice when he is angry. Be in control of your anger rather than letting your anger control you.
- Encourage the child to take responsibility for his own feelings, rather than blaming someone else for how he feels.
- Give your child a cooling down period before talking to him.
- Give him a choice of the place where he can go to cool down.
- Giving a child choices helps him to feel respected and aids in his believing that he has a part in figuring out solutions to anger or conflict.

In addition, there are other techniques one may use in helping a child deal with anger.

## Catch the child being good and compliment the child on his behavior.

Compliments reinforce the desired behavior within the child. A parent might say: "I like the way you came into dinner without my having to call you so many times." Or, "I am really proud of the way you handled the situation by refusing to fight your brother." "I appreciate the way you put your toys away, even though you really wanted me to read you a bedtime story." A parent looks for opportunities to reinforce the child's positive behavior throughout the day. "You were really patient and didn't interrupt while I was on the telephone talking." "I am so proud of the fact that you did not try to interrupt my adult conversation with your father." "I like the way you take into account other people's feelings about a situation." "Thank you for being brave enough to tell me the truth about what really happened."

Likewise, teachers can positively reinforce the constructive expression of anger and positive behavior with such statements as: "I know it was difficult for you to wait your turn, and I'm pleased that you did it so well." "Thanks for sitting in your seat so quietly. I appreciate your positive behavior." "You were thoughtful in helping Jimmy to feel that he has a friend in class." "You really worked hard on that project, and it shows."

## Learn to respect your child's feelings when you talk to him.

When you teach your children to express anger constructively, put yourself in their shoes. Ask yourself such questions as: "Am I speaking to my children so they will learn from me rather than resent me?" "Would I want anyone to speak with me the way I am speaking with my children?" If we do not consider our children's feelings and perspective, we are likely to do or to say things that will encourage negative angry behavior. Listen until your children finish talking. Let them run out of gas. Then ask if they have finished speaking before you begin speaking.

## Involve your child in the process of dealing effectively with anger.

Even young children can be involved in a discussion that deals with the following: (1) what makes us angry; (2) what are different ways for dealing constructively with anger; (3) what might be the consequences of each option; and (4) what option might be the most effective. When you are teaching anger management strategies to your children, serve as an appropriate role model for them. Remember that children do not always do what we say. They are more likely to do what we do. Thus, a key component of teaching anger management to children is for parents to model effective coping strategies.

Parents and teachers deliberately ignore anger and negative behaviors that can be tolerated, but they do not ignore the child. The ignoring of a child's behavior must be planned and consistent. Even though the child's negative behavior may be tolerated, the child must recognize that it is inappropriate.

Provide physical outlets for your children. Adults are inclined to exercise or do something that lets them slam things around, such as cleaning a kitchen. Children need physical activity to let off steam, too. Play with your child, and you will establish a relationship with him.

Use humor to defuse an angry child. Teasing or kidding can often take the sting out of an angry situation and allow a child to save face. Do not use humor to ridicule your child; instead, use it to make fun of the situation. You might say something like: "I know you are mad at that boy for calling you names, especially such stupid names. He must not be very smart if the meanest thing he could think to say was 'dumb butt.' "

## Appeal directly to your child.

You tell him or her how you feel and ask for consideration. For instance, a parent or a teacher might get a child's cooperation by saying: "I know that noise you're making doesn't usually bother me, but today I've got a headache; so could you find something else you'd enjoy doing."

## Use closeness and touching with your child.

Move physically closer to your child to reduce his angry impulse. Young children may often be calmed by having an adult come close by and express interest in their activities. Very young children who are emotionally deprived seem to need much more adult involvement in their interests. A child who is getting ready to use a toy or tool in a destructive manner is sometimes easily stopped by an adult who expresses interest in having it shown to him. An outburst from an older child struggling with reading can be prevented or reduced by a caring adult who moves near the child and says: "Show me which words are giving you trouble."

## Establish clear limits and boundaries with your child.

Children become angry when they are uncertain of their boundaries. It is normal for children to test the limits they are given, if only to see if the boundaries are real and consistent. When parents give in to their children's testing of boundaries, they learn a successful way to get their demands met. When children are given clear boundaries, they can exercise their choices within those boundaries. Family rules bring order and security to children, and the rules should be fair and consistent.

## Help your child identify the early warning signs of his anger.

Children oftentimes do not recognize that they are becoming angry.[42] They may act on their anger before they even recognize that they are enraged. Helping them to identify early warning signs makes them more aware of their feelings, which in turn gives them more opportunity to control their responses to a situation. When your child becomes angry, have him say something like the following: "I'm angry. It's easy for me to do something destructive now. But I am going to handle this situation constructively." Help your child to develop a "be constructive signal" that reminds him to remain calm and constructive when he feels anger rising within himself. As he feels the anger rise, he reminds himself to stay calm and be constructive.

Some common physiological cues in children that indicate they are becoming angry and may be about to lose control include: tensed body, clenched teeth, increased intensity of speech or behavior, changes in tone of voice to yelling, squinting, rolling the eyes, or pouting. Learn to recognize cues your child gives off to indicate that he is becoming angry. Then point these cues out to your child.

Eventually, children will be able to recognize their anger cues and choose appropriate responses before the anger erupts. One example of acknowledging anger signals worked with an extremely aggressive teenager (a 15-year-old boy whose father described him as having been a "problem child" since he was three). The youth learned to use the signs of impending aggression—cursing under his breath, tension in his body, the tightening of his right arm before striking someone—as cues to walk away from that person and calm down before continuing to talk to the other person.

### Teach your child how to assert himself rather than to use aggression.

Older children and teenagers sometime find themselves in arguments with their closest friends. Anger between friends can be particularly volatile and sometimes violent. In order for your child to assert himself constructively, he needs to: Describe to the person what he did that was upsetting. For example, "You promised to give me back my bike by 2 PM, and you didn't. Because you did not get my bike back on time, I was late going over to Shannon's house."

## Strategies for Dealing with Sibling Rivalry and Anger

Sibling rivalry is the jealousy, competition, and fighting between brothers and sisters. It is a concern for most parents who have more than one child. Difficulties between siblings occur right after the birth of the second child. Typically, such rivalry continues throughout childhood and even into adulthood. Its occurrence is stressful to parents. Most sibling relationships turn out to be close ones that endure despite conflicts. We learn conflict resolution skills when we find that pounding our younger brother or sister gets us into trouble.

### What causes sibling rivalry?

Children did not have the option of choosing each other for brothers or sisters. The closeness in age of the children and/or the gender of each child may contribute to sibling rivalry. Likewise, older siblings may use the age difference to point out the ineptness of their younger brother or sister and emphasize their superiority. Moreover, sibling rivalry develops because children feel they are getting unequal amounts of attention, discipline, and responsiveness. They may believe that their relationship with their parents is threatened by the arrival of a new baby.[43] Differences in personality and in temperament can also cause sibling conflict. While some prefer to spend their time reading quietly, others love group sports and games and crave excitement. Such temperament differences may erupt in conflicts. Competition in academics, sports, music or dance and even popularity can play a large role in sibling rivalry. Younger children resent having to grow up in an older sibling's shadow of excellence.

Parental attitudes can influence the severity of sibling rivalry. How parents treat their kids and respond to conflict can make a big difference in how well siblings get along. It is impossible to treat each child exactly the same all the time;

yet, it is important for parents to be fair and to show impartiality. Try not to make comparisons between children. Instead, celebrate the uniqueness of each one of your children.

### Strategies for resolving sibling conflict

Look for ways your children can cooperate rather than compete with each other. Reinforce them positively when they are cooperative with one another. Praise them when they work out problems on their own. Prevent confrontations between siblings by eliminating the situations over which they conflict. If you know your children are going to fight about who will get the first piece of cake, establish a system that allows them to take turns being first. Make sure that each child has enough time and space of his own to play with his own friends without the sibling and that each has his property protected.

It is important to set aside private or alone time for each one of your children. Each parent might spend one-on-one time with each kid on a regular basis. When you are alone with each child, ask what he likes most and least about each other. This will remind the children that they do have positive feelings for each other, and it helps you to keep tabs on their sibling relationship.

While parents should pay attention to their children's conflicts (so that no one gets hurt and you notice abuse if it occurs), it is best not to intervene. When parents jump into siblings' arguments, they sometimes protect one child (younger or smaller sibling) against the older one. Such parental behavior only escalates the sibling conflict, resulting in the older child resenting the younger one, and the younger one feeling that she can get away with more behavior.

Instead of getting drawn into a sibling conflict, a parent might say: "I'm sure the two of you can figure out a solution." Encourage win-win solutions when conflict erupts between children. Establish rules for resolving conflicts, such as no hurting, hitting, kicking, or pinching, and no name-calling, yelling, or tattling. If the children fight over a toy, the toy is placed into time out until the conflict between the two siblings is resolved. If borrowing is a problem, have the child who borrows something put up collateral.

Adolescents' anger is often directed toward parents and siblings because they may feel upset about having to strive so hard academically, or they may experience anger at parents for being critical, or they may feel that their parents' control of them is too strong or suffocating. [44] Current situations sometimes act as triggers to past feelings of hurt, pain, or resentment.

## How to Tell If Your Child's Anger Is Out of Control

When seeing your children erupt into anger, some of you have wondered: "Where is all this anger and hostility coming from? Is it normal for my child to be so easy provoked and aggressive, to take offense at the slightest thing, and to speak so disrespectfully?" The answer is no. Happy children with strong self-esteem and who have even moderate self-regulatory behavior are not so quick to become angry. Therefore, if you or your child's teachers or babysitter have complained more than several times about your child's angry outbursts, then there is need for concern.

How does a parent determine if his child's angry behavior is within a normal range or is truly cause for concern? In *The Angry Child,* Timothy Murphy[45] provides a number of soul searching questions that are summarized below. If you respond positively to four or more of these items, your child's anger may be out of control and help should be sought.

- Do you feel caught in a vicious shouting cycle, or do you resort to threats in order to get good behavior from your children and to achieve peace at home?
- Do you dread your child's reaction when you discipline him?
- Do you feel overwhelmed by your toddler's tantrums?
- Does your child make threats when he does not get his way?
- Does it seem that you are continually trying to mend fences because of your child's angry behavior?
- Do you feel exhausted by the daily struggles with mealtimes, bedtime, homework, and chores?
- Do you feel intimidated by your child's angry outbursts to the extent that you avoid interactions with him that might bring out his anger?
- Does your child refuse to accept any responsibility for his angry outbursts and blame others for "causing" them?

## *Parents' Spiritual Journey with Anger*

Part of the parenting spiritual journey involves getting in touch with your own anger as a child. How was anger handled in your family? Was anger shown or did everyone pretend that it did not exist? Think about your earliest angry memories. Who was involved? Was your anger resolved? If so, how was it resolved? Are you still angry about how your parents or siblings treated you? If so, what are some steps you could take to resolve your long-standing anger with your parents, siblings, or family?

One reason I am suggesting that you take this journey into the past is to help you parent your own child about anger in a positive and constructive fashion. We tend to parent the way that we were parented—unless we do something to change or redirect our parenting skills. Anger is a basic human emotion. Children need to learn how to deal with their anger so that they control it rather than the anger controlling them and their destiny. So many adults are locked in their own anger prisons. Forgiveness is the key that opens the door to healing and peace. As Buddha (563 BC–483 BC) once said: "Holding onto anger is like grasping a hot coal with the intent of throwing it at someone else . . .; you are the one getting burned."

# *Summary*

This chapter has dealt with anger in children—its emotional expression and its causes. The first part of the chapter examined children's temperament and their evolution of self-referencing. Next, attention was directed toward understanding the young child's development of self-regulatory behavior. Parenting style was discussed in terms of its influence on young people's expression of anger. Children of authoritarian parents are inclined to react with hostility when frustrated and exhibit high rates of anger and defiance. In contrast, parents who use an authoritative child-rearing style produce children who express anger appropriately because they have been given self-responsibility and because they have learned how to self-regulate their emotions. Strategies to assist parents with sibling rivalry and angry teenagers were presented. Intentional parental tips were provided to help parents deal constructively with the issue of anger.

# *Parental Reading List*

*Calming the Family Storm: Anger Management for Moms, Dads, and All the Kids* by Gary D. McKay and Steven Maybell. (2005). Atascadero, CA: Impact Publishers.

*Love and Anger: The Parental Dilemma* by Nancy Samalin with Catherine Whitney. (1991). New York: Penguin Group.

*When Anger Hurts Your Kids: A Parent's Practical Guide* by Matthew McKay. Oakland, Ca: New Harbinger Publications.

# *Intentional Parenting Tips for Dealing with Children's Anger*

## *Quiz for Analyzing Parental Anger*

To improve my ability to deal with my anger and that of my children, I first need to assess my understanding of my own anger. I will answer the following questions in my journal.

- What is my definition of anger?
- What usually makes me angry?
- Who usually makes me angry?
- What "hot buttons" are likely to arouse my anger?
- How do I usually express my anger?

- How healthy is my expression of anger?
- Where are my problems with anger rooted?
- What anger issues in my life remain unresolved?
- How can I forgive, forget, and heal my past anger?
- How do I show anger in front of my children?
- What am I teaching my children about anger?
- Am I satisfied by the manner in which my family handles anger?

## *Parental Tips for Dealing with Children's Anger toward Parents*

Some parents are deeply hurt when they hear their child's angry words. For instance, a child might say: "I hate you Mommy. You're a wicked witch." Instead of striking out at your child or trying to win your child's love, you might:

1. Empathize with the child's feelings. "You're really very angry with me right now."
2. State the anger issue. "You don't want to go to bed. You want to stay up and watch television."
3. Offer an alternative way of the child's expressing his anger toward you. "You can tell me that you are angry with me without saying that you hate me. Hate is such a strong ugly word, and I believe that you can express your feelings better than saying 'I hate you.'"

## *The Anger Diary*

If your children have a serious problem with anger, you might ask them to keep an anger diary to record every instance of their anger. Your children should record:

- What provoked the anger,
- The cues they exhibited that let them know they were becoming angry,
- The things they told themselves about their anger and the situation, and
- The consequences that followed their anger and actions.

## *Anger Management Lessons for Teachers and Counselors*

### The Anger Cycle
Objectives:

- To understand how anger hurts others
- To understand that anger has a cycle it goes through

- To understand that anger is a normal feeling
- To understand that the anger cycle can be broken

Activities:

- Draw a picture of what you think anger would look like if it had a shape.
- Tell about your picture. What did you draw and what were you thinking about when you drew your picture.
- Show a transparency of the anger cycle and explain it.

## Distancing Ourselves from Our Anger: An Exercise for Parents

- Distance ourselves from our own anger. If we feel separated from our own anger, then we will give less importance to it.
- Make a concerted effort not to allow anger to enter into us.
- Remind ourselves that anger is a signal for a deeper emotion, a deeper wound.
- Anger rarely improves a situation, although it might propel us to act.
- Breathe deeply because breathing can have a transformative effect on our thoughts and emotions. The nature of anger is to demand an immediate response without measured thought.
- Meditate. When we meditate, we try to avoid allowing any thought or emotion. We make our minds calm and vacant. When we no longer pursue our anger, our inner peace comes to the fore.

## Anger Management Self-Talk

Anger is produced, maintained, and influenced by the self-statements we make in situations that we allow to provoke us. These self-statements can be placed into three categories: (1) cognitive preparation for anger; (2) skill development, where the individual learns alternative coping skills in response to the provocation; (3) coping with arousal; and (4) reflecting on the provocation. Some positive anger management self-talk is listed below:

### Preparing for Provocation

This is going to upset me, but I know how to deal with it.

I can regulate my anger and work out a plan to manage the situation.

Easy does it. Remember to keep my sense of humor.

### Impact and Confrontation

Think of what you want to get out of this.

You do not have to prove yourself to anyone.

Look for the positives in this situation.

I am on top of this situation, and it is under my control.

### Coping with Arousal

It is just not worth it to get angry.

I will let him make a fool of himself.

I have a right to be annoyed, but let us keep the lid on.

He would probably like me to get angry, but I am going to disappoint him.

### Reflecting on the Provocation

a.  When conflict is unresolved

Try to shake it off. Do not let it interfere with your job.

I will get better at this as I get more practice.

Can I laugh about it?

Take a deep breath.

b.  When conflict is resolved or coping is successful.

I handled that one pretty well.

I actually got through that without getting angry.

I am getting better at handling anger each day.

# Finding Your Parenting Style

The questions below are designed to help you determine factors that may have influenced your parenting style. Think about the parenting style that helped shape you.

- What parenting styles did you experience as a child?
- How do you feel about the parenting styles you experienced as a child? Happy? Sad? Angry?
- What techniques did your parents use to discipline you?
- How did you feel about these discipline techniques?
- Did your parents teach you how to be well-behaved?
- If so, what were the guidelines for a well-behaved child?
- Did your parents teach and correct you with anger?
- How did your parents bring about compliance with their rules or standards?

- What impact did your folks' parenting style have on your developing self-control of your emotions?

List three things your parents did that you would like to repeat in raising your own kids:

1. _____
2. _____
3. _____

List three things that you would never do to your children that your parents did in raising you.

1. _____
2. _____
3. _____

Think about you and your partner's parenting style.

- How similar or different is your partner's parenting style?
- What impact do both of your parenting styles have on your children?
- If the parenting styles are different, how do you negotiate what style will be used in raising your children?

List three things that you would like to change about your parenting style.

1. _____
2. _____
3. _____

List three things that your parenting style does effectively with your children.

1. _____
2. _____
3. _____

# *School Violence: The Role of the Family and Educators*

*Nonviolence means avoiding not only external physical violence but also internal violence of spirit. You not only refuse to shoot a man, but you refuse to hate him.*

—Martin Luther King Jr.

School is supposed to be a place where children are safe to learn and where they build memories that last a lifetime. Most of us meet our first boyfriend or best girlfriend at school. We share secrets with our best friends over lunch and talk about who is going out with whom, what grade we got on different tests, and who the coolest teachers are. School is meant to be a place of treasured memories with only a few disappointments.

Yet, for a growing number of American young people, school has become a frightening place. Increasingly young people feel threatened by the possibility that one of their classmates may come into the school's hallway, lunchroom, or library angry at the world and blast people away with a rifle or a nine millimeter gun. The recent developments at Virginia Tech University in Blacksburg, Virginia, have only refueled both parents' and young people's concerns about school violence. On April 16, 2007, one lone 22-year-old college student shot and murdered 32 people on Virginia Tech's campus and injured a score of others. Later it was discovered that the youth had suffered with mental problems for more than a decade.

School has also been chosen as a place for committing suicide. On December 13, 2006, Shane Halligan ate breakfast with his family, promised that he would improve his grades so that he could get into a good college, grabbed his duffle bag, and went to school. The eleventh-grader lived in middle class

Springfield, PA. He was an Eagle Scout, prided himself on being a volunteer fire-fighter, and had planned a career in the military. The night before, Shane's parents had laid down the law with him about his grades. He was not failing, but they were concerned that his grades needed to be higher for him to get accepted by the college of his choice.

So, they decided they were not going to permit him to volunteer at the fire company anymore until he pulled up his grades. In their opinion, their decision was an act of "tough love." They loved their son enough to take something away from him that really mattered. Shane was devastated that they would forbid him from volunteering at the fire company. He absolutely loved volunteering with the fire company. It was the reason that got him up in the morning and motivated him to do well in school. He could not quite imagine life without volunteering at the fire company.

Shane begged his parents for some other kind of punishment or privilege to be taken away. His parents were resolute. He would not be permitted to volunteer until the grades were pulled up. They thought that this action would cause Shane to work harder and faster, since they both knew that he loved his volunteer work. Shane saw things differently. From his perspective, his whole world was being destroyed. It was if someone had taken a huge bulldozer and run roughshod over everything that he loved.

Shortly after breakfast, Shane took a rifle out of his father's locked gun cabinet and walked down to the basement to get the high powered ammunition he had discovered some time ago that his father had hidden. He left for school feeling distraught and hopeless. At Springfield Township High School, Shane took the rifle out of a large duffle bag after the first period. He fired several shots into the building's ceiling and high on the walls in the hallway. Students scattered. He then walked to a different hallway and shot himself in the head.

There was little doubt that Shane had intended to kill only himself. He made no effort to hurt anyone else. The police station was next door to the high school, and officers were on the scene almost immediately. They found the 16-year-old boy dead of a single gunshot in the hallway.

The next day Shane's distraught parents were on television saying tearfully that they never expected that he would have done anything like kill himself. They were good, loving parents. Although they did not directly ask for it, they were pleading to the public for understanding. All they wanted was for Shane to get better grades for college. Any parent could understand that, could they not? "Please do not judge us," they seemed to be saying. "We are not some kind of pushy parents concerned only about our son's grades. We are in enough pain, without your trying to play God and second-guess our decisions. Put yourself in our places. We have just lost our only son, our only child."

That night the television stations in Philadelphia were inundated with calls from anxious parents who were wondering if they were doing the right thing by taking privileges away from their teens so as to motivate them to get better grades in school. As a result, one station called in psychologists from the leading universities and asked them to respond to parents' questions. Parent callers made it clear: if the issue came down to their teen's life or his getting good grades in school, the choice was obvious. They would choose their child's life. But how were they to know what to do? They did not want their child to end up like Shane.

Shane had decided that he would put an end to his parents' concerns that his grades would not be "good enough for college." They would not have to worry any more what he got in English, math, or social studies. He was freeing himself from all pressures to achieve academically and get into college. If he could not do some of the things he wanted, he did not want to live at all. There would be no college. Psychologists theorized that Shane killed himself at the place that had caused him pain—school. It was if he were saying to his parents:

> You think high grades and college is all that matters. You took away the only thing that really mattered to me, my volunteering at the fire company. You bulldozed my world without so much as thinking about how I might feel. I'll show you. I'll take you back to your all important school and end it there. You want good grades for college. Well, you won't have to worry any more about my grades and college. I'm ending it all.

Violence can be directed either inward toward the self or outward toward others. When it is directed inward toward the self, the most tragic end is suicide. When it is directed outward toward others, as was the case with the person who killed 32 people at Virginia Tech, it erupts as homicide. During October 2007, a 14-year-old student shot and wounded two adults and two students at a high school near downtown Cleveland before taking his own life. The reason for the rampage has remained unclear. Both are acts of violence. Behind most violent acts is an individual who feels he has been deeply hurt. Violence is used to avenge the pain that one perceives others as causing. Young people who feel victimized by parents, teachers, and other students sometimes seek relief from their hurt feelings through violent acts of revenge.

Currently, we are searching for answers in America about school violence. Should all of our schools have metal detectors, security guards, and cameras in each classroom? And should all schools adopt a zero tolerance policy for violence? Just recently, a seven-year-old student was questioned without his parents' knowledge and permission and suspended from school for a day because he gave one of his friends a stick picture of two boys smiling with one of them holding a water gun. The mother was outraged. Could not the school officials see that the picture was only two stick figures who were smiling at each other? What gave the school the right to question her son about what the picture meant and any possible acts of violence that he might have been thinking about committing?

> "For God's sake," the mother of the seven-year-old complained with thinly controlled outrage on television, "I should have been called first before the school ever questioned my son. This is the United States of America .... We're supposed to

have basic rights. What is it now? We have Big Brother watching every kid to make sure that he does not draw a stick figure holding his toy water pistol? Get real and use some common sense about your zero tolerance policy."

The school administration was resolute. It would not apologize to the mother. It had taken the appropriate action against her son, and he would remain suspended for the day. Shortly thereafter the mother hired a lawyer. Who was right? Who was wrong? That evening one of the local television stations conducted a telephone call-in survey to determine what the public felt. The vast majority of the callers said that the school had overreacted and that the mother should have been called prior to school officials' questioning of the boy. Still, a small but vocal percentage felt that the school had taken the right procedures given the recent school violence at Virginia Tech and in Cleveland, Ohio.

# Definition of School Violence

School violence is defined as any intentional act that a young person engages in (1) to cause physical or psychological harm to a student, teacher, or other school staff member; (2) to disrupt the school's learning program, or (3) to destroy school property. School-related violent deaths are homicides or suicides that take place:

1. Inside a school, on school property, or on a school bus;
2. On the way to or from a school for a school session;
3. During or going to or from a sponsored school event; or
4. As a result of school-related incidents or conflicts, or activities, regardless of whether such events occurred on or off actual school property.[1]

# School Violence: The Good News

There is both good and bad news about school violence in the United States. Recent research has shown that the vast majority of American schools are safe.[2] Despite the headlines on school violence, it is actually safer to be in school than in a car. Twice as many 15 to 19 year olds die in car accidents than in shootings. According to the Centers for Disease Control and Prevention (CDC), less than one percent of all homicides among school-age children happen on school grounds or on the way to and from school.

Student safety at schools has improved. The victimization rate of students ages 12–18 at school declined from 73 victimizations per 1,000 students in 2003 to 55 victimizations in 2004. Away from school, total crime and violent crime victimization rates for students also decreased between 2003 and 2004. In 2003, there were 60 victimizations per 1,000 students away from school, compared with 48 victimizations in 2004. Researchers have attributed three important factors for the decline in school violence: (1) the installation of metal detectors for screening students in the most troubled schools, (2) the hiring of more security personnel to patrol schools, and (3) the introduction of programs to curb bullying that might lead to serious crimes.[3]

# The Bad News about School Violence

## School Murders

The bad news is that school violence continues throughout this country. This violence is captured in the school associated deaths from 2005–2006. According to the National School Safety and Security Services,[4] a total of 27 identified school-related violent deaths and 85 total nondeath shooting incidents took place during the 2005–2006 academic year. The school-associated deaths are broken down into the following categories: (A) shooting (15); (B) suicides (1); (C) murder-suicide (4); (D) fight-related (0); (E) stabbing (3); and (F) other (4). The preferred method used for school-related killings is a firearm.

## Threats and Attacks on Teachers

In 2003–2004, teachers' reports of being threatened or attacked by students during the previous 12 months varied according to their school level. Secondary school teachers were more likely than elementary school teachers to have been threatened with injury by a student (8 vs. 6 percent). However, elementary school teachers were more likely than secondary teachers to report having been physically attacked (4 vs. 2 percent). In 2003–2004, 10 percent of teachers in central city schools were threatened with injury by students, compared with 6 percent of teachers in urban fringe schools and 5 percent of teachers in rural schools. Public school teachers were more likely than private school teachers to have been threatened (7 vs. 2 percent) or physically attacked (4 vs. 2 percent) by students in school.[5]

Among teachers in central city schools, those in public schools were at least five times more likely to be threatened with injury than their colleagues in private schools (12 vs. 2 percent) and at least four times more likely to be physically attacked (5 vs. 1 percent). Annually, over the five-year period from 1998 to 2002, teachers were the victims of approximately 234,000 total nonfatal crimes at school, including 144,000 thefts and 90,000 violent crimes.[6]

# Violent School Shooters: Some Facts

A school violence report that analyzed conditions in episodes of school shootings over a two-year period revealed seven characteristics that shooters shared. Shooters shared a cluster of interests and habits that can serve as indicators of potential violence. All shooters reviewed:

- Were white males
- Complained of being taunted by schoolmates
- Did not perform well in sports
- Hated other races and subscribed to white-supremacist, Nazi philosophies
- Enjoyed violent videos and computer games along with music with violent or satanic themes
- Were fascinated with guns and gun magazines
- Collected information from the Internet on how to build bombs.

Most attackers engaged in some behavior prior to the incident that caused others concern or that indicated a need for help. They had difficulty coping with significant losses or personal failures, and some had considered or attempted suicide. Many felt bullied, persecuted, or injured by others prior to the attack, and they had access to and had used weapons prior to the attack.

# *Imminent Signs of Potential School Violence*

The federal government has issued early and imminent signs of potential violence in young people. These signs are summarized in *Early Warning, Timely Response: A Guide to Safe Schools.*[7] The publication cautions that warning signs do not necessarily mean causation; however, the greater number of the following characteristics a student manifests, the more likely those signs portend violent behavior on his part. Imminent signs suggest that a person may soon become violent. Such signs include fighting with peers or family members, destroying one's own or others' property, flying into a rage at the slightest provocation, putting out detailed threats of lethal violence, collecting weapons, injuring oneself, and threatening suicide. Bender, Shubert, and McLaughlin[8] (2001) analyzed random shootings that took place in schools during 1997 and 1998. Some characteristics of the random shooters were the following:

- Although no perpetrator was in special education, each one evidenced indicators to peers of fairly serious emotional problems, and each demonstrated a low regard for human life.
- The shooters were almost totally alienated from family and friends.
- Each shooter had "warned" others in advance of the violence by talking about killing in some context.
- Each shooter was a White male.

- Each perpetrator was average to above average in intelligence.
- Each perpetrator appeared to be deliberate in the violent actions on the day of the shootings.

Moreover, Bender, Shubert, and McLaughlin concluded that, for the most part, the shooters were what one might call "the invisible kids." Two of the invisible kids did not have a biological father in the home, and they tended to be overlooked by both their peers and their teachers. The kids are invisible because they do not exhibit the types of behavior problems that teachers immediately recognize as potentially violent. Some characteristics of the invisible kids were that they:

- Were motivated.
- Had no appropriate adult role models.
- Presented rarely behavior problems.
- Tended to be bullied rather than to be the bully.
- Were very planful.

# Causes of School Violence

There is no single cause of school violence; there are many causes. We also know that school violence is no respecter of ethnicity, race, or socioeconomic status. It occurs in wealthy school districts, just as it takes place in poor, inner-city schools. Researchers have, however, been able to identify persistent factors that are involved in school violence.

## Bullying as a Cause of School Violence

According to scholars,[9] bullying entails an individual seeking to undermine, humiliate, denigrate, or injure someone through such ways as teasing, taunting, insulting, depriving, physically assaulting, robbing, spreading rumors, and other behaviors. Bullying is the repeated and uncalled for aggressive behavior of one person toward another. It is a form of intimidation designed to threaten, frighten, or get a person to do something he would not do if the bullying were not taking place. Bullying exists when there is unequal power between two young people, such as bigger children picking on smaller ones or teasing a child who is thought to be different. It occurs when a child purposely and repeatedly holds power over another with the intent of hurting or shaming another.

Bullying is evident as early as preschool. Preschool-age children may bully other children to get attention, show off, or get what they want (toys, clothing). When preschoolers call people names or use unkind words, an adult should intervene immediately and consistently to teach acceptable behavior. Research shows that bullying increases as children move through elementary school. It peaks in middle school and decreases in late high school. There is an increase in teasing and bullying especially in the sixth grade when students try to fit in with others.

In 2005, about 28 percent of 12- to 18-year-old students reported having been bullied at school during the past six months.[10] Nearly half of all boys and girls surveyed said they had been bullied before. Girls are also bullies; however, they are more likely to harm another by spreading rumors, leaving other girls out of social events, teasing girls about their clothes or boyfriends, or threatening to withdraw their friendship. Children who are bullied are at a greater risk of suffering from depression and other mental health problems. Eight percent of urban middle and high school students miss one day of school each month because of fear of bullies.

Although much bullying happens where adults cannot see or hear it, it also happens when adults are present. Often adults do not do anything to stop the bullying. What children are frequent targets for bullies? A typical victim is likely to be shy, sensitive, and perhaps anxious or insecure. Some teens are picked on for physical reasons, such as being overweight or small, wearing different or "weird" clothing, or belonging to a different ethnic or racial group. Students who are isolated and without many friends tend to be bullied.

The consequences of bullying can be deadly for those who bully. A Secret Service study of school shootings found that almost three-quarters of the attackers felt persecuted and were bullied, threatened, attacked, or injured by others prior to the incident.[11] Bullying is, then, a major source of violence. Bullies have learned that their intimidation works with some people. They engage in bullying in order to feel more powerful and have more control of a situation. They continue their harassment as long as it works or as long as it makes them feel more powerful than the other person. The largest numbers of young people are not bullies but witnesses to bullying.

## How to Tell If Your Child Is Being Bullied

Although younger children may complain about being bullied to their parents, teachers, or adults they trust, it is highly uncommon for an older child who is being bullied to seek help. What prevents older youth from speaking out or telling on the bully? Usually, older youth feel shame and fear that things will only get worse or they believe that the situation is hopeless—"no one can help me." The bullied child may have voiced earlier complaints that adults dismissed, or he might have been told that being teased or bullied is a part of growing up.

Robert had repeatedly bullied Aaron everyday in their sixth grade classroom. The teacher did nothing to stop the badgering. Instead, she just told Aaron to ignore the behavior, and it would go away. But the constant belittling and degrading remarks did not stop. Red up with Robert's daily humiliation of him, Aaron picked up a chair and threw it at Robert. As a consequence, both were suspended from school. Aaron felt ashamed as he told his father why he threw the chair. "He just wouldn't stop, Dad. I got sick of it. I know that you told me not to fight in school, but I couldn't take it any longer. It was eating me up inside. So I threw the chair to get Robert to stop because the teacher did nothing, and I told her what was happening."

Aaron was surprised to see his father had a slight smile on his face while trying to look sternly at him. "What did the boy do after you threw the chair?"

"He did nothing. He just stood up stunned. Everyone was stunned . . . Even me. But I dared him to continue hitting me with spitballs and calling me names again, and he just stood there silent. I was shocked that the teacher called the office on the telephone and had us both taken out of the room. She never did anything when I complained about Aaron."

"That's all right son," his father said, as tears filled Aaron's eyes. But as his father walked away, he heard him say to his mother in the next room, "Yes! . . . Yes!"

Throwing the chair was not right, but it certainly was understandable. All too often teachers, school administrators, and parents expect children to take on a daily basis what none of them would endure for just one day. Sometimes it is only when violence actually erupts that adults take notice and do something about bullying. The greatest number of people involved in bullying are the bystanders—the onlookers who see the violence of one child toward another and do nothing about it. Many of these bystander bully supporters are adults.

The following are some signs that your child is being bullied at school:

- He has become quiet and withdrawn at home.
- He talks little about school, even when asked.
- He takes an unusual or long route to school.
- He comes home with cuts, bruises, or torn clothes or suddenly "loses" favorite clothes or possessions (bully stole them).
- He does not want to go to school, or talks about changing schools or moving.

## What Can Parents Do to Bully-Proof Their Children?

What can parents do to help bully-proof their children? Create quiet time so that your child can talk with you about bullying incidents at school. Ask him such questions as: How was school today? Who are the people you really like in school and get along with? Who are the people with whom you do not feel you have such a good relationship? Why do you feel that way? Have these children ever hit you or made fun of you? Listen to your child and record the facts as he sees them. Tell him that you will be there for him and that he is not alone. Reassure him that he does not deserve to be bullied and that it is not his fault that he is being bullied.

Encourage your child to form friendships with other children because children who have friends tend not to be vulnerable to bullies. Likewise, help him to develop a healthy sense of self-esteem because confident children are less likely to become victims of bullies. Start teaching the art of negotiation early so that he understands how to get out of difficult situations using words. For instance, if children are fighting over a toy, have them discuss how they can share the toy or take other steps to resolve the conflict.

Children need to have words readily available to help them counteract a bully's threats. Role play this scenario: have your child stand tall, look you in the eye, and say with the strongest voice possible two "I want" statements. Experts suggest saying, "I WANT you to stop that!" "I WANT you to leave me alone." "Stop it; get a life of your own." Also, make sure that he says no to a bully's demands right from the start. Research indicates that fighting back may increase the likelihood of continued victimization; however, passivity to a bully only invites further torment.

Suggest to children that they report the bullying to teachers, guidance counselors, or some other responsible adult. Monitor the situation by asking them for frequent updates about the bullying. Intervene if the bullying continues or becomes dangerous. Find out the school's policies and procedures for dealing with bullies. Report the bullying to school authorities and follow up to determine what is being done to stop it. Adults in the school need to know the extent of the bullying, where it takes place, when it happens, and what impact it is having on your children. Insist that the school take measures to discipline the bully.

## What If Your Child Is the Bully?

It is not easy to acknowledge the possibility that your child might be bullying another person. Usually children exhibit warning signs of bullying behavior as young as two or three years of age. Early on in life, bullies use aggression to resolve conflicts, and they typically refuse to accept responsibility for their own behavior, choosing instead to blame the other person for causing their bullying behavior. In addition, bullies demonstrate a lack of remorse for hurting other children; they may bully their siblings, act impulsively, and break family rules on a regular basis. Bullies delight in causing harm to animals or children who are younger or weaker. Another defining feature is that bullies may suddenly and unexplainably have extra spending money, or they come home with gifts of clothing and jewelry from "friends" at school.

Talk with your child about your concerns about his being a bully, the importance of resolving conflicts nonviolently, and the values of respect, compassion, empathy, and tolerance for others. Eliminate physical punishment in your home. Research shows that bullies are often raised in homes where physical punishment is the norm, thereby teaching children to resolve problems with violence. Spend time with your child doing things that both of you like. Consider professional counseling for your child.

# Lack of School Discipline: Another Cause of School Violence

Discipline continues to be a major issue in central city schools. About 46 percent of public schools reported taking some type of serious disciplinary action during the 2003–2004 school year. Of those actions, 74 percent were suspensions lasting five days or more, 5 percent were removals with no services, and 21 percent were transfers to specialized schools.[12] The likelihood of schools reporting violence increased as the school's enrollment increased. At schools with 1,000 or more students, 26 percent of principals reported student verbal abuse of teachers, compared with 14 percent of schools with 500–999 students, 10 percent of schools with 300–499 students, and 7 percent of schools with less than 300 students.[13]

Nearly 3 percent reported widespread disorder in classrooms, and 19 percent reported student acts of disrespect for teachers.[14] In 2003–2004, 2 percent of public schools reported daily or weekly occurrences of racial tensions among students. Both middle and high school teachers (83 percent) and parents (73 percent) of middle and high school students say the school experience of the majority of students suffers at the expense of a few chronic offenders. More than 1 in 3 teachers say they have seriously considered quitting the profession, or know a colleague who has left, because student discipline and disruptive behavior have become so intolerable.[15]

In 2003–2004, 83 percent of public schools controlled access to school buildings by locking or monitoring doors during school hours, and 36 percent controlled access to school grounds with locked or monitored gates. Metal detectors were the least observed security measure, with 11 percent of students reporting their use at school. Nearly all public schools required visitors to sign or check in when entering the school building (98 percent), while few schools required either students or visitors to pass through metal detectors regularly (1 percent each). The vast majority of students ages 12–18 reported that their school had a student code of conduct (95 percent).[16]

# School Climate and Student Violence

The school environment influences the potential for student violence in the school. [17] Although violence can take place in any neighborhood, some schools are safer than others. A safe school is one where the total school climate permits students, teachers, administrators, staff, and visitors to interact in a positive, nonthreatening manner that reflects the mission of the school.[18] A safe school is a place where education can be conducted in an environment free of intimidation, violence, and fear. It is a place where rules of student discipline are clearly communicated, consistently enforced, and fairly applied. Students do not feel threatened or afraid to walk about the school.

Safe schools emphasize a few major rules that have been agreed upon by students, teachers, and parents. Such rules should be specific and easy to understand. There is a consistency of behavioral expectations, and the consequences of breaking rules are incremental in nature, immediate, hard to avoid, and consistent throughout the school. High faculty expectations have been linked to school effectiveness more consistently than any other variable.[19] High expectations suggest a school climate where the faculty and staff expect all students to do well, believe in their ability to influence student achievement, and are held accountable for student learning.

## Gangs and School Violence

Many parents think that gangs are a problem only for the inner city, but gangs are everywhere—from the projects to million dollar mansions, gangs cut across ethnic and racial groups as well as across socioeconomic boundaries. Gangs with ties to California have for the past six years migrated eastward. Research indicates that gangs are spreading rapidly through many suburban communities. In 1999, law enforcement agencies reported active youth gangs in 100 percent of the nation's largest cities (those with populations of 250,000 or more), 47 percent of suburban counties, 27 percent of small cities (those with populations below 25,000), and 18 percent of rural counties.[20] It has been estimated that there are more than 24,500 different gangs within the United States, and more than 772,500 teens and young adults are members of gangs.[21]

In some instances, national gangs have entered some suburbanites' homes via the Internet, without their ever knowing it. Sometimes suburbanites are recruited into gangs because they lack criminal records. Gangs in suburban, small town, and rural areas are different from gangs in large cities. The most recently formed gangs in smaller cities and suburbs are more likely to be mixed ethnically and to involve females, as well as White and middle class youth.

Youth gangs are linked with serious crime problems in elementary and secondary schools in the United States. Students report much higher drug availability when gangs are active at their school. Schools with gangs have nearly double the likelihood of violent[22] victimization at school than those without a gang presence. Teens who are gang members are much more likely than other teens to commit serious and violent crimes. For instance, a survey in Denver found that while only 14 percent of teens were gang members, they were responsible for committing 89 percent of the serious violent crimes.

Nearly 41 percent of high school and 31 percent of middle school principals reported discipline problems involving gang activity during the 2003–2004 school year.[23] Higher percentages of students report knowing a student who brought a gun to school when students report gang presence (25 percent) than when gangs were not present (8 percent).[24] The presence of gangs doubles the likelihood of violent victimization at school (nearly 8 percent vs. 3 percent). The National Youth Gang Survey in 2003[25] confirmed that all cities with populations over 250,000 reported having gang activity. Nearly one-half of all gang members are Hispanic, and one-third are African American.

## Gangs—Not My Child! Are You Sure!— Clues and Warning Signs

If you are a typical parent, you would have difficulty believing that your child would ever join a gang. Let us hope that you are right. But just in case you are wrong, here are some clues and warning signs to look for that indicate the possibility that your child might be involved in a gang.

- Does your child use gang slang in everyday conversation? Does your child have an obsession with gangster influenced music, videos, and movies to the point that he is imitating them?
- Does your child have excessive pieces of clothing in two-color combinations, such as blue and black, gold and black?
- Does your son or daughter suddenly have a great need for privacy and refuses to tell you where he is going?
- Has your son or daughter withdrawn from former friends and refused to let you meet his new friends?
- Does your child have large amounts of unexplained cash or recently acquired expensive possessions?
- Does your child have gang graffiti written on books, on clothing, or inside the brim of his baseball cap?
- Does your teen wear gold or silver pendants and rings with the shapes of dollar signs, automatic guns, crowns, and so forth?

Young people just do not volunteer the information that they are in gangs. A big decision you might have to make is this: Should I search my child's room? How do I feel about snooping? Do the gains outweigh the possible loss of my child's trust? Remember that it is difficult for a person to get out of a gang. Gang members range in age from 10 to 60. So, if you are thinking that gang membership is just a passing phase, you may be wrong.

## Drugs and School Violence

Drugs are also not a respecter of a child's ethnicity/race or socioeconomic background. Young people in suburban communities may be able to evade detection of drug use because they have money to purchase drugs and because many parents do not know the warning signs of drug use until it is much too late. Hard core drug availability and sexual activity have been linked to violence among young people.[26] Half of all high schoolers and a quarter of middle schoolers reported that they attend schools where drugs are used, kept, or sold. Over half (51 percent) of youths aged 12 to 17 said it would be fairly easy to very easy for them to obtain marijuana, if they wanted some. About one-quarter reported it would be easy to get cocaine (24.9 percent) or crack (25.3 percent). Males are more likely than females to report that drugs were offered, sold, or given to them on school property in each survey year from 1993 to 2005. Approximately 74 percent of suburban twelfth graders and 71 percent of urban twelfth graders have tried alcohol more than two or three times. About four out of ten twelfth graders in both urban and suburban schools have used illegal drugs.

## *Is Your Child Using Drugs? Some Signs*

Parents are the first line of defense for blocking their children's drug use and for preventing school violence from use of these substances. Sometimes parents are the last to know if their teens are using alcohol and drugs. Therefore, the first step that parents are encouraged to take is to become familiar with the drugs available today. Learn the appearance of various drugs, their side effects, the terminology used to describe the drugs, and other drug lingo. Second, if parents want to prevent their children's use of drugs, they should talk with them about drugs at an early age—at about age ten.

There are three categories of signs that indicate drug use among young people: physical or biological signs, physical evidence, and behavioral changes. Physical signs can be red and bloodshot eyes, poor muscle coordination, pupils that are dilated, insomnia, sleepiness, sweating, watery eyes, and loss of appetite. To cover up the physical signs of drugs, some teens wear caps that they pull down over their eyes. They avoid conversations with their parents. Physical evidence provides the clearest indication that your child is using drugs—i.e., finding the drugs in your son's or daughter's room or car. Teens sometimes put drugs under mattresses, attach them to the back of drawers, or place them in the closet inside pockets of clothes that are never worn. Other physical evidence includes teens hiding drug paraphernalia (rolling papers, pipers, empty alcohol bottles, vials, aluminum foil that has been lit), wearing sunglasses or leaving Visine bottles around, and using incense burners and candles to cover up the scent.

The third set of signs is behavioral changes in your children if they are using drugs and alcohol. Check your teen's attendance record at school. Sometimes teens skip school or leave early to get high. Teens have been known to forge notes from their parents to account for their lateness or absence from school. When children are on drugs, they become irritable, secretive, more forgetful, and angry, and they spend less time involved with the family. They become less open to talking with their parents about new friends.

Teen addicts have pointed out that the most trusting parents are the ones who are the easiest to take advantage of. A good question is this: Are you paying for your child's drugs or alcohol? Some parents give their teens money to buy clothes and to eat out, but they use such funds for drugs. Teen alcoholics frequently get liquor from their parents' liquor cabinet. They first take alcohol that is clear and then they replace it with water. Some teens have found creative ways to get out of the house, even those with an alarm system—by using portable fire escape ladders from their rooms.

Parents might check their teen's vehicle after a Friday or a Saturday night to see if they can detect a strange odor coming out of it. Look for small pieces of joints—green leaf-like particles or seeds on the floorboards or seats. Also, look for white pasty substances on CDs, CD cases, dashboards, or mirrors that they might be using to do drugs. Ask for permission to look through your teen's pockets, purses, wallets, and backpacks. Consider giving your teen a random drug test.

Research has found that teens who have two or fewer dinners with their family per week are twice as likely to smoke and get drunk monthly, compared to teens who have at least five family dinners per week.[27] Have dinner with your child on a regular basis. Young people will tell you things over dinner that they might not mention during other times. The best antidote for prevention of alcohol and drug abuse is to develop an open and trusting relationship with your children.

## Dating Relationship Violence and Teens at School

What happens when young people who have not learned how to cope with their anger grow up to be teens and adults? One possibility is that they grow up to be abusive boyfriends and girlfriends. Some dating violence takes place right in the schools. Similar to adult domestic violence, teen dating violence is a pattern of coercive, manipulative behavior that one partner exerts over the other for the purposes of establishing and maintaining power and control, and it includes emotional abuse, physical abuse, sexual abuse, isolation, threats, intimidation, minimization, denial, and blame.[28]

Teen dating violence is alarming and cuts across race, gender, and socioeconomic lines. Both males and females are victims of dating violence; however, boys tend to be the more frequent abuser. Boys and girls are also abusive in different ways.[29] Girls are more likely to yell and threaten to hurt themselves. Boys injure girls more severely and frequently. One in three teenagers will experience abuse in a teen dating relationship. Females are much more likely than males to have serious injuries and to report being terrified. Girls in heterosexual relationships are much more likely than teenage boys to suffer from sexual abuse. In contrast, male victims seldom seem to fear violence by their dates or girlfriends. Boys often say that the attacks did not hurt and that they found the violence amusing.

Teen dating violence takes place in all types of relationships. In a study of gay, lesbian, and bisexual teenagers, youth involved in same-sex dating were just as likely to experience dating violence as youths involved in opposite sex dating.[30] Victims stay in an abusive relationship for many different reasons, including: fear of the perpetrator, self-blame, minimization of the crime, loyalty or love for the perpetrator, social or religious stigma, or lack of understanding. They hope that things will get better, but usually the violence escalates. Over a period of time, teens come to believe that they deserve the abuse.

### Teen Dating Violence in Schools

Victims and perpetrators of teen dating violence are more likely to bring a weapon to school. Five percent of girls reported missing at least one day of school during a 30-day period due to safety concerns. Forty-three percent of teen dating violence victims report that the dating abuse experienced occurred in a school building or on school grounds. Eighty-three percent of the abuse teen dating violence victims experienced at school was physical abuse. A recent study found that over 75 percent of school shootings were gender motivated, with the shooter often targeting former girlfriends or girls who had rejected him. [31]

### Parents and Teen Dating Violence

Only 33 percent of teens who were in an abusive relationship ever told anyone about the abuse. When female high school students were asked whom they would talk to if someone they date attempts to control them, insults them, or physically harms them, 86 percent said they would confide in a friend, while only 7 percent said they would talk to police.[32] Parents are likely to be in the dark about teen dating violence. Eighty-one percent of parents either believe that teen dating violence is not an issue or admit that they do not know if it is an issue. A majority of parents (54 percent) acknowledge that they have not spoken to their child about dating violence. If you have a teen who is dating, be alert for signs of physical and emotional abuse. The outward signs include: having bruises and injuries, changing the way she looks or dresses, dropping of old friends, and giving up things she cared about previously.

If you believe that your child is being abused, talk to her. She may find it difficult to talk about the dating violence. Try not to show anger, but rather let her know that you are there for her and that you want her to be safe. If you think your child is abusing his dating partner, confront him and seek professional help for him.

# Conflict Resolution Skills: An Effective School Violence Tool

Conflict is a natural and normal part of living and not a sign of failure.[33] A conflict may be defined as a struggle over values and claims to scarce status, power, or resources. Frequently, conflict is not about right and wrong, but actually about differences, especially differences in perspective and values. Conflict arises when it seems that satisfying one person's needs will block fulfilling those of another. Conflicts provide an opportunity to advance a person to a new level of learning and understanding. The question is, Can you help your children capitalize on the positives and make the conflict work for them?

Some people feel that compromise is an effective method for dealing with conflict; however, collaboration is a more effective method. Although compromise can be helpful, it can also lead to frustration and mistrust. Compromise tends to lead to the disputants' needs being only partially met. Collaboration leads to seeking solutions that meet everyone's needs because power is usually shared.

The family is a key influencer on how we handle conflicts. Families vary in how they resolve conflicts, depending upon the circumstances of the conflict and the person involved. Some families resolve conflicts by yelling, screaming, and hitting; while other families resolve conflicts by avoiding the underlying issue and by pretending that there is no difficulty. Both family approaches produce children who have difficulties solving conflicts in a positive and constructive fashion.

Conflict resolution education (CRE) programs teach children how to manage conflict so that they make good decisions rather than bad ones. Such programs also help children learn how to see conflict as an opportunity to build a relationship rather than to form an enemy. What is conflict resolution education? CRE developed out of the social justice concerns of the 1960s and 1970s with the work of the Society of Friends (Quakers). During the 1980s, the Educators for Social Responsibility created the National Association for Mediation in Education (NAME) which later merged with the National Institute for Dispute Resolution and its Conflict Resolution Education Network).[34] Some 20 years later, CRE programs are estimated to be in place in 15,000 to 20,000 of our nation's 85,000 public schools. In New York City, over 80,000 school children had experienced CRE. In three-fourths of San Francisco's public schools, there are student conflict managers, and all public school students in Chicago are required to take a conflict management course in ninth or tenth grade. [35]

## *Conflict Resolution: Identifying Emotions and Feelings*

Identifying our feelings accurately is the first step toward good interpersonal communication and successful resolution of conflict. Placing an accurate statement on our feelings helps us to know what next step to take. For instance, if you recognize that you are not really angry, but instead disappointed or hurt, you may be willing to take a look at your expectations or hurt. If you accurately described your hurt to your friend, she might be more willing to listen to you than if you labeled your feelings as anger. The following steps help to identify emotions aroused in a conflict situation:

1. *Name the emotion.* It is important to name our feelings, so that we have a clearer idea what feelings are involved. Be specific in identifying the emotion. Instead of saying, "She really made me mad," describe what is underneath the feeling of being mad.

2. *Claim ownership of the emotion.* Understand that it is your feeling, that no one made you feel this way. How you are feeling is your response (anger, sadness, etc.) to the conflict situation. A person might say, "I am feeling hurt. I own this feeling. My feeling may or may not be an appropriate response to the conflict,

but I acknowledge that it is still mine." To help yourself claim your emotional response, you might say, "This is my feeling. No one made me feel this way."

3. *Tame the emotion.* If you are not satisfied with the intensity of your feelings, you might engage in mental or physical activities that will help you reduce the intensity of the emotion. Some effective techniques include, taking deep breaths, counting to ten slowly, or taking a walk. It is important that you calm your emotions and not react.

4. *Reframe your emotion.* Place the emotion into perspective. Is this the first time you have felt this way? What are the specific contributors to this conflict? Do you have a history of previous conflicts with this individual? Can I reframe my feelings so that they become helpful in resolving the conflict?

5. *Aim the emotion.* Try to get an understanding of what you would like to do with your feelings. Do you need to talk with someone about the conflict or to obtain understanding of your role in the conflict?

## *Communicating Emotions Appropriately*

An essential part of resolving conflict is improving your communication skills. Effective communication takes place when people are able to exchange information accurately about facts and feelings. Poor communication results when people are not able to understand accurately the facts and/or feelings being shared. Factors that hinder effective communication include poor body language, poor listening, "you" statements, "loaded words," and an individual's unwillingness to acknowledge a different perspective.

## *''I'' Statements: A Conflict Resolution Technique*

"I" statements are used as a conflict management technique because they help individuals to get in touch with their feelings and they help people take responsibility for their own feelings and actions. "You" statements tend to blame the other person. "If you wouldn't have . . . ." And "You did it." The "I" messages help reduce or de-escalate a conflict before it gets really big. "I" messages helps people to identity their root feelings. An "I" statement helps an individual to reframe a situation. For instance, one might say: "I feel hurt and neglected when you don't let me know you will be late for dinner." Beginning with the statement "I" instead of "you" helps people to take responsibility for their own feelings and actions.

- I feel _____—put a name on the emotion and claim it.
- When _____—provide a nonjudgmental description of the troubling behavior.
- Because _____—describe the effects of the behavior.

## Steps for Resolving a Personal Problem

The following consists of six steps young people can use to solve personal problems.

- *Step One:* Decide if it is really your problem or someone else's problem. If you reach a decision that the problem is yours rather than someone else's, then acknowledge: "This is my problem, and I will do my best to solve it."

- *Step Two:* Name and describe the problem. Get a clear idea of what the problem is. Write a brief description of the problem. Name the feeling you have. "I feel. . . . "

- *Step Three:* Decide if you need to go to someone for help. Try not to get another person to solve the problem for you, but rather to listen and to make suggestions.

- *Step Four:* Listen empathically to the other person's side of the story. Listening is hard work and requires more than just looking at the person while he talks. Active listening is a term used to refer to a set of listening skills that entail good body language, listening, asking questions, and summarizing facts and feelings. Active listening is an important skill for managing conflict. When a listener asks clarifying questions and summarizes facts and feelings in a conflict situation, she enables the speaker to feel that she has been given a chance to be heard.

  Do not interrupt. Try to take the other person's perspective. Is the glass half empty or half full? Did Jim snub Nancy or not?

  Conflict often takes place when people perceive things differently. To resolve conflicts effectively, people must be willing to acknowledge, but not necessarily agree with, the other person's perception. To take another person's perspective, you must be willing to set aside momentarily your own perception and feelings to hear accurately the perception, feelings, and needs of another person. This technique allows disputing individuals to find common ground and to work toward a resolution.

  Ask open-ended questions so that the other person continues to explore her thoughts and feelings. Be careful of questions, especially the "Why" question, which tends to blame the other person. Tell the other person you want to listen to her viewpoint.

*Remember to:*

- Find a good time and place to talk.
- Avoid the blame game and get all the facts.
- Acknowledge feelings.
- Listen to what the other person is saying. One person tells his perspective of the conflict, including a message to say how he feels.
- The other person restates what the first person said (e.g., "What I hear you saying is. . .").
- Focus on the problem—not the person. Agree on what the problem is.
- You both agree to talk about the problem and follow ground rules.

- One person talks at a time, with no interrupting, no name-calling, and no put-downs.

- *Step Five:* State your positive intentions to resolve the conflict. "This difficulty between us really concerns me. I think if we sit down and talk, we can make things better. I am willing to spend the time necessary to improve the situation." Brainstorm possible solutions and summarize agreed upon points. All suggestions are accepted in the beginning and written down. If no solution seems possible, put the problem on the back burner and agree to meet again at a later date.

- *Step Six:* Evaluate options. Look for options that are fair and will work for both parties. Choose a solution where both parties can be winners. If this does not work and there is still a problem, ask someone for help.

Conflict resolution is not an easy simple process for beginners. It might be helpful to get the person to fill out a conflict resolution sheet. For instance, the sheet might ask the participant: Why do you think this conflict happened? How have you been feeling since the conflict? How do you think the other person has been feeling since the conflict? What do you both have in common? What do you both want? What do you think the other person wants? How could the situation be improved?

# *Conflict in Families*

Conflict occurs in all families. The matter of who owns what can be a major source of conflict in families. Families have conflict over issues related to "yours, mine, and ours." "Yours" is a category of ownership that suggests the possession is unavailable to another person. "Mine" means owned only by me, and "ours" includes shared possessions. Within these three categories, family members tend to have conflict over possessions, territory, and time. Possessions usually refer to material objects around the home. Possessions are either shared or owned individually. Territory refers to space and includes land, living areas, and work space. Territory can be owned by individuals, shared with the group, or owned by the public at large. Time is a resource that creates tension because people choose to allot time to such things as work, leisure, family, and fun.

Conflict can take place in families when family members make different assumptions about ownership, that is, what is yours, mine, and ours. Families may find the following table helpful in establishing what the rules are, who owns what, what can be borrowed, and what people would rather not share. Each family member should complete the form shown in Illustration 15 individually and then get together and discuss the responses. Family members might pay particular attention to what the others have written in their "Mine" column.

Illustration 15   Yours, Mine, and Ours Chart

| Resources | Yours | Mine | Ours |
|---|---|---|---|
| Possessions | | | |
| Territory | | | |
| Time | | | |

## *Understanding the Conflict and Differing Points of View*

Describe the conflict in a phrase consisting of five words or fewer. What is the conflict about? Is it about resources, values and beliefs, or psychological needs? The category of resources includes human resources, belongings and capital, natural resources, land, and territory. People, groups, and nations competing for the same resources may want to take someone else's resources or prevent an individual from getting needed resources. Values and beliefs form a second category of conflicts. The disputing individuals may have different deeply held beliefs about family, culture, politics, and religion. The third category of conflict involves psychological needs. This category includes power and control as well as emotional needs. Most individuals want respect, love, power over their own fates, a way to belong, and an opportunity to develop and achieve. When these needs are not met, conflict within families may occur.

Examine the relationships among the conflicting parties. The types of relationships among conflicting parties influence the intensity of the conflict and its outcome. Do the parties come to the conflict with equal power or a power imbalance? Is a positive relationship valued equally by both parties? Other issues revolve around the history of the conflict. Sometimes the longer a family conflict exists, the more intense and complete it becomes. Factors that complicate family conflict include:

- The *duration of the conflict*—how long has it continued?

- The *frequency of the conflict*—how often has the conflict reemerged? Are there periods when the conflict has escalated to extreme levels? Did the conflict develop in stages, and, if so, what were they?

- The *intensity of the conflict*—what is the emotional climate among the conflicting parties? Is the climate trusting or suspicious, friendly or hostile, open or closed, calm or emotionally intense? How life threatening is the conflict? Is the conflict emotionally or ideologically charged? How does the intensity of the conflict affect possible resolution of the conflict?

## Rules for Families Fighting Fairly

All families fight at some point. It is important to establish rules for family fighting rather than to extinguish it all together. These rules can also be combined with the family conflict resolution skills presented in the previous section. The rules are as follows:

Rule #1: State your needs honestly without any tricks or manipulations. What do you want and what do you need from the other person? You must sort out what your needs really are. Stating your needs means saying things like "I want..." or "I need..." without blaming anyone. State why your needs are important to you.

Rule #2: Do not attack the other person. When you verbally attack the other person, even if what you are saying is accurate, it is difficult to resolve the fight in a constructive manner.

Rule #3: Do not bring up old wounds. Old wounds leave scars, and if you open up the old wound, it will take even longer for the healing process to begin. Bringing up old wounds occurs when one party begins a sentence with: "You never...," "Every time I... you," "I remember the time when you...." These sentiments confuse what is happening right now with what happened two days ago or ten years ago. Stay with the present so that you will be able to hear what the other person needs and wants from you. In addition, the two of you will be listening to each other instead of defending yourselves against your past mistakes and crimes.

## Conflict Resolution Skills for Families

Families use the same conflict resolution and mediation skills that children learn in school. It is important for parents to create a calm, neutral space in their home where family members can feel good about talking about problems. Establish regular times to discuss family problems, and give everyone a turn to speak. Make sure that you listen to your children's grievances and take them seriously, or they will not listen to the complaints of other people. Try to get to the "why" of the conflict, not just "what happened." Set up clear expectations for each family member and create win-win situations at home.

Parents model and coach children to solve problems by asking reality-checking questions that focus on children's strengths, hopes, and future goals. All family members acknowledge and practice solution-building sessions. Parents facilitate the solution-building process between siblings by active listening and posing problem-solving questions and encouraging each child to contribute to the solution. All family members practice active listening and use "I" messages to maintain an environment that helps each person to state his needs and interests.

Some suggestions are that, in listening to their children, parents should pay attention to them, that they not interrupt, and that they reserve judgment until the child has finished and asked for a response.

Parents become aware of how they are responding to their children. They might say: "I am very concerned about. . ." or "I understand that it is sometimes difficult. . . ." These are better ways to begin talking with a child than by saying, "You should," or "If I were you," or "When I was your age we didn't do. . . ." Parents remain aware of body language and tone of voice during the solution-building process. Each family member must ask himself two questions: "How can this problem be resolved so we can all live in harmony?" and "How can this problem be resolved in a way that will allow each person to feel the solution is fair?" Endeavor to build solutions that will permit each person involved in the conflict to satisfy his interests.

The primary job of an adult facilitator of a conflict situation is to help the children remain focused on the problem and the problem-solving process. In the beginning, parents gather data about events and feelings. They then decide what parental options they will use. If you plan to help the children negotiate, avoid blaming the other child (even if you think someone is at fault). Instead, ask each child to state his perspective of the problem. Parents might find the following questions helpful: What happened? Why do you think this happened? How did you feel when you. . ..?

Parents help children to state the problem clearly. It is easier for children to solve a problem if they have a clear understanding of the problem. State the problem in terms of both children's needs. For instance, a parent might say: "You want to. . . and Kathy wants to. . . ." Or, "I know you are both upset about what happened. What are some of the things that we might do so that both of your needs will be met?"

Next, parents help children to brainstorm or to generate lots of ideas.Write the ideas down and encourage children to suggest silly ideas as well as practical one. Focus on the children's ideas and resist the temptation to add your ideas unless you are asked. Help children to evaluate the ideas. Encourage children to tell you how their ideas are similar to or different from their brother's or sister's ideas. Avoid criticizing children's ideas. If a child offers an idea that is not constructive, help him or her to evaluate the idea in the next step.

During the process of evaluating the different ideas, assist children in looking at the consequences. Have them answer the question: "What might happen if you . . . ?" "How might Jennifer feel if you . . . ?" Do the suggestions result in a win-win alternative? Parents ask children for a decision, and they help children plan. Parents help their children to review the alternatives, reach a decision, help plan how to implement the idea, and decide on a time to evaluate their plan. Children's resolutions should work for everyone to have a win/win solution.

## Helping Children after Violence or Tragedy Has Occurred at School

What do parents tell their children when news of school tragedies such as those at Virginia Tech or Columbine is played repeatedly on television? Such violence is shocking and frightening to children primarily because it disrupts the way they see the world. When threat of violence is high, children feel unsafe, and they begin to worry that it can happen to them or to those whom they love. When violence takes place in schools, a place where children are supposed to be safe, it can be particularly upsetting to children. Parents can reduce the emotional effects of school violence or tragedies at their children's school by using strategies to help them regain a sense of safety and security.

It is important that parents monitor the amount of time their children spend watching television. When children repeatedly watch images of violent death due to school shootings, their feelings of vulnerability increase. Ask your children what they have heard or what other children are saying about the violent incident. Children may ask such questions as, What does execution style murder mean? Although it is not necessary to become graphic, you might respond: "It means that it was done on purpose; it was not an accident."

Try to ascertain your child's concerns about the violent incident. You might say to your child: "After seeing the school violence on television about Virginia Tech, are you worried about anything at your school?" Young children tend to ask "why" questions, such as: "Why did the boy shoot all those people?" You might explain to your child that we do not know the exact reasons why these shootings occurred, but that the people who did the horrific acts were very troubled and were not able to think clearly about how to deal with their thoughts and feelings. They were not able to control their anger or their desire to hurt others. They also did not tell anyone about these thoughts and feelings in time for parents and teachers to help them to take another route to solve their problems without hurting anyone.

Parents can teach children the importance of getting help when they cannot control their angry feelings. Explain to your child: "Sometimes people have thoughts and feelings or problems that make them feel hurt or confused inside. They need someone to talk with in order to clarify their mixed-up thoughts." Then, ask your child: "Who would you talk to if you were feeling hurt, scared, or confused inside?" Have your child name several people whom they might go to if they were feeling very angry, and they could not seem to control their angry feelings toward others.

Reassure your child that the adults in his school have taken appropriate actions to make sure that he is safe. "The grown-ups in your school, such as the principal and teachers, work with the police to make sure that your school is safe." Talk with your child about the things his school does to protect students from violent acts. Your messages to your children should focus on safety measures at their school.

To help your children cope when school violence occurs, make sure you keep their daily routine intact. Routine provides your children with a sense of security. The routine of school, after school activities, and sports help children to feel that the world is safe. Spend as much time as possible as a family. Connecting with family members helps children to feel that there is a safety net of people around them. Monitor your children's behavior after they have observed school violence on television or in their own schools. For instance, some signs that children may be experiencing stress related to school violence are nightmares, inability to stop thinking about the event, refusing to attend school, or worrying excessively about something bad happening to them.

## How Parents Can Prepare When a School Emergency Happens

No parent wants to encounter emergencies at his school. School emergencies are supposed to happen at someone else's school. But if one were to occur, would you know how to handle it? Are you even familiar with the procedures that would be taken? During an emergency, it is critical that parents receive information from school officials before going to the school or scene of an emergency. As a parent, there are three steps you can take to prepare for a school emergency, and these are as follows:

- Provide accurate emergency contact information to your child's school and notify the school if it changes.
- Carry a school emergency card for parents at all times.
- Know a means to gain access to the school via a hotline or the Internet.

If your school has adopted other measures, find out what they are and become involved.

## Facts and Terms Every Parent Should Know

Every parent should become familiar with terms schools use when emergencies happen. For instance, parents should know different lockdown terms. During a high-level lockdown, all school interior and exterior doors are locked and students are confined to their classrooms; no entry or exit of the school is permitted. High-level lockdowns take place if there is a threat or possible threat at the school. You will know if your school is in a high-level lockdown because the main entrance doors are locked, and a sign might be posted on the front door indicating that the school is in a high-level lockdown. During a low-level lockdown, all school interior and exterior doors are locked. This type of lockdown takes place if the threat is outside the school. Parents may be admitted into the school with proper identification.

If the school building is evacuated, you will need to know how to locate your child. Typically, each school has a procedure for helping parents to locate their child. Parents will be directed to a specific location where they will be required to show proper identification. Students are released only to an adult that is documented as an emergency contact. If you are a noncustodial parent, you must be listed with your child's emergency contact information as a guardian and show proper identification. Generally, every school conducts emergency drills throughout the school year so that students and staff know effective steps to take.

## The Parental Spiritual Journey and School Violence

Almost everyone who is a parent has gone to school and hence knows what it is like to be in school with other children who may or may not like you. Getting through K–12 is not easy. I have always said that if you could make it through high school, you have passed a major hurdle in life. College tends to be a lot easier because it offers something that elementary, middle, and high schools do not, and that is a certain level of anonymity. You can spend an entire semester attending a class where some of your classmates may not even know your name.

In trying to help your own child through his journey in school, you need to reach back and revisit your sitting in your first grade class or kindergarten. Do you remember what you wore to school one day, and do you recall how the other children treated you? Were you popular or just kind of average so that few people ever really noticed you? Did children choose you first or last to be on their teams? If you could use five words to describe your experience in school, what would they honestly be?

Spending a little time one day mentally revisiting your elementary school, junior high or middle school, and senior high school will probably bring back both sad and happy moments. We all want school to consist of happy moments for our children. What can you do to make school happier for your child? All too often, parents see their children's participation in schools to be opportunities for their own "reflected glory." Sometimes we push our children to get good grades or higher grades than what they might be capable of earning. Are the grades for the children, or are they for us, the parents, and our desire to have positive reflective glory to show that we have been good parents.

If the burgeoning research on social emotional learning is accurate—that is, what really matters in life is a person's ability to have social emotional intelligence, not academic intelligence, then we may have to reconsider what emphasis we want to place on what kind of learning for our children. Further, the research suggests that violence in the schools occurs because of young people's problems with self-regulation of emotion and anger management, as well as with their inability or difficulty in getting along with their peers.

Some of the school murderers were excellent academic students. Many of these young people were hurting so much inside that instead of going to their parents and teachers, they took matters into their own hands and killed others. I am just wondering what might have happened if parents had spent as much time emphasizing the importance of their children's social emotional development as they did their academic performance. Feel grateful if your child eschews violence. Thank yourself, your family, your child's teachers, principals, fellow students, and a whole lot of people you probably do not remember if life either has turned out all right for your child or seems to be in the process of turning out okay.

Your child's education is broader than anything he will receive in a 45 minute class period at school. While teachers and counselors are extremely important, your child's most important teacher is you. And probably much of what you taught him that will have a meaningful impact on his life came during quiet moments that you least expected would have such an effect. There is the saying that "we learn most of what we need to learn about life in kindergarten." Take a spiritual journey with your child. Go back to school with him and sit in his seat to catch a glimpse of what he might be seeing and feeling.

# *Summary*

Schools are relatively safe places to be; they are far less violent than the recent shootings in them would indicate. Violence occurs in schools when children do not learn how to self-regulate their emotions, how to control their anger, and how to respond to bullying and conflict with others. Parents need to learn as much as possible about school violence because it takes place in most schools, regardless of the location or socioeconomic status of parents. It is important for them to learn about the safety procedures at their children's school and to keep such information readily retrievable.

Parents need to spend time talking with their children and having dinner and fun with them. All of the violent shooters in schools were estranged or disconnected from their parents in some kind of way. A good many of the shooters were bullied in their schools, while adults were bully bystanders and did very little or nothing to stop the abuse. Adults—parents, teachers, and counselors—need to take a more active role in bully prevention.

Social emotional learning and conflict resolution are good prevention devices to use to combat school violence. When children are taught conflict resolution techniques, they tend to feel empowered that they are equipped to handle conflict and negative situations. Not enough emphasis is placed on social emotional learning in our schools, even though research has demonstrated that it largely accounts for adults' success in life. There needs to be better balance in our school's curriculum so that we teach core academic subjects and also the skills necessary for young people to become emotionally capable, productive citizens.

# Parental Reading List

## Books about Bullying

*Nobody Knew What to Do: A Story About Bullying* by Becky McCain. Albert Whitman & Company, 2001.

*Stop Picking on Me* by Pat Thomas. Barron's Educational Series, 2000.

## Ages 6 to 9

*Arthur's April Fool* by Marc Brown. Little, Brown & Company, 1990.

*Blue Cheese Breath and Stinky Feet: How to Deal With Bullies* by Catherine DePino and Bonnie Matthews. Magination Press, 2004.

*How to be Cool in the Third Grade* by Betsy Duffey. Puffin, 1999.

## Ages 10 to 12

*Bullies Are a Pain in the Brain* by Trevor Romain. Free Spirit Pub., 1997.

*Crash* by Jerry Spinelli. Knopf, 1999.

*Freak the Mighty* by Rodman Pilbrick. Scholastic, 2001.

## Books for Parents

*And Words Can Hurt Forever: How to Protect Adolescents from Bullying, Harassment, and Emotional Violence* by James Garbarino. Free Press, 2002.

*Easing the Teasing: A Parent's Guide to Helping Children Deal with Name-Calling, Ridicule and Verbal Bullying* by Judy Freedman. Contemporary Books, 2002.

*Mom, They're Teasing Me: Helping Your Child Solve Social Problems* by Michael Thompson. Ballantine Books, 2002.

## Books on Teen Dating Violence

*Ending Violence in Teen Dating Relationships* by Al Miles. Augsburg Fortress Publishers, 2005.

*But I Love Him: Protecting Your Teen Daughter from Controlling Abusive Dating Relationships* by J. Murray. Harper Collins Publishers, 2001.

*Saving Beauty from the Beast: How to Protect Your Daughter from an Unhealthy Relationship.* Little, Brown & Company, 2004.

# Intentional Parenting Tips to Prevent School Violence

## How to Tell if Your Child is a Bully

Answer yes or no to the following questions. "Yes" responses suggest your child may have a problem bullying. Counseling may be a good step for you to take with your child.

*Yes/No*

1. Does your child disobey you on a regular basis?
2. Does your child have a bad temper, or is he hotheaded?
3. Do your child's teachers complain of disruptions in class caused by your child?
4. Has your child been sent home from school for fighting?
5. Has your child ever stolen money or property from you?
6. Is your child easily frustrated?
7. Does your child show a lack of warmth toward you or his siblings?

## Test Your Knowledge about School Violence

_____1. In 1996–1997, how many public schools in the United States reported one or more serious violent crimes?
   a. 33 percent
   b. 10 percent
   c. 25 percent
   d. 71 percent
_____2. Out of every 100 suburban high school boys, how many are likely to own a gun?
   a. 2
   b. 15
   c. 20
   d. 33
_____3. According to teachers, violence in schools occurs most frequently in:
   a. Bathrooms
   b. Lunchrooms
   c. Hallways and stairways
   d. Classrooms
_____4. Which is the most common weapon children take to school?
   a. Knife/razor
   b. Firearm
   c. Pepper spray
   d. Club

_____5. What is the most common antiviolence strategy used by schools?

    a. Security personnel

    b. Suspension

    c. Locker searches

    d. Expulsion

_____6. Under the federal law, Gun-Free Schools Act of 1994, public schools are required to administer which punishment to students taking a firearm to school?

    a. Expulsion for a full year

    b. Suspension for six months

    c. Suspension for two months

    d. Fine of $5,000 and suspension for two months

_____7. Where does homicide rank as a cause of death among people aged 10 to 24 years old?

    a. First

    b. Seventh

    c. Second

    d. Fourth.

Answers: 1. D; 2. C; 3. C; 4. A; 5. B; 6. A; 7. C.

## *School Safety Checklist*

Use this list of questions to find out about your child's school safety. Take this checklist with you to your next PTA meeting and review it with other parents.

### *The List of School Safety Questions*

1. Is student safety a priority for your school and your community?

2. Do parents have access to reports that include information about the number of violent or other unsafe incidents at the school?

3. Does your school have a procedure for responding quickly to unsafe situations?

4. Is your school addressing ways to protect from as well as respond to crises?

5. Are the school board, school principal, school superintendent, school staff, parents, students, and community professionals all involved in these efforts?

6. Are counselors and psychologists available to work with students who are troubled or disruptive?

7. Do students in all grades participate in classes to help them develop conflict resolution and other life skills?

8. Does the school emphasize promoting self-esteem and respect for others in all aspects of the school program?

9. Does the school have fair, firm, consistent discipline policies?

10. Is safety addressed in all aspects of the school program—the cafeteria, physical education, classrooms, playgrounds, and after school programs?

## Quiz on School Violence

Complete this quiz to test your knowledge of school violence. Answer True/False to each of the questions below.

1. The most common form of intervention in schools and society directed at bullies is punishment.

2. Adults involved in the care of children always know bullying behavior when they observe it.

3. Age is an important risk factor for being victimized because younger children are less likely than older children to have developed physical, cognitive, and social skills that can protect them from peer attacks.

4. Approximately 25 percent of students report being afraid that violence in their school will increase in the next two years.

5. Teachers' relative lack of awareness of peer victimization further encourages this behavior.

6. Students who report (high or low) levels of anger at school also tend to characterize themselves as angry in various other aspects of their lives.

7. About 10 percent of children are bullied at school.

8. Violence is a major cause of school-related injuries in children.

9. Racial and ethnic minorities feel less safe at school.

10. Despite media reports of homicides and other serious violent crimes in schools, schools are relatively safe.

Answers: 1. True; 2. False; 3. True; 4. True; 5. True; 6. True; 7. False (25 percent); 8. False; 9. True; 10. True.

# 6

# Reducing the Impact of Television and Media Violence

*By the time an average American child reaches 18 years old, he will have witnessed on television 200,000 acts of violence, including 40,000 murders.*

Over the past couple of decades, American society has engaged in a heated debate over whether or not television and other media forms cause young people to act violently. Most Americans probably have an opinion about whether or not children's viewing violence on television contributes to their later violent behavior. Thirty years of research, however, points to a clear causal link between media violence and aggressive behavior in children. Currently, well over 1,000 studies, including reports from the Surgeon General's office, the National Institute of Mental Health, and numerous other organizations (e.g., American Psychological Association) have concluded that viewing entertainment violence can lead to increases in aggressive attitudes, values, and behavior, particularly in children.

There is ample real life proof that television's depiction of violence can lead to crimes being committed and to death. Within the past several years, criticism of MTV's *Jackass* forced the network to pull the plug on the show because of increasing imitation and pressure from parents and organizations. This action was taken because two young boys poured gasoline on each other and then struck a match after they had watched an episode where a trained professional put on a fireproof suit and barbecued himself. In Nevada, one teenage child was killed and two others seriously injured while lying down along the center line of a highway. The boys admitted that they were imitating a scene from the Touchstone movie, *The Program*.

In Ontario, Canada, a five-year-old boy set his house on fire, killing his younger sister. The boy's mother blamed her child's actions on the MTV show *Beavis and Butt-head.* Several of the school shooters in the United States were addicted to violent television and video games. During April 1999, Eric Harris and Dylan Klebold, dressed in black trench coats, fatigues, and ski masks, opened fire on their schoolmates in Littleton, Colorado, leaving 12 students and a teacher dead, and 23 others wounded. They had made a video of themselves replaying a scene from *The Basketball Diaries,* in which the characters wore trench coats and pretended to be gunmen shooting their friends in the hallway. Children tend to imitate the behavior they see. They see a great deal of violence in countries that have electronic technology readily available.

Brandon Centerwall, an epidemiologist, has provided some clues regarding the relationship of television and violence in an entire society.[1] Centerwall analyzed homicide rates in the white populations of the United States and Canada between 1945 and 1974, and later the white population of South Africa. He found that homicide rates doubled during the first 10 to 15 years after television was introduced in the United States and in Canada. Centerwall studied South Africa because television was not introduced there until 1974. The homicide rate had been stable or had dropped in South Africa before the introduction of television in 1974. Within 10 years, it had doubled, just as it had done in the United States and Canada when television became widespread after 1950.

Some South African scholars have pointed out that apartheid may have been a factor in keeping a low violence rate; hence, the violence increased dramatically once apartheid was lifted. Still scholars estimate that the media account for between 5 percent and 15 percent of the violence in many Western societies. In a population of approximately 300 million in the United States, 5 percent adds up to a large number of people who may be violently victimized due to the influence of media violence.

David Grossman, a former army lieutenant colonel and professor at West Point, has studied the psychology of killing.[2] Grossman points out that normally human beings avoid killing members of our own species. During past wars, American soldiers shot over the heads of their enemies, even though doing so increased the risk to their own lives. Military officers worried about such behaviors because they wanted their troops to shoot to kill. In response, the military developed technologically advanced programs to desensitize soldiers and to train them to shoot first and to think later. Currently, the United States army uses computer programs and simulated battlefield conditions, such as replacing bull's-eye targets with pop-up humanoid figures that fall down, spurting red dye, when shot. These computer programs desensitize army trainees and help them to overcome their inhibitions about shooting another human being. As a result, American soldiers have been reversing the previous tendencies to shoot over the enemies' heads. Grossman has stated:

In Vietnam, a systematic process of desensitization, conditioning, and training increased the individual firing rate from a World War II baseline of 15 to 20 percent to an all-time high of up to 95 percent. . . . Men are shown a series of gruesome films, which get progressively more horrific. The trainee is forced to watch by having his head bolted in a clamp so that he cannot turn away, and a special device keeps his eyelids open.[3]

One consequence of desensitization training was that some soldiers did not face the reality of their having killed others until they returned home from combat, and that is when their grief and guilt occurred. Some soldiers suffered from a post-traumatic stress disorder once they could no longer repress their actions in battle.

According to Grossman, Americans are allowing similar desensitizing techniques to be used with their children every night in their homes via television and video games. Each week, and quite possibly each night, children witness violent scenes of people killing each other via various types of media. Grossman has stated:

We allow increasingly more vivid depictions of suffering and violence to be shown as entertainment to our children. It begins innocently with cartoons and then goes on to the countless thousands of acts of violence depicted on TV as the child grows up and the scramble for ratings steadily raises the threshold of violence on TV.[4]

Young people and adults do not imitate every behavior that they see, but, instead, they choose which actions to copy. People imitate others when they are similar to themselves or because they like them. Young people tend to imitate violent acts when they are performed by heroic, highly charismatic characters who seem invulnerable and who are either rewarded or not punished for their violent actions. When people see violence as justifiable, they identify with the aggressors rather than with their victims.

Hollywood films and television programs often make violence look exciting without showing any real life consequences (horrible wounds and disfigurement). Films that have produced copycat killers include *Taxi Driver*, a movie that John Hinckley saw at least 15 times before he tried to assassinate President Reagan. In the film, Bickle tries to protect a 12-year-old prostitute Iris, by shooting her pimp and by making himself a hero. Jody Foster played Iris. Paul Schrader had based the character Bickle on Arthur Bremer, who had tried to assassinate George Wallace. Hinckley imitated Bickle by collecting weapons and obsessively thinking about Jodie Foster, whom he would "rescue." Hinckley is still in a mental hospital.

It is important that parents understand what we know about the influence of the media on young people's display of violence. Parents make informed decisions about their approach to television, video games, and internet use when they have an understanding of the research on media violence. This chapter explores the influence of various forms of media violence on young people's behavior. It begins with some statistics and an analysis of what happens with the brain when we see violence depicted.

# Violence and Young People's Brains

Our brains hold many of the secrets of who we are and why we do what we do. It is important that we understand what kinds of things influence the brain's functioning. For instance, Matthews and Kronenberger have reported that watching violent television programs or video games may influence children's minds, even if they do not have a history of aggressive behavior.[5] These researchers found that nonaggressive children who had been exposed to high levels of media violence had similar patterns of activity in an area of the brain linked to self-control and attention as did aggressive children who had been diagnosed with disruptive behavior disorder.

In this study, researchers measured activity in the frontal cortex (the front part) of the brain in two groups of 14 boys and five girls while they performed a task requiring concentration. Youth who have less activity in the frontal cortex of the brain have problems with self-control and attention. One group of children was labeled aggressive because they had been diagnosed with disruptive behavior disorder, and the other group had no history of behavior problems. Half of the children in each group were exposed to high levels of media violence—that is, violence that exceeded the average amount of time spent each week watching television programs or playing video games showing human injury.

The results indicated that all of the aggressive children had a reduced activity in their frontal cortex while completing the task, regardless of their levels of media violence exposure. Yet, researchers also found that nonaggressive children who had high levels of media violence exposure showed a similar pattern of low activity in the frontal cortex. Children in this group who were not exposed to high levels of media violence had more frontal cortex activity. Matthews and Kronenberger asserted they were studying the neurological and self-control processes that underlie aggressive behavior and watching or participating in violent media. That is, viewing violent acts on television or in other media forms affects the activity in the frontal cortex of our brains, and there is some concern that these brain changes may be enduring or long lasting.

# Mental Health Effects of Violence in the Media and Young People

Two main research questions have been asked: How do children process media violence? What are the mechanisms by which viewing violence might lead to changes in children's attitudes, values, and behavior? Researchers have identified three main effects of media violence:

- Media violence leads to fear and the belief that the world is a dangerous place.
- People become desensitized to media violence. Viewing violence may lead to a greater willingness to tolerate violence in the broad society.
- Young people may become more aggressive after viewing violence, and they may develop favorable attitudes and values about the use of aggression to resolve conflicts.

These conclusions about media violence are supported by the American Medical Association's *Physician Guide to Media Violence,*[6] which stated that media violence:

- Causes an increase in mean-spirited, aggressive behavior among young people and adults;
- Produces increased levels of fearfulness, mistrust, and self-protective behavior toward others;
- Contributes to individuals' desensitization and callousness to the effects of violence and the suffering of others;
- Provides violent heroes whom children seek to emulate;
- Gives justification for resorting to violence when children think they are right;
- Creates an increasing appetite for viewing more violence and more extreme violence; and
- Promotes a culture in which disrespectful behavior becomes a legitimate way for people to treat each other.

Several studies have supported the American Medical Association's conclusions that children become desensitized after viewing violence.[7,8] Desensitization takes place when a child no longer responds to a threatening situation. For instance, when most people view violence, they experience the physiological response of "fight or flight." Gradually over time and with repeated exposure within the context of entertainment and relaxation, many children show decreasing emotional responses to the depiction of violence and injury. For instance, Molitor and Hirsch[9] reported that desensitization to violence led children to wait longer to call an adult to intervene in a witnessed physical altercation between peers. Mullin and Linz[10] found that media violence resulted in a reduction in sympathy for victims of domestic abuse. Because there are so many television channels and movies on video, today's youth have greater opportunities for desensitization to violence than ever before.

A study with older youth has indicated that the hostility engendered by violent media is not necessarily short-lived. Zillman and Weaver[11] randomly assigned male and female college students to view either intensely violent or nonviolent feature films for four consecutive days. On the fifth day in a supposedly unrelated project, the participants were asked to help or hinder another person's chances of future employment. Both the male and female college students who had been exposed to the daily dosage of movie violence were more willing (than those who were exposed to nonviolence) to undermine the person's job prospects, regardless of whether or not he had treated them well or had behaved in an insulting fashion. The researchers concluded that the viewing of repeated violence provided an enduring hostile mental framework that damaged interpersonal interactions that either were affectively neutral or involved provocation.

# Television, the Most Prevalent Media Form, and Violence

The television and entertainment media have a more intense relationship with children today than at any other time in American history. American children spend an enormous amount of time watching television or entertaining themselves with some form of the media. To understand the impact of television violence on children, we need to examine the number of hours children spend using some form of media.

By the time the average child leaves elementary school, he will have witnessed at least 8,000 murders and more than 100,000 other assorted acts of violence on television. By the time a child reaches 18 years old, he will have witnessed on television (with average viewing time), 200,000 acts of violence, including 40,000 murders.[12] Young children (ages 0–6) spend nearly 25 hours a week using screen media (watching television or movies, playing on the computer).[13] Young people 8–18 years of age spend 44.5 hours per week watching TV, playing video games, and listening to music. They spend more time involved with media than they do with their parents (17 hours) or at school (30 hours). Even when families are together, they may not spend much time communicating because 63 percent of children 8–18 live in homes where the TV is on during most meals. On average children ages 6 to 17 choose television as their top after school activity.

Many children do not have to watch television in the living room with their parents. About 36 percent of children age six and younger have a TV in their bedroom, compared to 68 percent of children 8–18. A good percentage of parents (53 percent) of children age 8–18 years old have no rules about TV. Young people multitask, with 26 percent of 8–18 year olds using more than one media device at a time.

The violent content on television programs is high. Nearly two out of three TV programs contained violence, averaging six violent acts per hour.[14] There are more than twice as many violent incidents in children's programming than in other types of programming. The average child watches two hours of cartoons a day and may see more than 10,000 violent acts a year. Many parents fail to see the violence in children's cartoons; hence, it is important to watch cartoons with your child.

Sexual content appears in 64 percent of TV all programs. Programs with sexual content average 4.4 scenes per hour. Only 15 percent of programs that contain sexual content include messages about risks like sexually transmitted diseases or unplanned pregnancies. On average, music videos contain 93 sexual situations per hour, including 11 "hard core" scenes depicting such behavior as intercourse and oral sex.[15] As of the year 2000, all new television sets now contain a V-chip that parents can program to filter out objectionable programs.

Two areas of technology are emerging to change the way we and our children use media, and these are the following: (1) interactive television with the convergence of television and Internet use; and (2) the revolution in wireless communication (cell phone and Internet access). With the advent of digital television, television sets will be able to receive signals over a great bandwidth. Digital TV allows people a more interactive use of television than was the case previously. Increasingly, television will become a place to do shopping, play games, e-mail friends, and view movies. People will be able to have interactive programs where they can switch from a television program to an Internet Web site that has more information about what is being watched. Eventually, viewers will be able to purchase any item they see in a TV program by merely clicking on it.

Research has found that teens who watched more than one hour of TV each day were four times more likely to commit aggressive acts in adulthood. In a study of third and fourth graders, reducing TV and video game consumption to less than one hour a day decreased verbal aggression and physical aggression by 40 percent. About 72 percent of teens think watching TV with a lot of sexual content influences their peers' behavior somewhat or a great deal.

Moreover, studies have also found that viewing violence produces intense fears and anxieties among children. The survey of Singer, Slovak, Frierson, and York[16] of more than 2,000 third through eighth graders in Ohio showed that as the number of hours that children watched television each day increased, so did the prevalence of symptoms of psychological trauma, such as anxiety, trauma, and post-traumatic stress disorder. Similarly, the survey of Owens, Maxim, McGuinn, Nobile, Msall, and Alario[17] of nearly 500 children in kindergarten through fourth grade in Rhode Island found that the amount of television viewing (especially at bedtime) and the presence of a television in the child's own bedroom were significantly related to children's frequency of sleep disturbances. Nearly 9 percent of the parents surveyed indicated that their child experienced television induced nightmares at least once a week. Moreover, a random national survey showed that 62 percent of parents of children between the ages of 2 and 17 reported that their child had been frightened by something they saw in a television program or movie.[18]

The age of children has a great deal to do with what they fear as a result of viewing television.[19] As children mature, they become more disturbed by realistic portrayals of violence and less frightened by unrealistic dangers.[20] For instance, preschool children aged three to five tend to be frightened by something that looks scary, but is actually harmless. In comparison, elementary school children age 9 to 11 years respond to the actual behavior or destructive potential of a character, animal, or object. Whereas preschoolers responded to images of bloodied victims with expressions of emotional distress, older elementary school children were concerned about their own vulnerability to attack and death.[21] Such changes result from developmental trends in children's understanding of fantasy and reality. As children grow older, they become frightened by the news or media depictions of world problems. For example, television's repeated depictions of the events of September 11 and their aftermath frightened young people differently based on their ages.

Television's depiction of violence may reinforce a child's tendency toward aggression, or it may increase aggression in a young child who is already exhibiting aggressive behavior. Children who evidence emotional, behavioral, learning, or impulse control problems may be more easily influenced by TV violence. Young people can be influenced by television violence even when the family atmosphere shows no tendency toward violence. Television violence is not the only cause of violent behavior. It is, however, a significant factor in children's development of aggressive behavior.[22]

# Viewing Violent Television: Long-Term Enduring Effects

The fact that viewing violent television is harmful to children's brains is alarming to most Americans. Yet, what is equally disturbing is the recent research that confirms the effects of viewing violent television may be long-lasting and enduring.[23] A study by Huesmann et al. found that television viewing between the ages of six and ten predicted children's antisocial behavior as a young adult. Both males and females who were heavy television violence viewers as children were significantly more likely to participate in serious physical aggression and criminal behavior later in life. Moreover, children who were heavy violence viewers were twice as likely as the others to engage in spousal abuse when they became adults, even when the researchers controlled for additional potential contributions to such abuse, including socioeconomic status and parenting practices.[24]

Other studies have also shown the long-term effects of violent media on children's fears and anxieties.[25,26,27] Studies indicate that intensely violent images often induce anxieties in children that linger and interfere with their sleeping and waking activities for years. Likewise, many young adults report that the frightening media images they saw as children have remained on their minds in spite of their repeated attempts to get rid of them. How many parents can still remember the horrible images in the movies *Psycho* or *Poltergeist?* What did it take to erase the *Psycho* shower scene from your mind? Some adults refused to swim in lakes or pools after they saw *Jaws,* even though they knew Jaws was a shark in the ocean and that a shark would not be in the swimming pool in their backyard. Some adults still report that they are uncomfortable swimming in lakes or pools because of the enduring emotional memory of the absolute terror they experienced when they saw the movie as a child.

Researchers have yet to discover what makes these emotional memories so enduring and still so frightening, even though we realize that they were movies. What happens to children's brains as they watch these frightening movies? What kinds of lasting changes take place in their brains? The research of Matthews and Kronenberger, which mapped the areas of the brain that are most influenced by violent images, might point us in the right direction.[28] Such studies offer the promise of clarifying why violent television and movies have enduring effects on the emotional memory of children. Yet, even if memories of violent television and movies were not enduring, we have to ask ourselves: Is this the kind of childhood memory we want our children to build?

# Television Viewing and Children's Physical Health: Obesity and Bone Structure

Researchers are even beginning to connect children's television viewing with physical and mental health risks. Approximately 30.3 percent of children (ages 6 to 11) are overweight and 15.3 percent are obese. For teens (12 to 19), the rate is almost identical: 33.4 percent overweight and 15.5 percent obese.[29] A preschooler's risk of obesity jumps 6 percent for every hour of TV watched per day, and the risk jumps to 31 percent if the TV is in their bedroom. Another study found that children who watch more than three hours of television a day are 50 percent more likely to be obese than children who watch fewer than two hours. These researchers concluded that "more than 60 percent of overweight incidents can be linked to excess TV viewing."[30]

Obesity puts children at risk for a number of health problems, including type II diabetes (adult onset), which is closely connected to weight. According to the Centers for Disease Control, 60 percent of overweight children between the ages of five and ten years of age already have at least one risk factor for heart disease, including elevated blood cholesterol, blood pressure or increased insulin levels. These factors lead to hypertension, diabetes, and atherosclerosis.[31]

Preschool children with TVs in their bedroom watched an additional 4.8 hours of TV or videos every week.[32] A study from Stanford University measured body weight differences between two sets of third and fourth graders. One group was taught how to lessen their time watching television and playing video games. The second group received no such instruction, and their TV and video game playing time went on as usual. The first group had a seven-hour a week limit on television and video game time. This freed up 14 hours for them to do something else.

The results indicated that the children who watched less television and played fewer video games had a significant reduction in measures of obesity, such as body mass index. The children who watched their usual amount of television had higher indicators of obesity. The only difference between the two groups was the amount of television and video game playing each performed.[33] As obesity becomes a major health problem for our youth, it is important to encourage them to become more active. Limiting screen time and removing televisions from bedrooms can be significant first steps toward helping children to start a more physically active lifestyle. When children have daily exercise, it helps to control their weight, build lean muscle, and reduce fat. It may improve blood pressure and cholesterol levels. In addition, regular exercise reduces anxiety and stress and increases children's overall energy level.

Moreover, researchers are finding that increased television viewing and subsequent lack of exercise may even affect children's bone development. Early childhood is a time of tremendous growth for children, and the amount of physical activity positively affects the strength and amount of bone mass developed. A study of preschoolers found that girls who watched more television measured lower in the amount of hipbone density.[34] Regular exercise for children helps build healthy bones, muscles, and joints.

# Television and Educational Achievement of Children

Children spend more time watching television than any other activity except sleeping. Television's impact on reading and other academic skills vary depending upon the amount of television watched, what is being watched, and the age of the child.[35] Studies have found that children who watch carefully constructed educational programs such as *Sesame Street* perform better on prereading skills at age five than do children who watched infrequently or not at all.[36,37] These same studies also indicated that children who watch cartoons or other purely entertainment television shows during their preschool years do poorer on prereading skills at age 5. Children between the ages of three and five are at a critical stage in brain maturation for the development of language and other cognitive skills. Heavy television viewing can influence the development of the brain's neural network in a negative way.

Television viewing displaces time the child would spend in other activities and verbal interactions. When television displaces the time a child would otherwise spend on reading practice, that child is delayed in acquiring reading skills. In a national education study, students reported spending four times as many hours each week watching television as doing homework.[38] Children who are heavy TV viewers (over three hours per day) show the greatest decline in reading ability. Television on in the background interferes with the retention of skills and information during homework time.[39]

Television viewing patterns established with preschoolers have an impact on their later development. Children who watch informative, educational television as preschoolers were inclined to watch more informative television as they got older. Conversely, children who watched more entertainment television watched few informative programs as they aged. In a longitudinal study of high schoolers, researchers found that viewing educational television programs as preschoolers was associated with higher grades, more reading, less aggression, and more value placed on academics when those children reached high school.[40]

The research evidence is clear. If you want your child to succeed academically in school, start him off with limited television viewing that has large dosages of educational information, such as *Sesame Street.* Shut the TV off when your child is doing homework, and by all means read to your child on a daily basis. When parents read to their children, they gain important vocabulary skills, and they learn to value education more than do children who are not read stories. Programs that children watch should be limited to carefully, thought-out, educationally-oriented programs. Such programs should be geared to the age of the child, be nonviolent, and reinforce language and social skills.

# Impact of Television Advertising on Children and Teens

The average American child sees 40,000 commercials each year on broadcast television.[41] Children as young as age three recognize brand logos, with brand loyalty influence starting at age two.[42,43] Young children are not able to distinguish between commercials and TV programs. They do not recognize that commercials are trying to sell something.[44] In 2000, children 12 years and under, directly and indirectly, influenced the household spending of over $600 billion. Children who watch a lot of television want more toys seen in advertisements and eat more advertised food than children who do not watch as much television.[45]

Children are the focus of intense advertising pressure seeking to influence billions of dollars of family spending. Advertisers understand that children influence the purchase of not just children's products anymore, but everything in the household from cars to toothpaste. They spend more than $10 billion targeting children and youth through TV ads, coupons, contests, public relations promotions, and special packaging design for children. Approximately 80 percent of the TV commercials that children see each year are for fast food, candy, cereal, and toys. During Saturday morning cartoons, an average of one food commercial is shown every five minutes.

Cartoon and toy characters are used on various kinds of products, seeking to catch the children's eyes and influence purchases. Databases of young customers are being built from information gathered on Internet sign-ups and chat rooms, from electronic toy registries at stores like Toys "R" Us, and from direct surveys. There is also daily school-permitted advertising in schools. Advertisers take advantage of schools' severe budget crunches, and they offer cash or products in return for advertising access to children.

## Television Messages

Parents can help their children by teaching them to recognize and decipher media messages. Every advertisement has a message that is directed toward getting someone to buy a product or service. Parents teach children that they have a choice to accept or reject an advertiser's message. Children can participate in activities with parents to help them develop skills to discern different media messages. Teach children making a game out of the following:

- Play "Spot the Commercials." Help your child learn to tell the difference between a regular program and the commercials that support it.
- Do a "taste test" to compare a heavily advertised brand with a generic or nonadvertised brand of cookie or soft drink (for example, a cheap brand of cola with the name brand Coca-Cola). Ask your child and his friends if they can tell the difference between the two products. When you see a movie, video, or video game with your child, discuss if what happens on the screen would happen in the "real" world. For instance: "Would a real person be able to lay on a railroad track and have a train roll over him without getting hurt?"
- Watch a music video with your child. Ask your child how the music video makes him feel. What violent and sexual images are contained within the video? Is there any alcohol or tobacco in the video? Then turn off the sound and the video and watch it silently. How does your child feel about the video without the sound?

# Suggested Guidelines for Television Viewing and Children

The American Academy of Pediatrics[46] has recommended that the total television viewing time for children be limited to no more than two hours per day, that programs should be nonviolent, that they be geared to the age of the child and reinforce language and social skills. Tips to foster healthy television use include:

- Videotape TV shows for your children so that they have a backup when there is nothing appropriate on the television for them to watch. When they have homework that needs to be completed, videotape their favorite programs to watch later.
- Keep television sets out of children's bedrooms.
- Avoid using the TV as a babysitter.
- Know what your children are watching. Be careful of the emotional images that you allow in your child's life.
- Set guidelines about what your children watch on television and when they watch it. For instance, there is no TV permitted before homework is completed.
- Turn off TV during family meals. Use family meals to share stories and activities from each family member's day.
- Put the family on a TV diet. Incorporate activities that are fun for your family to replace watching television. When you do watch TV, watch it with your children and talk with them about what is happening on the programs.
- Create a TV coupon system. Children get coupons and turn them in when they watch a program. Unused coupons can be "cashed" in for a special family activity.
- Do not make the TV the focal point of the room. Make your children the focal point of the room. Research shows that people watch less TV if it is not in the most prominent place in the room.

# Other Media Use and Young People

Youth are wired for media use more than ever before. The televisions in their bedrooms are usually hooked to cable or linked to VCRs and video game machines. The Internet is reached via a nearby computer or over a cable hookup. Most American children grow up in a home with an average of 3.6 CD or tape players, 3.5 TVs, 3.3 radios, 2.9 VCRs/DVD players, 2.1 video game consoles, and 1.5 computers.[47] About 83 percent of young people 8 to 18 have at least one video game player in their home, 31 percent have three or more video game players, and 49 percent have video game players in their bedrooms. A little over 96 percent of U.S. households own a television set, and 99.9 percent of these are color TVs. About 31 percent of young people have high speed Internet access at home. Of those who have Internet in their homes, 89 percent use e-mail; 84 percent search entertainment sites; 81 percent play online games; 76 percent search for current events; and 75 percent participate in instant messaging.[48]

American society has become a wired and a technologically sophisticated society. Computers have revolutionized how we communicate with each other. Young people can communicate on a daily basis with people whom they have never seen or have never met in person. Intimate conversations with faceless people may be replacing the conversations family members used to have with each other. Violence can enter our children's minds via media forms without parents having even a clue that this is taking place. All children have to do is to retreat to their bedrooms where there may be an assortment of media using violence that affects their brains.

# Video Games and Violence

Video games constitute an important media form that increasing numbers of children are using. In fact, video and computer games are the fastest growing form of media that young people use. The United States' video game market reached almost $10.5 billion in sales in 2005, and has a projected worldwide market of $46.5 billion by 2010.[49] Since 1995, almost 3 billion video games have been sold globally. The worldwide video game market garnered $25 billion in 2004. Online gaming, which currently brings in just fewer than $300 million per year, is projected to account for over $2 billion by 2009.

A recent report indicated that 45 percent of heavy video game players and almost a third of avid gamers are in the 6- to 17-year-old age group.[50] A study of over 2,000 children 8 to 18 years old (third through twelfth graders) reported that 83 percent of them have at least one video game player in their home; 31 percent have three or more video game players in their home, and 49 percent have video game players in their bedrooms. In that same study, only 21 percent of the youth said that their parents set rules about which video games they can play; 17 percent indicated their parents check warning labels or ratings on video games; and 12 percent reported they play video games they know their parents do not want them to play.[51]

## Who Is Playing Video Games?

During the mid-1990s, fourth-grade girls were playing video games at home for 4.5 hours per week and boys for 7.1 hours per week. The most recent data from third to fifth grades indicate that boys now play 13.5 hours and girls play them for nearly 6 hours each week. The fact that boys play more video games is noteworthy because boys account for the largest percentage of violence among youth. Although boys play more video games than girls, the industry views the female market as one of its primary areas for potential growth.[52]

It is projected that children's and teens' use of video games will continue and perhaps become more difficult to track because of improved and expanded technology. During the 1990s, young people played video games at home in front of the TV for three hours a week. Technological advances have changed the setting and the ease with which video games can be played without their use being easily detected by parents. Increasingly, games are available through sophisticated mobile phones, which also serve as Internet devices and cameras.

There are two significant trends in video games. First, there is an increasing number of adult themes. The video gamers who were 15 years old are now in their mid-twenties, and many of them still play video games. As a result, the video games have adopted mature themes that contain sex, graphic violence, violence against authority figures, especially police, and even sexualized violence against women. Although these games are intended for adults, children frequently gain access to them when they are purchased by unsuspecting parents. For instance, *Grand Theft Auto: San Andreas* has violence and mature adult themes; yet it continues to be accessible to and popular with young children.[53]

The second major trend involves the growing popularity of online role-playing games. During the past ten years, broadband connections have made it possible for the rise of massively multiplayer online role playing games (MMORPG). Millions of people play these games in cooperation and in competition with each other. *World of Warcraft* is one of the most popular of these games. Four million players worldwide pay $15 a month to play *Warcraft*. Although $720 million per year may appear to be a lot of money, it is not when one considers the number of hours some MMORPG players spend online in their games.

## The Positive Side of Video Games

Not everything about video games is negative. Video game playing introduces children to computers and information technology. For girls, such games offer a good way for them to be introduced to increased fine motor and spatial skill development. In addition, video games are entertaining and fun; they give occasions for parents and children to play together. Some reasons children give for playing video games include: the games are fun, relieve boredom, and give them a sense of mastery and control.

Whether or not video games have a good or bad influence on children depends on the content of the games and how the children use them. Moreover, video games can be excellent teachers for academic skill development and now even for exercising. They give practice in following directions and in logic. Video games can teach children new languages, help them recover from painful procedures, and get them interested in complicated plot lines and problem solving. Researchers have found that skill in a game requiring 3D navigation is related to 3D mental visualization skills. Another study showed that demonstrated skill on video games and past experience with video games were the best predictors of surgeons' advanced laparoscopic surgical skills. Further, playing games that require the player to constantly scan the screen for information improves visual attention skills to computer screens. Parents should know the positive effects of video games and how they can tap into those positive effects.

## The Negative Effects of Video Games: Violence and Sex

A decade of research on video games has focused largely on whether or not they increase aggression. Meta analyses, which combine the results of all studies on a topic, have found that there is a significant relationship between violent video game playing and aggression. Across studies, violent video games have significant negative effects on young people's physiological arousal, aggressive thoughts and behaviors. Additionally, the more young people play video games, the less likely they will exhibit positive youth behavior.

Practicing violent acts via video games may contribute to aggressive behavior.[54] Game environments are typically founded on plots of violence, aggression, and gender bias. Many games give repeated dosages of weapons, killings, kicking, stabbings, and shootings. One study found that with 607 eighth and ninth grade students the total amount of time playing video games directly predicted poorer grades, but was not directly related to antisocial or aggressive behaviors. In one study, playing violent games predicted aggressive behaviors, but it did not predict poorer school performance.[55] This finding did not hold up, however, in other studies.

Children have been found to manifest a hostile attribution bias after playing a highly violent martial arts game. That is, they attribute to others negative rather than positive intent in certain situations. For instance, if someone looks at them or approaches, they anticipate that the person intends harm to them. Kirsh asked 9- to 11-year-old girls and boys to play one of two video games: (1) a nonviolent sports game called *NBA Jam: TE;* and (2) the other a somewhat sanitized version of *Mortal Kombatt II,* a highly violent martial arts game. After playing either game, the children were read five stories that had provoking incidents in which the intention of the provoker was unclear or ambiguous.[56]

One story portrayed a child getting hit in the back with a ball, but it was unclear whether or not the child (usually a same sex peer) had thrown the ball on purpose or by accident. In responding to questions about the playmate's intent, the children who had just played the violent video game were more likely than those who played the nonviolent game to attribute bad motives and negative feelings and to anticipate that they would retaliate if they were in that situation. Kirsh concluded that violent video games encourage children to have a hostile attribution bias or a negative cloud over their interpersonal relations with others.[57]

Additional criticisms of video games include: women are often portrayed as weaker characters who are helpless or sexually provocative, and some games have explicit sex. Games can cause young people to confuse reality and fantasy. Many games do not offer action that requires the player to demonstrate independent thought or creativity. In a number of violent games, players must become more violent to win. In "first person" violent video games, players may be more affected by violence because they control the frame and experience the action through the eyes of their character. Players' overdependence on video games fosters social isolation because they often play alone. Some of the violent school shooters were isolated from their peers, families, and teachers because they spent an inordinate amount of time playing solitary video games.

# Video Game Ratings

The Entertainment Software Rating Board (ESRB) is an industry organization that has developed a rating system for computer, Internet, and video games. Most games sold in the United States are rated using this system. Video game ratings have different logos showing age recommendations. The bottom line is that parents must always check out a game for themselves before letting their children play it. A brief description of these ratings is given below:

- Titles rated **EC (Early Childhood)** have video game titles that have content that may be suitable for persons ages three and older. Titles in this category contain no material that parents would find objectionable.

- Titles rated **E (Everyone)** have video game titles that have content that may be suitable for persons ages six and older. Titles in this category may contain minimal cartoon, fantasy or mild violence and/or infrequent use of mild language.

- Titles rated **E10+ \*= (Everyone 10 and older)** have titles that may be suitable for persons ages 10 and older. Titles in this category may contain more cartoon, fantasy or mild violence, mild language, and/or minimal suggestive themes.

- Titles rated **(T)** are teen rated games that have content that may be suitable for persons ages 13 and older. Titles in this category may contain violent content, mild or strong language, and/or suggestive themes.

- Titles rated **Mature (M)** have content that may be suitable for persons ages 17 and older. Titles in this category may contain mature sexual themes, more intense violence, and/or strong language.

- Titles rated **Adults Only (AO)** have content suitable only for adults. Titles in this category may include graphic depictions of sex and/or violence. Adults Only products are not intended for persons under the age of 18.

- **Rating Pending:** Used only for advertising and/or marketing materials created for titles that have been submitted to the ESRB and are awaiting a final rating.

- **Content Descriptor:** Over 30 standardized phrases that indicate content that triggered a particular rating and may be of interest or concern.

Most children's parents continue to be unaware of the games they play. Studies have found that M-rated games are very popular and easily accessible for youth of various ages. Many parents still do not stop their children from getting a video game because of its rating. Parents must understand the ratings and know why it is so important to pay attention to them. Questions parents might ask about their child's video games include: How graphic is the violence? Is the violence against humans or inanimate objects? Is the violence sexual? What are the consequences of the violence?

### Computer and Video Game Addiction

A person is said to be addicted to playing video games when time spent playing harms his family and social relationships or disrupts his school or work life. The criteria for addiction are the person spends up to ten hour a day or more rearranging or sending files, playing games, etc., and he spends 70 to 80 hours a week gaming. The psychological payoff of the video game replaces the emotional life that his family used to provide. In order to keep feeling good, the addicted person spends more time playing video games or searching the Internet. When an addicted individual has to spend time away from the computer or game, he experiences moodiness or withdrawal symptoms. Other symptoms of video game addiction include:

*For children:*

- Spending most nonschool hours on the computer or playing video games.
- Receiving declining grades because of time spent on the computer.
- Lying about video game use.
- Choosing to use the video game rather than being with friends.
- Dropping out of social and sport groups.
- Becoming irritable when not playing a video game.

*For adults:*

- Experiences intense feelings of pleasure and guilt when playing games.
- Obsesses and is preoccupied about playing video games.
- Disrupts family, social, or work life to spend hours playing video games.
- Lies about video game use.
- Has withdrawal symptoms when not playing video games.
- Cannot control video game use.
- Replaces former emotional life with video game playing.

# *Violence, Music, and MTV*

Music is a significant part of young people's daily media diet. Teens use music to shape their cultural identity and to help define their social group. In fact, some social groups are identified primarily by their choice of music. Preadolescents and adolescents listen to music (including radio, CDs, tapes, and music videos) between three and four hours per day.[58] By eleventh grade, girls generally listen to music a half-hour more than boys do each day. Teens consider musicians their heroes more frequently than they do athletes, and they rate the influence of music higher than that of religion or books.[59] Teens use music to enhance or intensify their mood or to change mood directions. Although teens identify more than

20–30 music styles, only rap and heavy metal bring about the most controversy over song lyrics.

## Heavy Metal Music and Violence

Most heavy metal fans are not at-risk, but troubled, at-risk youth gravitate to heavy metal music, which correlates positively with casual sex, greater drug use, suicidal thoughts, drunk driving, and conflict with parents and problems at school. Typically youth become alienated from mainstream school culture, and then they choose heavy metal music. The angry, depressive, violent lyrics of hard rock and heavy metal music may be a risk factor for suicide and violence for those adolescents who are already depressed and suicidal. According to the American Academy of Child and Adolescent Psychiatry, the troublesome lyrics of some teen music:

- Advocate and glorify the abuse of drugs or alcohol
- Present suicide as a solution
- Display graphic violence
- Focus on the occult with Satanism and human sacrifice
- Describe harmful sexual practices and a devaluing of women

The Parents Music Resource Center has reported that American teenagers listen to an estimated 10,500 hours of rock music between the seventh and twelfth grades alone—just 500 hours less than they spend in school over 12 years. A survey by the Recording Industry Association of America found that many parents do not know what lyrics are contained in the popular music to which their children listen. Parents need to pay attention to the music lyrics of their children's favorite recording artists so that they understand the messages their children are receiving about sex, women, and violence.

## Rap Music and Violence

Rap music tends to glamorize gangsters, drugs, and sex. The lyrics are often violent because they are based on the lives of the performers. Teens who spend a great deal of time watching the sex and violence depicted in the "reel" life of "gangsta" rap music videos are more likely to practice these behaviors in real life. A study was conducted with 522 African American girls between the ages of 14 and 18 from nonurban, lower socioeconomic neighborhoods. Researchers found that compared to those who never or rarely watched these videos, the girls who viewed the gangsta videos for at least 14 hours per week were far more likely to practice numerous destructive behaviors. They were

- Three times more likely to hit a teacher
- Over 2.5 times more likely to get arrested

- Twice as likely to have multiple sexual partners
- About 1.5 times more likely to get a sexually transmitted disease, use drugs, or drink alcohol

DiClemente's research team is currently expanding its research to investigate how these and other rap videos may influence behaviors across other racial, gender, and socioeconomic lines. This concern is prompted by the fact that although gangsta rap videos depict tough inner-city "street" life, their largest viewing audience is White suburban youth, who have better access to cable television channels, such as MTV and BET (Black Entertainment Television).[60]

## MTV and Violence

MTV celebrated its twenty-fifth birthday in 2006. Its programming consists of music videos by top-selling artists. MTV reaches 350 million households on a global basis.[61] Music videos are designed for teenagers between 12 and 19 years of age. Seventy-three percent of boys and 78 percent of girls in the 12 to 19 years of age group watch MTV. Boys watch for an average of 6.6 hours per week, and girls watch for an average of 6.2 hours per week.[62] In one study, 75 percent of concept music videos (those that told a story) involve sexual imagery and more than half involve violence—usually against women.[63] In more than 80 percent of the violent music videos, men are the aggressors.[64]

According to some research, even modest viewing of MTV and other music videos results in significant exposure to glamorized depictions of alcohol and tobacco use. When lyrics are acted out in a storytelling music video, their impact is enhanced. Music videos appear to contribute to teens' desensitization to violence. The use of violence by music video stars makes it normal and more acceptable to teens. At least two experiments show that watching MTV results in more permissive attitudes about sex. One study found that college students who were assigned to watch MTV developed more liberal attitudes toward premarital sex than peers who did not watch MTV.[65] Greeson and Williams reported that seventh and ninth graders were more likely to approve of premarital sex after watching MTV for less than one hour.[66]

# Violence, the Internet, and Children and Adolescents

The Internet (or the Net) is a vast network that connects people and information worldwide through computers. It comprises a huge, but almost invisible universe that includes thousands of networks, millions of computers, and billions of users across the world.[67] The Internet is sometimes called the information superhighway. The World Wide Web (WWW or the Web) is a part of the Internet that includes pictures, sound, and text.

Parents who are not computer savvy need to learn the vocabulary associated with computers and the Internet. For instance, "online" means being connected to the Internet. "Surfing the Web" means browsing or searching for information on the Internet. A "blog" is a Web log or an online journal or diary that can include images. They can be found on social networking Web sites, and they are becoming more popular than chat rooms. Chat rooms are a way for a number of computer users to communicate with each other instantly in "real time." For instance, if you type a message and send it, everyone else in the chat room will see it instantly, and they can respond to it just as quickly.

The Internet can connect your family to many different types of resources. Using your computer, you can read the latest news, look up information, listen to music, play games, buy things, or e-mail friends. There are endless possibilities for learning and exploring on the Internet. In addition, the Internet brings the world—the good, the bad, and the ugly—to the American family's doorstep.[68] A major issue with using the Internet is parental control.

More than 80 percent of American youth, ages 12 to 17, use the Internet, and almost half log on daily.[69] Many adolescents prefer being online to other media, including the telephone, TV, and radio. According to the Pew Internet and American Life Project, the overwhelming number of teens use e-mail (89 percent); 75 percent use instant messaging (IM), which permits them to have multiple simultaneous conversations with a defined group of peers. Over 50 percent of teens have more than one e-mail address or screen name, which they can use to send private messages to friends or to participate anonymously in online forums, such as chat rooms. Continuous access to the Internet gives adolescents opportunities to connect with their peers as well as with complete strangers from across the world.

The Internet is transforming the social world of adolescents because it is influencing how they communicate, establish and maintain relationships, and find social support. It is a new social environment in which adolescents can explore a number of their issues, including identity formation, sexuality, and self-worth. Because it is a social environment, the Internet enables multiple communication functions, such as e-mail, IM, chat, and blogs, to permit young people to participate and to co-construct their own environments. Hence, it is highly important to gain awareness of both the positive and negative effects of Internet use.

## Positive Uses of the Internet

The Internet is a powerful tool for both networking and academic enhancement for children. Linda Jackson at Michigan State University found that low-income youth who consistently used the Internet exhibited higher grade point averages over the course of time than did less frequent users. Evidence also suggests that Internet communications may be advantageous for shy, socially anxious, or marginalized youth, primarily because they are able to practice social skills without the risks associated with face-to-face interactions. The freedom from social pressures helps adolescents to build up their confidence about meeting others.

## Negative Effects of the Internet

The Internet has caused varying social concerns about privacy, security, pornography, Internet crime, and virtual community.[70] According to recent polls, the number one media concern parents have is about the Internet. Approximately 85 percent of parents reported that among all forms of media, the Internet posed the greatest risk to their children.[71] Such parental concerns are understandable, given that teens are essentially free to view and post whatever they choose and to communicate with whomever they want without their parents' knowledge.

Another reason for parental concern is that the Internet has become a highly effective and profitable means of distributing sexually explicit material as well as a sophisticated means for engaging in compulsive sexual behavior and sex crimes.[72] According to a survey conducted by the London School of Economics, 90 percent of children between ages 8 and 16 have seen pornography on the Internet. An investigation of chat conversations has revealed that chat participants often resort to the age/sex/location chat code to share identity information. A nationwide poll found that half of teens ages 13–18 often communicate through the Internet with someone they have not met in person; one-third have talked about potentially meeting someone face-to-face whom they have only met through the Internet. Moreover, almost 12.5 percent found out that someone they were communicating with online was an adult pretending to be much younger.

Millions of teens have revealed personal identification and pictures of themselves on such Web sites as *MySpace* and *Facebook*. It is important that young people understand that being online is the same as being in public. Although using the Internet at home may feel safe and secure, there are very real privacy issues. Personal information can be obtained easily when young people create "member profiles" with Internet service providers, on a Web site or in a chat room. "Cookies" allow outside sources to see inside one's home computer. This information can be misused by marketing experts who direct products at children and by child predators.

A number of children have been contacted by someone they met over the Internet. Those most frequently involved are in the 12–17-year-old age group, especially girls. Such contacts are usually initiated through chat rooms or instant messaging, with subsequent contact continuing via e-mail. Although the majority of perpetrators are male, women can also be involved.

The Internet may encourage false identities. People online are not always who they say they are. Anyone can put information online. Young people can unexpectedly and unintentionally find materials on the Web that are offensive and/or pornographic (including child pornography). It is important that parents have a set of rules to guide their children's use of the Internet. Make sure your children know what you consider appropriate and what areas are off limits.

## Cyber-bullying

Another area of concern for parents is cyber-bullying. Online bullying, called cyber-bullying, happens when teens use the Internet, cell phones, or other devices to send or post text or images intended to hurt or embarrass another person. Some youth who cyber-bully: (1) pretend they are other people online to trick others; (2) spread lies and rumors about victims; (3) trick people into revealing personal information; (4) send or forward mean or nasty text messages; and (5) post pictures of victims without their consent. Another potentially damaging technique is to obtain someone's password and then send inappropriate material to someone else using the victim's e-mail account. Although reliable statistics on Internet bullying are not available, estimates range from 6 percent to 25 percent of American children have been bullied in cyberspace. Almost a third of those who were bullied told no one about the cyber-bullying. To prevent cyber-bulling, teens can block communication with the cyber-bully; delete messages without reading them; talk to a parent or friend about the bullying; or report the problem to an Internet service provider or website moderator.

### How can parents provide cyber safety!

Parents can provide cyber safety by using Internet blocking or filtering software, talking with your children about safety on the Internet, and establishing family rules about Internet use, such as children cannot give out family information without the parents' consent. Internet filtering comes in two categories: (1) software that the parent can load onto the computer at home; and (2) programs that can be activated through the Internet provider, which will filter Web sites for you. The filtering mechanism on these programs work by scanning sites and blocking those that contain specific words, by blocking sites that are found to contain sexually explicit, violent, or hateful material, and by limiting a child's search to a predefined set of sites or to sites that need certain categories. None of the devices are totally effective in blocking all objectionable sites. The Web is too big and changes too quickly.

## Some Tips for Parents

Parents must look for strategies to encourage safer and more positive operation of the World Wide Web. Talk with your children about what they are seeing and doing on the Internet. Ask them about the people they meet on the Internet. Make sure that your children talk with you directly about anyone they have met on the Internet who wants to meet them in person. Teach your children that they should:

- Never give out personal information (including their name, home address, phone number, age, race, family income, school name or location, or friends' names) or use a credit card online without your permission.
- Never share their password, even with friends.
- Never arrange a face-to-face meeting with someone they meet online, unless you approve of the meeting and go with them to a public place.
- Never respond to messages that make them feel confused or uncomfortable.

# Spiritual Parenting Solutions for Media Violence

If you believe that violence on television or in video games can impact your children's behavior negatively, then use intentional parenting techniques to guard against their negative influences.[73] When trying to make a decision about whether or not you will permit your child to view media violence, ask yourself the following questions: What are the consequences for the aggressive behavior? Is it rewarded or punished? Aggressive behavior on screen that lacks consequences, is portrayed as justified, or is rewarded will have a greater effect on children. Likewise, when the violence is committed by an attractive or a charismatic hero with whom children identify, the effect of that violence will be greater. If the child sees the violence in the show as being realistic, the impact will also be greater.[74]

Intentional parents who believe that media violence contributes to aggressive behavior do not allow a television in a child's bedroom. They point out that, although an actor has not been hurt or killed on television or video games, such violence in real life results in pain or death. Parents might also consider refusing to let children see television programs that are known to be violent. It is important that you come to terms with the idea that your children are living in a much different world than the one you knew as a child. The digital era has changed how we interact with one another. Make a concerted effort to understand your child's media world so that you can communicate with each other.

# Intentional Parenting Recommendations for Children's Use of Media

The following are some ways that you can tame media use in your house rather than letting it control you and your children. These suggestions are designed to bring the family together.

1. *Family homework activity.* Use a graph to explore how much and the type of media time (television, movies, video games, and computer time) your family uses in a week. The graph should have each day of the week, and time slots noted at one half hour intervals. Each night for a week, each family member fills out a graph before he goes to bed; younger children may need help completing their log. Color in the half-hour blocks for the amount of time watched and list the show, news program, video game, or computer activity in the block. After a week or two, review the charts together as a family and discuss possible changes, set new guidelines or goals, and identify choices for substitute activities.

2. *Make a media plan.* Schedule media times and choices in advance, just as you might with other activities. A media plan helps everyone to choose and use various media forms carefully. In addition, you do not have to argue over the remote control and what program the family is watching.

3. *Set media time limits.* Limit your children's total screen time. This limitation includes time watching TV and videotapes, playing video games and computer games, and surfing the Internet. Use a timer. When the timer goes off, tell your child that the media time is ended—no exceptions.

4. *Set family guidelines for media content.* Learn what the ESRB ratings are for video and computer games. Check the content ratings and parental advisories for all media. Use these ratings to determine what media are suitable for your child.

5. *Establish family media rules.* Be clear and consistent with children about media rules. If you do not approve of your children's media use, explain why and help them choose something more appropriate.

6. *Make media a family activity and help children to become knowledgeable consumers.* Use media with your children as often as possible, so that you can discuss with them what they see, hear, and read. Help your children to analyze, question, and challenge the meaning of messages that the media program has provided. During a violent scene or act or an unhealthy advertisement, ask your children to evaluate what was just shown. These "talk back" procedures will help your children to become critical media consumers. Ask your children: How does what was portrayed in this scene or media message compare with the values that I have tried to teach you?

7. *Look for media side affects.* Be able to assess if the media your children are using contribute to any of the following: poor school performance, hitting or pushing other children, aggressively talking back to adults, frequent nightmares, increased eating of unhealthy foods, smoking, drinking, or drug use.

You can make a difference in the way media impacts your children if you limit, supervise, and share media experiences with them. As you continue your spiritual journey with nurturing nonviolent children, consider having a tune-out media week, when you do not watch television or movies, participate in video games, or use the Internet. You just might get to know each other better and learn some interesting things that might have gone unnoticed with the television blaring or with someone playing video games in isolation in his room. You might just discover how to be a family again and learn that you are all pretty nice people.

# Summary

This chapter has examined the role of various forms of media in creating aggressive and violent behavior in children and teens. No matter what media form we are considering—television, video games, music and MTV, the Internet—all have been found to influence young people to become more aggressive. Yet, each one of these media forms has also brought clear benefits to children, teens, and adults. There are no easy solutions when it comes to having a balanced use of media in our homes. As parents, we must monitor carefully our children's use of various media forms.

# Parental Reading List

*Play between Worlds: Exploring Online Game Culture* by T. L. Taylor. MIT Press, 2006.
*Protect Your Child on the Internet: A Parent's Toolkit* by John Lenardon. Self-Counsel Press, 2006.

## Parent's Internet and Media Guide

The following Web sites offer pamphlets, information, and other materials on Internet and media safety.

Action Coalition for Media Education: http://www.acmecoalition.org.
American Academy of Pediatrics: www.aap.org.
Children Now—Children and the Media: www.childrennow.org/media.
Get Net Wise: www.getnetwise.org/.
Internet Keep Safe Coalition: www.ikeepsafe.org.
KidsHealth (The Nemours Foundation): www.kildshealth.org/parent.
Mediascope: www.mediascsope.org/index.htm.
National Institute on Media and the Family: http://www.mediafamily.org.
SafeKids.Com: www.safekids.com.
SafeTeens.com: www.safeteens.com. SafeTeens.com is The Online Safety Project's site for teen safety on the Internet.
TV Parental Guidelines: www.tvguidelines.org

# Intentional Parenting Tips on Television and Media Violence

## The Family Media Quiz

1. At what age do children begin imitating behaviors they see on television or in videos?
   a. 14 months
   b. 2 years
   c. 3 years

2. Media experts recommend that parents should limit children over two to how many hours of television, movies, and video or computer games a day?
   a. 1 to 2 hours
   b. 2 to 3 hours
   c. 3 to 4 hours

3. Some of the negative effects of having children view more than four hours of television or media entertainment per day?
   a. It increases a child's risk of being overweight.
   b. It increases a child's later risk of using alcohol and drugs and engaging in sexual activity at an earlier than average age.
   c. Children who watch a lot of TV go on to have lower reading scores and lower overall academic ability, have more problems playing with peer, and have fewer hobbies than children who watch less TV.
   d. All of the above.

4. Research shows that advertisers believe children become consumers at what age?
   a. Infancy
   b. 3 years
   c. 5 years

5. What percentage of the food advertised during Saturday morning is considered unhealthy for children (i.e., too much sugar, fast food)?
   a. 50 percent
   b. 75 percent
   c. 90 percent

## Video Game Addiction Quiz

Check the extent to which you agree or disagree with each of the following statements: 4 = strongly agree; 3 = agree; 2 = disagree; and 1 = strongly disagree

1. I feel unhappy, cranky, or upset when I am not playing a video game.
2. It angers me when my parents or someone asks me to stop playing video games.

3. I wish I could find more time to play video games each day.

4. Sometimes I find myself spending more time playing video games than I had planned.

5. My family and friends tell me that I spend too much time playing video games.

6. Usually, I spend about 20 hours a week playing video games.

7. Sometimes I neglect family and friends just to play video games.

8. Even though I have tried to cut back playing video games, I have not been able to do so.

9. I continue to play video games in spite of the negative consequences that playing brings.

10. Playing video games is not a problem for me. I can stop any time that I want.

11. I do not spend very much time playing video games.

12. It is a mistake for young people to spend a lot of time playing video games.

High scores suggest that there may be a problem with your playing video games and that there may be issues of addiction.

## Parent Quiz on Video and Computer Games

The purpose of this quiz is to determine how concerned you are about your child's playing video and computer games. Check the extent to which you agree or disagree with each of the following statements, with: 4 = strongly agree; 3 = agree; 2 = disagree; 1 = strongly disagree.

1. My child spends a great deal of time playing video and computer games.

2. I am concerned that my child's playing video and computer games is interfering with his completing schoolwork.

3. I have caught my child telling lies about his video and computer game playing time.

4. My child sneaks to play video and computer games, sometimes early in the morning or late at night.

5. I am concerned that my child's friends seem to be primarily "online."

6. My child spends most of his time in his bedroom playing video and computer games.

7. My child would rather play video and computer games than be with family and friends who are not "online friends."

8. My child seems to be irritable or cranky when he is not playing video and computer games.

9. My child sometimes flies into an angry rage when I ask him to stop playing video and computer games.

10. I am concerned that my child does not seem able to cut back on his video and computer playing time.

High scores suggest that there may be a problem with your playing video games and that there may be issues of addiction.

## Media Discussion Points with Your Child: Internet

The following are some questions you can use to begin a discussion with your child about Internet safety. Discuss these questions with your child.

### Internet Rules

What rules should we set for using the Internet? Will these rules apply only when you are at home, or do they apply wherever you use the Internet?

*You may want to decide your family's rules about Internet use with everyone present so they know and understand them. Your family's rules may cover the length of time your child may be on the Internet, when your child can be on the Internet, who controls the passwords, and what Web sites are acceptable. Other rules could include checking the history function to see where your child has been on the Internet and how many buddies your child has on his buddy list.*

### Sharing Personal Information

If you are online and you "meet" someone your age in a chat room, is it okay to give him your address or phone number so you can get together?

*As part of your discussion about this question, make sure your child knows not to give out any personal information, even if he or she thinks the new online friend is trustworthy. Your child should always check with you before arranging any meeting or giving out any personal information.*

### Buddy List

How many people do you think you should have on your instant message buddy list?

*A long buddy list suggests that your child has gotten "buddies" from a friend's buddy list. That friend may have received buddy lists from other friends. Sometimes children make a contest out of how many buddies they can have on a list. To stay safe, it is usually better to make sure that only people your child knows can send him an instant message. Knowing everyone on your child's buddy list is an important safety guideline.*

### Private Information

What if you are at a Web site of a popular company or organization (such as Disney), and it asks for your name and e-mail address to enter a contest. Would you give them that information? What if you are online and you get a message that states it is from your Internet service provider, and they need your password to fix a problem. Would you give it to them?

*Never give out personal information, even if the request comes from a seemingly legitimate source. A company must have parental permission before getting personal information from a minor online.*

# Kid's Pledge on Media Use

- I will not give personal information such as my address and/or telephone number, parent's work address and/or telephone number, or the name and location of my school without my parents' permission.
- I will tell my parents right away if I come across any information that makes me feel uncomfortable.
- I will not agree to get together with someone I "meet" online without first checking with my parents. If my parents agree to meeting, I will be sure that it is in a public place and that I bring my mother or father along.
- I will not respond to any messages that are mean or in any way make me feel uncomfortable. If I do receive such messages, I will tell my parents right away.
- I will talk with my parents so that we can set up rules for going online.
- I will not give out my Internet password to anyone (even my best friends) other than my parents.
- I will be a good online person and not do anything that hurts other people or is against the law.

I agree to the above.

_____

Child's Signature

I will help my child follow this agreement and will permit reasonable use of the Internet as long as these rules and other family rules are followed.

_____

Parent's Signature

The Kid's Pledge is adapted from SafeKids.com.

# Parent's Pledge about the Internet

- I will get to know the web sites my child visits. If I do not know how to navigate the sites, I will get my child to show me.
- I will set reasonable rules and guidelines for computer use by my child, and I will discuss these rules with my child. I will post these rules near the computer as a reminder. I will remember to monitor my child's compliance with these rules, especially when it comes to the amount of time he spends on the computer.
- I promise not to use a computer or the Internet as an electronic babysitter.
- I will encourage the use of the Internet as a family activity, and I will ask my child to help plan family events using the Internet.

• I will try to get to know my child's online friends, just as I try to get to know his other friends.

_____

Parent's Signature

I understand that my parent(s) has agreed to these rules, and I agree to help my parent(s) explore the Internet with me.

_____

Child/Teen's Signature

The Parent's Pledge was adapted from SafeKids.com, at wwww.safekids.com/contract.htm.

# 7

# *Helping a Child Develop Responsible Behavior*

*Train a child in the way he should go; and when he is old, he will not depart from it.*

—Proverbs 22:6

Many parents have a secret dream of raising the perfect child—perhaps a son who will not only bring home straight A's on his report card, but also be a handsome star athlete on the football team, president of his class, and the one voted most likely to succeed in the yearbook. In this dream, other parents consult you for your wisdom on how to raise the perfect child, much in the same way that parents who wanted to have a Tiger Woods sought out Earl Woods. And then reality sets in as you pull into your driveway and the dream fades away.

Meredith was one of these parents who, like the people caught napping on the mattress in the Sealy commercial, found herself dreaming the perfect life for children and herself. But unlike the people in the Sealy commercial, Meredith knew that she would not awaken from her dream and say: "I'll take it"—meaning the mattress. As Meredith climbed the stairs leading to her kitchen, she wondered if she were going to have to argue with Brad again about completing his homework. Such arguing had become a daily ritual, one that she had come to dread. In fact, Meredith found herself arriving home later and later to avoid the confrontation with Brad.

But it was not just the homework that they argued about. Brad and Meredith seemed to knock heads on just about everything, including the fact that he usually found a reason not to wash the dishes on the nights that it was his job to do so. His room was a complete mess, with clothes strewn all over. And the smell of those sneakers! How could he keep wearing those smelly sneakers to school every day?

What bothered Meredith most, however, was the feeling that somehow she had failed as a mother, as a parent. Meredith believed that she had tried everything that she knew to raise Brad so that he would be a responsible person when he grew up. But no matter how hard she tried, nothing seemed to work with him.

"Maybe some kids were born to be a certain way, and there is nothing anyone can do about," Meredith thought to herself. "Maybe, if Glenn had been home more, instead of working late so many nights. Maybe if I had known more about children's development and I didn't have to work, things would have turned out differently."

Meredith was sick of all the "maybes." She was tired of second-guessing and blaming herself for whatever went wrong with Brad. Her thoughts traveled to her best friend, Jessica, whose children seemed to be perfect. One day Meredith remembered seeing Michael dressed in his perfect white shorts with his perfect haircut, and she mused to herself: "I wonder if he ever does anything wrong. He's this perfect kid. . . . I'm sick of seeing Jessica's bumper sticker, 'My Child's an Honor Student.' " "Who cares?" Meredith asked out loud. "Who really cares about your honor student?" And then Meredith answered her own question. "I care," she said. "I don't want to admit it, but I care. I want Brad to show to the rest of the neighborhood that I'm a good parent, too."

Meredith was tired of Brad's irresponsible behavior, and if she heard him say just one more time "whatever," she would scream. "Whatever, whatever, whatever," Meredith mocked him one day? "You'd think you could learn another word." Brad looked at her as if she had lost her mind, and then shouted at her "Whhaatev . . . er," drawing out and emphasizing the "ever."

Meredith knew that she would never receive the "Mother of the Year Award." No one would ever come to her for advice about how to raise responsible children. She wondered silently to herself: "What happened? Where did I go so wrong? How could Jessica be such a better mother than I am? I mean maybe if I had had the luxury of staying home with my kids, things might have been different. . . . I had to work to help out with the bills. How could one person make so many mistakes? Was it . . . was it too late to turn things around with Brad?"

Like Meredith, most parents want to raise responsible children, but it is not easy. And the situation is not helped by all the books that give a different bent on how to raise responsible children. While some books say that parents should lighten up, others say that the answer is tighter control and more structure. Who is right? Does anyone have real wisdom about how to raise decent children so that they become productive and successful adults? Meredith had consulted her mother and some of her friends for answers, but most of the things they told her to do just did not work for Brad. And the fountain of parental wisdom that Meredith was searching for eluded her, much in the same way that fountain of youth had eluded Ponce de Leon.

No one has a perfect formula for raising responsible children. In fact, psychologists and other researchers are just discovering the many different factors that make up raising responsible children. It is not all a matter of nurturing children. Increasingly, we are learning about the importance of genetic factors and brain development on children's and adolescents' behavior. This chapter is about the different factors that contribute to raising a responsible child. It begins with a broad definition of what constitutes responsible children and then moves to examine how discipline can help or hinder parents in their raising of responsible children. Other areas explored are setting limits, using family rules to guide children, and learning how to establish boundaries in our family relationships.

# What Are Responsible Children?

What do we mean by "raising responsible children?" Responsibility is a value children learn from their parents, teachers, peers, and society. It is a life-long skill that involves meeting our obligations and accepting the consequences of our actions. Why is it important for children to learn to be responsible? Children's irresponsibility is related to failure in school, at work, and in interpersonal relationships. Research shows that children who act responsibly receive more positive attention from adults and peers than those who act irresponsibly.[1] For young people, being responsible includes such things as attending school, completing homework, coming home on time, completing chores, and showing self-discipline. Responsible children respect themselves and others, learn self-control, develop empathy for others, develop prosocial values, and build a value system for becoming productive and involved citizens.

# Understanding the Purpose
# of Discipline

The word "discipline" means to teach. A person who is learning is a disciple. Children rely on their parents and others to teach them how to become responsible. Our actions constitute discipline if we create a positive learning process for our children. The goal of disciplining our children should be to teach them appropriate behavior in a caring, respectful way. We need to focus on how we want them to behave rather than on what we do not want them to do. From this perspective, children's misbehaviors become opportunities to teach them how to behave well. The ultimate goal of discipline is to teach our children self-discipline so that they can make good choices throughout their lives.

# Understanding Your Child
# and Misbehavior

Children are not born knowing how to behave. If you understand why your children misbehave, you may be better equipped to reduce their behavior problems. Children often communicate their feelings through their behavior. Try to understand what need a child's behavior is communicating. Learning why children misbehave helps parents to determine, what, if any, consequences are warranted. Significant changes in a child's life may create anxiety, such as parents divorcing, the birth of a new baby, or a move to a new neighborhood. In addition, determine if there may be medical issues related to your child's behavior. Some children suffer from undiagnosed attention deficit hyperactivity disorder. Listed below are some possible reasons children misbehave:

- They want to test if parents will enforce rules.
- They do not understand the rules or they are held to parental and teacher expectations that are beyond their developmental levels.
- They want to assert themselves and their independence.
- They feel ill, bored, hungry, or sleepy.
- They have been previously rewarded for their misbehavior with adult attention.
- They copy the actions of their parents.

Before parents take disciplinary action against their children, they should ask themselves the following questions: Is the child really doing something wrong? Or, are you just tired and out of patience? If there is a problem with your child's behavior, is she child capable of doing what you expect? If you are not being realistic, reevaluate your expectations of her. If your child knew that what she was doing was wrong, and she intentionally disregarded a reasonable expectation, she misbehaved.[2] If the behavior were an accident, such as wetting her pants while sleeping, it was not misbehavior; it was an accident. When parents use a problem-solving approach, children develop skills in thinking through a situation and considering consequences for their actions. To encourage problem solving, ask your child how she might solve the problem or what she might do differently if given another chance.

# Before Disciplining, Learn about
# Your Child

In disciplining children, it is important to know what to expect from them, given their cognitive ability and their stage of psychosocial development.

Discipline should take into account children's ability to understand and reason. For instance, from birth to about age two, children need a great deal of support, holding, and loving interactions from parents. During these years, children learn from their senses and their physical activity. From about age two to six, children learn language, some reading skills, and some social skills. They struggle with independence from their parents and begin to take more initiative in their daily living skills. During these years, children learn by exploring, hitting, touching, turning objects over and throwing them, and asking many questions. From about age 6 to 12, children respond with increasing self-control. They develop their capability to process information and to make decisions.

Each child is a unique individual with varying strengths and weaknesses. To nurture your child effectively, take time to learn her special qualities, especially her strengths. Observe her in different settings and jot down answers to the following questions:

- How is my child similar to me? How is my child different from me?
- How does my child get my attention?
- What are my child's special strengths?
- What special challenges does my child present to me and to himself?
- What do I appreciate about my child?

# Disciplining by Natural and Logical Consequences

Most parents' concept of discipline is based on how their parents treated them. Intentional parenting requires that parents observe how they try to teach their children right from wrong. Very often parents punish for misdeeds; however, research has established that punishment merely suppresses bad behavior; it does not end it.[3] Effective discipline teaches children there are consequences for their actions. It is important for parents to learn the differences between natural consequences, logical consequences, and punishment.

# Natural Consequences

Natural consequences permit a child to experience what naturally happens as a result of his actions. Natural consequences are those things that happen in response to your child's behavior without parental involvement.[4] They are imposed by nature, society, or another person. You do not actually have to deliver a natural consequence yourself. Instead, you allow nature or society to impose the consequence on your child by not interfering. For instance, your child refuses to put away a favorite toy that lies in the driveway. Dad accidentally drives over the toy the next day. The child then remembers to put toys away in the future.

If a parent interferes with a natural consequence, it will not work. For instance, by preparing a later meal after your child has refused to eat dinner, you will stop the natural consequence of hunger. By forcing your child to wear a coat, he will not experience the natural consequence of being cold. Natural consequences work only if they are undesirable to your child and if you do not interfere with the consequence. Parents should carefully choose the conditions when they allow natural consequences to occur. Although natural consequences are effective, sometimes they can be too severe or delayed to be effective. Parents cannot use natural consequences if the health or safety of their child is involved. In cases where natural consequences are inappropriate to use, a parent uses logical consequences.

# Logical Consequences

Logical consequences are related to the offense; they teach children to accept responsibility for their mistakes and behavior and help them to link their behavior with consequences that make sense. If a child breaks a window, it is not logical for him to lose television privileges or to be given a spanking. Neither of these responses is related to the breaking of the window. On the other hand, making a child use his allowance to pay for the broken window teaches a valuable lesson about responsibility for one's actions. If your child skips a chore, have him do an extra chore. If he leaves a mess, have him clean the room. Do not ground him for a week for these offenses because grounding is not related to the offense.

The goal of logical consequences is to help children develop an internal understanding, self-control, and a desire to follow the rules. Logical consequences help children to look more closely at their behaviors and to consider the results of their choices. In contrast to punishment, where the intention is to make children feel ashamed, the intention of logical consequences is to help children learn from their mistakes in a supportive atmosphere. The message in using logical consequences is that the behavior is a problem, not that the child is a problem.

Some advantages of logical consequences include: (1) they are directly related to a behavior and they make sense; (2) the child understands the reason for the consequences and knows how to avoid them in the future; (3) the child learns about responsibility and can make future choices based on this knowledge. Logical consequences require that a parent gather more information before reacting to her child's behavior. Some questions a parent might ask when trying to assess a child's behaviors are the following: Is it clear to the child what is expected of him? What rule has been broken? What problem is the behavior creating? What will help to resolve the problem?

Logical consequences should be respectful to children and reasonable for them to complete. Parents give consequences with empathy and in a respectful tone of voice to their children. Children who are not treated respectfully are inclined to become aggressive, resentful, and uncooperative. Reasonable consequences are fair and appropriate to the situation and your child's age. The consequence should not be too severe for the misdeed. Warn your children before you implement the consequence. You might say: "Kids, this yelling is just too loud for me. If you can't work things out between yourselves, I am going to take the cake that you are arguing over." If parents talk to children about possible consequences, they are less likely to be resentful when they are implemented.

The logical consequences approach recognizes your children's ability to change their own behavior. Frequently, children who engage in misbehavior externalize their actions—that is, they blame others for their misdeeds. Expect denial from your children if you ask them to own up to behavior when they are upset and angry. Instead, give them a cooling down period before trying to discipline them. Children's anger in a conflict situation reduces their ability to reason. On such occasions, they use cognitive distortions such as minimizing, justifying, or rationalizing their destructive behavior. "It's not my fault," such children may say. "If he hadn't done this, I would not have done that. . . ." Or, "He made me do it."

The logical consequences approach to discipline helps children to see that blaming someone else is an unnecessary defense. Parents tell their children: "You don't have to defend yourself by blaming someone else. That doesn't help solve the problem. You have to learn how to be a problem solver and to take care of yourself. Now tell me your part in this so we can work it out and it won't happen again." From here, the parent asks her child to describe the poor choice of behavior that he made. After listening to her child, a mother says, "Okay, now can you tell me what you can do to correct the error in behavior?"

Parents can use the technique of "pull outs" to release shame after their children have taken responsibility for their behavior. Parents might say to their children: "Now that you have made a decision to do things differently next time, you don't have to hold on to bad feelings. You have made amends and have taken action to correct your past inappropriate behavior to make sure that it doesn't happen again." Ask your children where the bad feelings are in their body. Feelings of shame and anger are usually in the chest, stomach, or head areas. Tell your children to let the bad feelings come up so that they really feel them. "Okay, let's make them really strong. Let those feelings come up and feel BAD. Have you got them up now so you can move them? Tell yourself, 'I don't have to do that behavior anymore, so I can let go of my bad feelings.' Now, let's pull them out."

Have your children put their bad feelings in the trash can to indicate that they can let go of bad feelings, if they take responsibility for making amends and for changing their behavior. You then express faith in your child's ability to make good choices in the future. The pull out technique is not recommended for children who appear to have no conscience or remorse for their behavior. These children need to learn empathy and compassion for others before using this technique. Empathy training helps the unremorseful child learns how to put himself in the other person's place.

# Punishment

In contrast to logical consequences, the goal of punishment is to enforce compliance with rules by using external controls or authoritarian discipline.[5] Children who have done something wrong may be punished to reduce the likelihood that the behavior will take place again. The belief underlying punishment is that children must feel pain to learn from their inappropriate behavior. Punishment of children often leads to feelings of anger, discouragement, and resentment. It teaches children to be afraid of authority, to resent authority, to lie, and to evade detection. Punishment for aggression may stop the behavior temporarily in the presence of an adult, but such behavior may increase in other settings, without the adult presence. Moreover, children may strike back at the punishing adult or displace their anger on someone else.

Punishment is usually for hurting, while discipline is for training young people to become socially responsible. When we punish children, we focus on what we do not want them to do. The goal of punishment is to make the consequences that follow the behavior so aversive that the child will not want to do it any longer. Oftentimes, punishment instills fear in children and creates a sense of shame and humiliation within them.[6] Problems can develop when punishment is used to hurt a child—either physically or emotionally. Studies show that spanking and other physical discipline techniques can create ongoing behavioral and emotional problems. Harsh, physical discipline teaches children that violence is the only way to solve problems.

Children who get into trouble frequently receive so much punishment that they sometimes become inured to it.[7] Instead of shrinking from the punishment, they may shrug it off with an "I don't care" attitude or a "So what," or laugh it off with a "that doesn't hurt me." Punishment does not work if parents use it all the time.[8] The more parents punish, the less effective it becomes. For instance, if you ground a teenager for six months, it basically becomes meaningless. The less you punish, the more powerful punishment is when you need to use it. Punishment should never be used alone. If punishment is used, it needs to be followed by discipline that teaches children how to behave. Differences between logical consequences and punishment are summarized in Illustration 16.

# Positive Discipline

Much of the work on positive disciplining can be traced to Rudolf Dreikurs and his associates.[9] Positive discipline begins at birth when the bonds of

Illustration 16    Differences between Logical Consequences and Punishments

| Logical Consequences | Punishments |
|---|---|
| Teach children to take responsibility for their actions | Focus on adults' delivering punishment |
| Give consequences with empathy and respect for children's feelings | Are often delivered with anger |
| Link misbehavior to the time and place of the infraction. | Are often arbitrary |
| Allow children to develop an internal sense of control | Emphasize outer control |
| Understand that logical consequences focus on teaching children | Focus on hurting children and sometimes on revenge. |

attachment and trust are formed between parents and infant as they respond consistently and compassionately to an infant's needs. Positive discipline refers to techniques parents can use to reduce their children's undesirable behavior and increase their desirable behavior by rewarding the positive. It takes place when parents and teachers of infants, toddlers, or preschoolers are involved in setting limits and in encouraging desired behaviors.[10] Positive discipline occurs when parents help children resolve their behavior problems in a way that leaves them with their dignity intact.

A parent asks questions such as these: Am I disciplining in a way that hurts or helps my child's self-esteem? Will my discipline help my child develop self-control? The positive discipline philosophy maintains that the goals of discipline are to teach the child lifelong skills for good character, such as responsibility and self-control, to protect the child, and to instill values. Parents give children skills for making decisions, to gradually help them gain self-control, and to have them assume responsibility for their own actions.[11]

Positive discipline views misbehavior as an opportunity for teaching new behavior. Parents ask themselves: "What can I teach my child?" "How can I guide or help my child with his behavior?" Parents use positive discipline when they tell their children what to do rather than what not to do. The parent tries not to phrase the desirable behavior negatively, such as "Don't hit the dog." Instead, the parent states: "Pet the dog gently."

Parents use positive discipline when they show their children that they recognize and listen to the reason they give for doing the wrong thing. A parent might say: "You want to play with the truck, but...." When you show that you recognize the reason your child has misbehaved, you validate the legitimacy of his desires and you show that you are an understanding person. It is also important to state the "but" in teaching children positive discipline. "You want to play with the truck, but Elisha is using it right now." "You want me to play with you, but right now I have to cook." The "but" part of the sentence lets your child know that others have needs, too. This approach to discipline teaches your child perspective taking and helps him to have empathy by putting himself in other people's shoes. Next, parents offer a solution to their child. "I will play with you as soon as I finish cooking."

Parents who use positive discipline avoid power struggles, which ensue when they use punishment to discipline children. Power struggles are typically about meeting the needs of the parent or the child at the expense of the other person not getting his way. The job of parents is to teach children how to get their needs met in socially acceptable ways. Once children's underlying needs and feelings are acknowledged and addressed, their behavior often improves.[12]

The most effective discipline tools used for younger children up to preschool age include redirection, substitution, and supervision, as well as offering choices and changing the environment. At the preschool age, parents should be focused on prevention. Make some rules that guide children's behavior. A few necessary, clear, and reasonable behavioral limits that are enforced on a consistent basis give children feelings of security that parents are helping them to behave. Rules within families should be about protecting the health, safety, and property rights of the child and other family members.

Supervision of a child is an important positive discipline strategy. Parents should not allow their children to play or explore out of sight. Toddlers need a parent or caregiver to stay close to them—to be physically within an arm's reach of them at all times. Once a child is in preschool, the parent or caregiver determines the level of supervision required. For instance, you might ask such questions as: What is my child able to do? How active is my child? How impulsive is my child? How well does my child follow requests and rules? How safe is the environment? Has the home been safety proofed for my young children? Your responses to these questions will help determine the kind of supervision and positive discipline your child requires.

Other positive discipline techniques include redirecting, which involves helping the child find an alternative activity that is similar to what he was doing.[13] "I can't let you throw your ball in the house, but you may throw it outside." A cooling off period may be used to deal with an angry outburst. Your child can be sent to a calming place in the house to rest or to do something until she gains control of herself and changes the undesirable behavior. Time outs that have no agreed upon end are not effective. You can make time outs more effective when you set a time limit using one of the following methods:

- Assign one minute of "time out" for each year of your child's age. (A six year old would have a six minute time out).
- Let your children end the time out when they feel under control and ready to try again. If your children indicate they are ready to end the time out, ask what they plan to do if the problem happens again. This approach teaches children to control their emotions and reinforce the point that calmer emotions are needed to solve problems.

Give your child chances to choose. When children are given choices, they feel a sense of power over their lives; and their making a choice encourages them to engage in decision-making. The parent states the rule and then gives the child a choice. A parent might say: "It's time to take a nap. Do you want me to hold your hand while you walk to your bed, or do you want to race me to see who gets to your bed first?"

The most effective discipline tools for older, school-age children and teens are active listening, "I" messages, time out, changing the environment, modeling, logical consequences, and problem solving. In addition, family meetings are very effective at this age. Intentional parents help children to express their anger in a socially acceptable manner and encourage them to think about alternatives and solutions to problems.[14]

Positive discipline emphasizes catching children doing something right rather than focusing primarily on what they are doing wrong.[15] Parents describe the appropriate behavior: "Good job completing your homework." Or, "You played very nicely with the other boys and girls today. You allowed the other kids to play with your toys, and sharing is important." "You did your homework before watching TV just like we asked you to do. We're proud of you for that." "Thanks for being home on time. That makes me trust you more and prevents me from worrying where you are and if you are okay." "I'm glad that you told me the truth about how the lamp was broken. It's important to tell the truth." "Thank you for apologizing. That lets me know that you understand what you did was inappropriate and that you care about my feelings."

Remember the 4:1 ratio. Catch children doing something correctly four times for every time you find them doing something incorrectly. Use the privacy principle, which is to never embarrass a child in front of others. Always move to a private place to talk when there is a problem. For a period of one week, keep a written tally when you talk to your children about their behavior. Make two columns—one for "good" and one for "bad" behavior. Put a mark in the good column when you tell your children that they are doing something right. Put a mark in the bad column when you have to chastise them for doing something wrong. At the end of the week, total each column to see how often you are approaching your children in a positive or in a negative manner about their behavior.

Use the positive closure principle.[16] At the end of the day, remind your children that they are special and loved. Help them to find something good about the day that is finished and about the day that lies ahead. Other positive parenting techniques include: Get on the child's eye level principle. When talking with your child, get down on his eye level and look at him while talking firmly but softly. Another technique is to use actions instead of words. Do not say anything. When your child continues to get out of bed and comes to the family room, take him back to bed, as many times as it takes. Do not talk, get upset, scold, threaten, or give reasons. Just stay calm. Your child will soon learn that nighttime is for sleeping and that you are serious about enforcing bedtime rules. Positive discipline is all about building the right relationship with your child. Positive approaches to discipline increase children's self-esteem, help them to feel valued, encourage them to feel cooperative, and enable them to learn gradually the many skills involved in taking some responsibility for what happens to them.

# Nurturing Messages for Children

We nurture our children so that they know they are truly loved. According to a number of studies, nurturance in raising children is a highly important quality. A nurturing adult is warm, understanding, and supportive of a child. As pointed out in the section on parenting styles, children learn more easily from a nurturing parent than they do from a harsh or rejecting or permissive parent. Children raised by nurturing parents are less likely to become delinquent than are those raised by harsh or rejecting parents. Here are some nurturing messages: I value you as a person; I believe in you; I trust you; I listen to you; You are very important to me; I know that you will do your best; I love you; It is okay to make mistakes.

# Setting Limits for Children: Family Rules

Parents are responsible for identifying and enforcing reasonable limits for their children and for gradually giving them freedom to be responsible. Children who know their limits tend to feel more secure, and they also evidence fewer behavior problems. In setting limits, parents must first decide what the important rules are for their family.

Every healthy family lives by a set of rules in the home. In establishing family rules, healthy families have a reasonable chain of command. Although children may be given rights, the ultimate responsibility for the family falls upon the parents. Healthy families have clear rules that allow parents to show children what is expected of them and to make clear the ways that they can contribute to the family's welfare. Family rules help parents to be consistent in the way that they discipline their children. Effective family rules are positive statements about how a family wants to carry out its mission and how it wants to look after and treat its members.

It is important to involve children in establishing family rules. Parents can make rules as soon as their children have the language skills to understand them. Children as young as three years of age can participate in meaningful conversations with their parents about what the family rules are and why they are necessary. As children grow older, they can make a contribution to these rules and assist in establishing consequences for breaking them. Involving children in developing family rules and the consequences for them promotes their internalization of family rules.

A family should establish five or fewer rules. For example, our family treats each other with respect.[17] Everyone picks up after himself in our family. Our family members share with each other. Or, our family listens to one another. No one in our family hits another person. The power of family rules rests in the word "we," when meaning "our family." The word "we" shows evidence that a bond has been created between a child, his parents, and siblings. For instance, "We all do our share to keep our home clean." Another rule might be: "We respect the rights of others."

Rules might be established about how the family gets things done or how it deals with conflict. For instance, "We have the right to disagree with each other, but we try to find win/win solutions to solve conflicts between family members." "We keep our commitments made to each other, and when we cannot, we take time to inform the person ahead of time by calling or by writing a note."

Rules might be made concerning chores and household responsibilities. "We complete our chores and responsibilities to the best of our ability without having to be told."

Steps for establishing family rules are:

- Get everyone together in your family and brainstorm a list of family rules. For instance, "We tell the truth to each other."
- Write the rules with a marker on poster board and hang the rules in a prominent place in the home. Add to your family rules as needed.
- When your child's behavior needs correcting, refer to the rules to highlight that the child's behavior does not meet your family's standards.
- If the family agrees, establish some appropriate consequences for breaking each rule and write these consequences down.

Children need to be encouraged to keep family rules. Therefore, praise them when you see them following a family rule. For instance, a parent might say: "I like the way you shared your toy with your brother. That's the way we do things in our family." Remove children from a situation when they seem incapable of maintaining a rule. "I see that you're too angry to listen to what I am saying right now. Go to your room to cool off and come back when you are ready to hear what I have to say." Gradually, children internalize family rules that have to do with powers of judgment, ethical responsibility toward self and others, persistence, and concern for others. Meaningful family rules build character in children and adolescents. They provide guidelines for them to use in the absence of their parents.

## *Family Value or Mission Statements*

Although most parents have a sense of their own values, few have crystallized them into written statement.[18] The family values statement or mission statement is based on a set of your family's deeply held beliefs. For instance, "Our family never gives up. We keep coming, long after most people have quit." A family's mission contains information about how family members like to express themselves when they are upset, the importance they attach to being family members, and appropriate behavior or boundaries with nonmembers. It covers a wide diversity of values to be decided, first by the parents and then by all members. It becomes the blueprint for making family decisions, and for settling questions about how the family operates. An effective way to develop a family mission statement is as follows:

- Parents talk between themselves about what is important to them and what values they want to impart to their children. Both parents need to agree.

- Parents talk with their children about these values. They state values in positive terms rather than in negative terms—by saying what family members want rather than what they do not want.

- The entire family discusses the values at the dinner table or at a family meeting so that everyone understands them.

The family mission statement can deal with a number of topics, such as the importance of education; the way money is spent and saved; the responsibilities each member of the family will have toward maintaining the household; and the importance of activities outside the home. A sample family mission statement is provided for the Jones family.

### Jones Family Mission Statement

We, the Jones family, do dedicate our family to the task of honoring and enriching our members.

We live by these *five values*:

1. We love and Honor God above all others. We believe in the faith of a mustard seed.

2. We treat others the way that we would like to be treated.

3. We work hard and persist to achieve our goals. We do not give up or take the easy way out. Our motto is that we can do all things with the help of God.

4. We stress the importance and value of an education, cooperate with and show respect for our children's teachers.

5. We do not bring shame upon the family.

We also hereby establish *six family rules* from these two principles:

1. We honor Mom and Dad by obeying them.

2. We honor others and our possessions by putting things away after we have used them.

3. We honor our commitment to the family by performing all chores responsibly.

4. We honor friends and family by having good manners, maintaining appropriate boundaries, and exercising responsibility toward others.

5. We honor all of God's creation, people, and things.

6. God's Word is to be honored in our house.

## Using Family Meetings to Build Young People's Sense of Responsibility

Young people need an anchor, a sense that they belong to a group. Emphasize the importance of family to your children. Stress the fact that your family is a team and encourage members to spend time with each other and extended family members, such as grandparents, aunts, and cousins. Eat dinner together several times a week. When children believe in the importance of their families, family meetings take on additional significance.

The purpose of family meetings is to take a structured amount of family time to touch base with everyone in the family, to help members celebrate their small and big successes, to provide support for them in their challenges, to organize busy schedules, and to solve problems. Family meetings are times set aside to promote positive family communication between members. Regular family meetings are helpful to build effective relationships between children and their parents. Such meetings can be used to involve children in decision-making and to listen to their feelings about issues. A family meeting is a good way to teach children problem solving behavior, to encourage family members, and to promote their cooperation with each other.

A major benefit of family meetings is that children are able to see their family working together as a group. A second benefit is that such meetings can be used to resolve family conflicts. A third benefit of regularly scheduled meetings is that they help families divide up the tasks of family life so that things are accomplished in an orderly fashion. For instance, meetings might be held to decide who drives which child to what practice or who completes what chores for the week. A fourth benefit of family meetings is they can be called for discussing special events, such as planning a family vacation or a holiday, clearing the air after a fight, or easing a major family transition, such as dealing with one child moving out or a divorce between parents.

Family meetings are held to state a family's goals. Families that talk about their goals are more likely to be aware of them and to achieve them. Initially, parents tell children that they will begin holding family meetings to talk about what is going on in everyone's life. Most children come to value family meetings as they come to understand that such meetings are times to air their concerns and to discuss possible solutions for problems they are experiencing at home or at school.

There are two leadership roles at the family meetings: (1) a chairperson who keeps the discussion on track and monitors it so that everyone's opinion is heard at the meetings. Mom and Dad are the co-leaders for the meetings at the beginning. In subsequent meetings, other family members take turns at these two leadership roles so that no one has total responsibility for leadership.

One of the first tasks is to decide how the meetings will be run. Are family meetings to be structured with a definite set of beginning rituals, or are they to be unstructured, with family members dealing informally with issues? At the first meeting, certain rules might be established, such as everyone is to contribute to the conversation, listen without interrupting, and be supportive, rather than critical. Set a scheduled time for meetings, post it where everyone will see, and keep the time.

Use a "go around" technique to get everyone involved in the meeting. This technique involves going around the circle giving each family member the opportunity to respond to the topic. Try to have several topics for discussion at the family meeting. For instance, assume that each family meeting has four structured topics. Topic 1 might be a go-around on something that made you feel good this week. Go around Topic 2 deals with something hat bothered you this week. Parents listen for and acknowledge the feelings that are expressed, ask open-ended questions to clarify the problem, and then brainstorm solutions with the entire family.

For Topic 3, everyone states something that he wants to work on or to accomplish during the next week. Go around Topic 4 involves family members' schedule for the coming week. What meetings, appointments, tests, special events, or projects do family members have for either this week or the coming week? Parents help children identify any scheduling conflicts and help children to plan their week. This go around topic teaches children time management. Family meeting time can also be reserved to do fun things such as telling jokes, playing games, or having contests. Assign family members to say a quotation that has meaning for them. Create something during the meeting, such as a family poster or calendar. Pray together.

## General Guidelines for Effective Family Meetings

- Hold family meetings on a regular basis at a time everyone can attend.
- Encourage everyone to bring up issues. Write them down, and keep a list until the next meeting, and discuss them in order.
- Use the next meeting to evaluate decisions that have been made.
- Follow through on family agreements. At the time agreements are made, build in logical consequences for broken agreements.
- Establish rules that family members are to listen respectfully and not interrupt when another person is talking.

# Establishing Healthy Boundaries with Children and Family Members

Boundaries may be defined as a set of rules that govern how you will allow people to treat you.[19] They help define our sense of self and put us in charge of ourselves.[20] Healthy families establish appropriate boundaries between family members and between categories of family members, such as parents and children.[21] Children need boundaries to understand their place and role within families and to develop a healthy sense of where they begin and others end. For instance, children learn that there are boundaries between children and adults and that within each of these boundaries, there are certain rights, responsibilities, and limitations.[22] Boundaries help define our sense of self, they protect us, and they put us in charge of ourselves. When we are treated with dignity and respect, we develop a healthy sense of boundaries.

Moreover, boundaries are limits or barriers that protect you as a parent, your time, and your energy. Personal boundaries are the physical, emotional, and mental limits that define and separate one person from another.[23] Healthy boundaries are those that recognize you as a separate person with your own emotions, needs, attitudes, and values. Psychological boundaries help us to define our sense of self. Our boundaries help us to say no to others.

In healthy families, parents create boundaries around themselves from their children. A parental boundary enables them to have a private life separate from their children. For instance, parents share confidences and sexual intimacy with each other because they trust that such confidences and intimacies will remain private and not be shared with outsiders, including their children and other family members. Boundaries function to keep some information private, while other information may be shared freely across boundaries. Parents may share information with children, such as their love for them and each other. It is important, however, for parents not to share their intimate business with children because this blurs the parent/child boundary. When parents argue in front of their children or use them as confidants for adult issues, they create indistinct parental boundaries.[24]

Parents who fail to establish appropriate boundaries with their children become enmeshed with them. Enmeshment refers to losing one's sense of self within a relationship. For instance, a mother might encourage an overly close relationship with her children because she feels empty inside. When parents become enmeshed with their children, both have difficulty separating themselves from each other and in determining their own individual responsibilities.

Healthy boundaries with our children and others need to be flexible enough so that we can choose what to let in and what to keep out. Rigid, inflexible boundaries prevent others from ever really getting to know us. We all use phrases to indicate when our boundaries have been crossed. Typically, most of us allow several minor infringements on our boundaries until we feel that the self is threatened in such a manner that we must take a stand. The following are common phrases people use to let others know that they have crossed their boundaries:[25]

- "I've had just about all that I am going to take from you."
- "I've had it up to here with you."
- "That's the last straw that I am taking from you."
- "I've stood this about as long as I can."
- "I can't take anymore of this or anymore of you and your behavior."

We establish either weak or strong boundaries within their families. Family members who establish strong boundaries are those who are clear about their own responsibilities and the responsibilities of others. They do not allow themselves to be encroached upon by their children's responsibilities or by their other family members' responsibilities. A parent might say: "You volunteered for the project. I didn't. You can't borrow my talents. You have to use yours."

Parents who establish weak boundaries with their children allow their children's responsibilities to encroach upon their own time, physical space, and talents. If you feel that you are a doormat for your family, then you have established weak boundaries between yourself and other family members. You have laid the groundwork for weak boundaries if your child continually wants to use your talents and ability to complete a project for which he or she is responsible. The message is that you have established no boundary between your talents and those of your child. Your child believes that he has the right to borrow your talents and that you must comply simply because he is your child and you want him to do well in life.

Setting boundaries means owning and taking responsibility for yourself and not allowing others to abuse you or to take advantage of you, even if they are family members and you love them. People who have a high need for approval may have difficulty establishing firm boundaries. Boundary maintenance can be scary for some people. We may ask ourselves: "What happens if I say no?" "Will my child still love me?" Sometimes we tend to blame others when they continually violate our boundaries; however, the truth is that the blame (responsibility) lies within ourselves. We must accept responsibility for maintaining our own boundaries. We cannot give that responsibility to someone else and expect that our boundaries will be where we want them to be. Some signs that your boundaries are weak are the following:

- You have knots in your stomach after agreeing to do things for family members and others.
- You feel angry at a child, sibling, or mate, even though you have agreed to help in some manner. For instance, you lend your teenager money. Three months later you

get into an argument and discover that deep down inside you are really angry about lending the money to him. You feel angry because you did not enforce your financial boundaries with your child. "This is my money. I worked for it. You don't have the right to use me or my money—just because I am your parent. I want to establish financial boundaries with you. What's mine is not yours."

- You have a deep feeling of dread when your child approaches because you anticipate that he is going to ask for something from you, and you do not have the courage to say no.

## *Boundary Setting Areas*

Children respect parents when they establish their personal boundaries with them. A parent might say: "My room is off limits, unless you knock, and you ask permission to come in." "This is my towel, my toothbrush, and I do not like anyone drinking out of my glass." "When I am talking to another adult, you wait until I am finished, unless there is an emergency. You do not butt into adult conversations." "When I am talking on the telephone, you do not come and ask me questions or interrupt my conversation, unless there is an emergency or danger of some sort." For young children, parents might:

- *Establish personal and physical space boundaries in the home.* Your office may be off limits for the children. Under no circumstances are they to enter your office without your permission, unless there is an emergency.

- *Establish privacy rules about your bedroom.* Children are required to knock and get permission before entering their parents' bedroom.

  Also, children have rights to personal space boundaries. Parents knock before entering the bathroom when children are using it. Depending upon the child's age, parents knock before entering a child's bedroom. Children are taught that they have the right to establish boundaries with regard to their physical bodies. They have the right not to be touched inappropriately by others, including adults.

- *Establish talent boundaries in your home.* As a parent, you may help your children with various projects, but your talent is not available for family members to use at their will and convenience. The same situation exists for your children and partner. Parents do not have the right to "volunteer" their children's talents to neighbors and other family members. For example, "Kevin likes to work on cars, and he will help you to fix your brakes."

- *Develop property boundaries in your home.* You may use my personal belongings only if I give you permission to do so. Unless I give you permission to use my personal belonging, do not remove it from where I have put it or use it in any fashion.

- *Establish limits on your time and energy.* A parent also needs to have private time that allows him to recoup from the day. A parent might post a private time on a bedroom or office door.

## Teaching Responsibility by Having Chores

Giving your child chores teaches him a sense of responsibility and helps instill a sense of discipline. Chores teach children that no one is entitled; everyone has to work for what he wants.[26] Research suggests that children who are involved in household chores from an early age tend to be happier and more successful. Why? From an early age, they are made to feel that they contribute to the family and that they belong. Children want to belong and to feel like they are valuable, and they achieve this goal when they perform some necessary family task.

Chores do not have to be done perfectly. Be aware of what your child can realistically be responsible for, given his age and level of cognitive and social development. Consider your child's interests and need for variety when setting responsibilities. Involve your child in planning his chores and other responsibilities and in setting timelines for their completion. For instance, the bathrooms will be cleaned when you come home from school or before dinner. Be receptive to your child's way of completing chores. Occasionally, when your child is rushed for time, you might assist him in completing a chore so that he learns the value of cooperation. Let your child know that the completion of chores is valued by you and the family.

- Have your child choose the household tasks for which he will be responsible. Make a list of tasks that are within your child's ability and let him choose two or three to do. The more children feel they are involved in making decisions, the more they will feel ownership for those household responsibilities.
- Help your child learn self-motivation by assisting him to discover the emotional rewards of a job well done. A good Web site that contains reward boards is http://www.myrewardboard.com/approach_responsibility.html.
- Consider your rewards. Are you going to link chores with a requirement for allowance? How will you record children's completion of chores? Will you use a sticker system? Decide what reward system works best for your family.

Chores should be related to the age, cognitive, and social development of the child. Many toddlers become excited when they can help Mommy or Daddy with household chores. It is important to remember that learning a new chore may take months or even years for a child to move from completing a task with help to doing a task independently. How do you get children to help with chores? Children are motivated to help around the house when parents say: "I need your help," rather than "Did you do your chores?" Be clear and specific when giving instructions for a chore. Provide choices in assigning chores. Use a "job jar" or job rotation strategy.

Offer praise and express appreciation when children attempt or complete chores. Sticker charts are an excellent way to keep toddlers excited about helping. Some chores that two to three year olds can do with your help are self-care activities, such as getting dressed and putting away clothes. They can help make the bed, pick up their toys, and put away books. From ages three to five children should have chores that give them greater independence in self-care, such as helping to set and clear the table, helping to put away the dishes, and keeping their room clean.

Here are ten quick suggested chores for children ages six to ten that you might choose to help your child develop a sense of responsibility and competency in completing tasks: set the table for dinner, clean up the table after dinner, wash dishes, dust, feed the pet, take out the garbage, vacuum, water plants, clean the bathroom. Some chores preteens and teens are capable of include: Help wash the car, wash dishes, help prepare simple meals, operate the washer and dryer.

## *Service to Others: A Responsibility Builder for Children*

A family doctrine of service to others can be used as a deterrent to the entitlement syndrome. Instead of buying your children gifts during holidays, it may be helpful if you had them volunteer at shelters, hospitals, and animal clinics. Consider having your children participate in activities such as community walks for hunger or cancer—even if they only walk a few hundred yards. For example, one child took blankets to a homeless shelter. Children learn that they can make the world a better place through their volunteering efforts. Some families are providing service to others on their vacations. Some parents ask that children set aside a certain part of their allowance for giving to those less fortunate than they. Suggestions for giving to others include:

- Designate a container in which your children can deposit their loose change. When the jar is full, they donate the money to an agreed upon charity.
- Have children save their own money to buy a gift for a holiday toy drive.
- Encourage your children to run errands for the elderly whom both you and they know in your neighborhood.
- Have your children pack up clothing or toys they no longer play with and donate them to a homeless shelter.

Studies have found that service to others may actually increase young people's academic achievement.[27] Service learning is related to academic success because it provides young people with two key resources: a feeling of usefulness and being valued, and a way of tangibly demonstrating the importance of what they have learned in school. Children like to feel they are needed and can help others.

Encourage your children to reflect on their service experience. When children express their feelings about what they learned from a service experience, they are able to evaluate their efforts. They engage in the process of reflection. The ability to reflect on the good and the bad of life experiences will be useful to them throughout their lives. Having your children to provide service to others is an important value to impart to your children.

## Teaching Your Children Self-Discipline

Self-discipline involves taking ownership of behavior and holding oneself responsible and accountable for what one does or does not do. Parents provide the initial groundwork for a child's developing self-discipline. In fact, the ultimate goal of a parent's discipline of a child is to foster the child's own self discipline. A parent's discipline code for children provides the outer coat, the framework. Children need an inner sense of discipline that will guide them long after a parent's influence has waned. Self-discipline takes over when no one is watching. It is a major foundation for children's lifelong personal and social development. Helping your child achieve self-discipline is well worth your effort.

Self-discipline may be defined as the ability and will to do what needs to be done for as long as it needs to be done and to learn from the results of one's efforts. It involves adhering to actions, thoughts, and behaviors that bring personal improvement or accomplishment of one's goals rather than instant gratification. An important cornerstone of self-discipline is an individual's acceptance of responsibility. Responsibility refers to an individual's capacity and desire: (1) to behave properly without direct supervision; (2) to correct one's own behavior when it is improper or inappropriate; and (3) to assist others in behaving properly. Some of the essential elements of self-discipline include self-organization, self-mobilization, commitment, concentration, impulse control, self-motivation, and the ability to face and overcome obstacles.

Successful experiences contribute to children's having positive views of themselves and of self-discipline. A feeling of belonging or oneness with others is necessary for self-discipline. Self-discipline requires persistence, continual self-monitoring, positive self-talk, and a focus on the opportunities that are available. Moreover, parents teach children how to master their time by focusing their efforts on actions that bring them closer to their goals.

Self-discipline requires children to learn delayed gratification. Researchers sometimes study the early emergence of self-control by giving children tasks that require delay of gratification or waiting for an appropriate time and place to engage in a tempting act. Between ages 18 months and 3 years, children manifest an increasing capacity to wait before eating a treat, opening a present, or playing with a toy.[28] Children who can delay immediate gratification of their desires generally have more self-control and self-discipline than those who give in to their desires and demand immediate gratification.

Self-discipline keeps children working toward their goals. Parents who model patient, nonimpulsive behavior tend to produce children who are self-disciplined. The payoff for helping children to become self-disciplined is immense. As children grow older, they must decide if they will sacrifice short-term pleasure for long-term happiness or the accomplishment of their goals. Does one study, or does one go out drinking with one's friends? Children who have developed a strong sense of self-discipline are better able to deal with peer pressure, especially as such pressures are related to sex, drugs, and other challenging behavior. Young people who are self-disciplined are more inclined to graduate from college and to experience fewer problems at work than those who do not have self-control over their emotions and behavior.

## Teaching Children to Set Goals: An Important Ingredient of Self-Discipline

Why is it important to teach children to set goals? Up to 30 percent of students drop out of school, and many who do graduate admit to being aimless.[29] Research shows it is critical to get children thinking early—in elementary and middle school—about what is important to them and why. Dreams and goals give life purpose, direction, and meaning. They help young people build toward the future and offer a sense of control and hope. Moreover, for the past several decades, research has shown that children who participate in setting their own learning goals in a classroom are consistently more motivated and self-disciplined.[30]

Knowing how to set and achieve goals are important skills children must have to prepare for school, adulthood, and work. Setting goals helps children become more motivated and disciplined because it helps them make a connection between their own efforts, choices, and a desired end result. A goal is created three times—first as a mental picture; second, when it is written down with clarity detailing its dimensions, and third when you take action toward its achievement. Goal-setting teaches your child about the value of hard work, being persistent, following through, and achieving success. They learn that without having a goal, they cannot set a course of action. When children achieve their goals, they feel better about themselves, and they develop a sense of competency.

Discuss with your children what it means to set a goal, and have them brainstorm a personal list of goals they would like to accomplish. Next, have them select one goal as the primary goal to be reached by a designated time, perhaps Christmas or the end of the school year. Increase your children's motivation by asking them to write or draw with as much detail as possible what their goal would look like when they have achieved it. Another alternative is to go through old magazines to find pictures that represent their goal. Children are then encouraged to place their goal in a visible place they will see everyday, such as on a mirror in their bedroom. It is important for them to get a clear visualization or image regarding the goal so that it becomes real to them.

Encourage your children to see themselves as if they have already accomplished the goal. Inquire: Who is there to congratulate you when you achieve your goal? What are you wearing? How do you look as you are achieving your goal? These visualizations prepare children for success. Many professional athletes do this on a regular basis as part of their training to achieve a competitive edge. For example, they picture themselves on a platform receiving an Olympic gold medal. To aid children in visualizing the successful completion of their goals, encourage them to use as many of their senses as possible.

Parents can help young people by having them write out the steps and actions they need to take to achieve their goals. You might draw or purchase a goal ladder to help your children decide what steps they need to take to achieve the desired goal. Recommend that they do something each day toward achieving their goal, regardless of how small the step is. For instance, it could be a phone call to ask someone for help on the project. The more parents help children to break down the steps necessary to reach the goal, the greater the likelihood they will be able to succeed at reaching that goal.

Some children have a tendency to give up when they hit a roadblock while trying to accomplish their goal. Therefore, parents need to teach young children how to monitor their journey toward realizing their goals. The goal monitoring process should involve having children evaluate what factors helped them to achieve their goals. What things hampered them from accomplishing their goals? How did they exercise self-control to achieve the accomplishment of their goals? Achieving goals takes consistent effort, especially when it might appear that one has a chance of not succeeding.

When children seem discouraged about achieving their goals, teach them to engage in positive self-talk rather than negative self-talk. The biggest deterrent to people's achieving their goals is negative self-talk. Negative self-talk slowly leaks poison into individuals' psyches, telling them that they do not have what it takes to accomplish their goals. Children's negative self-talk can sabotage their goals.

## *Teaching Your Children to Earn What They Want: Responsibility Builder*

If you smother your children with material things, they will grow up thinking the world owes them a living.[31] They will have a sense of entitlement rather than a sense of responsibility. We help build our children's sense of responsibility when we teach them to earn what they want. Paid work gives them a sense of accomplishment. It is important that parents use a consistent approach to teach children about money. Before trying to teach their children about money, they should consider answering some of the following questions:

- What are the values our family has with respect to money?
- How might we teach our values about money to our children?
- Will we give our children allowances or use another method to help them learn about money?
- What might our children be observing from us regarding our own money?

Begin teaching children about money as early as possible. Communicate your values about money—how to earn it, save it, and make it grow. Engage children in good spending habits and teach them the difference between needs and wants. Before children make a purchase, ask if the purchase represents something they need or want. Parents teach saving as a way for children to get what they want or need. One benefit of saving is that it reinforces planning and delayed gratification skills. When you work with children on short-term saving projects, help them to determine how long it will take to save a particular amount to purchase the desired object or toy. You can motivate children to save by annually matching the amount they saved or by providing interest on the amount saved.

Preschoolers view all money as having the same value, and they think that coins have more value than paper money. To help them understand money concepts, parents might play grocery store or bank with play money. To help children understand the concept of coins and their values, parents separate coins into piles by color and size and discuss their value. Preschoolers can learn about money if their parents let them pay for one item at the grocery store or put money in the parking meter. Parents might teach children that family members work to pay for food and clothes. Let your child visit your workplace to see where and how you earn money to provide food for him and the rest of the family. Other techniques parents might use to teach preschoolers about money are to put savings in a jar and let them count the money with you.

During elementary school, children know what money is but may not correctly name coins and bills.[32] These children need to learn about money in a concrete way. They can be taught to save for something if the saving time is short. Some suggested parental teaching activities for elementary school children are to open a savings account at a financial institution that accommodates children. Explain sales receipts and bills for expenses you pay for them such as clothing and toys. Have children compare prices when they shop with you. Have children clip coupons and give them the amount saved. Post a list of family needs and wants so that children understand that not all wants can be met; this helps them learn priorities. Consider giving your children a weekly allowance to teach them how to manage money. You might have them contribute some of their allowance money to religious groups or to charitable organizations.

Children in the middle elementary years are capable of long-term (for one year or until next summer) planning for spending or saving.[33] They understand to some extent how much money will buy. They understand the difference been needs and wants and comprehend that money is limited. They may need parental guidance to understand the value of things, and consider if it is wise to spend $150 on a pair of sneakers. Middle school children are concerned about fairness in how siblings are treated. They can use math skills to keep track of expenses, available money, and savings. To help develop middle elementary school children's knowledge about money, parents might find extra jobs children can perform to earn money, or have them figure out the amount of money needed for special projects. Require your children to save a part of their allowance. Have them check prices in newspapers or catalogs for something the family wishes to buy.

The developmental characteristics of teenagers also have a bearing on their attitudes and use of money. Typically, teens want to make earning and spending decisions without consulting parents. They can earn and save for long-term goals. They may still need help in distinguishing between their wants and needs. It is important for teens to experience the good and bad consequences of spending actions.

To assist teens in their understanding and management of money, parents might involve them in the planning and budgeting for the family vacation or other projects.[34] They can also help with grocery shopping. Allow teens to make their own spending decisions. They will learn from their mistakes. Make sure your teens have such basic skills as knowing how to write a budget and knowing how to write a check and balance a checking account.

Parents tend to be lax in teaching their children how to be responsible in the area of money matters. They assume that their children are learning monetary skills in school, but many graduate from high school without ever having learned how to write a check. Young people need to be taught to earn what they want rather than to expect that their parents will supply their every want and need. When parents supply their children's every need, they grow up with a sense of entitlement. Teaching children how to manage money, especially how to earn money, save it, and budget it, are skills they will be grateful for when they enter adulthood.

# Spiritual Parenting and Raising Responsible Children

There is no such thing as the perfect child, even though most of us have some idea of what the perfect child would be for us. Children are not given to us for the purpose of their serving as our reflective mirrors or testimonials of our great parenting skills. Instead, they are given to us for the purpose of nurturing them and teaching them how to become all that they can become. Figure out the five things that you really want for your child. Then ask him what he really wants for himself. How much of your time are you willing to devote to nurturing him so that he achieves those five things?

Raising responsible children is not an easy task. It requires a lot of work, planning, and time. Children learn to be responsible because their parents model responsible behavior and because their parents carefully and consistently nurture them. Parents must give children the freedom to make choices, to demonstrate their judgment, and to learn from their mistakes. Does the child have opportunities to contribute to the running of the household? Is he permitted to structure his time, plan activities, or demonstrate preferences in clothing and food? Is your child permitted to make some choices and decisions for himself, or do you make all the important decisions without including his opinion or desires?

Children who are responsible have parents who raised them with positive discipline and who taught them consequences for their actions using both natural and logical consequences. Such families have taken the time to institute a family mission statement that contains the values to which the family subscribes and the family rules that are used to bring order and discipline to the home. Responsible children have had the good fortune to have parents who gave them chores and who helped them establish goals for themselves. They have internalized the values they were taught about gratitude, sharing, service to others, and kindness so that they have become self-disciplined, no longer requiring their parents' close instruction.

# Summary

This chapter explored the key ingredients for raising responsible children. Some of those key components are positive discipline using natural and logical consequences, as well as setting limits and establishing family rules. It was recommended that families develop their own mission statements to highlight their values and what they stand for in life. Family meetings were suggested as a means to be consciously aware of their relationships and goals. The importance of boundary setting for both children and parents was discussed. Finally, it was suggested that parents need to teach children responsibility in their use of money.

# Parental Reading List

*Children with Challenging Behavior: Strategies for Reflective Thinking* by Linda Brault. (2005). Phoenix, AZ: CPG Publishing Company.
*Challenging Behavior in Children* by Barbara Kaiser. (2003). Boston, MA: Allyn & Bacon.
*Parenting that Works* by Edward R. Christophersen. (2003). Washington, DC: APA Life Tools.
*Kids are Worth It: Giving the Gift of Inner Discipline* by Barbara Coloroso. (2002). Littleton CO: Kids are Worth It.
*Easy to Love, Difficult to Discipline* by Becky Bailey. (2000). New York: William Morrow.
*The Case against Spanking: How to Discipline without Hitting* by Irwin A. Hyman. (1997). San Francisco, CA: Jossey-Bass.

## Character-Building Books for Children

*Heat* by Mike Lupica. Philomel Books, 2006. Teamwork. Family. Hard work pays off.

*Lou Gehrig: The Luckiest Man* by David Adler. Turtleback Books, 2002. Perseverance, dedication, living a good life, not letting bad news ruin a positive outlook.

*Maze* by Will Hobbs. Avon Books, 1998. At 14, Rick Walker's life has hit a dead end. A way out of this maze comes in the high deserts and canyons of Utah. In this high adventure tale of friendship and lost identity, Rick finds a future.

*Peeling the Onion* by Wendy Orr. Mass Market Paperback, 1999. Within seconds Anna's whole life changes. Surviving a car wreck, but physically disabled, she must now discover who she really is.

# Parental Tips

## Tips for Helping Your Child to Establish Goals

Goals can be short-term or long-term. Younger children should focus on short-term goals, while older and more mature children can set their sights on long-term goals. Encourage your child to achieve each step in the goal ladder, rather than just focusing on the end result. Some short-term goals could be as limited as completing the night's homework. Long-term goals include being chosen for the football team or being selected to play in the school's band. Draw a ladder with your child's goal written at the top. Your child can fill in a rung on the ladder for each step he takes toward accomplishing that goal. The following list contains goals for young children of different ages:

- *College planning*—Help your adolescent set goals around college planning. He could identify a college and then set goals for getting into that college.

- *School grades*—Encourage your child to set goals for schoolwork. During the summer, a child might establish a goal of reading one new book each week.

- *Friendship*—Encourage your child to get his friends involved in creating a project that they can work on and enjoy the benefits from working together. The friendship project will strengthen their relationship.

- *Dream chest*—Make a decorated dream chest out of a cardboard box. Have children put pictures of their dreams and goals in this chest. Children will be able to review how the dream chest has changed as they have grown older.

- *Historical hero*—Have your child identify a historical figure whom he admires. Read about the individual to discover his goals and how he achieved them. The historical hero can also become a family project.

- *Dream letter*—Start the school year with a dream letter that describes your child's dreams and hopes. Children identify their dreams (focus on one). They write a dream letter that includes what their dream is, why they have it, what they need to do to accomplish it, the specific steps to fulfill their dream, and a specific date to achieve their dream.

- *Create a storyboard of goals*—Purchase a piece of poster board and attach it to a wall in your child's or adolescent's room where they will see it often. Review two or three magazines a week and help your youngster make a collage of the goals that excite him. As your child works on the collage on a weekly basis, he can see how the goals are blossoming.

- *Hallway of dreams*—Create a "Hallway of Dreams" at school. Each student's name and photo is featured on a large yellow star. On three smaller yellow stars hanging from the large star, each student writes a goal for the school year, a personal goal for something they would like to be or do when they get older, and a dream for our world. Hang the stars in the school hallway to remind students of their goals and to inspire them.

- *"Better Me" list*—Help children create a "Better Me" list—things they can do on a regular basis to improve themselves and build their character. These might include reading one new book a week, helping out a younger brother or sister to gain a skill, calling a grandparent once a month, or studying an extra 15 minutes a day.

- *Children's magazines*—Look in children's magazines such as *Highlights for Children* to locate biographies in which the person achieved a goal he set. Discuss how many people have overcome major obstacles in order to reach their goals.

## Goals for Parents

It is important that parents have goals and that children see their parents working toward their own identified goals. Parents need to achieve goals, if they are to have a sense of fulfillment in life. The focus cannot just be on helping their children to achieve their goals. Most people today spend more time planning a two-week vacation than they do planning their lives by setting goals. Oftentimes, achieving goals is not a problem—it is setting them that is the problem. Far too many people leave their lives to chance—and usually end up broke in money and in dreams by the time they reach retirement. These tips were taken from Hilton Johnson and his *The Top Ten Best Ideas for Setting Goals* (http://www.topachievement.com/hiltonjohnson.html.)

- Write down ten things you want to accomplish this year. By making a list of the things that are important to you, you begin to create images in your mind.

- The three most important things—decide on three things that you want to achieve before you die. Then work back listing three things you want in the next 20 years, 10 years, 5 years, this year, this month, this week, and, finally, the three important things you want to accomplish today. Then act as if it is impossible to fail.

- Make a list of your values. What is really important to you? Your family? Your religion? Your leisure time? Decide on the most important values in your life and then make sure that the goals you set are related to the things you value most.

- Begin with the end in mind—Tom Watson, the founder of IBM, was once asked to what he attributed the phenomenal success of IBM. He said it was three things. The first thing was that he created a very clear image in his mind of what he wanted his company to look like when it was done. He then asked himself how a company like that would have to act on a day-to-day basis. Then in the very beginning of his company, he began to act that way.

## Tips on Maintaining Boundaries: ''If I Am You, Who Am I!''

Our emotional health is tied to the health of our boundaries. If our boundaries are intact, we have a sense of well-being, of being distinct from others. If our boundaries are blurred, we lack a sense of who we really are, what we will tolerate, and what we will not tolerate. Sometimes we get so caught up in our roles as mother, father, and wife that we lose boundaries with the self. Take a sheet of paper and put on it the following title: "If I Am You, Who Am I?" Draw a circle and label it "me." Draw at least two other circles to indicate significant others in your life and label these circles with their names. For instance, it is recommended that one circle be a spouse and another circle a child.

Draw what you believe are the boundaries that you have established with each person. When there is overlap, indicate what you believe is shared in the boundaries. Where there is no overlap, write down what you think is uniquely you, the inner you that is separate from your significant others. Write down the areas of boundary conflict that you have with the significant others you have chosen for this exercise.

## Boundary Quiz Questions: Too Close for Comfort!

Answer the following questions or statements choosing either (3) always, (2) sometimes, or (1) never. Then add up your score.

_____1. Do you tend to use the word "We" when talking with your child's teacher?

_____2. Do you tell your children what to wear and how to style their hair?

_____3. Do you leave the door open when using the bathroom?

_____4. Do you think about your child's problems, even when you have no control over them?

_____5. Do you find yourself angry at family members because you feel used by them?

_____6. Do you volunteer your child's or partner's talents/skills to other people without their consent?

_____7. Do others volunteer your services to different organizations?

_____8. Do you find yourself lending money to children or friends, even though you promised yourself that you would not do this again?

If your score is high, you may need to work on redefining your boundaries with those whom you love.

## Money Habits Quiz for Parents

This is an exercise that may help you determine what you are or are not doing to teach your children money habits for life. Yes answers indicate ways you are helping your child learn money management skills. "No" answers indicate you need to help them more in this area, or you have not dealt with this area. The stage of your child's development will dictate how involved you get with the topics presented in the question.

### Yes/No

1. My children have some money to manage without my interference.
2. I have helped my child set up a savings account.
3. I have given my child financial responsibilities as he has grown older.
4. I am a good money manager and a good role model for handling money.
5. I have taught my children that money requires work.
6. I have taught my child to take into consideration his needs and wants when he purchases an item.
7. I allow my child to make his own money mistakes.
8. I have talked about the need to budget with my child.
9. I have talked with my child about the need for planning before they spend.
10. I compliment my children when they make wise money decisions.
11. I give my child an allowance that he must manage.

# 8

# *The Resilient Child*

*The strongest oak of the forest is not the one that is protected from the storm and from the sun. It's the one that stands in the open where it is compelled to struggle for its existence against the winds and rains and the scorching sun.*

—Napoleon Hill

*Fall seven times; stand up 8 times.*

—Japanese proverb

Jada felt uncomfortable because the conversation of the group had suddenly changed to her. Getting up from her chair in the living room, Jada asked: "Anyone for a second round of coffee." "Come on, Jada; you're not going to get off that easily," Nicole yelled as Jada disappeared into the kitchen for the coffee. "We've all shared our stories, but you. Stop trying to slip out of it."

Going to the kitchen had not changed the subject. When Jada returned to her worn, sunken brown chair, she said: "There's nothing really to tell about my life. Compared to you guys, I've lived an average life. My mother was a school teacher, and my father a postal worker. I have one brother . . . ." After Jada finished, Nicole asked: "But Jada, you had everything going for you, why didn't you ever get your college degree?"

"I don't know. I completed everything except for one semester. I always said I would go back, but then I got married, and had babies . . . and . . . ."

Nicole paused, looked Jada in the eye, and confronted her. "You're getting a divorce, Jada, in a few months, and you don't have a degree . . . . You'll need a job, Jada . . . I just don't understand what happened, Jada. You had more than all of us; yet, you're the only one without a degree."

Jada seemed to be thinking deeply about what Nicole had said to her. Part of her wanted to lash out at Nicole for saying what the rest of the Thursday coffee group was thinking, but was too polite to say. Neither of Nicole's parents had graduated from high school, and both worked as laborers. "I guess," Jada began, "I guess that I never had to want for anything, never had to fight for anything the way you did Nicole. I don't think that I could have survived going through some of the things you talked about . . . . Maybe I just never pushed myself for anything, and now that I am getting a divorce three kids later. I'll find some kind of work. Don't you guys worry about me. I'll be all right." Deep down within she knew her friends were worried, and so was she. How was she going to take care of herself? She had not worked in years.

Jada was right about one thing, though. There is something about struggling that makes us stronger. What is the saying? "What doesn't kill us makes us stronger." Jada never had to fight for anything in her life. Her parents had never let her struggle or want for anything. Whenever Jada was challenged, her parents always seemed to find a way to bail her out. In contrast, adversity had honed Nicole like a strong oak tree.

The paradox of adversity is that we become stronger by confronting our challenges, by trying to master them, rather than by running from or denying them. Enduring human strength emerges from having to reach down deep inside. We have all heard people talk about how they are grateful for the adversity they faced. Some cancer survivors talk about how cancer made them more appreciative of life. "Cancer taught me the true purpose of my life." One survivor of sexual abuse said that she found meaning in her sexual abuse because as a result of that pain she was able to reach out and help others going through similar experiences.

This chapter is about helping your children to become resilient. The word "resilience" comes from the Latin *resilire* (meaning to recoil, jump, or bounce back). It is a general concept that refers to positive adaptation in the face of challenge or stress. The physical sciences and engineering disciplines use the term resilience to describe the capacity of a metal or a spring to withstand stress or strain without breaking, or to refer to the ability of a spring or rubber band to recover to its original state.[1] The term "resilience" suggests a person's ability to recover from traumatic experience, to succeed despite overwhelming odds, and to adapt to the stresses and strains of everyday life. It refers to a person's adaptation and healthy development despite stressors or challenges that might be severe. According to Garmezy, resilience is made of ordinary rather than extraordinary processes.[2] It is the process of an individual's persisting in the face of adversity. Individuals who overcome addictions (e.g., alcoholism and drug abuse) are often labeled "resilient." The average child can be taught to become resilient.

# Why Is Resilience Important for Children?

Learning resilient behavior is important for all children, regardless if they live in the inner city or in a wealthy suburban community. All children need to learn how to bounce back from adversity rather than allowing negative life circumstances to defeat them. Consider, for instance, the life stories of Albert Einstein, Helen Keller, and Thomas Edison. Each one of these individuals was labeled by their teachers as being uneducable and doomed to failure. Yet, each one succeeded and made important contributions to society. Examples of adversity for children would be growing up with a mentally ill parent or growing up in poverty.

Winston Churchill repeated a grade several times while growing up. He was told that he was uneducable. Yet, he did learn. In fact, he soared to heights that some of his doubting teachers never achieved during their entire lifetimes. As the Prime Minister of England, Churchill was asked to give a speech to a graduating class. He stood up and said three words. "Never give up." The crowd responded with loud applause. He sat down and rose two more times to repeat the same phrase, "Never give up." Each time the crowd gave a thunderous applause. Then Churchill left the stage. His speech highlighted a powerful characteristic of resilient people, and that is that they are persistent. They learn how not to give in, even though the going gets tough. As Yogi Berra said: "It ain't over, till it's over."

Research has found that some children develop resilience through natural process but that other children need help.[3] Children's early years hold great promise for teaching them how to become resilient. If parents and educators promote positive growth during the early years, their prospects for favorable development are improved. Everyone benefits when children learn to be resilient. The resiliency approach emphasizes finding and using children's strengths, despite their life circumstances. Resiliency protects children from drug addiction and violence.

# Risk and Protective Factors

Risk and protective factors are central concepts for understanding resiliency. A risk factor is that which increases the likelihood that a person will experience harm. Risk factors increase the chances that a youth will become violent, take drugs, or become involved in teenage pregnancy. Risk factors do not necessarily cause children's unhealthy behaviors; rather they have a strong correlation or association with negative young people's behaviors, such as delinquency or violence. Resilience is the ability of individuals to remain healthy in light of the presence of risk factors.

Risk factors are usually grouped into five categories: (1) individual factors associated with the child or adolescent: (2) family risk factors; (3) school risk factors; (4) peer risk factors; and (5) community risk factors. Risk factors may be internal or external. Internal risk factors involve the way that a child or youth processes or interprets information. For children, internal factors might be their temperament or their attention deficit hyperactivity disorder. Children's unique traits can promote the later development of at-risk behavior. Typically, young people who exhibit internal risk factors have established a learning process that results in negative self-fulfilling prophecies for themselves.

External risk factors are those outside the child, such as growing up in a poor neighborhood or in a low-income family. Prevention of problematic behavior is based on understanding when and how risk factors emerge at different stages of youth development. Risk factors also have varying effects on children depending on their stage of development. Parental absence may have extremely critical effects on a young child, while an adolescent is generally better able to cope with this risk factor. The presence of these factors does not necessarily mean that a young person will become violent. Violent behavior is a result of multiple factors functioning at many levels in the absence of protective factors.

In contrast to risk factors, protective factors are those that potentially decrease the likelihood of engaging in a risk behavior. Not all at-risk youth succumb to their risk factors.[4] Protective factors can influence the level of risk a youth experiences, or they can moderate or buffer the relationship between risk and the behavior. Protective factors help explain why children and adolescents who encounter the same degree of risk may be affected differently. In some instances, children with exposure to risk factors can sometimes elude the full impact because of the presence of protective factors.

Protective factors have additive and cumulative effects. They do not guarantee that a youth will not develop problem behaviors. Smith and his colleagues identified protective factors that contributed to positive outcomes for youth.[5] Educational protective factors included being committed to their education, bonding with teachers, and reaching high reading and mathematics achievement levels. Protective family factors were close parental supervision and a strong parent-child bonding. Lack of sufficient parental supervision was much more critical during adolescence than during middle childhood.

According to Garbarino, each child has a tipping point between doing well and doing poorly. A close relationship with a caring adult who serves as a positive role model is a strong protective factor that shifts a child from being at risk to being resilient.[6] Studies have found that a child who has a good relationship with even one caregiver manifests greater resiliency than one who lacks such a relationship.[7] Benard has listed three key protective factors for children: (1) a caring and supportive relationship with at least one person, preferably an adult; (2) consistently clear, high expectations communicated to the child; and (3) sufficient opportunity to contribute meaningfully to one's social environment.[8]

Similar to risk factors, protective factors can be internal or external. External protective factors involve the family, school or educational system, peers, and community. Family protective factors include good parental supervision, attachment to parents, parental attachment to child, parental involvement in child's activities, effective management of family stress, clear parental expectations for children's behaviors, nurturing and protective parents, quality parental time with children, and a high warmth–low criticism parenting style.

Internal protective factors within a youth are those that may have been influenced by heredity and environment. Key internal protective factors are positive self-esteem, prosocial attitudes, good problem-solving skills, good interpersonal communication skills, positive sense of self-efficacy, good coping skills, average intelligence, a positive outlook on life, a sense of purpose, and a belief in a positive future.[9]

# What Can Parents Learn from Risk and Protector Factor Research?

Parents can learn how to assess their children's present life situation using a risk and protective framework. From Illustration 17, check the risk factors your children have in their lives. Then identify the protective factors that might serve to buffer them from the risk factors. If children have five or more risk factors, they are considered to be at risk for the development of problem behavior. It is the accumulation of risk factors that challenge seriously a person's chances of positive development.

Resiliency should be viewed as something that we promote throughout young people's development by strengthening protective forces in their lives. Protective inputs have to be reinforced continually so that the potential for young people to be resilient when faced with risk factors and vulnerabilities is strong. In short, fostering resilience in children is a process that is developmental and long term; that emphasizes children's strengths rather than their deficits or weaknesses; that nurtures children by placing protective factors in their lives; and that reduces negative outcomes by altering their exposure to risk.

# Family Resiliency: One Pathway to Developing Resilient Children

Young people have a greater chance of becoming responsible, productive citizens if they come from resilient families. If a family is at risk, then the family

Illustration 17    Risk-Related Factors by Life or Social Area

| Context | Risk Factors | Protective Factors |
| --- | --- | --- |
| Individual Related | Low verbal skills | Average intelligence |
|  | Favorable attitudes toward antisocial behavior | First-born Conventional social attitudes |
|  | Psychiatric symptomatology Anxiety, depression, bipolar | Easy temperament Good mental health |
|  | Cognitive bias to attribute hostile intentions to others, aggressive behaviors | Good problem solving skills |
|  | Low expectations for future success, either educationally or vocationally | High levels of self-esteem Positive expectations for future success, school/work |
|  | Poor social skills | Good social skills |
|  | Early display of problem behavior | Absence of early problem behavior |
|  | Minority status | Majority status |
|  | Low self-esteem | Positive self-esteem |
|  | Low self-efficacy | Strong sense of control |
| Family Factors | Lack of supervision and monitoring of child | Good supervision of child during after school hours |
|  | Ineffectual parental discipline | Appropriate parental discipline |
|  | Lack of attachment, bonding and low warmth | Good attachment to parents, bonding with family |
|  | High family conflict | Supportive family environment Good family relationships |
|  | Family models problem behavior of child | Good family role models |
|  | Parental difficulties, e.g., drug abuse, psychiatric disorders of parents | Noncriminal behavior of parents, Good mental health of parents |
|  | Family criminality | Conventional, prosocial family behavior |
| Peer-Related | Association with deviant peers | Bonding with prosocial peers |
|  | Poor peer relationship skills | Good social competence skills |
|  | Low association with prosocial peers | High association with prosocial peers |

|  | Friends dropped out of school, possible drug use | Friends stay in school, peers against drug use |
|---|---|---|
| School-Related | Low academic achievement | Average academic achievement |
|  | Low commitment to education | Commitment to schooling |
|  | Truancy | Good school attendance |
|  | School conduct problems, suspensions, etc. | Conventional or positive school behavior |
|  | Chaotic school, lack of caring teachers and administrators, poor school climate | Caring teachers, supportive school environment, good school climate |
|  | Low teacher expectations for student academic achievement | High teacher expectations for student academic achievement |
|  | School has high rate of school dropouts | School has low percentage of school dropouts |
|  | School puts little emphasis on high academic standards | School has high academic standards |
| Neighborhood and Community | High mobility of people living in community | Stable community membership with long-term community residency |
|  | High crime neighborhood | Safe neighborhood |
|  | Inadequate after school resources for youth in community | Good community resources for positive youth involvement |
|  | Few opportunities for youth to contribute positively to community | Community offers opportunities to engage youth positively |
|  | High disorganization of neighborhood | Strong community organizations |
|  | Low community support for youth | Strong community support for youth, with planned community activities and after school programs, recreational programs |
|  | Lack of an adequate number of mentors and role models | A positive role model or mentors in community |

may lose its ability to protect its children. A number of circumstances can put a family and children at risk, such as divorce, death of a parent, a parent's loss of employment, conflict in the home between two parents, and domestic violence. Families that are facing these challenges may find it difficult to administer their protective function to children.

What is family resiliency? Family resiliency may be conceptualized as the family's ability to use strengths and resources to resist challenges that confront the family when crisis situations occur. It consists of the properties of the family system that enable it to maintain its established patterns of functioning even after it has been challenged and confronted by risk factors. In addition, family resiliency may be conceptualized as the family's ability to recover quickly from a misfortune, trauma, or crisis.

Characteristics that contribute to a family's resiliency include the family's ability to organize itself to meet a crisis, the resources that it is capable of marshalling, its problem solving ability, and its capacity to communicate among its members. Each family should examine how resilient it is because children reflect the resiliency of the family. How cohesive is your family? How effectively does your family deal with boundary issues with children and extended family members? How does your family deal with emotion and time spent together? How adaptable is your family? Does your family act with optimism and positive expectations?

# Emotionally Intelligent Parenting: Key to Developing Resilient Children

## Parents as Emotional Coaches

Being a good parent involves more than just providing a warm and safe place for your children. According to Gottman, parents should be emotional coaches for their children.[10] Emotion coaches are parents who teach their children to deal with life's ups and downs. They neither deny nor object to their children's displays of anger, sadness, or fear. They use parenting to provide their children with emotional moments or opportunities for learning important life lessons and for building closer relationships with them. Gottman recommends five steps for parents to use in emotional coaching of their children, and these are as follows:

1. Become aware of your child's emotion

2. Recognize your child's emotion as an opportunity for intimacy and teaching

3. Listen empathetically and validate your child's feelings

4. Help your child find the words to label the emotion he is having

5. Set limits while exploring strategies to solve the problem the child presents

Gottman maintains that when parents used an emotional coaching style of parenting, their children were more resilient, performed better academically, and were less violent than those who had not received emotional coaching from their parents. Children who received emotional coaching were shielded from the negative effects of their parents' divorce. Gottman found that when fathers showed that they were aware of their children's feelings and tried to help them solve problems, they did better in school and in relationships with others. Conversely, an emotionally distant father who was harsh, critical, or dismissing of their children's emotions had children who were more likely to do poorly in school, fight with friends, and have poor health.

# Characteristics of Resilient Children

Educators have proposed varying characteristics that distinguish resilient young people. While I include many of the traditional resilient characteristics cited by Wolin and Wolin and others, I also suggest different ones, such as being able to self-regulate, having a sense of purpose, having gratitude, having the ability to forgive yourself and others, having perspective taking ability, and being able to set boundaries with others. Some of the resilient characteristics have been discussed in other chapters of this book; hence, these characteristics are mentioned only briefly, and the reader is referred to the more in-depth discussion of the characteristics.

## Resilient Characteristic #1: Bonding with One Caring, Prosocial Adult

The research has become increasingly clear: The most important protective factor that increases young people's resiliency is their positive attachment to a prosocial caring adult. Scholars have begun to refer to young people's attachment as their "connectedness" to family, school, and community. The National Longitudinal Study on Adolescent Health randomly sampled roughly 90,000 adolescents (seventh through twelfth grades) from 134 schools around the United States and interviewed the children, parents, and school administrators.[11] The study examined variables in three categories: (1) individual variables (emotional distress, substance abuse, sexual behavior, religious identity, grades, violence, amount of paid work, perceived chance of dying before age 35, and self-esteem); (2) family variables (parent-family connectedness, family activities, family presence, parental school expectations, parental sex expectations, and family suicide attempts); and (3) school variables (connection to student, prejudice, attendance, dropout rate, class size, and education of teachers).

After demographics were controlled for, the studies found that family and school connectedness were protective against every health-risk behavior measure except pregnancy. On an individual level, self-esteem was the most protective factor. Having too much free time, associating with negative peers, working 20 hours or more a week for pay, anticipation of an untimely death, and academic problems were predictors of smoking, drinking, and acts of violence. Resilient children have a connection to the family, a caring relationship with a caregiver, and structure, such as boundaries and clear expectations. Connections to a school and a mentor were also strong protective factors.

Young people develop their complex social behaviors and skills from modeling the behaviors of others. Infants imitate the facial expressions, gestures, and sounds of the people around them. Although such imitation declines during the elementary school years, observational learning and modeling continue throughout life. We know that modeling impacts everyone. During the teen years, studies have shown that a teen's expectations about their future lives, level of educational attainment, work, and family life are all significantly influenced by adult role models. Such role models are people who the teens perceive to be "like them" or whom they wish to be like. They are also people with whom young people feel comfortable talking about problems that are bothering them. Positive role models for youth are associated with the following outcomes:

- Higher levels of self-esteem and self-efficacy;
- Decreased problem behaviors;
- Decreased early sexual intercourse among females;
- Reduced smoking, alcohol use, and drug use;
- Improved high school graduation rates;
- Positive school adjustment; and
- Higher occupational aspirations and expectations.

## Resilient Characteristic #2: The Ability to Self-Regulate

A child's ability to self-regulate or to control his emotions and emotional response to situations is perhaps the greatest overall resilient characteristics. Buckner, Mezzacappa, and Beardslee conducted an investigation to study the characteristics of resilient youths living in poverty.[12] The authors found that resilient youth were notably different from nonresilient youth in terms of having greater self-regulatory skills and self-esteem, as well as in receiving more active parental monitoring.

Self-regulation refers to children's ability to control their emotions and behavior. Children who can self-regulate can maintain a behavior to achieve a specific goal, with external instruction or motivation. Self-regulation is needed for people to have the capacity to inhibit their behavior. It involves stepping back to think about a situation before acting. Self-regulation is important because it forms the basis of a number of other resilient characteristics, such as the ability to delay gratification. In order for children to self-regulate, they must first be able to inhibit certain behaviors and thoughts; this ability is partly a function of neurological development. Second, self-regulation requires sufficient language skills to accurately represent actions and events. Third, self-regulation requires such cognitive processes as memory for past events, the ability to anticipate consequences of actions, and knowledge of why various emotions have aroused.

Young people become more self-regulating when they learn self-monitoring strategies. Children are not always aware of how often they do something wrong or right. To help them with this process, adults ask them to observe and to record their own behavior. Self-focused observation often brings significant improvements in children's academic and social behaviors. To become self-regulating, children must learn to judge their own behavior.

Parents can help young children to self-regulate by teaching them impulse control by playing such games as "Red Light, Green Light," "Red Rover," and "B-I-N-G-O." These games teach children restraint. For instance, you can move only when the light is "green." In "B-I-N-G-O," a child has to learn not to sing the omitted letter. At age three, most children cannot successfully play the game, "Red Light, Green Light" because they cannot stop themselves from "going" whenever the light comes on. By age five, most children can control themselves, in terms of the green or red light direction. Below is a version of this game.

### ''Red Light, Green Light''

1. One of the children acts as the "stoplight," and the other children are the "cars." The cars line up about 25 feet away, while facing the stoplight.

2. The stoplight then turns around with his back to the cars and says "green light," at which time the cars start moving forward. Without any warning, the stoplight then suddenly yells "red light" and turns around quickly. If the stoplight sees anyone moving, that child then returns to the starting line.

3. The fun part is the cars have to decide if they are going to move forward fast and risk getting caught or move a short distance and then stop so they do not get caught.

4. As soon as someone reaches the stoplight the game is over, and the person who made it all the way gets to be the stoplight for the next game.

### ''B-I-N-G-O Clapping Song''

There was a farmer had a dog,
And Bingo was his name-Oh.
B-I-N-G-O! B-I-N-G-O! B-I-N-G-O!
And Bingo was his name-Oh!

There was a farmer had a dog,
And Bingo was his name-Oh.
Clap-I-N-G-O!
Clap-I-N-G-O!
Clap-I-N-G-O!
And Bingo was his name-Oh.

There was a framer had a dog,
And Bingo was his name-Oh.
Clap, Clap, N-G-O!
Clap, Clap, N-G-O!
Clap, Clap, N-G-O!
And Bingo was his name-Oh! . . .

## Reasons Children Disobey

Parents might interpret their children's disobedience as a willful act of defiance or a moral failure. While sometimes children do disobey willfully, other times they disobey because of delays in their cognitive and psychosocial development or because they are unable to inhibit their actions. Further, sometimes children's limited cognitive development interferes with their memory of a parental rule. Rules have to be repeated many times so that they become a part of children's long-term memory.

Children begin to gain some control over their impulse for immediate gratification of a desired end around the age of three-and-a-half years. Being able to wait for a desired treat or action is a learned skill for a child. Sometimes children are able to delay gratification by distracting themselves. They may go play with their toys while they are waiting for a desired cookie treat. Children who experience permissive and inconsistent parenting are less able to delay immediate gratification than are children raised by parents who use an authoritative style. Parents can teach a child to delay gratification by setting limits, while at the same time permitting some flexibility within boundaries.

Children who learn self-regulation at an early age receive the benefits of such parental teaching throughout their lives. The research indicates that children who are able to self-regulate are better liked by peers, have more self-confidence and self-esteem, are more independent, have better cognitive and social skills, perform better academically, are better able to handle stress and frustration during adolescence, and have better career success in adulthood.[13]

## Resilient Characteristic #3: Self-Esteem

Children grow up with definite beliefs about themselves, their personal attributes, and their strengths and weaknesses. Self-esteem refers to the feelings people have about their capabilities and worth. The concepts of self-concept and self-esteem overlap. In general, the term "self-concept" refers to a complex hierarchy of beliefs, whereas self-esteem remains a single global feeling about oneself. The behaviors of family members, teachers, and peers influence children's self-esteem. To boost children's self-esteem, parents must accept their children as they are and treat their concerns as important. On the other hand, parents who punish children for the things they cannot do, without also praising them for the things they do well, are likely to have children with low self-esteem.

Children's self-esteem is also affected by teachers' expectations of them and by their peers' evaluations. Peers communicate information about a young person's social competence. Some adolescents are preoccupied with their peers' approval and form their own sense of self-worth largely on what peers think of them. Moreover, biology or physical appearance is a highly significant factor in the self-esteem of people of all ages. Inherited temperamental tendencies, physical skills, and intellectual capabilities also contribute to children's positive or negative self-appraisal.

Children and adolescents behave in ways that are consistent with their self-beliefs and their expectations for future success or failure.[14] Therefore, it is important that parents let their children know they have high, positive expectations for them. Students who believe they have high academic ability are more inclined to pay attention in class, use effective learning strategies, seek out challenges, and persist when confronted with difficulty.[15] Conversely, students who believe they are "poor students" are more likely to misbehave in class, study infrequently, and ignore homework assignments.

Children who believe in themselves are more resilient than those who have low self-esteem because their self-esteem encourages them to get up and try another day. They believe that they can impact their circumstances positively, and they act to bring about the desired outcomes. Good self-esteem is the basis for mental health, and the lack of it forms the foundation for such problems as alcoholism, drug abuse, juvenile delinquency, and poor academic achievement. It is, therefore, important that parents encourage positive self-esteem in children.

If parents want to build self-esteem in their children, they need to do two things: First, teach them a skill they do not already have. The skill can be about anything that helps to expand your children's skills repertoire, such as writing poetry or doing imaginative art work. When children learn a particular skill, it builds their sense of competence, which leads them to positive self-esteem. Second, teach them how to use the skills so that they can be of service to someone.

Other parental tips for raising children with positive self-esteem include: treat your children respectfully, ask their views and opinions, and give them meaningful feedback, instead of just brushing them off with a perfunctory comment. Parents can help their children develop and maintain healthy self-esteem by helping them to cope with defeats rather than minimizing them. Teach your children that they have the ability to resolve and to rise above their defeats. In this way, children will come to see themselves as survivors rather than as victims.

Try not to be judgmental with children. If you are giving children constructive feedback, present it as positively as possible. To avoid creating sibling rivalry, do not compare siblings. Show that you have positive expectations for children and that you believe in them. Make sure that you emphasize your children's strengths rather than their weaknesses. Give your children at least three compliments a day on something they have done well.

Use weekly "I Appreciate Days" so that children understand that they are valued and loved. For instance, some families choose a different family member each week, and during dinner, everyone states what he appreciates about the other person. Oftentimes, families neglect to say what they appreciate about other family members' efforts. Giving your child a foundation of positive self-esteem can be likened to giving him a lifelong gift that he can continually use to deal with life circumstances.

Parents might make it a habit to give ten words of acknowledgement or appreciation each day to your child. The bond between the two of you will grow, and so will your child's self-esteem. Goethe has said, "If you treat an individual . . . as if he were what he ought to be and could be, he will become what he ought to be and could be," and William James once said, "The deepest desire in human nature is the craving to be appreciated." To experience more connection with your child and to increase his self-esteem, begin by giving small acknowledgements to your child each day. As a parent, you might consider saying to your child:

- I appreciate it when you work so hard.
- Thanks for being so quiet today when you knew I was busy on the telephone.
- I like watching you grow up.
- I am so glad that I am your mother.
- I am really glad that you are my child.
- My love for you grows bigger each day.

Another way parents can increase their children's self-esteem is to leave love notes for them in unexpected places. A parent can write a love note on the napkin of her child's lunch. Some messages a parent might leave are: "All of this will be funny in 10 years, so why not laugh now." "If you share your sorrow, you only carry half its weight." "I'll be there for you no matter what." Some messages for a teen might be: "I enjoy watching you grow into an adult." "I trust you, and I believe that you can trust yourself." "You have the ability to make your dreams come true." "It's okay to feel confused sometimes." Parents should remember that it is a special honor to influence and nurture a child. It is part of the natural life cycle to give back what we received.

## Resilient Characteristic #4: Empathy and Kindness

*No act of kindness, no matter how small, is ever wasted.*

—Aesop

Empathy has come to be regarded as an important attribute of a successful learner and resilient children. Empathy is defined as a person's affective capacity to share in another's feelings—to recognize, perceive, and feel indirectly the feelings of another person. Empathy is often characterized as an individual's ability to put himself in another person's shoes. It is also a person's ability to understand another person's perspective and to communicate their views.

The current belief is that children have a biologically based readiness to respond empathically to virtually anything, once they view it in terms of its strivings and struggles. Children are born with the innate capacity to act kindly toward others. Opportunities for encouraging empathy and kindness in children appear early in life and continue to develop across the life span. There are differences in how and how often children act kindly toward others; yet, all children go through a set sequence of developing kind and caring behavior. Young children's selfish and territorial behaviors are part of normal development. Typical examples of children's caring behavior are the following: (1) sympathetic crying among groups of babies; (2) a toddler comforting a baby doll; (3) a toddler sharing blocks with another child; (4) a preschooler bringing bandages to an injured classmate; (5) a preschooler hugging and comforting a crying sibling; (6) school-age children collecting canned goods for a food bank; and (7) an adolescent volunteering to shovel snow for an elderly neighbor. Parents might take into consideration that females usually exhibit higher levels of empathy than males; however, empathy training can reduce this difference. Classrooms that use cooperative learning groups and cross-age peer tutoring groups also facilitate empathy in children. Child-rearing practices positively associated with the development of empathetic understanding and behavior include:

- Explaining to children the effects of their behavior on others;
- Pointing out to children that they have the power to make others happy by being kind and generous to them;
- Modeling (parental) of caring behavior toward family members;
- Helping children who have hurt or distressed others understand why their behavior is harmful; and
- Encouraging children to discuss their feelings and problems with adults.

Children are better able to put themselves in another person's place and are more likely to feel sympathy for that person when they know what the person feels and why the person feels as he does. If a mother says, "Stop banging on the toy," children may not stop the banging. But if a mother says, "Stop banging on the toy; the noise is hurting Mommy's head and she feels sad," children tend to stop the banging. In the second instance, the mother has provided the children with the information they need to understand her feelings. When parents share their needs with children so that they know how they can make life easier for them, children are likely to feel empathy for their parents.

Child-rearing practices that are related negatively to the development of empathetic understanding and behavior include threats and physical punishments directed toward inducing children to "behave," inconsistent behavior toward children's expression of emotional needs, and the provision of extrinsic rewards or bribes designed to get good behavior from children. Empathy instructions

Illustration 18   Developmental Milestones of Kindness (8 Months to 12 Years)

| Age | Characteristics | Example |
|---|---|---|
| 8 to 18 Months | Child understands that own behavior can make another happy or sad. | "If I kiss my baby sister, she will stop crying." |
| | Child understands adult instructions for kind behavior when words are used with actions. | Mother says: "Pet the dog gently," and the child imitates the mother's actions. |
| 2 to 3 Years | Child begins to show empathic behavior. | Child may spontaneously comfort his crying brother. |
| | Child complies more often with adult requests for socially responsive behavior. | Child more willingly takes turns, says "please" and "thank you," helps clean up at home. |
| 4 to 6 Years | Child recognizes concept of fairness. | "You gave him more ice cream than you gave me." |
| | Child begins to understand that selfish behavior may be wrong. | "If I take all the blocks, my brother will have nothing to play with." |
| | Child participates in more kinds of empathic behavior. | Child can share, comfort, protect, and encourage. |
| | Child can plan in advance to do something nice for another person. | "I want to give my old books and toys to the kids who live in the shelter." |
| 6 to 12 Years | Child can take the perspective of another and can recognize possible reasons for another person's feelings and actions. | "Jim doesn't have any friends to play with. Maybe I will play with him at school." |
| | Child can understand right and wrong and think about what might happen after doing something wrong. | "It is wrong that Stan cheated on his test." |

and training improve children's affective and cognitive behavior. Such training should focus initially on the child's feelings as a point of departure for relating to others. Next, a parent emphasizes the similarities between the child's feelings and the feelings of others. Finally, a parent then asks the child to demonstrate a caring, empathic response to the other person. Children who are resilient know how to demonstrate empathy and kindness toward others. In return, the world responds positively to them.

## *Resilient Characteristic #5: Problem Solving and Decision–Making Ability*

Young people who have good problem-solving and decision-making skills are more resilient and successful than those who lack these skills. Ineffectual problem solving and decision-making leads to poor choices and the resultant consequences of those choices. Children and adolescents who do not have confidence in their own judgment are easily manipulated by others. They will look to others to make decisions for them.

If you want your children to have confidence in their own judgments, make them feel good about themselves by praising their attempts at independent thought and action, acknowledging even small steps toward independence. Do not make your children feel stupid for making mistakes. On the contrary, teach them to expect to make mistakes, and not to be too disturbed when they do make errors. The more faith that your children have in their own decision-making ability, the more willing they will be to rely on their own personal standards when faced with tough issues. You can increase children's confidence in their decision-making ability by giving direct experience and training in decision-making.

Think of the problem-solving process as having four P's: (1) define the problem; (2) generate possibilities; (3) create a plan; and (4) perform your plan. To define a problem effectively, you need to understand that there is a mismatch between what you want and what you have. Problem solving is about reducing the gap between these two factors. Begin with what you have. Tell the truth about what is present in your life right now, without shame or blame. "I am not doing well in social studies because I don't like studying for it." Next, describe in detail what you would like to be the case. "I want to get a B in social studies on my next report card."

After you have taught your child to define the problem and to state what he would like to be the case, you are ready to take the next step. Step 2 involves helping your child to generate possibilities. Have your child brainstorm as many possible solutions to the problem as he can. Gather relevant information related to each of the possibilities. The third step involves helping him to create a plan. After rereading your problem definition and list of possible solutions, choose the solution that seems best. Make sure that your solution reflects your values. Consider the specific actions that will reduce the gap between what you have and what you want. Then visualize the steps you will take to make the chosen solution a reality and put them in chronological order. Put your plan in writing. The final step is to have your child perform the plan. Resilient children understand how to go about problem solving and good decision-making, despite their life circumstances.

## *Resilient Characteristic #6: An Attitude of Gratitude*

Gratitude plays an important role in a person's sense of well-being. Most religions have long exalted the virtue of gratitude as something that people should seek. Recently, psychologists have begun to link gratitude with self-empowerment, health, and resiliency. McCollough, Tsang, and Emmons found that individuals who kept a daily gratitude diary reported high levels of alertness, enthusiasm, happiness, and determination.[16]Additionally, the gratitude group experienced less depression and stress, was more likely to help others, exercised more regularly, and made more progress toward personal goals. According to the findings, people who feel grateful are also more likely to feel loved.

McCollough, Tsang, and Emmons also noted that gratitude encouraged a positive cycle of reciprocal kindness among people since one act of gratitude encourages another. Although gratitude is a part of most religions, it works independently of faith. Research suggests that people can increase their sense of well-being and create positive social effects just from counting their blessings. Gratitude helps people to take a more positive perspective on the adversity they may be facing. When we feel gratitude, a positive message travels along a nerve in our brain. When this message reaches the end of the nerve, it releases chemicals that are picked up by the next nerve, permitting the message to be continued throughout the brain. These chemicals are called neurotransmitters, and they have a calming effect on the brain by increasing levels of other chemicals such as serotonin, which has been found to produce a feeling of peace and calm. The more genuinely positive messages that are sent to the brain, the more neuro-chemicals are released and the more our feelings of peace and contentment are increased.

When we feel gratitude, even for the smallest things in our lives, the brain responds by releasing chemicals that give us a good feeling that allows us to view ourselves and what is happening to us more positively than if we viewed the event totally negatively. Feelings of gratitude also have the effect of placing our minds on more positive events in our lives. If we fake feelings of gratitude and tell ourselves to stay positive, our brains will still release chemicals, but not the calming ones associated with gratitude. The downside of faking is that the brain will not develop new pathways that help us to cope.

When adversity happens to us, it is important for us to fully experience it, and not dull our experiences. Each emotion functions to create and strengthen pathways within the brain so that, with each successive event, we are better able to cope. Going through adversity truly does make us stronger physically and emotionally, and we become more resilient. People who avoid the negative aspects of a situation by denying or repressing the negative emotions eventually lose the ability to experience a full range of emotions. They do not build up the brain circuitry or neurochemical pathways needed to cope with adversity.

When we repress emotions, our bodies interpret such repression as stress, and our bodies release cortisol, a stress hormone designed to guard the body against injury. When we repeatedly repress our emotions, cortisol levels increase to dangerous levels and eventually begin to erode the immune systems, making us vulnerable to illness and injury. Some people may even collapse under the pressure.

Hence, the act of being grateful promotes our health and well-being, but it is a choice. When we choose to wallow in a situation, we tend to grow increasingly bitter and resentful. When we choose to experience a negative emotion and say that we are grateful that we can learn from it, we build both a neurological and a physical resilience. At this point, we can state that we are truly grateful for having experienced the adversity and the adversity has made us stronger.

Children and adolescents need to be taught how to respond to adversity with gratitude rather than with learned helplessness. Adversity is a two-sided coin. One side of the adversity contains the negative event, while the other side provides the opportunity to use our talents, strengths, and inner fortitude to overcome it. Adversity brings lessons to be learned that make us stronger to deal with other challenging situations in our lives. As young people observe themselves being grateful for the adversity and other problems in their lives, they become more resilient. They know that they are going to learn a valuable lesson and discover something very positive about themselves that they might not have known before.

Modeling gratitude is the best way for parents to teach their children to be grateful. Letting your children see that you are grateful for small things will start them on the right road. Say "thank you" to them for doing a good job with their chores or to the bus driver when he brings your child home safely. Establishing family rituals is another good way for parents to teach children to be grateful. Start dinner with each family member sharing what he is most grateful for. Establish a bedtime ritual for your children by having them reflect on the day and share what they were grateful for that happened during the day.

Moreover, parents can begin teaching their children to feel gratitude by doing small things, such as saying a grace or blessing of thankfulness at mealtimes. Have your children make a daily entry into a gratitude journal. Write down three things each day for which you are grateful. Have your children write thank you notes for gifts. Writing what they enjoyed about a gift reminds your children to be grateful for both the gift and the person who gave it.

Children who feel daily gratitude are inclined to feel happy and to be resilient. That is because gratitude is a powerful mood lifter. Focusing on what you are thankful for turns negative thoughts to positive ones. It can also instill hopefulness when situations seem insurmountable. Teaching children how to experience and express gratitude will probably aid them in their social interactions with playmates, teachers, and others in their social world. It is simply more pleasurable to be around people who are grateful for the little things in life than to be around those who continually complain or gripe about what they do not have.

## *Resilient Characteristic #7: Positive Outlook on Life*

Research has also found that individuals who have a positive outlook on life are more resilient than those who hold a pessimistic outlook. Optimistic people are able to see the positive in a given situation. It is not what happens to us but our response to it that predicts our emotional health. Children can learn to be more resilient by becoming more optimistic in response to difficulty.

Children who are optimistic expect that their experiences will be pleasant and fulfilling. Negative events in their lives can shake their natural optimism. Children who believe that negative situations are temporary and that they can take steps to make their future better have better mental health than those who have a pessimistic outlook. Children who have negative outlooks on life tend to be at risk for such mental disorders as anxiety and depression.

Children's thoughts are very powerful because they affect their entire attitude. In turn, their attitudes affect the people around them. Children who have positive thoughts attract people to them because such thoughts energize them. Hence, a positive attitude promotes better health, longer life, more friends, less stress, and more success. Conversely, negative thoughts have a draining effect on those around us. A negative attitude repels people while a positive one attracts them. If parents want children who are able to socialize and who are chosen by other children, they need to teach them the benefits of having a positive attitude. Parents can teach children to have a positive attitude by helping them to plan their day in a positive manner. Have your child visualize himself waking up with plenty of energy or imagine enjoying himself at school, learning from his teacher, and playing positively with his classmates.

## *Resilient Characteristic #8: Forgiveness and Letting Go*

Virtually all major religions stress the importance of forgiveness. Recently, however, forgiveness has emerged in psychology as a key factor in children's and adults' mental health. Forgiveness represents a person's decision to stop feeling resentment toward an offender or a perceived offense. Learning to forgive others and oneself for playing a role in causing harm promotes resiliency because there is something of the message: "I am still standing, in spite of all that you did to me." Forgiving may transform a negative situation into a positive one.

Forgiving oneself and others starts the healing process, especially in situations that have been fraught with conflict. Forgiving is not the same as forgetting, pardoning, condoning, excusing, or denying the harm that one person does to another. Forgiveness helps to make children and adolescents less angry, resentful, fearful, interested in revenge, or remorseful. Frequently, violence stems from our holding on to anger, hurt, and pain and from our lack of forgiveness of a transgression. As a consequence, we may rehearse the offense repeatedly in our minds. Forgiving persons choose to experience, appropriately express, and then let go of negative feelings of anger, guilt, and retaliation. In this manner, forgiveness increases our resiliency.

Forgiveness allows relationships to continue, despite mistakes, betrayals, or failures to meet expectations. It allows the one who is offended to let go of the negative effect that would interfere with a relationship continuing. Forgiveness makes it possible for relationships to continue and prosper after threats to it have occurred and is, therefore, an important tool in the maintenance of serious, long-term relationships within the family, between parents and children, and between partners.

To truly forgive, one must allow oneself to experience and acknowledge the hurt as opposed to denying or forgetting it. Forgiveness also requires the development of a more complex view of an offender, especially if the offending person is a parent. The child no longer has an idealized view of his parent, but instead may see the parent with both positive and negative capabilities and behaviors. Other factors affecting forgiveness are more specific to the relationship or the circumstances surrounding the event, such as importance of the relationship, receipt of an apology, or perceived remorse. Attachment style has also been found to be related to forgiveness, with those having a secure attachment style being more able or likely to forgive.

Everett Worthington[17] offers the REACH model for forgiveness, with each letter in "reach" standing for a particular behavior or attitude.

- R = Recall the hurt or pain the person has caused you.
- E = Empathize with the one who has inflicted the harm on you.
- A = [offer the] Altruistic gift of forgiveness.
- C = [make a] Commitment to yourself to forgive.
- H = Hold on to the forgiveness.

Forgiveness needs to be voluntary rather than forced. When forgiveness is forced, it is experienced as a betrayal of oneself. Therefore, parents should not try to force a child to forgive another person. If the child is to heal from the pain of the hurt or offense, then he must offer forgiveness as a gift freely given to the other person. People become more resilient when they forgive because they learn that they are in control of their emotions and the responses to things that people do to harm them. A resilient person says, "I am not going to let the pain that you caused me to destroy the rest of my life. Therefore, I forgive you, and I let go of my hurt and all negative feelings associated with what you did." Forgiving another person allows us to put the past behind us and to get on with our lives. It is the first step toward healing ourselves. We release ourselves from the pain that was inflicted upon us.

We teach our children to forgive by role modeling forgiveness toward them. Parents emphasize to children that forgiveness is a letting go and a healing process that will free them from their anger and pain. They do not have to play the role of the victim any longer. They release the emotional attachment to the offender and dismiss him with forgiveness. Parents teach children that forgiveness is a conscious decision.

## Resilient Characteristic #9: Establish a Spiritual or Moral Foundation

Children are more resilient when they have established within themselves a moral or spiritual framework from which to make decisions and to judge their actions and those of others. For a long time, studies have reported that individuals who are grounded within a religion tend to be happier than those who are less spiritual. There is the old adage that the family that prays together stays together. Spiritual development is conceptualized as a young person's search for meaning and purpose in life. It is often the focus of religious groups; however, a person's spirituality may be viewed as broader than religion. Spirituality involves understanding one's connectedness to people and the world around, including one's relationship with nature. The self is embedded within something that is larger than the self. Spirituality is shaped both within and outside of religion.

Spiritual development is a universal human process that has been said to take place across time and cultures. Studies have found spirituality to be related inversely to a number of negative outcomes and positively associated with numerous positive outcomes.[18] Children's primary nurturing relationships influence their early spiritual development. Oftentimes the child attributes to his parents the perfections and abilities that he later assigns to God. For adults, spirituality is associated with less criminal activity, less use and abuse of drugs and alcohol, high levels of reported personal happiness, higher levels of hope and optimism, and a stronger sense that one's life has purpose and meaning. For adolescents, religiosity is associated with reduced likelihood of violence (murder), safer driving and more seat belt use, decreased juvenile delinquency, less substance abuse, and fewer endorsements of engaging in high-risk conduct.

Spirituality serves as a protective mechanism for young people because it increases their social connectedness (if affiliated with a religious group) and it provides a framework of meaning that emphasizes gratitude, forgiveness, patience, and hope. Children who are involved in a religious group or who profess some kind of spirituality are more effective at resolving feelings of loneliness, show greater regard for the self and others, and have a stronger sense that life has meaning and purpose. As part of their spiritual development, young people ask such questions as: Why am I here? What is the purpose of my life? How should I live? What will happen when I die? In essence, spirituality deals with the human need to know what is true about life's purpose and ultimate ends.

# *Parenting as a Spiritual Journey*

Parents, even those who profess not to be spiritual, teach their children a sense of spirituality and connectedness from the earliest of days. Spirituality involves a way of looking at the world, ourselves, and other people. It consists of what we believe deeply about the universe, who controls it, and how we go about living in our daily world. Parents who are truly spiritual know that they can only guide their children. They view parenting as a privilege rather than as a chore. Some of the words of Kahlil Gibran, the poet, capture the spirituality of parenting children.

### On Children

And a woman who held a babe against her bosom said, Speak to us of Children.
And he said:
Your children are not your children.
They are the sons and daughters of Life's longing for itself.
They come though you but not from you,
And though they are with you, yet they belong not to you.
You may give them your love but not your thoughts.
For they have their own thoughts.
You may house their bodies but not their souls,
For their souls dwell in the house of tomorrow, which you cannot visit, not even in your dreams.

# *Summary*

Most parents want to raise resilient children, children who can pick themselves up after adversity and bounce back. We spend a lot of time teaching our children to master academic knowledge and to do well on aptitude and achievement tests. We would do well to spend much more time on nurturing our children's emotional development, for it is the latter that will make the difference between their success or failure and their happiness in life. Nine resilient characteristics were reviewed.

# *Parental Reading List*

*Duck on a Bike* by David Shannon. Blue Sky Press, 2002, 1991. The farmyard animals have a range of thoughts and feelings as they watch Duck peddle past on a bike.
*Moondance* by Frank Asch. Scholastic, 1993. Little Bird helps his friend Bear challenge some negative beliefs and follow his desire to dance with the clouds, the rain, and the moon.

*Nancy Mitford (Vintage Lives)* by Selina Hastings. Vintage, 2002.
*Would You Rather . . .* by John Burningham. Red Fox, 1994. A source for discussion about making choices and the consequences of decisions.

# Intentional Parenting Tips

The following exercises and quizzes are designed to help parents and teachers to become resiliency builders for children and their families.

## Learning the Power of Words to Promote Parental Resilience

In a family gathering (or with your partner or best friend) use two minutes to:

• Tell a story of yourself as a victim.
• Use three words to describe how you felt describing yourself as a victim.

Again, use two minutes to:

• Tell a story of yourself as a survivor.
• Use three words to describe how you felt describing yourself as a survivor.
• What gave you the strength to be a survivor?
• What specific strength(s) did you use to be a survivor?
• Considering your story, would you consider yourself resilient? If so, why, and if not, why not?

## How Have I Done As Well As I Have Done!

Parents and children sometimes take their own accomplishments and efforts for granted. Yet, each of us at some time in our lives has been called upon to use our innate capacity for overcoming adversity. To promote our own and our children's self-esteem, we need to examine how we have done as well as what we have done. This exercise is designed to help parents and children to recognize their strengths and to understand how they use their strengths to overcome adversity or to become resilient.

In a small circle with partner or family members, each person takes a turn to respond to the following questions:

• How have I done as well as I have done?
• What are the two biggest challenges that I have had to overcome in my life?
• What strengths did I use to overcome them?
• What strengths do I use everyday to cope effectively with the stresses in my life?

- What specific qualities, supports, skills, attitudes, aptitudes, and talents have I relied on to take me this far?

Now repeat this exercise with your children. Children feel stronger just relating a positive story about themselves. Children need to be taught how to recognize their strengths and how to use their strengths to become resilient, a survivor rather than a victim. Using the resilience route is not easy to do. We all live in a world that tends to be obsessed with "what is wrong" rather than "what is right." Families need to learn how to:

- Give themselves and others credit for all we have overcome, all the ways we have demonstrated resiliency. We must teach our children how to name the strengths they used to secure their accomplishments.
- Spend time focusing on how we have done as well as we have done as a family, and suspend temporarily the focus on what has not yet been accomplished.
- Identify the best things about the family and individual members in the family.
- Teach children and other family members that maximizing their strengths is the best path to success.

## *Personal Resiliency Builders*

Put a check by the top three or four resiliency builders you use most often. Ask yourself how you have used these in the past or currently use them. Think of how you can best apply these resiliency builders to current life problems, crises, or stressors.

_____ 1. Relationships—uses sociability and the ability to form positive social relationships.

_____ 2. Service—provides service to others or to a cause.

_____ 3. Humor—uses laughter and humor to deal with adversity.

_____ 4. Insight or perceptiveness—uses understanding of people and situations to resolve issues.

_____ 5. Positive view of the future and one's life chances—sees the glass as half full rather than half empty.

_____ 6. Flexibility—adjusts to change easily and can bend as needed to meet life circumstances.

_____ 7. Self-esteem—has positive feelings of self-worth.

_____ 8. Spirituality—evidences a personal belief or faith in something greater than oneself.

_____ 9. Persistence or perseverance—does not give up easily, keeps on keeping on.

_____10. Inner direction—uses an internal frame of reference to make decisions.

_____11. Attitude of gratitude—expresses thankfulness for the good and bad of life.

_____12. Ability to self-regulate—can control one's emotions or channel them to reach a goal.

_____13. Sense of purpose in life—knows where he is going in life and why.

_____14. Attitude of forgiveness—forgives others in order to get on with life.

_____15. Boundary setting with others—shows the ability to establish psychological and personal boundaries with others.

## Emotional Parenting Quiz

This quiz is designed to help parents reflect upon their parenting practices for building emotional intelligence within their children. Answer true or false to the following statements. Give yourself a 1 for each false answer and a 2 for each true answer. Add your total points.

_____ 1. I have taught my child to be aware of his own feelings.

_____ 2. I have used ordinary life situations to help my child identify and label specific feelings in himself.

_____ 3. I have helped my child to identify specific feelings in others.

_____ 4. My child and I talk about emotions on a regular basis.

_____ 5. My child knows a number of words to describe his emotions and those of others.

_____ 6. My child knows what causes his emotions.

_____ 7. My child can help his brothers and sisters to identify their emotions.

_____ 8. I have taught my child how to turn his negative emotions into positive emotions.

_____ 9. My child understands how his thoughts affect how he feels.

_____10. My child talks to me about his feelings.

_____11. My child can manage his emotions.

_____12. My child has the ability to use his emotions to make good decisions.

_____13. My child uses his emotions constructively to deal with others.

_____14. My child understands that how he feels is based partly on the way he views things.

_____15. My child has learned how to adapt to different situations in a positive manner.

High scores indicate that the parent has spent time teaching his child emotional intelligence. Low scores suggest that more parental work may need to be done for increasing the child's emotional intelligence.

## Building Resiliency Characteristics: Theme of the Month

Choose a theme that your family responds to on a monthly basis. For instance, post the definition of persistence on the family bulletin board. At the family meetings, read excerpts from a biography about someone who modeled courage, such as Mahatma Gandhi or Martin Luther King, Jr. During the month, post quotations, proverbs, cartoons, or articles for family members to read. At the family meeting, each person shares a story about how he was persistent, or courageous, or whatever the theme of the month is.

# 9

# *It Takes a Village: Nurturing a Nonviolent Child Is a Process And a Journey*

*To put our nation in order, we must first put our families in order; to put our families in order, we must nurture our children. No one raises a child alone. We need a village to truly nurture our children and to guide them through life's journey.*

## Children as Entrusted Gifts from God

Children are gifts from God entrusted to us for nurturing and care. They are not ours to possess or to own, but rather they are our trustees for only a short period of time. No one raises a child alone because no man is an island unto himself. Instead, we are all a part of the main—all part of a village. We share in the journey upon which children embark, including the twists and turns in the various roads they take.

It takes a village to raise a child because no matter how loving or caring we are as parents, children need more than our love and our care to survive along the way. They need a village that cares about them, that is responsive to their needs, and that works in partnership with their parents and families for their good. Villages are strong only to the extent that the families that comprise them are strong. Families are the basic unit of a society, and if that unit is damaged or impaired, ripple effects are felt in other sections of the village, including our schools and our justice system.

The national statistics suggest that we are not doing all that we can to nurture American children. More than 15 million American youth are labeled "at risk." Compared to other Western nations, American children suffer from higher rates of depression, anxiety, attention deficit hyperactivity disorder, conduct disorders, suicide ideation, and other serious mental and behavioral problems.

The statistics on Americans are alarming in virtually all major categories that measure their well-being. One out of every four adolescents in the United States is currently at serious risk of not achieving a productive adulthood.[1] Approximately 21 percent of youth ages 9 to 17 have a diagnosable addictive disorder. Four million children and adolescents in this country struggle with a serious mental disorder that causes significant functional impairments at home, at school, and with peers. More children suffer from psychiatric illness than from leukemia, diabetes, and AIDS combined.[2] About 3 million American children suffer from attention deficit hyperactivity disorder.[3]

According to a 2007 study in the *Journal of the American Medical Association,* about 25 million children age 17 and under are either overweight or obese. This figure represents nearly one-third of the 74 million American youth in that age group[4,5] An epidemic of childhood obesity may result in long-term medical and financial consequences for this nation. Currently, the direct medical costs attributed to overweight and obesity account for slightly more than 9 percent of all national health expenditures. The number of overweight children has tripled among preschoolers and quadrupled among 6 to 11 year olds. This population age group is likely to become an increasing burden to the American health care system.

Yet, health issues are not the only problems young people face. Violence directed outward (murder) and inward (suicide) continue to plague America's youth. Homicide is the leading cause of death for African American males age 15–24. Suicide is the third leading cause of death for 15 to 24 year olds and the sixth leading cause of death for 5 to 15 year olds in our country. More teenagers and young adults die from suicide than from cancer, heart disease, AIDS, birth defects, stroke, pneumonia, influenza, and chronic lung disease combined. Although we have witnessed shocking school violence on our television sets, children are more at risk of violence at home and on the streets than in school. An incident of child abuse is reported, on average, every 10 seconds. More than 2.9 million reports were made in 2003; the actual incidence is presumed to be much higher.

American boys are an endangered group. Statistics indicate that American boys are at a greater risk than girls for learning disabilities, illiteracy, dropping out of school, substance abuse problems, violence, juvenile arrest, and early death caused by violent behavior. Further, increasing numbers of children are growing up in homes without a father present, and studies report that an overwhelming number of violent criminals in the United States are males who grew up without fathers.[6]

The American village is at serious risk because of the problems that our youth are currently facing. These problems are not going to go away without concerted, intentional effort on our part. No one group can solve the issues and problems associated with our youth. Violence among youth is a public health issue in our nation. It will take the all groups working together to solve youth violence.

# Building Young People's Resiliency: An American National Agenda

Our national agenda must be to nurture young people, to reduce the risk factors that impinge upon their lives, and to increase the protective factors that will build their resiliency. Each school must conduct its own assessment of the risk factors that challenge their students and the protective factors that it plans to implement. Schools should consider making social and emotional learning a central part of the educational curriculum. Additionally, schools must work to increase the resiliency of youth. Resiliency training might help youth to become less vulnerable to such mental health issues of depression, anxiety, violence, and suicide.

Moreover, instead of focusing primarily on young people's deficits, schools must emphasize their strengths. The culture of a school should provide a setting in which young people feel safe, supported, valued, listened to, and respected. Nurturing nonviolent children is both a process and a journey. You nurture your children intentionally when you make conscious decisions about how you are going to raise them—for instance, what values you intend to instill and how you will discipline them.

# Recommended Parental Resolutions for Responding to Children

1. *Resolve to be positive toward your child.* Look for things your child says and does correctly. Many of us were conditioned within our families to look for the negative. Pay attention to your child's correct behavior, while not ignoring his misbehavior. Do not negatively reinforce your child; pay attention to your child's polite requests (please), not his whining, teasing, and tantrums. Reinforce your child's calm discussions, not arguments and power struggles. Focus on the positive attitudes and behavior in your children. You will improve your relationship with your child by being more positive toward him.

2. *Help your child to feel connected to family and to feel secure at home and at school.* A parent who builds a solid relationship with his child provides a secure base from which the child can explore the world and begin the

learning process. Children need to know that their parents will be there for them regardless if they succeed or fail. When there is a strong bond between a parent and child, a child is more likely to trust what his parents say, share their values, and let them know when they require help. Children feel a bond with a parent when they believe they are listened to and when they sense their feelings matter. Each day or night review your child's day and share his emotions, and the bond will grow stronger.

3. *Encourage your child, teaching him logical consequences of actions.* When you encourage your children, they will have faith and confidence in themselves. Use encouragement rather than punishment, as a means to change your child's behavior. Punishment of negative behavior only temporarily suppresses the child's displaying that behavior. The behavior returns as soon as the memory of the punishment fades into the background. Help your child to do the right thing, not because someone is presenting him with an external reward of some sort, but rather because it is the right thing to do.

4. *Be consistent in your communications, actions, and discipline toward your child.* Consistency is the key to working with your child. In order for children to learn to make correct decisions, they must be able to predict the consequences of their behavior. They must be able to see the cause-effect relationship between how they behave and what happens to them. When children can predict how their parents will respond, they not only make better choices but also have better guidelines for their behavior. Parents help to meet children's basic need for security when they respond consistently to them.

5. *Resolve to be patient with your child.* Give your child time to change negative behavior patterns. Children do not change misbehavior patterns easily. Misbehaviors that have been conditioned and mastered take time to give up. Just because you decide to be more positive and more consistent, your child's behavior will not change overnight.

6. *Eliminate any "strings" that you attach to loving your child. Try not to attach conditions to loving your child.* "I love you when you bring home good grades." "I love you when you do well in basketball, tennis, swimming." Let your children know that you love them, no matter what. Do not condition your love for your child on their school or other achievements.

7. *Understand your child's needs.* Sometimes parents expect children to be able to do things before they are ready. We ask an infant or toddler to keep quiet and sit still. In these instances, we are not only being unrealistic, but we are also setting up our child for repeated failures to please us. Parents must understand developmental stages so that they have a realistic understanding of their children's abilities. Can you identify your child's needs? Do you know how to respond to those needs in a nurturing manner? We get it backwards when we expect that our children will meet our needs rather than the other way around.

8. *Help your child to feel competent.* What motivates a child is his having a sense of competence. Children feel good when they learn how to do things,

such as drawing a picture, reading a story to a parent, or cleaning their room. For instance, toddlers who have just learned how to take off their shoes will do so over and over again. Teach your child how to do ordinary things around the house. Instead of your doing things for your child, help him gain independence by doing things for himself. Parents can help children to feel competent by pointing out what they have accomplished, instead of giving them general praise—which may not provide sufficient useful information.

9. *Teach your children how to resolve conflicts nonviolently.* He will be grateful to you for such teachings, and so will the rest of the world.

10. *Analyze your own parenting style to examine its impact on your children.*

## What Can Be Done If Your Child Shows Violent Behavior?

If you are concerned about any aggressive or violent behavior your child has shown, you should immediately arrange for a comprehensive evaluation by a qualified mental health professional. Early treatment by a trained professional can often help to reduce or to eliminate the behavior while providing an understanding of the underlying causes of such behavior. The goals of treatment usually focus on helping a child to learn how to control his anger, express anger and frustrations in appropriate ways, be responsible for his actions, and accept consequences. The mental health professional will also explore family issues, peer relationships, and school problems.

## Can Anything Prevent Violent Behavior in Children?

Children's violent behaviors can be decreased or even prevented if you reduce or eliminate the risk factors associated with violent behavior (including exposure to violence in the media, domestic violence, punitive physical punishment as a means of discipline, or being the victim of physical and/or sexual abuse). Most significantly, your efforts should be directed toward decreasing the exposure of your child to violence in the home, including repeated family conflicts. Also, consider the protective factors that you might put in your child's life to offset any risk factors.

In conclusion, two important functions of families are to give children roots and wings. Roots have two basic purposes. First, roots give children a sense of stability. The roots that children need are formed initially in the kind of attachment relationship that parents or a primary caregiver provides to them in their early years. The second purpose of roots is to provide nourishment. Parents plant the root of stability for their children when they provide for children's physical needs, such as a home, food, and clothing. Parents give the root of nourishment when they create a family atmosphere that is loving and when they encourage their children to achieve, help them to develop a sense of competency, and treat them with respect. Family stability and nourishment help children to develop a sense of belonging, security, and self-esteem. Family roots supply an important anchor or reference point for young people when they experience difficulties in life.

Just as roots anchor children to something bigger than themselves, wings set them free and permit them to soar on their own. Parents give their children gradual "wing flying lessons" during the times that they are raising them. They limit children's freedom for as long as it takes to teach them responsible behavior, and then they give them back their freedom so that they can launch on their own. Parents give children wings by allowing them to do things their own way, even if they know that a better way exists. Parents might suggest a different approach to their children, but then allow them to make the decision and to manage the consequences that take place because of that decision.

No child gets his wings all at once. Earning one's wings is a gradual process. Our job as parents is to support our children as they strengthen their wings. We must not try to keep them from doing what comes naturally—from both wanting to and learning how to fly. How do we help our children find their wings? We engage them in wing school when we make sure they have the necessary skills and competencies to succeed in life. We give our children big steps toward finding their wings when we teach them self-confidence to open the door when the right time arrives. When we give our children chores and responsibilities, they will begin to learn to believe in themselves. Parents should not try to raise children so that they live in the smallest nest in a corner of their homes, with their wings pressing close to their side. Roots hold children close. Wings set them free. Children are born to soar to the farthest reaches of life, with their wings in flight.

Children take steps toward earning their wings as parents talk with them about the choices they make. Being an active participant in "wing school" involves parents talking with their children about the consequences of their decisions. Real learning takes place when parents help their children to analyze consequences. We give our children wings when we help them develop values that we have set by being good role models and by establishing clear limits and expectations for them. We help our children work toward earning their wings when we give them permission to explore and to make mistakes and when we emphasize logical consequences rather than punishment. We give our children wings when we allow them to find their own truths, when we trust in them, and when we permit them to find themselves.

Children who have strong roots often return back to us like the geese flying in a flock on a beautiful fall day. Sometimes our children fly back to us because they just want to touch base with us, get a portion of much needed love, catch their breath, and then they are off again. Even though we give our children wings, we never really lose them. They fly back again and again, that is, if there is something worth making the trip for another time.

# Notes

# Chapter 1

1. Schwab-Stone, M., Chen, C., Greenberger, E., Silver, D., Lichtman, J., & Voyce, C. (1999). No safe haven II: The effects of violence exposure on urban youth. *AmericanAcademyof Child and Adolescent Psychiatry, 38*(4), 359–367.

2. Berman, S., Jurtines, W., Silverman, W., & Serafini, L. (1996). The impact of exposure to crime and violence on urban youth. *American Journal of Orthopsychiatry, 66*(3), 329–336.

3. Kilpatrick, D., & Saunders, B. (1997). *The prevalence and consequences of child victimization: Summary of a research study.* Washington, DC: U.S. Dept. of Justice, Office of Justice Programs, National Institute of Justice.

4. Kilpatrick, D., & Saunders, B. (1997). *The prevalence and consequences of child victimization: Summary of a research study.* Washington, DC: U.S. Dept. of Justice, Office of Justice Programs, National Institute of Justice.

5. Office of Juvenile Justice and Delinquency Prevention. (1999). *Juvenile Offenders and Victims:National Report.* Available at http://www.ncjrs.gov/html/ojjdp/nationalreport99/toc.html

6. Grunebaum, J. A., Kann, L., Kinchen, S., Ross, J. G., Lowry, R., Harris, W. A., et al. (2003). *Youth risk behavior surveillance.* Available at http://www.cdc.gov/mmwr/preview/mmwrhtml/ss5302a1.htm

7. Department of Health and Human Services. (2001). *Youth Violence: A Report of the Surgeon General.* Available on http://www.surgeongeneral.gov/library/youthviolence/toc.html

8. Strauss, M. A., & Gelles, R. J. (1992). *Physical violence in American families: Risk factors and adaptation to violence in 8,145 families.* New Brunswick, NJ: Transaction Publishers.

9. American Psychological Association. (1996). Presidential Task Force on Violence and the Family. *Violence and the family.* Washington, DC: Author.

10. Niehoff, D. (1999). *The biology of violence (How understanding the brain, behavior, and environment can break the vicious cycle of aggression).* New York: The Free Press.

11. Famularo, R. A., Kinscherff, R. T., & Fenton, T. (1990). Symptom Differences in Acute and Chronic Presentations of Childhood Posttraumatic Stress Disorder. *Child Abuse and Neglect, 14,* 439–444; Finkelhor, D., & Browne, A. (1985). The traumatic impact of child sexual abuse: A conceptualization. *American Journal of Orthopsychiatry, 55,* 530–541; Garbarino, J. (1995). *Raising children in a socially toxic environment.* San Francisco: Jossey-Bass.

12. Gaskins, P. (2001). The science of violence: As the toll of teen violence grows, scientists search for reasons why—Life Science: Teen Health. *Science World.* Available at http://www.findarticles.com/p/articles/mi_m1590/is_4_58/ai_79967172

13. American Psychological Association. (1996). Presidential Task Force on Violence and the Family. *Violence and the family.* Washington, DC: Author.

14. Hamburg, B., Elliott, D. S., & Williams, K. R. (1998). *Violence in American schools: A new perspective, youth violence.* New York, NY: Cambridge University Press.

15. U.S. Department of Health and Human Services. (2001). *Youth violence: A report of the Surgeon General.* Rockville, MD: U.S. Department of Health and Human Services, Centers for Disease Control and Prevention. U.S. Government Printing Office.

16. Department of Health and Human Services. (2001). *Youth Violence: A Report of the Surgeon General.* Available at http://www.surgeongeneral.gov/library/youthviolence/toc.html

17. Nansel, T. R., Overpeck, M., Pilla, R. S., Ruan, W. J., Simons-Morton, B., & Scheidt, P. (2001). Bullying behaviors among U.S. youth: Prevalence and association with psychosocial adjustment. *Journal of the American Medical Association, 285*(16), 2094–2100.

18. Centers for Disease Control and Prevention. (2004). *Web-based injury statistics query and reporting system (WISQARS).* Available at http://www.cdc.gov/ncipc/wisqars/default.htm

19. Osofsky, H. J., & Osofsky, J. D. (2001). Violent and aggressive behaviors in youth: A mental Health and prevention perspective. *Psychiatry, 64,* 285–295.

20. American Psychological Association. (1996). Presidential Task Force on Violence and the Family. *Violence and the family.* Washington, DC: Author.

21. Centers for Disease Control and Prevention, National Centers for Injury Prevention and Control. (2005). *Web-based injury statistics query and reporting system (WSQARS).* Retrieved February 9, 2008, from www.cdc.gov/ncipc/wisqars

22. Fox, J. A., & Zawitz, M. W. (2002). *Homicide trends in the United States.* Washington, DC: Bureau of Justice Statistics.

23. Centers for Disease Control and Prevention. (2004). *Web-based injury statistics query and reporting system.* Available at http://www.cdc.gov/library/youthviolence

24. Centers for Disease Control and Prevention, National Centers for Injury Prevention and Control. (2007). *Web-based injury statistics query and reporting system (WSQARS)..* Available at http://www.cdc.gov/ncipc/wisqars/default.htm

25. Osofsky, H. J., & Osofsky, J. D. (2001). Violent and aggressive behaviors in youth: A mental Health and prevention perspective. *Psychiatry, 64,* 285–295.

26. Anderson, R. N., & Smith, B. L. (2003). Deaths: Leading causes for 2001. *National Vital Statistics Report, 52*(9), 1–86.

27. Gurian, M. (1999). *The good son.* New York: Penguin Putnam.

28. Gurian, M. (1999). *A fine young man: What parents, mentors and educators can do to shape adolescent boys into exceptional men.* New York: Penguin Putnam.

29. Weiler, J. (1999). *Girls and violence.* New York: Eric Digests: Clearinghouse on Urban Education.

30. Peters, S. R., & Peters, S. D. (1998). Violent adolescent females. *Corrections Today, 60,* 28–29.

31. Heimer, K., & De Coster, S. (1999). The gendering of violent delinquency. *Criminology, 37*(2), 277–314.

32. Garbarino, J. (2006). *See Jane hit: Why girls are growing more violent and what we can do about it.* New York: The Penguin Press.

33. Federal Bureau of Investigation (FBI). (2006, June 26). *Uniform Crime reporting program.* Available at www.fbi.gov

34. Prothow-Sith, D., and Spivak, H. R. (2005). *Sugar and spice and no longer nice: How we can stop girls' violence.* Hoboken, NJ: Jossey-Bass.

35. Weiler, J. (1999). *Girls and violence.* New York: Eric Digests: Clearinghouse on Urban Education.

36. Weiler, J. (1999). *Girls and violence.* New York: Eric Digests: Clearinghouse on Urban Education.

37. NCHS National Vital Statistics System for numbers of deaths U.S. Bureau of Census for population estimates. (2004). *Statistics compiled using WISQARS produced by the Office of Statistics and Programming.*

38. Centers for Disease Control and Prevention. (2002). Youth risk behavior surveillance—United States. In *CDC Surveillance Summaries, 51,* 6.

39. Centers for Disease Control and Prevention. (2002). Youth risk behavior surveillance—United States. In *CDC Surveillance Summaries, 51,* 6.

40. Centers for Disease Control and Prevention. (2002). Youth risk behavior surveillance—United States. In *CDC Surveillance Summaries, 51,* 6.

41. Russell, S. T., & Joyner, K. (2001). Adolescent sexual orientation and suicide risk: Evidence from a national study. *American Journal of Public Health, 91*(8), 1276–1281.

42. Remafedi, G., French, S., Story, M., Resnick, M. D., & Blum, R. (1998). The relationship between suicide risk and sexual orientation: Results of a population-based study. *American Journal of Public Health, 88,* 57–60.

43. Faulkner, A., & Cranston, K. (1998). Correlates of same-sex sexual behavior in a random sample of Massachusetts high school students. *American Journal of Public Health, 88,* 262–266

44. Mays, V. M., & Cochran, S. D. (2001). Mental health correlates of perceived discrimination among lesbian, gay, and bisexual adults in the United States. *American Journal of Public Health, 91*(11), 1869–1876.

45. Russell, S. T., & Joyner, K. (2001). Adolescent sexual orientation and suicide risk: Evidence from a national study. *American Journal of Public Health, 91*(8), 1276–1281.

46. Capuzzi, D., & Golden, L. (1998). *Preventing adolescent suicide.* Muncie, IN: Accelerated Development, Inc.

47. Tomlinson-Keasey, C., & Keasey, C. B. (1998). "Signatures" of suicide. In D. Capuzzi and L. Golden (Eds.), *Preventing adolescent suicide.* Muncie, IN: Accelerated Press.

48. Capuzzi, D., & Golden, L. (1998). *Preventing adolescent suicide.* Muncie, IN: Accelerated Development, Inc.

49. Lipschitz, A. (1995). Suicide prevention in young adults (age 18–30). *Suicide and Life Threatening Behavior, 25,* 155–170.

50. Anderson, R. N., & Smith, B. L. (2003). Deaths: Leading causes for 2001. *National Vital Statistics Report, 52*(9), 1–86.

51. Petersen, G. J., Pietrzak, D., Speaker, D., & Kathryne, M. (1998). The enemy within: A national study on school violence and prevention. *Urban Education, 33,* 331–359.

52. Shubert, T. H., Bressette, S., Deeken, J., & Bender, W. N. (1999). Analysis of random school shootings. In W. N. Bender, G. Clinton, and R. L. Bender (Eds.), *Violence prevention and reduction in schools.* Austin: PRO-ED.

53. Cook, P. J., & Ludwig, J. (2001). *Gun violence: The real costs.* New York: Oxford University Press.

54. Cook, P. J., & Ludwig, J. (2001). *Gun violence: The real costs.* New York: Oxford University Press.

55. Myles, B. S., & Simpson, R. L. (1998). Aggression cycle and prevention/intervention strategies. *Intervention in School and Clinic, 33,* 259–264.

56. Anderson, R. N., & Smith, B. L. (2003). Deaths: Leading causes for 2001. *National Vital Statistics Report, 52*(9), 1–86.

57. Karr-Morse, R., & Wiley, M. S. (1997). *Ghosts from the nursery: Tracing the roots of violence.* New York: Grove/Atlantic Monthly Press.

58. Myers, W. C., Scott, K., Burgess, A. W., & Burgess, A. G. (1995). Psychopathology, biopsychosocial factors, crime characteristics, and classification of 25 homicidal youths. *Journal of American Academy Academic Child and Adolescent Child and Adolescent Psychiatry, 34*(11), 1483–1489.

59. Niehoff, D. (1999). *The biology of violence (How understanding the brain, behavior, and environment can break the vicious cycle of aggression).* New York: The Free Press.

60. Shore, R. (1997). Rethinking the brain: *New insights into early development* [Executive Summary]. New York: Families and Work Institute.

61. Shore, R. (1997). Rethinking the brain: *New insights into early development* [Executive Summary]. New York: Families and Work Institute.

62. Simmons, T., & Sheen, R. A. (1997, February 16). A brain research manifests importance of first years. *The News and Observer.*

63. Karr-Morse, R., & Wiley, M. S. (1997). *Ghosts from the nursery: Tracing the roots of violence.* New York: Grove/Atlantic Monthly Press.

64. Shore, R. (1997). Rethinking the brain: *New insights into early development* [Executive Summary]. New York: Families and Work Institute.

65. Gerhardt, S. (2004). *Why love matters: How affection shapes a baby's brain.* New York: Brunner-Routledge.

66. Simmons, T., & Sheen, R. A. (1997, February 16). A brain research manifests importance of first years. *The News and Observer.*

67. Shore, R. (1997). Rethinking the brain: *New insights into early development* [Executive Summary]. New York: Families and Work Institute.

68. Gerhardt, S. (2004). *Why love matters: How affection shapes a baby's brain.* New York: Brunner-Routledge.

69. Gerhardt, S. (2004). *Why love matters: How affection shapes a baby's brain.* New York: Brunner-Routledge.

70. Gerhardt, S. (2004). *Why love matters: How affection shapes a baby's brain.* New York: Brunner-Routledge.

71. Suomi, S. J. (2003). Social and biological mechanisms underlying impulsive aggressiveness in rhesus monkeys. In B. B. Lahey, A. Caspi, & T. Moffitt (Eds.), *Causes of conduct disorder and juvenile delinquency.* New York: Guilford Publications.

72. Suomi, S. J. (2003). Social and biological mechanisms underlying impulsive aggressiveness in rhesus monkeys. In B. B. Lahey, A. Caspi, & T. Moffitt (Eds.), *Causes of conduct disorder and juvenile delinquency.* New York: Guilford Publications.

73. Niehoff, D. (1999). *The biology of violence (How understanding the brain, behavior, and environment can break the vicious cycle of aggression).* New York: The Free Press.

74. Macmillan, J. C. (2000). *An odd kind of fame: Stories of Phineas Gage.* Cambridge, MA: MIT Press.

75. Zimbardo, P. G., Weber, A. L., & Johnson, R. L. (2003). *Psychology: Core concepts.* Boston: Allyn and Bacon.

76. Whalen, P. J. (1998). Fear, vigilance, and ambiguity: Initial neuroimaging studies of the human amygdala. *Current Directions in Psychological Science, 7,* 177–188.

77. Whalen, P. J. (1998). Fear, vigilance, and ambiguity: Initial neuroimaging studies of the human amygdala. *Current Directions in Psychological Science, 7,* 177–188.

78. Handbook of Texas. Available at http://www.tsha.utexas.edu/handbook/online

79. Karr-Morse, R., & Wiley, M. S. (1997). *Ghosts from the nursery: Tracing the roots of violence.* New York: Grove/Atlantic Monthly Press.

80. Kemper, T. (1990). *Social structure and testosterone.* New Brunswick, NJ: Rutgers University Press.

81. Westen, D. (1996). *Psychology: mind, brain and culture.* New York: John Wiley and Sons.

82. Karli, P. (1991). *Biological psychology.* New York: Holt, Rinehart and Winston, Inc.

83. Mann, J. J. (1999). Role of the serotonergic system in the pathogenesis of major depression and suicidal behavior. *Neuropsychopharmacology, 21,* 995–1055.

84. Coccaro, E. F., Kavoussi, R. J., Hauger, R. L., Cooper, T. B., & Ferris, C. F. (1998). Cerebrospinal fluid vasopressin levels. Correlates with aggression and serotonin function in personality-disordered subjects. *Archives of General Psychiatry, 55.*

85. Coccaro, E. F., Kavoussi, R. J., Hauger, R. L., Cooper, T. B., & Ferris, C. F. (1998). Cerebrospinal fluid vasopressin levels. Correlates with aggression and serotonin function in personality-disordered subjects. *Archives of General Psychiatry, 55.*

86. Kruesi, M. J., Hibbs, E. C., Zahn, T. P., Keysor, C. S., Hamburger, S. D., Bartko, J. J., & Rapoport, J. L. (1992). A two-year prospective follow-up study of children and adolescents with disruptive behavior disorders: Prediction by cerebrospinal fluid 5-hydroxyindoleacetic acid, homovanillic acid, and autonomic measures. *Archives of General Psychiatry, 49,* 429–435.

87. Coccaro, E. F., Bergeman, C. S., Kavoussi, R. J., & Seroczynski, A. D. (1997). Heritability of aggression and irritability: A twin study of the Buss-Durkee aggression scales in adult male subjects. *Biological Psychiatry, 41,* 273–284.

88. Karr-Morse, R., & Wiley, M. S. (1997). *Ghosts from the nursery: Tracing the roots of violence.* New York: Grove/Atlantic Monthly Press.

89. Bandura, A., Ross, D., & Ross, S. A. (1961). Transmission of aggression through imitation of aggressive models. *Journal of abnormal and social psychology, 63,* 575–582.

90. Karr-Morse, R., & Wiley, M. S. (1997). *Ghosts from the nursery: Tracing the roots of violence.* New York: Grove/Atlantic Monthly Press.

91. Karr-Morse, R., & Wiley, M. S. (1997). *Ghosts from the nursery: Tracing the roots of violence.* New York: Grove/Atlantic Monthly Press.

92. Coccaro, E. F., Bergeman, C. S., Kavoussi, R. J., & Seroczynski, A. D. (1997). Heritability of aggression and irritability: A twin study of the Buss-Durkee aggression scales in adult male subjects. *Biological Psychiatry, 41,* 273–284.

93. Bandura, A., Ross, D., & Ross. (1961). Transmission of aggression through imitation of aggressive models. *Journal of abnormal and social psychology, 63,* 575–582.

94. Goetting, A. (1995). Homicide in families and other special populations. New York: Springer.

95. Children's Defense Fund. (1997). *Every day in America. CDF Reports* (p. 18). Washington, DC: CDF.

96. Lipsey, M. W., Derzon, J. H. (1998). Predictors of violent and serious delinquency in adolescence and early adulthood: A synthesis of longitudinal research. In R. Loeber & D. P. Farrington (Eds.), *Serious and violent juvenile offenders: Risk factors and successful interventions* (pp. 86–105). Thousand Oaks, CA: Sage Publication.

97. Goetting, A. (1995). *Homicide in families and other special populations.* New York: Springer.

98. Goetting, A. (1995). *Homicide in families and other special populations.* New York: Springer.

99. Carter, L. S., Weithorn, L. A., & Behrman, R. E. (1999). Domestic violence and children: Analysis and recommendations. *The Future of Children, 9*(3), 4–20.

100. Osofsky, J. D. (1995). The effects of exposure to violence on young children. *American Psychologist, 50,* 782–788.

101. Bandura, A., Ross, D., & Ross. (1961). Transmission of aggression through imitation of aggressive models. *Journal of abnormal and social psychology, 63,* 575–582.

102. Cornell, C. P., & Gelles, R. J. (1982). Adolescent to parent violence. *The Urban and Social Change Review, 15,* 8–14.

103. Strauss, M. A., & Steward, J. H. (1999). Corporal punishment by American parents: National data on prevalence, chronicity, severity, and duration in relation to child and family characteristics. *Clinical Child and Family Psychology Review, 2,* 55–70.

104. Strauss, M. A., & Steward, J. H. (1999). Corporal punishment by American parents: National data on prevalence, chronicity, severity, and duration in relation to child and family characteristics. *Clinical Child and Family Psychology Review, 2,* 55–70.

105. Evans, E. D., & Warren-Sohlberg, L. (1988). A pattern analysis of behavior toward parents. *Journal of Adolescent Research, 3,* 210–216.

106. Strauss, M. A., & Steward, J. H. (1999). Corporal punishment by American parents: National data on prevalence, chronicity, severity, and duration in relation to child and family characteristics. *Clinical Child and Family Psychology Review, 2,* 55–70.

107. Struder, J. (1996). Understanding and preventing aggressive responses in youth. *Elementary School Guidance and Counseling, 30,* 194–203.

108. Myers, J. (1993). *Social psychology* (3rd ed.). New York: McGraw-Hill.

109. Widom, C. S., & Ames, M. A. (1994). Criminal consequences of childhood sexual victimization. *Child Abuse & Neglect, 18,* 303–318.

110. Ganley, A., & Schechter, S. (1996). *Domestic violence: A national curriculum for child protective services*. San Francisco: Family Violence Prevention Fund.

111. Carter, L. S., Weithorn, L. A., & Behrman, R. E. (1999). Domestic violence and children: Analysis and recommendations. *The Future of Children, 9*(3), 4–20.

112. Carter, L. S., Weithorn, L. A., & Behrman, R. E. (1999). Domestic violence and children: Analysis and recommendations. *The Future of Children, 9*(3), 4–20.

113. Wilt, S., & Olsen, S. (1996). Prevalence of domestic violence in the United States. *Journal of the American Medical Women's Association, 51*, 71–82.

114. Parker, B., McFarlane, J., & Soeken, K. (1994). Abuse during pregnancy: Effects on maternal complications and infant birth weight in adult and teen women. *Obstetrics and Gynecology, 841*, 323–328.

115. Violence Policy Center. (2000). *When men murder women: An analysis of 1998 homicide data*. Washington, DC. Available from Violence Policy Center, 1140 19th Street, NW, Suite 600, Washington, DC 20036. Available at http://www.vpc.org/studies/dv3cont.htm

116. Fantuzzo, J. W., & Mohr, W. K. (1999). Prevalence and effects of child exposure to domestic violence. *The Future of Children, 9*, 21–32.

117. Holden, G. W., Geffner, R. A., & Jouriles, E. N. (1998). *Children exposed to marital violence: Theory, research, and applied issues*. Washington, DC: American Psychiatric Association Press.

118. Hilton, N. Z. (1992). Battered women's concerns about their children witnessing wife assault. *Journal of Interpersonal Violence, 7*, 77–86.

119. Holden, G. W., & Ritchie, K. L. (1991). Linking extreme marital discord, child rearing, and child behavior problems: Evidence from battered women. *Child Development, 62* 311–327.

120. Fantuzzo, J. W., & Mohr, W. K. (1999). Prevalence and effects of child exposure to domestic violence. *The Future of Children, 9*, 21–32.

121. Osofsky, J. D. (1995). The effects of exposure to violence on young children. *American Psychologist, 50*, 782–788.

122. Zeanah, C. Z., & Scheeringa, M. (1996). Evaluation of posttraumatic symptomatology in infants and young children exposed to violence. *Zero to Three, 16*, 9–14.

123. Wenar, C., & Kerig, P. (2000). *Developmental psychopathology from infancy to adolescence*. (4th ed.). New York: McGraw-Hill.

124. Fantuzzo, J. W., & Mohr, W. K. (1999). Prevalence and effects of child exposure to domestic violence. *The Future of Children, 9*, 21–32.

125. Holden, G. W., Geffner, R. A., & Jouriles, E. N. (1998). *Children exposed to marital violence: Theory, research, and applied issues*. Washington, DC: American Psychiatric Association Press.

126. Kazdin, A. E. (1987). *Conduct disorders in childhood or adolescence*. Newbury Park , CA: SAGE.

127. Holden, G. W., Geffner, R. A., & Jouriles, E. N. (1998). *Children exposed to marital violence: Theory, research, and applied issues*. Washington, DC: American Psychiatric Association Press.

128. Kazdin, A. E. (1987). *Conduct disorders in childhood or adolescence*. Newbury Park , CA: SAGE.

129. Kilpatrick, D., & Saunders, B. (1997). *The prevalence and consequences of child victimization: Summary of a research study*. Washington, DC: U.S. Dept. of Justice, Office of Justice Programs, National Institute of Justice.

130. Holden, G. W., & Ritchie, K. L. (1991). Linking extreme marital discord, child rearing, and child behavior problems: Evidence from battered women. *Child Development, 62* 311–327.

131. Knox, L. (2002). *Connecting the dots to prevent youth violence: A training and outreach guide for physicians and other health professionals.* Chicago, Illinois: American Medical Association.

132. Widom, C. S., & Ames, M. A. (1994). Criminal consequences of childhood sexual victimization. *Child Abuse & Neglect, 18,* 303–318.

133. Holden, G. W., & Ritchie, K. L. (1991). Linking extreme marital discord, child rearing, and child behavior problems: Evidence from battered women. *Child Development, 62* 311–327.

134. Knox, L. (2002). *Connecting the dots to prevent youth violence.* American Medical Association. Available at http://www.ama-assn.org/violence

135. Holden, G. W., & Ritchie, K. L. (1991). Linking extreme marital discord, child rearing, and child behavior problems: Evidence from battered women. *Child Development, 62* 311–327.

136. Hunt, H., Malmud, E., Brodsky, N. L., & Giannetta, J. (2001). Exposure to violence: Psychological and academic correlates in child witnesses. *Archives of Pediatrics and Adolescent Medicine, 155,* 1351–1356.

137. Kilpatrick, D., & Saunders, B. (1997). *The prevalence and consequences of child victimization: Summary of a research study.* Washington, DC: U.S. Dept. of Justice, Office of Justice Programs, National Institute of Justice.

138. Knox, L. (2002). *Connecting the dots to prevent youth violence.* American Medical Association. Available at http://www.ama-assn.org/violence

139. Osofsky, J. D. (1999). The impact of violence on children. *The Future of Children, special issue on domestic violence and children, 9,* 33–49.

140. Hawley, T. (2000). *Safe start: How early experiences can help reduce violence.* Chicago: The Ounce of Prevention Fund.

141. Catalano, R. F., & Hawkins, J. D. (1996). The social development model: A theory of antisocial behavior. In J. D. Hawkins (Ed.), *Delinquency and crime: Current theories* (pp. 149–197). New York: Cambridge University Press.

142. Osofsky, J. D., & Jackson, T. (1994). Parenting in violent environments. *Zero to Three, 14,* 8–11.

143. Coleman, J. (1998). Social capital in the creation of human capital. *American Journal of Sociology Supplement, 94,* 95–120.

144. Wilson, W. J. (1996). When work disappears: The world of the new urban poor. New York: Knopf.

145. Fitzpatrick, K. M., & Boldizar, J. P. (1993). The prevalence and consequences of exposure to domestic violence among African American youth. *Journal of the American Academy of Child and Adolescent Psychiatry, 32,* 424–430.

146. DuRant, R. H., Cadenhead, C., Pendergrast, R. A., Slavens, G., & Linder, C. W. (1994). Factors associated with the use of violence among urban black adolescents. *American Journal of Public Health, 84,* 612–617.

147. Foy, D. W., & Goguen, C. A. (1998). Community violence-related PTSD in children and adolescents. *PTSD Research Quarterly, 9,* 1–6.

148. Sanders-Phillips, K. (1997). Assaultive violence in the community: Psychological responses of adolescent victims and their parents. *Journal of Adolescent Health, 21,* 356–365.

149. Garbarino, J. (1995). *Raising children in a socially toxic environment.* San Francisco: Jossey-Bass.

150. Garmezy, N. (1993). Children in poverty: Resilience despite risk. *Psychiatry, 56,* 127–135.

151. Osofsky, J. D., & Jackson, T. (1994). Parenting in violent environments. *Zero to Three, 14,* 8–11.

152. Lorion, R. P., & Saltzman, W. (1993). Children's exposure to community violence: Following a path from concern to research to action. *Psychiatry, 56,* 55–65.

153. Lynch, M., & Cicchetti, D. (1998). An ecological-transactional analysis of children and contexts: The longitudinal interplay among child maltreatment, community violence, and children's symptomatology. *Development and Psychopathology, 10,* 235–258.

154. Guerra, N. G., & Tolan, P. (1994). Neighborhood disadvantage, stressful life events, and adjustment in urban elementary school children. *Journal of Clinical Child Psychology, 23,* 391–400.

155. Duncan, D. F. (1996). Growing up under the gun: Children and adolescents coping with violent neighborhoods. *The Journal of Primary Prevention, 16,* 343–356.

156. Osofsky, J. D. (1997). *Children in a violent society.* New York: Guilford Press.

157. Garbarino, J. (1995). *Raising children in a socially toxic environment.* San Francisco: Jossey-Bass.

158. Wilson, W. J. (1996). *When work disappears: The world of the new urban poor.* New York: Knopf.

159. Elliott, D. (1994). Serious violent offenders: Onset, developmental course, and termination. The American Society of Criminology, 1993 Presidential Address. *Criminology, 32,* 1–21.

160. Huizinga, D., & Jakob-Chen, C. (1998). Cotemporaneous co-occurrence of serious and violent juvenile offending and other problem behaviors. In R. Loeber & D. P. Farrington (Eds.), *Serious and violent juvenile offenders: Risk factors and successful interventions* (pp. 47–67). Thousand Oaks, CA: Sage Publications.

161. Parker, R. N., & Auerhahn, K. (1998). Alcohol, drugs and violence. *Annual Review of Sociology, 24,* 291–311.

162. Knox, L. (2002). *Connecting the dots to prevent youth violence.* American Medical Association. Available at http://www.ama-assn.org/violence

163. Knox, L. (2002). *Connecting the dots to prevent youth violence.* American Medical Association. Available at http://www.ama-assn.org/violence

164. Glicken, M., & Sechrest, D. (2003). *The role of the helping professions in treating and preventing violence.* Boston: Allyn & Bacon.

165. Quinn, J. F., & Downs, B. (1995). Predictors of gang violence: The impact of drugs and guns on police perceptions in nine states. *Journal of Gang Research, 2,* 15–27.

166. Dwyer, K., Osher, D., and Warger, C. (1998). *Early warning, timely response: A guide to safe schools.* Washington, DC: U.S. Department of Education.

167. U.S. Department of Health and Human Services. (2001). *Youth violence: A report of the Surgeon General.* Rockville, MD: U.S. Department of Health and Human Services, Centers for Disease Control and Prevention. U.S. Government Printing Office.

# Chapter 2

1. Bowlby, J. (1969). *Attachment and loss. Vol. 1: Attachment.* New York: Basic Books.

2. Bowlby, J. (1998). *A secure base: Parent-child attachment and healthy human development.* New York: Basic Books.

3. Sroufe, L. A. (1983). Infant-caregiver attachment and patterns of adaptation in preschool: The roots of maladaptation and competence. In M. Perlmutter (Ed.), *Minnesota Symposium in Child Psychology* (Vol. 16, pp. 41–83). Hillsdale, NJ: Erlbaum Associates.

4. Sroufe, L. A. (2000). Early relationships and the development of children. *Infant Mental Health Journal, 21,* 67–74.

5. Bowlby, J. (1969). *Attachment and loss. Vol. 1: Attachment.* New York: Basic Books.

6. Bowlby, J. (1998). *A secure base: Parent-child attachment and healthy human development.* New York: Basic Books.

7. James, B. (1994). *Handbook for treatment of attachment-trauma problems in children.* New York: Lexington Books, Macmillan.

8. Luminare-Rosen, C. (2000). *Parenting begins before conception: A guide to preparing body.* Rochester, VT: Inner Traditions.

9. Klaus, M. II., Kennell, J. H., & Klaus, P. H. (1995). *Bonding.* Boston: Addison-Wesley.

10. Sroufe, L. A. (1983). Infant-caregiver attachment and patterns of adaptation in preschool: The roots of maladaptation and competence. In M. Perlmutter (Ed.), *Minnesota Symposium in Child Psychology* (Vol. 16, pp. 41–83). Hillsdale, NJ: Erlbaum Associates.

11. Sroufe, L. A. (2000). Early relationships and the development of children. *Infant Mental Health Journal, 21,* 67–74.

12. Bowlby, J. (1969). *Attachment and loss. Vol. 1: Attachment.* New York: Basic Books.

13. Bowlby, J. (1998). *A secure base: Parent-child attachment and healthy human development.* New York: Basic Books.

14. Bowlby, J. (1969). *Attachment and loss. Vol. 1: Attachment.* New York: Basic Books.

15. Bowlby, J. (1969). *Attachment and loss. Vol. 1: Attachment.* New York: Basic Books.

16. Schore, A. N. (2001). Effects of a secure attachment relationship on right brain development, affect regulation and infant mental health. *Infant Mental Health Journal, 22,* 7–66.

17. James, B. (1994). *Handbook for treatment of attachment-trauma problems in children.* New York: Lexington Books, Macmillan.

18. James, B. (1994). *Handbook for treatment of attachment-trauma problems in children.* New York: Lexington Books, Macmillan.

19. James, B. (1994). *Handbook for treatment of attachment-trauma problems in children.* New York: Lexington Books, Macmillan.

20. Tucker, D. M. (1992). Developing emotions and cortical networks. In M. R. Gunar & C. A. Nelson (Eds.), *Minnesota symposium on child psychology, Vol. 24. Developmental behavioral neuroscience* (pp. 75-128). Mahweh, NJ: Erlbaum.

21. Schore, A. N. (2000). Attachment and the regulation of the right brain. *Attachment & Human Development, 2,* 23–47.

22. Schore, A. N. (1997). Early organization of the nonlinear right brain and development of a predisposition to psychiatry disorders. *Development and Psychopathology, 8,* 595–631.

23. Semrud-Clikeman, M., & Hynd, G. W. (1990). Right hemispheric dysfunction in nonverbal learning disabilities: Social, academic, and adaptive functioning in adults and children. *Psychological Bulletin. American Psychological Association, Inc., 107*(2), 196–209.

24. Kandel, E. R. (1999). Biology and the future of psychoanalysis: A new intellectual framework for psychiatry revisited. *American Journal of Psychiatry, 156,* 505–524.

25. Fink, G. R., Markowitsch, H. J., Reinkemeier, M., Bruckbauer, T., Kessler, J., & Heiss, W. D. (1996). Cerebral representation of one's own past: Neural networks involved in autobiographical memory. *Journal of Neuroscience, 16,* 4275–4282.

26. Schore, A. N. (2000). Attachment and the regulation of the right brain. *Attachment & Human Development, 2,* 23–47.

27. Main, M. (1999). Epilogue. Attachment theory: Eighteen points with suggestions for future studies. In J. Cassidy & P. R. Shaver (Eds.), *Handbook of attachment: Theory, research, and clinical applications* (pp. 845–877). New York: Guildford Press.

28. Bowlby, J. (1969). *Attachment and loss. Vol. 1: Attachment.* New York: Basic Books.

29. Cline, F. (1994). Hope for high risk and rage-filled children. Evergreen, CO: EC Publications.

30. Trowell, J. (1982). Effects of obstetric management on the mother-child relationship. In C. M. Parkes & J. Stevenson-Hinde (Eds.), *The place of attachment in human behavior* (79-94). New York: Basic Books.

31. Perry, B. D. (1997). Incubated in terror: Neurodevelopment factors in the cycle of violence. In J. D. Osofsky (Ed.), *Children in a violent society.* New York: Guilford Publications.

32. Perry, B. D. (1997). Incubated in terror: Neurodevelopment factors in the cycle of violence. In J. D. Osofsky (Ed.), *Children in a violent society.* New York: Guilford Publications.

33. Hughes, D. (1999). *Building the bonds of attachment: Awakening the love of deeply troubled children.* Northvale, NJ: Jason Aronson.

34. Perry, B. D. (1997). Incubated in terror: Neurodevelopment factors in the cycle of violence. In J. D. Osofsky (Ed.), *Children in a violent society.* New York: Guilford Publications.

35. Klaus, M. H., Kennell, J. H., & Klaus, P. H. (1995). *Bonding.* Boston: Addison Wesley.

36. Lamb, M. E. (1997). The development of father-infant relationships. In M. E. Lamb (Ed.), *The role of the father in child development* (pp. 3, 104–120). New York: Wiley.

37. Cox, C. F., White, K. C., Ramus, D. L., Farmer, J. B., & Snuggs, H. M. (1992). Reparative dentin: Factors influencing pulpal response to cavity preparations. *Quintessence International, 23,* 257–270.

38. Pedersen, F. A., Suwalsky, J. T., Cain, R. L., Zaslow, M. J., & Rabinovich, B. A. (1987). Paternal care of infants during maternal separations: Associations with father-infant interaction at one year. *Psychiatry, 50,* 193–205.

39. Esterbrooks, M. A., & Goldberg, W. (1984). Toddler development in the family: Impact of father involvement and parenting characteristics. *Child Development, 55,* 740–752.

40. Kotelchuk, M. (1981). The infant's relationship to his father: Experimental evidence. In Michael E. Lamb (Ed.), *The role of the father in child development.* New York: Wiley.

41. Geiger, B. (1996). *Fathers as primary caregivers.* Westport, CT: Greenwood.

42. Clarke-Stewart, K. A. (1980). The father's contribution to children's cognitive and social development in early childhood. In F. A. Pedersen (Ed.), *The father-infant relationship: Observational studies in a family setting* (pp. 111-146). New York: Praeger Press.

43. Radin, N. (1994). Primary caregiving fathers in intact families. In A. E. Gottfried & A.W. Gottfried (Eds.), *Redefining families* (pp. 55-97). New York: Plenum Press.

44. Nugent, J. K. (1991). Cultural and psychological influences of the father's role in infant development. *Journal of Marriage and the Family, 53,* 475–585.

45. Bronstein, P. (1984). Difference in mothers' and fathers' behaviors toward children: A cross-cultural comparison. *Developmental Psychology, 20* 995–1003.

46. Collins, W. A., & Russell, G. (1991). Mother-child and father-child relationships in middle childhood and adolescence: A developmental analysis. *Developmental Review, 11,* 99–136.

47. Radin, N. (1994). Primary caregiving fathers in intact families. In A. E. Gottfried & A.W. Gottfried (Eds.), *Redefining families* (pp. 55-97). New York: Plenum Press.

48. Radin, N. (1994). Primary caregiving fathers in intact families. In A. E. Gottfried & A.W. Gottfried (Eds.), *Redefining families* (pp. 55-97). New York: Plenum Press.

49. Nugent, J. K. (1991). Cultural and psychological influences of the father's role in infant development. *Journal of Marriage and the Family, 53,* 475–585.

50. Cassidy, J., Parke, R. D., Butkovsky, L., & Braungart, J. M. (1992). Family-peer connections: The roles of emotional expressiveness within the family and children's understanding of emotions. *Child Development, 63,* 603–618.

51. Volling, B., & Belsky, J. (1992). The contribution of mother-child and father-child relationships to the quality of sibling interaction: A longitudinal study. *Child Development, 63,* 1209–1222.

52. Volling, B., & Belsky, J. (1992). The contribution of mother-child and father-child relationships to the quality of sibling interaction: A longitudinal study. *Child Development, 63,* 1209–1222.

53. Parke, R. D., & Brott, A. A. (1999). *Throwaway dads: The myths and barriers that keep men from being the fathers they want to be* (pp. 6–7). Boston: Houghton Mifflin Co.

54. Shinn, M. (1978). Father absence and children's cognitive development. *Psychological Bulletin, 85,* 295–324.

55. Ainsworth, M. D. S. (1969). Object relations, dependency, and attachment: A theoretical review of the infant-mother relationship. *Child Development, 40* 969–1025.

56. Ainsworth, M. D. S. (1979). Infant-mother attachment. *American Psychologist, 34,* 932–937.

57. Ainsworth, M. D. S. (1969). Object relations, dependency, and attachment: A theoretical review of the infant-mother relationship. *Child Development, 40* 969–1025.

58. Ainsworth, M. D. S. (1979). Infant-mother attachment. *American Psychologist, 34,* 932–937.

59. Ainsworth, M.D.S., Blehar, M. C. Waters, E., & Wall, S. (1978). *Patterns of attachment: A psychological study of the strange situation.* Hillsdale, NJ: Lawrence Erlbaum Associates.

60. Sroufe, L. A. (2000). Early relationships and the development of children. *Infant Mental Health Journal, 21,* 67–74.

61. Pipp, S., & Harmon, R. J. (1987). Attachment as regulation: A commentary. *Child Development, 58,* 648–652.

62. Rutter, M. (1987). Temperament, personality and personality disorder. *British Journal of Psychiatry, 150,* 443–458.

63. Levy, T. M., & Orlans, M. (1998). *Attachment, trauma, and healing: Understanding and treating attachment disorder in children and families.* Washington, DC: Child Welfare League of America Press.

64. Sroufe, L. A. (2000). Early relationships and the development of children. *Infant Mental Health Journal, 21,* 67–74.

65. Kesner, J. (1998). *The effects of secure attachments on preschool children's conflict management skills.* Paper presented at the 4th National Headstart Research Conference, Washington, DC. (ERIC Document Reproduction Service No. ED 422 118).

66. Sroufe, L. A. (1983). Infant-caregiver attachment and patterns of adaptation in preschool: The roots of maladaptation and competence. In M. Perlmutter (Ed.), *Minnesota Symposium in Child Psychology* (Vol. 16, pp. 41–83). Hillsdale, NJ: Erlbaum Associates.

67. Egeland, B., & Erickson, M. F. (1999). Findings from the parent-child project and implications for early intervention. *Zero to Three,* 3–10.

68. Levy, T. M., & Orlans, M. (1998). *Attachment, trauma, and healing: Understanding and treating attachment disorder in children and families.* Washington, DC: Child Welfare League of America Press.

69. Hughes, D. (1999). *Building the bonds of attachment: Awakening the love of deeply troubled children.* Northvale, NJ: Jason Aronson.

70. Jernberg, A., & Booth, P. (1999). *Theraplay: Helping parents and children build better relationships through attachment-based play* (p. 2). San Francisco: Jossey-Bass.

71. Levy, T. M., & Orlans, M. (1998). *Attachment, trauma, and healing: Understanding and treating attachment disorder in children and families.* Washington, DC: Child Welfare League of America Press.

72. Cowan, P. A., Cowan, C. P., Cohn, D. A., & Pearson, J. L. (1996). Parents' attachment histories and children's externalizing and internalizing behaviors: Exploring family systems models of linkage. *Journal of Consulting and Clinical Psychology, 64,* 53–63.

73. Ainsworth, M. D. S., Blehar, M. C. Waters, E., & Wall, S. (1978). *Patterns of attachment: A psychological study of the strange situation.* Hillsdale, NJ: Lawrence Erlbaum Associates.

74. Sroufe, L. A. (2000). Early relationships and the development of children. *Infant Mental Health Journal, 21,* 67–74.

75. James, B. (1994). *Handbook for treatment of attachment-trauma problems in children.* New York: Lexington Books, Macmillan.

76. Sroufe, L. A. (2000). Early relationships and the development of children. *Infant Mental Health Journal, 21,* 67–74.

77. Lyons-Ruth, K. (1996). Attachment relationships among children with aggressive behavior problems: The role of disorganized early attachment patterns. *Journal of Consulting and Clinical Psychology, 64,* 64–73.

78. Crittenden, P. M., Landini, A., & Claussen, A. H. (2001). A dynamic-maturational approach to treatment of maltreated children. In J. Hughes, J. C. Conley, and A. LaGreca (Eds.), *Handbook of psychological services for children and adolescents* (pp. 379–398). New York: Oxford University Press.

79. Kerns, K. A., & Stevens, A. C. (1996). Parent-child attachment in late adolescence: Likens to social relations and personality. *Journal of Youth and Adolescence, 25,* 323–342.

80. Koback, R., & Sceery, A. (1998). Attachment in late adolescence: Working models, affect regulation, and representations of self and others. *Child Development, 59,* 135–146.

81. Larson, R., & Richards, M. H. (1991). Daily companionship in late childhood and early adolescence: Changing developmental context. *Child Development, 62,* 284–300.

82. Larson, R., Richards, M. H., Moneta, G., & Holmbeck, G. C. (1996). Changes in adolescents' daily interactions with their families from ages 10 to 18: Disengagement and transformation. *Developmental Psychology, 32,* 744–454.

83. Arnett, J. J. (2001). Conceptions of the transition to adulthood: Perspectives from adolescence through midlife. *Journal of Adult Development, 8,* 133–143.

84. Arnett, J. J. (2000). Emerging adulthood: A theory of development from the late teens through the twenties. *American Psychologist, 55,* 469–480.

85. Becker-Weidman, A. (2006). Treatment for children with trauma-attachment disorders: Dyadic Developmental Psychotherapy. *Child and Adolescent Mental Health.* Published online.

86. Hughes, D. (2004). An attachment-based intervention for the spectrum of attachment disorders and intrafamilial trauma. *Attachment and Human Development, 3,* 263–278.

87. Hughes, D. (1999). *Building the bonds of attachment: Awakening the love of deeply troubled children.* Northvale, NJ: Jason Aronson.

88. James, B. (1994). *Handbook for treatment of attachment-trauma problems in children.* New York: Lexington Books, Macmillan.

89. http://www.attachmentexperts.com/childteen.html (2007, March 8).

# *Chapter 3*

1. Maslow, A. (1954). *Motivation and personality.* New York: Harper.

2. Maslow, A. (1971). *The farther reaches of human nature.* New York: The Viking Press.

3. Erikson, E. (1959). Identity and the life cycle. *Psychological Issues, 1,* 680–684.

4. Maslow, A. (1971). *The farther reaches of human nature.* New York: The Viking Press.

5. Maslow, A., & Lowery, R. (Ed.). (1998). *Toward a psychology of being* (3rd ed.). New York: Wiley and Sons.

6. Willems, S., Vanobbergen, J., Martens, L., & De Maeseneer, J. (2005). The independent impact of household and area based social determinants on early childhood caries (ECC): A cross-sectional study in inner city children. *Family and Community Health, 28* (2), 168–175.

7. Morrow, L. M. (Ed.). (1995). *Family literacy connections in schools and communities*. Newark, DE: International Reading Association.

8. Kenny, M., Gallagher, L., Alvarez-Salvat, R., & Silsby, J. (2002). Sources of support and psychological distress among academically successful inner-city youth. *Adolescence, 37,* 161–182.

9. Kline Kovner, K. (2003). *Hardwired to Connect: The New Scientific Case for Authoritative Communities*. New York: Institute for American Values.

10. Oliner, P., Oliner, S., Blum, L., & Baron, L. (1995). *Embracing the other*. New York: University Press.

11. Oliner, P., Oliner, S., Blum, L., & Baron, L. (1995). *Embracing the other*. New York: University Press.

12. Norwood, G. (1999). Maslow's hierarchy of needs. *The Truth Vectors* (Part I). Retrieved May 2002 from http://www.connect.net/georgen/malsow.htm

13. Wahba, A., & Bridgewell., L. (1976). Maslow reconsidered: A review of research on the need hierarchy theory. *Organizational Behavior and Human Performance, 15,* 212–240.

14. Deci, E., & Ryan, R. (1991). A motivational approach to self: Integration in personality. In R. Dienstbier (Ed.), *Perspectives on motivation*. Nebraska Symposium on Motivation. Lincoln: University of Nebraska Press.

15. Thompson, M., Grace, C., & Cohen, L. (2001). *Best friends, worst enemies: Understanding the social lives of children*. New York: Ballantine Books.

16. Franken, R. (2001). *Human motivation* (5th ed.). Pacific Grove, CA: Brooks/Cole.

17. Franken, R. (2001). *Human motivation* (5th ed.). Pacific Grove, CA: Brooks/Cole.

18. Burton, J. W. (1993). Conflict resolution as a political philosophy. In D. J. D. Sandole and H. van derMerwe (Eds.). *Conflict resolution theory and practice: Integration and application* (pp. 55-64). Manchester, England: Manchester University Press. Available at http://www.colorado.edu/conflict/transform/burton.htm

19. Rosenberg, M. (2003). *Nonviolent communication: A language of life*. Encinitas, CA: Puddle Dancer Press.

20. Franken, R. (2001). *Human motivation* (5th ed.). Pacific Grove, CA: Brooks/Cole.

21. Maslow, A. (1954). *Motivation and personality*. New York: Harper.

22. Burton, J. W. (1993). Conflict resolution as a political philosophy. In D. J. D. Sandole and H. van derMerwe (Eds.). *Conflict resolution theory and practice: Integration and application* (pp. 55-64). Manchester, England: Manchester University Press. Available at http://www.colorado.edu/conflict/transform/burton.htm

23. Rosenberg, M. (2003). *Nonviolent communication: A language of life*. CA: Puddle Dancer Press.

24. Parten, M. (1932). Social participation among preschool children. *Journal of Abnormal and Social Psychology, 27,* 243–269.

25. Ladd, G. W., Birch, S. H., & Buhs, E. S. (1999). Children's social and scholastic lives in kindergarten: Related spheres of influence? *Child Development, 70,* 1373–1400.

26. Summerlin, J. R., & Norman, R. L., Jr. (1992). Self-actualization and homeless men: A known-groups examination of Maslow's hierarchy of needs. *Journal of Social Behavior and Personality, 7*(3), 469–481.

27. Mother Teresa. (1988). *One heart full of love.* Servant Publications: Ann Arbor, MI.

28. Erikson, E. (1950). *Childhood and society.* New York: Norton.

29. Erikson, E. (1959). Identity and the life cycle. *Psychological Issues, 1,* 680–684.

30. Erikson, E. (1968). *Identity, youth, and crisis.* New York: Norton.

31. Erikson, E. (1950). *Childhood and society.* New York: Norton.

32. Erikson, E. (1959). Identity and the life cycle. *Psychological Issues, 1,* 680–684.

33. Erikson, E. (1968). *Identity, youth, and crisis.* New York: Norton.

# Chapter 4

1. Cummings, E. (1987). Coping with background anger in early childhood. *Child Development, 58*(4), 976–984.

2. Fabes, R. A., & Eisenberg, N. (1992). Young children's coping with interpersonal anger. *Child Development, 63*(1), 116–128.

3. Lewis, M., & Michalson, L. (1983). *Children's emotions and moods.* New York: Plenum.

4. Zenman, J., & Shipman, K. (1996). Children's expression of negative affect: Reasons and methods. *Developmental Psychology, 32*(5), 842–850.

5. Zenman, J., & Shipman, K. (1996). Children's expression of negative affect: Reasons and methods. *Developmental Psychology, 32*(5), 842–850.

6. Lewis, M., & Michalson, L. (1983). *Children's emotions and moods.* New York: Plenum.

7. Russell, J. A. (1989). Culture, scripts, and children's understanding of emotion. In C. Saarni & P. L. Harris (Eds.), *Children's understanding of emotion* (pp. 293–318). Cambridge, England, U.K.: Cambridge University Press.

8. Honig, A., & Wittmer, D. (1992). *Prosocial development in children: Caring, sharing, and cooperation: A bibliographic resource guide.* New York: Garland.

9. Cummings, E. (1987). Coping with background anger in early childhood. *Child Development, 58*(4), 976–984.

10. Melmed, M. E. (1998). Talking with parents about emotional development. *Pediatrics, 102,* 1317–1326.

11. Melmed, M. E. (1998). Talking with parents about emotional development. *Pediatrics, 102,* 1317–1326.

12. Thomas, A., & Chess, S. (1977). *Temperament and development.* New York: Brunner/Mazel.

13. Thomas, A., & Chess, S. (1977). *Temperament and development.* New York: Brunner/Mazel.

14. Bates, J. E., Wachs, T. D., & Emde, R. N. (1994). Toward practical uses for biological concepts. In J. E. Bates & T. D. Wachs (Eds.), *Temperament: Individual differences at the interface of biology and behavior* (pp. 275–306). Washington, DC: American Psychological Association.

15. Ramos, M. C., Guerin, D. W., Gottfried, A. W., Bathurst, K., & Oliver, P. H. (2005). Family conflict and children's behavioral problems: The moderating role of child temperament. *Structural Equation Modeling, 12,* 278–298.

16. Schmitz, S., Fulker, D. W., Plomin, R., Zahn-Waxler, C., Emde, R. N., & DeFries, J. C. (1999). Temperament and problem behavior during early childhood. *International Journal of Behavioral Development, 23,* 333–355.

17. Thomas, A., & Chess, S. (1977). *Temperament and development.* New York: Brunner/Mazel.

18. Putnam, S. P., Samson, A. V., & Rothbart, M. K. (2000). Child temperament and parenting. In V. J. Molfese & D. L. Molfese (Eds.), *Temperament and personality across the life span* (255–277). Mahwah, NJ: Erlbaum.

19. Coplan, R. J., Bowker, A., & Cooper, S. M. Parenting daily hassles, child temperament, and social adjustment in preschool. *Early Childhood Research Quarterly, 18,* 376–395.

20. Calkins, S. D. (2002). Does aversive behavior during toddlerhood matter? The effects of difficult temperament on maternal perceptions and behavior. *Infant Mental Health Journal, 23,* 381–402.

21. Camras, L. A., Oster, H., Campos, J. J., & Bakeman, R. (2003). Emotional facial expressions European, American, Japanese, and Chinese infants. *Annals of the New York Academy of Sciences, 1000,* 1–17.

22. Gergely, G., & Watson, J. (1999). Early socio-emotional development: Contingency perception and the social-biofeedback model. In P. Rochat (Ed.), *Early social cognition: Understanding others in the first few months of life* (pp. 105–116). New York: Springer.

23. Izard, C. E., & Ackerman, B. P. (2000). Motivational, organizational, and regulatory functions of discrete emotions. In M. Lewis & J. M. Haviland-Jones (Eds.), *Handbook of emotions* (2nd ed., pp. 253–264). New York: Guilford.

24. Izard, C. E., & Ackerman, B. P. (2000). Motivational, organizational, and regulatory functions of discrete emotions. In M. Lewis L& J. M. Haviland-Jones (Eds.), *Handbook of emotions* (2nd ed., pp. 253–264). New York: Guilford.

25. Harter, S. (1999). *The construction of self: A developmental perspective.* New York: Guilford.

26. Sternberg, R. J. (2003). A broad view of intelligence: The theory of successful intelligence. *Consulting Psychology Journal: Practice and Research, 55,* 139–154.

27. Striano, T., & Rochat, P. (2000). Emergence of selective social referencing in infancy. *Infancy, I,* 253–264.

28. Repacholi, B. M., & Gopnik, A. (1997). Early reasoning about desires: Evidence from 14–18-month-old. *Developmental Psychology, 33,* 12–21.

29. Kochanska, G., & Knaack, A. (2003). Effortful control as a personality characteristic of young children: Antecedents, correlates, and consequences. *Journal of Personality, 71,* 1087–1112.

30. Eisenberg, N., & Spinrad, T. L. (2004). Emotion-related regulation: Sharpening the definition. *Child Development, 75,* 334–339.

31. Fox, N. A., & Calkins, S. D. (2003). The development of self-control of emotion: Intrinsic and extrinsic influences. *Motivation and Emotion, 27,* 7–26.

32. Axia, G., Bonichini, S., & Benini, F. (1999). Attention and reaction to distress in infancy: A longitudinal study.*Developmental Psychology, 35,* 500–504.

33. Repacholi, B. M., & Gopnik, A. (1997). Early reasoning about desires: Evidence from 14–18-month-old. *Developmental Psychology, 33,* 12–21.

34. Baumrind, D. (1989). Rearing competent children. In W. Damon (Ed.), *Child development today and tomorrow* (pp. 349–378). San Francisco: Jossey-Bass.

35. Hart, C. H., Newell, L. D., & Olsen, S. F. (2003). Parenting skills and social-communicative competence in childhood. In J. O. Greene & B. R. Burleson (Eds.), *Handbook of communication and social interaction skills* (pp. 753–797). Mahwah, NJ: Erlbaum.

36. Barber, B. K., & Harmon, E. I. (2002). Violating the self: Parental psychological control of children and adolescents. In B. K. Barber (Ed.), *Intrusive parenting: How psychological control affects children and adolescents* (pp. 15–52). Washington, DC: American Psychological Association.

37. Amato, P. R., & Fowler, F. (2002). Parenting practices, child adjustment, and family diversity. *Journal of Marriage and the Family, 64,* 703–716.

38. Baumrind, D. (1989). Rearing competent children. In W. Damon (Ed.), *Child development today and tomorrow* (pp. 349–378). San Francisco: Jossey-Bass.

39. Aunola, K., Stattin, H., & Nurmi. (2000). Parenting styles and adolescents' achievement strategies. *Journal of Adolescence, 23,* 205–222.

40. Murphy, T., Oberlin, L. H. (2001). *The angry child: Regaining control when your child is out of control.* New York: Three Rivers Press.

41. Greene, R. W. (2005). *The explosive child: A new approach for understanding and parenting easily frustrated, chronically inflexible children.* New York: Harper.

42. Greene, R. W. (2005). *The explosive child: A new approach for understanding and parenting easily frustrated, chronically inflexible children.* New York: Harper.

43. Goldenthal, P. (1999). *Beyond sibling rivalry: How to help your children become cooperative, caring, and compassionate.* New York: Henry Holt & Company.

44. Barber, B. K., & Harmon, E. I. (2002). Violating the self: Parental psychological control of children and adolescents. In B. K. Barber (Ed.), *Intrusive parenting: How psychological control affects children and adolescents* (pp. 15-52). Washington, DC: American Psychological Association.

45. Murphy, T., & Oberlin, L. H. (2001). *The angry child: Regaining control when your child is out of control.* New York: Three Rivers Press.

# *Chapter 5*

1. National School Safety and Security Services. (2007). *School-related deaths, school shootings, & school violence incidents.* Cleveland, OH: Author.

2. School Violence Fact Sheet. (2007). National Youth Violence Prevention Resource Center. Available at http://www.safeyouth.org

3. Sherman, M. (2005, November 21). Schools crimes decline, U.S. report says. *Boston Globe.* Available at http://www.boston.com/com/news/nation/washington/articles/2005/11/21school school.crimesdecline.us_report_says/

4. National School Safety and Security Service. (2007). *School-related deaths, school shootings, & school violence incidents.*

5. *Indicators of School Crime and Safety.* (2006). Available at http://nces.ed.gov/programs/crimeindicators/

6. Nolle, K. L., Guerino, P., and Dinkes, R. (2007). *Crime, violence, discipline, and safety in U.S. public schools: Findings from the school survey on crime and safety: 2005-06* (NCES 2007-361). Washington, DC: National Center for Education Statistics, Institute of Education Sciences, U.S. Department of Education.

7. OSERS. (1998, August 18). *Early warning, timely response: A guide to safe schools.* Available at http://www.ed.gov/about/offices/list/osers/osep/gtss.html

8. Bender, W. N., Shubert, T. H., & McLaughlin, P. J. (2001). Invisible kids: Preventing school violence by identifying kids in trouble. *Intervention in School and Clinic, 37,* 105–111.

9. Nansel, T. R., Overpeck, M. Pilla, R. S., Ruan, W. J., Simons-Morton, B., & Scheidt, P. (2001). Bullying behaviors among U.S. youth: Prevalence and association with psychosocial adjustment. *Journal of the American Medical Association, 285*(16), 2094–2100.

10. *Indicators of School Crime and Safety.* (2006). Available at http://nces.ed.gov /programs/crimeindicators/

11. U.S. Secret Service National Threat Assessment Center. (2000). *Safe school initiative—An interim report on the prevention of targeted violence in schools.* Available at http://www.secretservice.gov/ntac_ssi.shtml

12. National Center for Education Statistics. (2006). *Crime, violence, discipline and safety in U.S. Public Schools: Findings from the School Survey on Crime and Safety: 2003–2004.*

13. U.S. Departments of Education and Justice. (2006). *Indicators of School Crime and Safety: 2005.* http://www.ojp.usdoj.gov/bjs/abstract/iscs06.htm

14. *Indicators of School Crime and Safety.* (2006). Available at http://nces.ed.gov /programs/crimeindicators/

15. Public Agenda. (2004). *Teaching interrupted: Do discipline policies in today's public schools foster the common good?* Available at http://www.publicagenda.org

16. *Indicators of School Crime and Safety.* (2006). Available at http://nces.ed. gov/programs/crimeindicators/

17. Black, S. (2003). New remedies for high-school violence. *Education Digest, 69* (3), 43–47.

18. Potter, L. (2003). Safety in our schools. *Principal Leadership (Middle School Ed.), 4*(3), 81–82.

19. Hernandez, T. J., & Seem, S. R. (2004). A safe school climate: a systemic approach for the school counselor. *Professional School Counseling, 7*(4), 256–262.

20. Egley, A. (2000). Highlights of the 1999 National Youth Gang Survey. *OJJDP Fact Sheet.* Washington, DC: U.S. Department of Justice, Office of Justice and Delinquency Prevention.

21. Egley, A., & Arjunan, M. (2002). Highlights of the 2000 National Youth Gang Survey. *OJJDP Fact Sheet.* Washington, DC: U.S. Department of Justice, Office of Justice Programs, Office of Juvenile Justice and Delinquency Prevention.

22. Howell, J. C., & Lynch, J. P. (2000). Gangs in schools. Juvenile Justice Bulletin. Nation Youth Gang Survey Trends from 1996 to 2000. *OJJDP Fact Sheet.* Washington, DC: U.S. Department of Justice, Office of Justice Programs, Office of Juvenile Justice and Delinquency Prevention.

23. National Center for Education Statistics. (2006). *Crime, violence, discipline and safety in U.S. Public Schools: Findings from the School Survey on Crime and Safety: 2003–2004.*

24. Howell, J. C. (2006, August). The impact of gangs on communities. *NYGC Bulletin, 2,* 1–6; Howell, J. C., & Egley, A., Jr. (2005, June). *NYGC Bulletin, 1,* 1–6.

25. NYGC Bulletin, OJJDP. (2006, August). *The impact of gangs on communities.* Available at http://www.iir.com/nygc; NYGC Bulletin, OJJDP. (2005, June). *Gangs in small towns and rural counties.* Available at http://www/kidshealth.org/kid/feeling/school/pool_bullying.html

26. The National Center on Addiction and Substance Abuse at Columbia University. (2007, September). *The importance of family dinners.* Sponsored by the Safeway Foundation. New York; The National Center on Addiction and Substance Abuse at Columbia University. (2007, August). *National survey of American attitudes on substance abuse XII: Teens and parents.* Sponsored by the Safeway Foundation. New York.

27. The National Center on Addiction and Substance Abuse at Columbia University. (2007, September). *The importance of family dinners.* Sponsored by the Safeway Foundation. New York.

28. National Center for Victims of Crime. (2005). *Teen Victim Project.* Available at http://www.ncvc.org/tvp

29. Avery-Leaf, S., & Cascardi, M. (2002). Dating Violence Education. *Preventing Violence in Relationships* (p. 82). Washington, DC: American Psychological Association.

30. Halpern, C. (2001). Partner violence among adolescents in opposite-sex romantic relationships: Findings from the national Longitudinal Study of Adolescent Health 91. *American Journal of Public Health,* 1679; Halpern, C., et al., (2004, August). Prevalence of partner violence in same-sex romantic and sexual relationships in a national sample of adolescents. *Journal of Adolescent Health, 35,* 124–131.

31. Klein, J. (2006). An invisible problem: Everyday violence against girls in schools. *Theoretical criminology, 10,* 147.

32. Zwicker, T. (2002). Education Policy Brief: The imperative of developing teen dating violence prevention and intervention programs in secondary schools. *Southern California Review of Law and Women's Studies, 12,* 131.

33. Jones, T. S., & Compton, R. (2003). *Kids working it out: Stories and strategies for making peace in our schools.* San Francisco, CA: Jossey-Bass.

34. Jones, T. S., & Kmitta, D. (Eds.). (2000). *Does it work? The case for conflict resolution education in our nation's schools.* Washington, DC: Conflict Resolution Education Network.

35. Sandy, S. V., & Cochran, K. (2001). The development of conflict resolution skills in children: Preschool to adolescence. In M. Deutsch and P. Coleman (Eds.), *The handbook of conflict resolution: Theory and practice* (pp. 316–342). San Francisco, CA: Jossey-Bass.

# *Chapter 6*

1. Centerwall, B. (1992). Television and violence: The scale of the problem and where to go from here. *Journal of the American Medical Association, 267*(22), 3050–3063.

2. Grossman, D. (1995). *On killing: The psychological cost of learning to kill in war and society.* Boston and New York: Little Brown.

3. Grossman, D. (1995). *On killing: The psychological cost of learning to kill in war and society* (p. 304). Boston and New York: Little Brown.

4. Grossman, D. (1995). *On killing: The psychological cost of learning to kill in war and society* (p. 308). Boston and New York: Little Brown.

5. Matthews, V. P., Kronenberger, W. G., et al. (2005). Media violence exposure and frontal lobe activation measured by functional magnetic resonance imaging in aggressive and nonaggressive adolescents. *Journal of Computer Assisted Technology, 29*(3), 287–292; Matthews, V. P., et al. (2002). Violent video games trigger unusual brain activity in aggressive adolescents. Presentation to the annual meeting of the Radiological Society of North America, December 2, 2002.

6. American Medical Association. (1996). *Physician guide to media violence.* Chicago: Author.

7. Molitor, F., & Hirsch, K. W. (1994). Children's toleration of real-life aggression after exposure to media violence: A replication of the Drabman and Thomas studies. *Child Study Journal, 24,* 191–207.

8. Mullin, C. R., & Linz, D. (1995). Desensitization and resensitization to violence against women: Effects of exposure to sexually violent films on judgments of domestic violence victims. *Journal of Personality and Social Psychology, 69,* 449–459.

9. Molitor, F., & Hirsch, K. W. (1994). Children's toleration of real-life aggression after exposure to media violence: A replication of the Drabman and Thomas studies. *Child Study Journal, 24,* 191–207.

10. Mullin, C. R., & Linz, D. (1995). Desensitization and resensitization to violence against women: Effects of exposure to sexually violent films on judgments of domestic violence victims. *Journal of Personality and Social Psychology, 69,* 449–459.

11. Zillman, D., & Weaver, J. B., III. (1999). Effects of prolonged exposure to gratuitous media violence on provoked and unprovoked hostile behavior. *Journal of Applied Social Psychology, 29,* 145–165.

12. Huston, A. C., et al. (1992). *Big world, small screen: The role of television in American society.* Lincoln, NE: University of Nebraska Press.

13. Henry J. Kaiser Family Foundation. (2005). *Generation M: Media in the lives of 8–18 year olds.* Retrieved February 21, 2008, from http://www.kff.org/entmedia/upload/ Executive-Summary-Generation-M-Media-in-the-Lives-of-8-18-Year-olds.pdf

14. Henry J. Kaiser Family Foundation. (2003). *Fact sheet: TV violence.* Menlo Park, CA: Author.

15. Henry J. Kaiser Family Foundation. (2005). *Generation M: Media in the lives of 8-18 year olds.* Retrieved February 21, 2008, from http://www.kff.org/entmedia/upload/ Executive-Summary-Generation-M-Media-in-the-Lives-of-8-18-Year-olds.pdf

16. Singer, M., Slovak, I., Frierson, T., & York, P. (1998). Viewing preferences, symptoms of psychological trauma, and violent behaviors among children who watch television. *Journal of the American Academy of Child and Adolescent Psychiatry,* 1041–1048.

17. Owens, J., Maxim, R., McGuinn, M., Nobile, C., Msall, M., & Alario, A. (1999). Television viewing habits and sleep disturbance in school children. *Pediatrics, 104,* 552.

18. Gentile, D. A., & Walsh, T. M. (1999). *Media quotient: National survey of family media habits, knowledge, and attitudes.* Minneapolis, MN: National Institute on Media and the Family.

19. Cantor, J. (1998). *"Mommy, I'm scared": How TV and movies frighten children and what we can do to protect them.* San Diego, CA: Harcourt Brace.

20. Cantor, J., & Hoffner, C. (1990). Children's fear reactions to a televised film as a function of perceived immediacy of depicted threat. *Journal of Broadcasting & Electronic Media, 34,* 421–442.

21. Cantor, J. (2001). Helping children cope: Advice in the aftermath of the terrorist attacks on America. Available at http://joannecantor.com/terror_adv.htm

22. Huesmann, L. R., Moise-Titus, J., Podolski, C., & Eron, L. (2003). Longitudinal relations between children's exposure to TV violence and their aggressive and violent behavior in adulthood: 1977–1992. *Developmental Psychology, 39,* 201–202.

23. Huesmann, L. R., Moise-Titus, J., Podolski, C., & Eron, L. (2003). Longitudinal relations between children's exposure to TV violence and their aggressive and violent behavior in adulthood: 1977–1992. *Developmental Psychology, 39,* 201–202; Johnson, J. G., Cohen, P., Smailes, E. M., Kasen, S., & Brook, J. S. (2002). Television viewing and aggressive behavior during adolescence and adulthood. *Science, 295,* 2468–2471.

24. Huesmann, L. R., Moise-Titus, J., Podolski, C., & Eron, L. (2003). Longitudinal relations between children's exposure to TV violence and their aggressive and violent behavior in adulthood: 1977–1992. *Developmental Psychology, 39,* 201–202.

25. Harrison, K., & Cantor, J. (1999). Tales from the screen: Enduring fright reactions to scary media. *Media Psychology, 11*(2), 97–116.

26. Cantor, J. (2004). *Teddy's TV troubles.* Madison, WI: Goblin Fern Press.

27. Cantor, J. (2002). Fright reactions to mass media. In J. Bryant & D. Zillman (Eds.), *Media effects: Advances in theory and research* (2nd ed., pp. 287–306). Hillsdale, NJ: Lawrence Erlbaum.

28. Matthews, V. P., Kronenberger, W. G., et al. (2005). Media violence exposure and frontal lobe activation measured by functional magnetic resonance imaging in aggressive and nonaggressive adolescents. *Journal of Computer Assisted Technology, 29*(3), 287–292.

29. American Obesity Association. (2005, May). *Fact Sheet: Obesity in youth.* Available at http://obesity1.tempdomainname.com/subs/fastfacts/obesity_youth.shtml

30. Tremblay, M. S., & Wilms, J. D. (2003). Is the Canadian child obesity epidemic related to physical inactivity? *International Journal of Obesity, 27,* 1100–1105.

31. Centers for Disease Control. (2006, May). *Physical activity and the health of young people.* Retrieved February 21, 2008 from http://cdc.gov/HealthyYouth/physicalactivity/facts.htm

32. Dennison, B. A., Erb, M. S., Tara, A., & Jenkins, P. L. (2002, June). Television viewing and television in bedroom associated with overweight risk among low-income preschool children. *Pediatrics, 109,* 1028–1035.

33. Robinson, T. N. (1999, October 27). Reducing children's television viewing to prevent obesity. *JAMA, 282,* 1561–1567.

34. Janz, K. F., Burns, T., Torner, J. C., Steven, M., Paulos, Willing, M. C., & Warren, J. J. (2001). Physical activity and bone measures in young children: The Iowa bone development study. *Pediatrics, 107,* 1387–1393.

35. Reinking, D., & Wu, J. (1990, Winter). Reexamining the research on television and reading. *Reading Research and Instruction, 29,* 30–43.

36. MacBeth, T. (Ed.). (1996). *Tuning into young viewers.* Newbury Park, CA: SAGE Publications.

37. Wright, J. C., Huston, A. C., Murphy, K. C., Peters, M. St., Pinon, M., Scantlin, R., & Kotler, J. (2001). The relations of early television viewing to school readiness and vocabulary of children from low-income families: The early window project. *Child Development, 72,* 1347–1366.

38. Office of Educational Research and Improvement. (1988). *National education longitudinal study of 1988.* Washington, DC: Government Printing Office.

39. Armstrong, G. B., Boirsky, G. A., & Mares, M. L. (1991, September). Background television and reading performance. *Communication Monographs, 58.*

40. Anderson, D. R., Huston, A. C., Schmitt, K., Linebarger, D. L., & Wright, J. S. (2001). Early childhood television viewing and adolescent behavior: The recontact study. *Monographs of the Society for Research in Child Development, 66,* (Serial No. 264).

41. Henry J. Kaiser Family Foundation. (2005). *Generation M: Media in the lives of 8–18 year olds.* Retrieved February 21, 2008, from http://www.kff.org/entmedia/upload/Executive-Summary-Generation-M-Media-in-the-Lives-of-8-18-Year-olds.pdf

42. Fischer, P. M., Schwartz, M. P., Richards, J. W., Jr., & Goldstein, A. O. (1991, December 11). Brand logo recognition by children aged 3 to 6 years: Mickey Mouse and Old Joe the Camel. *Journal of the American Medical Association, 266,* 3145–3148.

43. McNeal, J. (2002). *Kids as customers.* New York: Lexington Books; McNeal, J. (1999). *The kids' market: Myths and realities.* Ithaca, NY: Paramount Market.

44. Comstock, G. (1991). *Television and the American child.* New York: Academic Press Inc.

45. Strasburger, V. C., & Wilson, B. J. (2002). *Children adolescents and the media.* Thousand Oaks, CA: Sage Publication.

46. http://www.aap.org/family/smarttv.htm

47. Henry J. Kaiser Family Foundation. (2005). *Generation M: Media in the lives of 8–18 year olds.* Retrieved February 21, 2008, from http://www.kff.org/entmedia/upload/Executive-Summary-Generation-M-Media-in-the-Lives-of-8-18-Year-olds.pdf

48. National Institute on Media and the Family. (2001). *Sixth annual video and computer game report card.* Available at http://www.mediafamily.org/research/report_vgrc_2001-2.shtml

49. Business Week Online. (2006, June 23). *Global video game market set to explode.* Retrieved February 21, 2008, from http://www.businessweek.com/print/innovate/content/jun2006/id20060623_163211.htm

50. NPD Group Inc. (2006, September 19). *Video gamer segmentation report.* Available at http://www/npd.com/corpServlet?nextpage+entertainment-specialreports_s.html

51. Henry J. Kaiser Family Foundation. (2005). *Generation M: Media in the lives of 8–18 year olds.* Retrieved February 21, 2008, from http://www.kff.org/entmedia/upload/Executive-Summary-Generation-M-Media-in-the-Lives-of-8-18-Year-olds.pdf

52. Business Week Online. (2006, June 23). *Global video game market set to explode.* Retrieved February 21, 2008, from http://www.businessweek.com/print/innovate/content/jun2006/id20060623_163211.htm

53. Mediawise video and computer game report card: A ten year overview. (2006). Retrieved February 21, 2008, from http://www.mediafamily.org/research/report_10yr_overview.shtml

54. Anderson, C. A., & Dill, K. E. (2000). Video games and aggressive thoughts, feelings, and behavior in the laboratory and in life. *Journal of Personality and Social Psychology, 78*(4), 772–790.

55. Gentile, D. A., Lynch, P. J., Linder, J. R., & Walsh, D. A. (2004). The effects of violent video game habits on adolescent hostility, aggressive behaviors, and school performance. *Journal of Adolescence, 27,* 5–22.

56. Kirsh, S. J. (1998). Seeing the world through Mortal Kombat-colored glasses: Violent video games and the development of a short-term hostile attribution bias. *Childhood, 5,* 177–184.

57. Kirsch, S. J. (1998). Seeing the world through Mortal Kombat-colored glasses: Violent video games and the development of a short-term hostile attribution bias. *Childhood, 5,* 177–184.

58. Christenson, P. G., & Roberts, D. F. (1998). *It's not only rock & roll: Popular music in the lives of adolescents.* Cresskill, NJ: Hampton Press.

59. Knight-Ridder/Tribune News Service. (1999, July 9). *Popular music's influence on teens is undeniable and sometimes negative* (p. K-5667).

60. Wingood, G. M., DiClemente, R. J., Bernhardt, J. M., Harrington, K., Davies, S., & Hook, E. W., III. (2003). *American Journal of Public Health, 93*(3), 437–439.

61. PBS On-Line. (2001). With Todd Cunniham. PBS.org.

62. Rich, M., Woods, E., Goodman, E., Emans, J., & DuRant, R. (1998, April). Aggressors or victims: Gender and race in music video violence. *Pediatrics, 101,* 669–674.

63. *Pediatrics.* (2001). Vol. 102, p. 5. Available at http://www.pediatrics.org/cgi/content/full/102/5/e54

64. DuRant, R. H., Rich, M., Emans, S. J., Rome, E. S., Alfred, E., & Woods, R. R. (1997). Violence and weapon carrying in music videos: A content analysis. *Pediatric Adolescent Medicine, 151,* 443–448.

65. Calfin, M. S., Carroll, J. L., & Schmidt, J. (1993). Viewing music-video tapes before taking a test of premarital sexual attitudes. *Psychological Reports, 72,* 475–481.

66. Greeson, L. E., & Williams, R. A. (1986). Social implications of music videos on youth: An analysis of the content and effects of MTV. *Youth and Society, 18,* 177–189.

67. Greenfield, P., & Yan, Z. (2006). Children, adolescents, and the Internet: A new field of inquiry in developmental psychology. *Journal of Applied Developmental Psychology, 42*(3), 391–394.

68. Third Way Culture Project. (2005). *The porn standard: Children and pornography on the Internet.* Retrieved February 21, 2008, from http://www.thirdway.org/data/product/file/14/porn_standard.pdf

69. Lenhart, A., Madden, M., & Hitlin, P. (2005, July). *Teens and technology: You are leading the transition to a fully wired and mobile nation.* Retrieved October 12, 2005, from http://www.pewInternet.org/pdfs/PIP_Teens_Tech_July2005web.pdf

70. Greenfield, P., & Yan, Z. (2006). Children, adolescents, and the Internet: A new field of inquiry in developmental psychology. *Journal of Applied Developmental psychology, 42*(3), 391–394.

71. Common Sense Media. http://www.commonsense.com/

72. Galbreath, N., & Berlin, F. (2002). Paraphilias and the Internet. In A. Cooper (Ed.), *Sex and the Internet: A guidebook for clinicians* (pp. 187–205). New York: Brunner Routledge.

73. Gentile, D. A., Walsh, D. A., Ellison, P. R., Fox, M., & Cameron, J. (2004, May). Media violence as a risk factor for children: A longitudinal study. Paper presented at the American Psychological Society 16th Annual Convention, Chicago, Illinois.

74. Huesmann, L. R., Moise-Titus, J., Podolski, C., and Eron, L. D. (2003). Longitudinal relations between children's exposure to TV violence and their aggressive and violent behavior in young adulthood: 1977–1992. *Developmental Psychology, 39*(2), 201–221.

# *Chapter 7*

1. Glenn, S. (1989). *Raising self-reliant children: In a self-indulgent world.* Rocklin, CA: Prima Publishing.

2. Adams, C., & Gruge, E. (1996). *Why children misbehave and what to do about it.* Oakland, CA: Harbinger Publications.

3. Brooks, R., & Goldstein, S. (2007). *Raising a self-disciplined child.* New York: McGraw-Hill.

4. Coloroso, B. (1995). *Kids are worth it: Giving your child the gift of inner discipline.* New York: Avon Books.

5. Straus, M. A., & Stewart, J. H. (1999). Corporal punishment by American parents: National data on prevalence, chronicity, severity, and duration in relation to child and family characteristics. *Clinical Child and Family Psychology Review, 2,* 55–70.

6. Bilmes, J. (2004). *Beyond behavior management: The six life skills children need to thrive in today's world.* St. Paul, MN: Redleaf Press.

7. Sprague, J., & Golly, A. (2005). *Best behavior: Building positive behavior in school.* Boston, MA: Sopris West.

8. Cline, F., & Fay, J. (2006). *Parenting with love and logic.* Colorado Springs: Pinon.

9. Dreikurs, R., & Cassel. P. (1972). *Discipline without tears: What to do with children who misbehave.* New York: Hawthorne Books Inc.

10. Cline, F., & Fay, J. (2006). *Parenting with love and logic.* Colorado Springs: Pinon.

11. Brooks, R., & Goldstein, S. (2007). *Raising a self-disciplined child.* New York: McGraw-Hill.

12. Divinyi, J. (2003). *Discipline that works: Five simple steps.* Peachtree, GA: The Wellness Connection.

13. Divinyi, J. (2003). *Discipline that works: Five simple steps.* Peachtree, GA: The Wellness Connection.

14. Brault, L. (2005). *Children with challenging behavior: Strategies for reflective thinking.* Phoenix, AZ: CPG Publishing Company.

15. Zahn-Waxler, C., & Robinson, J. (1995). Empathy and guilt: Early origins of feelings of responsibility. In J. P. Tangney & K. W. Fischer (Eds.), *Self-conscious emotions* (pp. 143–173). New York: Guilford.

16. Nelsen, J. (1999). *Positive discipline.* New York: Ballantine Books.

17. Bailey, B. (2000). *Easy to love, difficult to discipline.* New York: William Morrow.

18. Covey, S. (1997). *The seven habits of highly effective families.* United Kingdom: Golden Books.

19. Cloud, H., & Townsend, J. (2002). *Boundaries.* Emeryville, CA: Zondervan.

20. O'Neil, M., & Newbold, C. E. (1998). *Boundary power: How I treat you, how I let you treat me, how I treat myself.* Emeryville, CA: Sonlight Publishing.

21. Cloud, H., & Townsend, J. (2002). *Boundaries.* Emeryville, CA: Zondervan.

22. Black, J., & Enns, G. (1998). *Better boundaries: Owning and treasuring your life.* New Oakland, CA: New Harbinger Publications.

23. O'Neil, M., & Newbold, C. E. (1998). *Boundary power: How I treat you, how I let you treat me, how I treat myself.* Emeryville, CA: Sonlight Publishing.

24. Black, J., & Enns, G. (1998). *Better boundaries: Owning and treasuring your life.* New Oakland, CA: New Harbinger Publications.

25. O'Neil, M., & Newbold, C. E. (1998). *Boundary power: How I treat you, how I let you treat me, how I treat myself.* Emeryville, CA: Sonlight Publishing.

26. Genett, D. M. (2005). *Help your kids get it done right at home and at school.* Sanger, CA: Quill Driver books.

27. Scales, P. C., Roehlkepartain, E. C., Neal, M., Kielsmeier, J. C., & Benson, P. L. (2006). Reducing academic achievement gaps: The role of community service and service learning. *Journal of Experimental Education, 29,* 38–60.

28. Vaughn, B. E., Kopp, C. B., & Krakow, J. B. (1984). The emergence and consolidation of self-control from eighteen to thirty months of age: Normative trends and individual differences. *Child Development, 55,* 990–1004.

29. Bosak, S. (2004). *Dream: A tale of wonder, wisdom, & wishes.* Whitchurch-Stouffville, Ontario, Canada: The Communication Project.

30. Holverstott, J. (2005). Promote self-determination in students. *Intervention in School & Clinic, 41,* 1, 39–42.

31. Gallo, E., Gallo, J., & Gallo, K. (2001). *Silver spoon kids: How successful parents raise money responsible children.* Columbus, OH: McGraw-Hill.

32. Godfrey, J. (2003). *Raising financially fit kids.* Berkeley, CA: Ten Speed Press.

33. Godfrey, J. (2003). *Raising financially fit kids.* Berkeley, CA: Ten Speed Press.

34. Godfrey, J. (2003). *Raising financially fit kids.* Berkeley, CA: Ten Speed Press.

# *Chapter 8*

1. Luthar, S. S., Cicchetti, D., & Becker, B. (2007). The construct of resilience: A critical evaluation and guidelines for future work. *Child Development, 71,* 543–562.

2. Garmezy, N. (1993). Children in poverty: Resilience despite risk. *Psychiatry, 56,* 127–136.

3. Wright, M. O., & Masten, A. S. (2005). Resilience processes in development: Fostering positive adaptation in the context of adversity. In S. Goldstein & R. B. Brooks (Eds.), *Handbook of resilience in children and adolescents* (pp. 17–37). New York: Kluwer Academic/Plenum Publishers.

4. Kersting, K. (2003, September). Lessons in resilience. *APA Monitor on Psychology, 32*(8), 30–31.

5. Smith, C., Lizzotte, A. J., Thornberry, T. P., & Krohn, M. D. (1995). Resilient youth: Identifying factors that prevent high-risk from engaging in delinquency and drug use. In J. Hagan (Ed.), *Delinquency and disrepute in the life course* (pp. 217-247). Greenwich, CT: JAI.

6. Garbarino, J. (1994). *Raising children in a socially toxic environment.* San Francisco, CA: Jossey-Bass.

7. Werner, E. E., & Smith, R. S. (1992). *Overcoming the odds: High risk children from birth to adulthood.* Ithaca, NY: Cornell University Press.

8. Benard, B. (1991). *Fostering resiliency in kids: Protective factors in the family, school, and community.* San Francisco: Far West Laboratory for Educational Research and Development. ED 335 781.

9. Kersting, K. (2003, September). Lessons in resilience. *APA Monitor on Psychology, 32*(8), 30–31.

10. Gottman, J. (1997). *Raising an emotionally intelligent child.* New York: Simon & Schuster.

11. Blum, R. W., Beuhring, T., Shew, M. L., Bearinger, L. H., Sieving, R. E., & Resnick, M. D. (2000). The effects of race/ethnicity, income, and family structure on adolescent risk behaviors. *American Journal of Public Health, 90,* 1879–1884.

12. Buckner, J. C., Mezzacappa, E., & Beardslee, W. R. (2003). Characteristics of resilient youths living in poverty: The role of self-regulatory processes. *Development and Psychopathology, 15,* 139–162.

13. Shonkoff, J. P., & Phillips, D. A. (Eds.). (2000). *From neurons to neighborhoods: Acquiring self-regulation.* Washington, DC: National Academy Press.

14. Bandura, A. (1997). *Self-efficacy: The exercise of control.* New York: Freeman.

15. Eccles, J. S., Wigfield, A., & Schiefele, U. (1998). Motivation to succeed. In W. Damon (Editor-in-Chief) and N. Eisenberg (Vol. Ed.), *Handbook of child psychology. Vol. 3: Social, emotional, and personality development* (5th ed., pp. 1017–1095). New York: Wiley.

16. McCullough, M. E., Tsang, J., & Emmons, R. A. (2004). Gratitude in intermediate affective terrain: Links of grateful moods to individual differences and daily emotional experience. *Journal of Personality and Social Psychology, 86,* 295–309.

17. Worthington, E. L., Jr. (2001) *Five steps to forgiveness: The art and science of forgiving.* New York: Crown Publishers.

18. Benson, P. L., Roehlkepartain, E. C., & Rude, S. P. (2003). Spiritual development in childhood and adolescence: Toward a field of inquiry. *Applied Developmental Science, 7,* 204–212.

# *Chapter 9*

1. U.S. Department of Health and Human Services. (1999). *Mental health: A report of the surgeon general.* Rockville, MD: U.S. Department of Health and Human Services. Substance Abuse and Mental Health Services Administration, Center for Mental Health Services, National Institutes of Health, National Institute of Mental Health.

2. U.S. Department of Health and Human Services. *Mental health: A report of the surgeon general.* Rockville, MD: U.S. Department of Health and Human Services. Substance Abuse and Mental Health Services Administration, Center for Mental Health Services, National

3. Facts about children and adolescents with ADHD. (2005). Retrieved on February 21, 2008 from http://www.aboutourkids.org/articles/facts_about_children_adolescents_adhd

4. Institute of Medicine of the National Academies. (2004, September). *Childhood Obesity in the United States: Facts and Figures.* http://www.iom.edu

5. Lavizzo-Mourey, R. (2007). Childhood Obesity: What It Means for Physicians. *Journal of the American Medical Association, 298*(8), 920–922.

6. *Fact Sheet: Helping America's Youth.* (2007). Available at http://www.whitehouse.gov/news/releases/2007/04/print/20070412-2.html

# Index

Aaron (bullying example), 152–53
Abuse of children. *See* Child abuse
Abuse of drugs. *See* Drug and substance abuse
Abuse of women. *See* Domestic violence
Academic achievement of children:
father-child relationships, influence of, 249; goal-setting and, 231–32; inner-city students, 83; self-esteem and, 253; service learning and, 230; television and media influences, 186–87, 191, 197. *See also* Intellectual learning capacities
Activity component of temperament, 123
Adaptability component of temperament, 123
ADHD (attention deficit hyperactive disorder): peer rejection of children with, 81, 94; statistics of, 268; undiagnosed, 212
Adolescents: attachment and, 53, 59–61, 68–69; bullying and, 152; discipline tools for, 219; emerging sexuality of, 60; empathy and kindness of, 255–56; Erikson's psychosocial theory, 106; fears of, 88; household chores for, 229; money management by, 234; music listened to by, 194–95; peer relationships of, 97; proximal zones

of development, 68–69; sibling rivalry and, 138; spirituality of, 262; suicide rates, 268; transitions within parent-children relationships during, 60
Adoption, 48
Adrenaline, 116
Adults. *See* Parents and parenting; Teachers
Adversity. *See* Resilient children
Advertisements, 187–88. *See also* Television and media violence
Aesop, 254
"Affect hunger," 58–59
African Americans: domestic violence rates, 21; as gang members, 157; homicide rates, 7, 268; juvenile delinquency cases, 7; music listened to by, 195; social capital within inner-city neighborhoods, 24–25; suicide rates, 8
Aggression, 133, 137. *See also* Anger
Ainsworth's patterns of attachment, 50–51
Alario, A., 183
Alaskan Natives: domestic violence rates, 21; homicide rates, 7
Alcohol abuse. *See* Drug and substance abuse

# *About the Author*

**ELSIE JONES-SMITH** is Clinical Psychologist, Counselor Educator, and President of the Strength-Based Institute, which provides consultation to organizations dealing with youth suffering from problems, including drug and alcohol addiction. She is a fellow of two divisions of the American Psychological Association, Society of Counseling Psychology, and the division on Ethnic Minority Issues. She has been a professor at Temple University, Michigan State University, University of Buffalo, and Boston University. Jones-Smith has served on numerous editorial boards, including the *Journal of Counseling Psychology, The Counseling Psychologist,* and *Counselor Education and Supervision.* She served 18 years as an Education Consultant for violence prevention in New York schools. She holds two PhDs—in Clinical Psychology and Counselor Education.